The Attraction Paradigm

PERSONALITY AND PSYCHOPATHOLOGY

A Series of Monographs, Texts, and Treatises

THE ATTRACTION
PARADIGM

Donn Byrne
Department of Psychology
Purdue University
West Lafayette, Indiana

ACADEMIC PRESS   New York and London   1971

ACADEMIC PRESS, INC.
111 Fifth Avenue, New York, New York 10003

United Kingdom Edition published by
ACADEMIC PRESS, INC. (LONDON) LTD.
Berkeley Square House, London W1X 6BA

LIBRARY OF CONGRESS CATALOG CARD NUMBER: 70-159619

PRINTED IN THE UNITED STATES OF AMERICA

Contents

v

STIMULUS GENERALITY

RESPONSE GENERALITY

THEORY-BUILDING

APPLICATIONS

Preface

The affective responses elicited by other human beings constitute a pervading influence in man's affairs. Our moments of greatest pleasure and most intense distress are occasioned by interpersonal interactions. The spectrum ranges from the simplest joys and pettiest annoyances of family and friends to the most utopian visions of a harmonious world society and the most awesome possibilities of the destruction of our species. In the broadest sense, then, a major impetus for the development of attraction theory is the desire to achieve a basic understanding of interpersonal pleasure and pain, of love and hate.

From these grandiloquent heights, it is necessary to descend to the more mundane tasks of scientific inquiry. On a number of grounds, it can be argued that the lawful regularities underlying interpersonal relationships are unlikely to be formulated in the course of a direct attack on important practical problems. Rather, the possibility of progress lies in deliberately turning away from such problems and in pursuing the curious path of paradigmatic research. This book is a progress report describing one such pursuit.

In attempting to present a coherent description of a body of research, it is not really possible to bridge the gap between the context of discovery and the context of justification. Anyone who has had contact with ongoing research is well aware that scientific advance takes place in a somewhat haphazard and disorganized atmosphere in which accidents and insights and stubborn biases play as large a role as do efforts at experimental rigor, quantitative precision, and logical deductions. For the sake of coherent communication, the final product of a scientific quest must be several steps removed in abstractness and orderliness from the actual conduct of research. Just as theories consist of an abstract representation of natural events, research descriptions consist of an abstract representation of scientific activity. From time to time in the present account, however, there is an attempt to depict bits of the original process.

For many, this book might seem better titled *Everything You Always Wanted to Know about Attraction—and Some That You Didn't*. For that reason, I would like to suggest different starting points for those with special or limited interests. For example, if one feels that the major justification for research is its relevance to applied problems, Chapter 14 should be read first. If theoretical questions are a major interest, Chapters 10 through 13 should be the starting point. The historical framework is best seen in Chapter 2. If one is planning to conduct an experiment in which there is a manipulation of attitudes in order to influence attraction, Chapters 3 and 4 should be first. Still another possibility is to read the book in the order in which the chapters are printed, as intended.

One reason for the suggestion that various starting points are possible is the obvious one that there is no perfect order in which such material can be arranged. That is, the theoretical developments and the empirical research and the historical antecedents and the applications are all intertwined and interconnected. From the very beginning, for example, the data collection was influenced by the general theory, whereas the articulation of the theory was dependent at each step on empirical findings. The only really satisfactory solution is to read all fourteen chapters at once. In any event, in whatever fashion the reader should decide to approach this material, the final result should be a familiarity with a body of work which has been a source of challenge and frustration and excitement for a number of us for the past decade.

To an increasing extent, research within the paradigm is being conducted by colleagues, students at various universities, academic grandchildren, and various others who are attracted to attraction; this development is a gratifying one. In a very real sense, though, the basic work could not have been carried out without the dedicated labor and cerebration and enthusiasm of an exceptional group of students at Texas, Stanford, and Purdue; individuals who have contributed in varying degrees to the building of the attraction paradigm: Rick Allgeier, Dave Andres, Dale Baskett, Barbara Blaylock, Mike Bond, Jerry Clore, John DeNinno, Mike Diamond, Mike Efran, Chuck Ervin, Carole Golightly, Charlie Gouaux, Bill Griffitt, Charles Haywood, Lou Hodges, Bill Hudgins, Maitland Huffman, Rich Hughes, John Lambert, Oliver London, Pat Mahaffey, Roy McDonald, Carl

McGraw, Jim Mikawa, Herman Mitchell, Lois Mueller, Don Nelson, John Palmer, Lu Picher, Keith Reeves, Ray Rhamey, Don Sachs, Mark Schwartz, John Sheffield, Ramadhar Singh, Dan Stefaniak, Dan Wiener, and Terry Wong.

Four individuals contributed a great deal of patient effort toward the production of this book. A literally voluminous number of very messy and partially decipherable pages were transformed into an equal number of neat and entirely legible pages by Bettye Stubblefield, Sue Gouaux, and Marsha Mitchell. Then, my wife Lois had the unenviable and exacting task of copyreading and proofreading. All of this work is gratefully acknowledged and thoroughly appreciated.

DONN BYRNE

BACKGROUND

Chapter 1 / **Paradigm Research**
in Personality and Social Psychology

_In marked contrast to the older and more firmly established sciences, it appears to be necessary in psychology to describe and defend the rationale as well as the content of one's research. Painful personal experience has shown that an unadorned exposition of the theoretical and empirical work relevant to interpersonal attraction evokes a predictable array of concerns and criticisms. The present chapter is in part an attempt to avoid such difficulties.

There is an inordinate amount of controversy about the methods and goals of research in personality and social psychology. At least a portion of that controversy stems from a failure to distinguish differences between basic and applied research and, paradoxically, a failure to identify the crucial similarities. A related but more general problem is the absence of widely accepted guidelines for conducting systematic psychological research. Much of the stress in graduate education is on the importance of experimental design and the experimental method, but the emphasis is almost exclusively intraexperimental. Our forte is in producing complex analysis of variance designs complete with triple interactions. Our weakness is in the absence of a schema that suggests what might be done in subsequent experiments.

In the present chapter, an effort is made to explore the basic–applied distinction and to propose an organizational structure which includes both

kinds of research. The remainder of this book deals with research on interpersonal attraction which, among other things, illustrates the structural
schema.

RESEARCH IN PERSONALITY AND SOCIAL PSYCHOLOGY

Among the problems facing psychology and especially the "soft"
areas are innumerable discussions and internecine quarrels about what is
wrong with current research in the field and what is the appropriate way to
proceed in the future. Though the arguments are seldom so labeled, much
of the disputation may be reduced to the advocacy of either basic or applied
research. When the two are not distinguished, there is a tendency to use the
criteria and standards of one to evaluate and, hence, to derogate the other.
Thus, the proponents of basic research may dismiss an applied interest as
nonscience in that it aims toward mere application or requires only an
engineering mentality appropriate for technicians. On the other hand, the
proponents of applied research dismiss basic research as trivial, uninteresting, "nitpicking," obvious, artificial, and neglectful of the major problems
facing mankind. How can anyone afford to piddle around in a laboratory
while cities are burning and children are dying of starvation?

Disagreements about Research Strategy

Partly because an interest in basic research is a rare phenomenon
even in the recent history of Western civilization, it seems more vulnerable
to attack than does applied research. Even when there is a ritual ac-
knowledgment that in some vague way basic research must be good, there
is still an impatience with those who perversely maintain concerns with
"what makes the grass green" when there are important practical things
to be done. President Johnson, for example, expressed this impatience when
he spoke about arteriosclerosis, cancer, and other diseases at a White
House meeting, "A great deal of basic research has been done. . . . But I think
the time has now come to zero in on the targets by trying to get our knowledge
fully applied [Walsh, 1966, p. 150]."

Pfaffmann (1965) has outlined some aspects of this difficulty and also
some of the reasons for distinguishing the two types of research activity:

> The distinction between basic and applied research, difficult enough to make in
> the natural sciences, is even harder to make in the behavioral sciences. Yet, for two
> reasons, the distinction is probably more important in the latter disciplines.
> First, there is the danger that purely applied social research to support some action
> program will be so hedged in by popular prejudices and assumptions that it fails to
> get to the root of the problem and, hence, becomes trivial. . . .

The second reason for distinguishing between basic and applied work is that the normal aversion to basic research is greater in regard to the social sciences than it is in regard to natural science. One can see the relevance of basic principles in physics and chemistry to achievements in making weapons, television sets, and medicines; but one cannot see so clearly the relevance of special "abstractions" and "jargon" concerning things we know about already, such as taxes, schools, race relations, and the family. The skepticism is increased by the fact that the layman has his own common-sense views about social matters. He objects when these are placed in question by empirical evidence supporting contrary and usually less sweeping generalizations. This is particularly true if the matter is one to which people attach strong positive or negative values.

Behavioral science often deals with human behavior in the context of daily affairs and everyday life, both with regard to individual behavior and the institutions in which it is embodied. It is, thus, tied to many practical situations and has future potential application for human and national welfare. . . .

But practical problems often require action, whereas scientific study requires some degree of isolation from the demands for immediate solutions. The scientist must look at and analyze the situation with some objective detachment in the attempt to develop generalizations applicable beyond the immediate ad hoc situation [pp. 669–671].

The task of explaining or justifying basic research to the general public or to members of Congress presents a difficult but not insurmountable impediment to scientific progress. A more serious difficulty is the negative reaction of those within the field. This particular problem is not a new one. In 1939, Kantor stressed that "the social psychologist must draw a line between scientific inquiry and the urge to improve the conditions of man and his society [p. 307]." He felt that social psychologists were not drawing such a line:

Social psychology, in other words, becomes assimilated to the efforts to improve the political, economic, and social welfare of persons and groups as well as to prevent war.

It cannot be denied that much of this social-service writing is very agreeable to liberal-minded people, but we may well raise the question whether, as social psychologists, we are interested primarily in the improvement of society or in a scientific analysis of a particular kind of psychological behavior [pp. 316–317].

The failure to distinguish the two kinds of activity would be even more striking to Kantor today, because there is mounting resistance to the kind of basic research he advocated. For example, in an editorial in the *Journal of Personality and Social Psychology*, Katz (1965) stressed the necessity for more research which included cultural variables, the social context, the real world. Sanford (1965) feels that psychology is too far removed from application and has become too much oriented toward the artificial, laboratory, operational, experimental approach. Allport (1966) complains that in current research "we have too few restraints holding us to the structure of life as it is lived [p. 8]." From a similar point of view, Bordin (1966) indicates:

Psychology as a science is presently overvaluing the strategy of simplification. ... Simplification and abstraction involve leaving out some aspects of the naturalistic setting in which the phenomena which aroused our curiosity and for which we hope to account were first encountered. ... We must be able to demonstrate that the understandings derived from simplified laboratory situations will in fact have relevance to the everyday phenomena of human experience [p. 120].

Murray (1963) described himself as:

... an aging psychologist who views with sorrow and misgivings the apparent accentuation of certain powerful forces that are keeping a multiplicity of his colleagues dissociated from the nature and experiences of actual people by binding their energies to an enthralling intellectual game played with abstract counters of dubious importance and of spurious relevance to human life [p. 28].

The aggrevation suggested by these various statements might possibly be ameliorated by the recognition that the goals and values and methods associated with application are quite different from those associated with basic research. The key word is "different" which does not imply either intellectual or moral inferiority or superiority. One reason for the accentuation of the difference is the likelihood that people with dissimilar values are attracted to the two kinds of research. Mathes (1969) notes:

Some 20 years ago John Mills discussed a basic difference in ... approaches to a problem. The managerial (or action) people base their primary analysis on "differences" (or changes in the situation) and the scientific (or thinking) people form their judgment on the "similarities" they find in comparing situations or objects. Another characteristic is that the managerial person wants (or writes) a report with first a recommendation for action, followed by the technical conclusions on which the recommendation is based, and ending with a description of the process by which the technical data were obtained. The scientist, on the other hand, usually will begin by stating the origin of the problem, its history, the various possible attacks, the test procedures decided on, then the data in charts and tables, the technical conclusions, and finally, a recommendation [p. 630].

It should, of course, be possible to pursue either type of activity without arousing the cry that "My research is better than your research. Therefore, you must share my values and do as I do!" An extreme example of this reaction in Radin's (1966) proposal that all physical and behavioral scientists be drafted for 3 years of applied research as soon as they obtain a degree. Sadly enough, much of the work described in the remainder of this book deals with just such reactions whether the topic is research goals, politics, religion, or western movies. Nevertheless, it would be a more comfortable world if we could each respond with the gentle wisdom of McGuire (1967):

I would urge, rather, that each of us try to do the best work he can and leave off attacking those whose predilections about what good work is are different from our own, even when these others take the offensive. I have confidence that there is a free

market of ideas in which the best work wins out in the end and the best workers receive the most emulation. . . . In the long run, class will tell. Let each of us do his own
work and leave negative comments about others' work for more desperate situations
than the one that now confronts us [p. 138].

Until we each can learn that degree of tolerance, it is suggested here
that a clear delineation of the differences between basic and applied
research might result in more harmonious or at least less acidulous reactions
to research of both kinds. How might we differentiate the methods and,
more importantly, the goals and criteria of success for basic and applied
science?

Applied Research

Applied research constitutes the utilization of scientific methods
and procedures and concepts for the express purpose of solving a
problem or of simply answering a question posed in the world of everyday life. Much of the work on interpersonal attraction, for example, has
centered on the problem of improving marital success. An early question
was, "Do husbands and wives tend to express similar attitudes about
most topics?" A positive answer to that question leads to other research
such as an attempt to determine the effects of differential husband–
wife similarity on marital happiness or marital stability. Positive findings
in this sort of problem-solving research can lead to technological
developments. For example, it might prove beneficial and even com-
mercially profitable to utilize premarital attitude testing and profile
matching as aids in the selection or evaluation of potential spouses.
Specific studies of this type are described in Chapters 2 and 14. What are
the integral characteristics of such research?

Methodological Considerations. Quite often, applied research involves
the study of individuals in a natural setting. The questions asked and the
problems for which solutions are sought are enmeshed in the complexities
of the everyday world. At times in applied research it is necessary to
create an experimental setting in which the real life situation is simulated
as closely as possible. The value of a wind tunnel or a mock space capsule
or a computerized teaching machine lies in the successful reproduction
of certain aspects of the real world in an economical or safe or efficient
fashion. The specific demands made on laboratory methods are different
for basic and applied research. In the latter, an experimental methodology
which was inadequate or inaccurate in simulating the real world would be
poor methodology because of the low probability that the resultant findings
could be generalized directly to nonlaboratory counterparts in the everyday world.

Laws and Theories. Applied research methods are generally inappropriate for the discovery of general laws, and general laws are of little use in applied research until they are translated into the specifics of an actual situation. Keehn (1966) gives a good example:

> All phenomena must be analyzable in scientific terms and the analyses subjected to proper verification, but the phenomena need not always exemplify the scientific laws containing the terms. It would be hard, for example, to maintain a belief in the gravitational constant after feeling the effects of a pound of loose feathers and a pound of lead dropped from a yard or so above one's head.
>
> Conversely, basic scientific laws are not discovered in this fashion ... the speeds at which bodies *really* fall to the ground can be ascertained by computing average rates of fall. But these are engineering data, and are hardly the bricks by which to construct a scientific edifice [p. 916].

Dodd and Garabedian (1961) extend this point:

> In other words, predictive scientific laws are not always simply descriptions of the observed behavior of solids, gases, etc., as found in nature or even as observed in the laboratory, nor even "averages" of large numbers of such cases. Rather they are often statements of *limiting cases*, of what *would happen if certain theoretical ideal conditions existed*—such as masses having no friction, gases being perfectly elastic, etc. In our actual experience these conditions are only approximated in varying degrees, though in the laboratory they may sometimes be approximated very closely. In nature conditions generally deviate so widely and variously from the ideal ones that for all but the most recent tiny fraction of man's sojourn on earth his observations of motion, etc., gave him no notion of these eminently workable laws. Their great usefulness lies in the fact that they constitute, not a picture of some sort of "average" behavior of physical substances, but a theoretical baseline from which the deviations of data can be measured and analyzed and other systematic variables thereby located, measured, and manipulated [p. 144].

It should also be pointed out that although theoretical concepts may have far-reaching implications for applied problems, applied research can in many instances make excellent progress in the absence of theoretical guidance or theoretical concern.

Goals and the Criteria of Success. The goal of any given project of applied research is the answer to a specific question or the solution of a specific problem. Once the goal is attained, the research is complete, and pure application may begin. The only additional tinkering with success is in making technological refinements. A meaningful finding is one which is applicable, and the criterion of good applied research is its validity when applied to practical problems. In this context, the development of a vaccine to prevent poliomyelitis is of great importance, but evidence relating to subatomic particles is irrelevant or even trivial because there is no practical use for it.

An interesting aspect of setting an applied goal is that the work leading to that goal is usually not intrinsically exciting until or unless the goal is reached. The rewards for success, both in private satisfaction and in public acclaim, are great. Without success, one can only say that he has saved others some precious time by demonstrating what is not effective. With success, however, portions of the world are altered, and the researcher's name is likely to become a household word.

Basic Research

Basic research is primarily an intellectual undertaking which aims toward a conceptual explanation of a given phenomenon or phenomena. Its initial impetus may lie in the external world and its eventual product may be of great relevance to that world, but its essence lies in isolation and abstraction. A basic research question in the area of attraction would be "Why do similar attitudes elicit attraction?" Attempts to provide a suitable explanation lead to the construction of a theoretical framework from which hypotheses are derived and then tested experimentally. The interpretation of the findings of this research either strengthens the conceptual system or leads to its modification, and then further hypotheses are derived in a continuing process.

Methodological Approach. A peculiar characteristic of basic research is the deliberate and necessary suspension of interest in real life problems. An abstract approach inevitably involves artificiality when viewed from the perspective of applied research. Accurate reproduction of the external world is not sought because the resultant complexity would contaminate or obscure that which is under investigation. The need to isolate and control variables leads one to a stimulus situation which is different from that which is found outside of the laboratory. Those who criticize the artificiality of psychological experiments must find it puzzling that experimenters in other fields find any utility in the use of cloud chambers, sterile tissue cultures, temperatures of absolute zero, unadulterated chemicals, and other oddities hardly representative of the outside world.

Science tends to be differentiated from other conceptual activities primarily with respect to its emphasis on the collection of empirical data. A few brief points must be considered with respect to this concern with the empirical. Almost no one any longer takes the once popular position that the real world is sitting there full of facts to be discovered and then properly organized. The selection of phenomena to investigate, the way in which variables are operationalized, and the selection and interpretation of findings which are deemed to be relevant, all are influenced by preexisting conceptualizations and by what Holton (1964) calls the "thematic imagination." Kessel (1969) describes this process:

> What is being asserted is that the scientist's premises and presuppositions can and do play a significant role at all levels of his endeavor. The analogy drawn by Eddington (1928) between the scientist and the icthyologist conveys the point best: Having used a fishing net with a certain size mesh, the icthyologist proclaims that there are no fish in the universe smaller than the mesh size. It is a simple and yet seldomly appreciated point that the scientist is casting a net with a certain size mesh and that his catch is to a large extent a function of that mesh [p. 1004].

That realization leads many scientists, such as Edward Teller, to say that basic research "is a game, is play, led by curiosity, by taste, style, judgment, intangibles." Thus, the game of science could very easily be seen only as an amusing pastime in which sophisticated players are deluding themselves and others with a stacked deck in which the game's outcome is predetermined. There is, of course, more to data collection than that. Once the player enters into the game and accepts the rules and agrees upon the playing pieces, arbitrary though some of them may be, he is bound by the findings to make his conceptual system conform to the data or to as much of them as possible. The resulting interplay between data and theory is not solely confined to science, but the heavy emphasis on data collection and the responsiveness of theoretical systems to the necessity of modification are very special.

Laws and Theories. Perhaps the most distinguishable characteristic of successful basic research is the formulation of empirical laws indicating the relationship between variables and the formulation of theories which transcend specific empirical relationships and which can serve as unifying networks between seemingly unrelated events. Spence (1944) describes this process and its function:

> In some areas of knowledge, for example present day physics, theories serve primarily to bring into functional connection with one another empirical laws which prior to their formulation had been isolated realms of knowledge. The physicist is able to isolate, experimentally, elementary situations, i.e., situations in which there are a limited number of variables, and thus finds it possible to infer or discover descriptive, low-order laws. Theory comes into play for the physicist when he attempts to formulate more abstract principles which will bring these low-order laws into relationship with one another. Examples of such comprehensive theories are Newton's principle of gravitation and the kinetic theory of gases. The former provided a theoretical integration of such laws as Kepler's concerning planetary motions, Galileo's law of falling bodies, laws of the tides, and so on. The kinetic theory has served to integrate the various laws relating certain properties of gases to other experimental variables [pp. 47–48].

He goes on to say:

> Without the generalizations which theories aim to provide we would never be in a position to predict behavior, for knowledge of particular events does not provide us with a basis for prediction when the situation differs in the least degree. The higher the level of abstraction that can be obtained the greater will be both the understanding and the actual control achieved [p. 62].

Goals and the Criteria of Success. The goal of basic research is an increase in the generality and predictive accuracy of a conceptual system. Unlike applied research, there is no single goal the attainment of which signals the end point of a given line of basic research—there is no end point in basic research. There is, in fact, very much the atmosphere of a never-ending contest in which there are repeated opportunities for minor achievements and occasionally the chance for a major one. The intrinsic rewards for playing the game are great. When Einstein was asked the goal of science, he replied, "To keep the scientist amused." The extrinsic rewards lie in the esteem of colleagues which is sometimes expressed in the form of citations, awards, medals, plaques, and other secondary reinforcements of which we humans are fond. James Watson (1968) gives a personal and revealing account of both types of reward in *The Double Helix*. Conant (1952) describes the intellectual and creative joys of this kind of science:

> To my mind, the significance of the fabric of scientific theories that have been produced in the last three hundred and fifty years is the same as the significance of the art of the great periods in history, or the significance of the work of the musical composers. For most scientists, I think the justification of their work is to be found in the pure joy of its creativeness; the spirit which moves them is closely akin to the imaginative vision which inspires an artist. To some degree, almost all men today applaud the success of the past in the realm of creative work and do not measure the degree of success by material standards. So too, at some distant time, the advance of science from 1600 to 1950 may be regarded entirely as a triumph of the creative spirit, one manifestation of those vast potentialities of men and women that make us all proud to be members of the human race [p. 98].

Because of these various characteristics, the evaluation of basic research is more difficult than the evaluation of applied research. A meaningful finding is one which makes a precise and consistent contribution of theoretical relevance, and more is contributed by the conceptual processes of the investigator than by the empirical data. The criterion of good basic research is thus quite subjective. Furthermore, its value is often not clear until subsequent work and theorizing has confirmed or disconfirmed its value by demonstrating where it leads. In this context, evidence relating to subatomic particles can be of great importance, but the development of a vaccine to prevent poliomyelitis is irrelevant or even trivial because it makes no theoretical contribution.

Application as an Outcome of Basic Research. Commitment to basic research does not preclude an interest in the problems of the outside world on the part of the experimenter, and it does not preclude the relevance of this research to the problems of the outside world. Rather, the history of science suggests that basic research constitutes one of the more effective ways of extending the knowledge base and, incidentally, of solving real life problems. Application is not the justification for basic research nor is it an inevitable outcome of that research; it occurs with sufficient frequency, however, that the basic researcher can frequently have his cake and eat it as well. There are numerous instances in which experimental methodology or experimental findings developed in basic research are found to be applicable in work on an applied problem. Such research fallout may be serendipitous in that the concerns of those conducting the original research may be far removed from the use to which it is eventually put. For example, the discovery of X-radiation (itself an accident) was of considerable importance in theoretical physics; at the same time, the utilization of X-rays in medical diagnosis constituted an application in a quite different field. Similarly, the uses of atomic energy and laser beams are diverse and without obvious connection with the original research interests of those who worked on the phenomena. Townes (1968) has documented the basic research which led to the development of the laser beam which then became a tool in multiple applied problems. He then raises a question:

> Consider now the problem of a research planner setting out 20 years ago to develop any one of these technological improvements—a more sensitive amplifier, a more accurate clock, new drilling techniques, a new surgical instrument for the eye, more accurate measurement of distance, three-dimensional photography, and so on. Would he have had the wit or courage to initiate for any of these purposes an extensive basic study of the interaction between microwaves and molecules? The answer is clearly No. . . . It was the drive for new information and understanding, and the atmosphere of basic research which seem clearly to have been needed for the real payoff [p. 702].

Two questions illustrate the different emphases that may be placed on the same finding: Is it relevant to the theoretical formulation? Could it serve a utilitarian purpose? Perhaps an ideal situation is one in which both questions are asked and an ideal finding is one which allows one to answer "yes" to each question.

Weinberg (quoted in Greenberg, 1966) describes how the absence of a pragmatic goal can be advantageous to science:

> I would like to draw an analogy between science and basketball. Our high school basketball coach used to say, "In setting up a good shot at the basket, by all means keep the ball moving. It doesn't matter so much where the ball moves as long as it does not remain in one place; only in this way are openings created." This approach to basketball is certainly inefficient; the amount of wasted motion is much greater than the amount of motion specifically directed at the goal. And yet by following this prescription our team won most of its games. In the same sense, science is inefficient; by maintaining scientific activity in areas that are broadly of interest, one creates opportunities that can be exploited practically [p. 619].

The ability to achieve success in applied work is in direct proportion to the stage of development of basic research in that field. Weinberg points out some of the differences across fields:

> ... there is a difference between the physical and biological sciences with respect to the degree to which their underlying scientific structure can be efficiently mobilized for achieving practical goals. The physical sciences and engineering, though they may have started independently ... have now been so intertwined and integrated, and the physical sciences themselves are so advanced, that given an applied goal in engineering, there is often nothing but money that stands in the way of achieving the goal, provided basic science has shown this goal to be achievable. I can't stress too strongly the importance of this latter proviso. Thus, applications in the physical sciences fall into two great categories: those projects whose basic feasibility has been demonstrated; and those equally desirable projects whose basic feasibility is yet to be demonstrated.... The bulk of biomedical research is in the pre-feasibility stage, and therefore, the underlying basic research must be done broadly. Since most of our knowledge is in the pre-feasibility stage, the vital link between basic and applied biomedical research is much more haphazard and unpredictable than I suspect our President would like it to be.... I think it is fair to say that most basic molecular biologists would work directly on a cure for cancer rather than on what they are now doing, if only they knew how to make real progress. We don't cure cancer because we don't want to, but rather because we don't know how to cure it [p. 619].

Weinberg's analysis suggests the two primary ways in which applied research may advance. A problem may be identified and applicable solutions sought, or reliable knowledge may be identified and applicable problems sought. Physics–engineering is able to advance with the former procedure, whereas biomedicine is sufficiently undeveloped to require major reliance on the latter. If one can assume that behavioral science is closer to biomedicine in its developmental level than it is to physics–engineering, it clearly follows that our best strategy is the encouragement of basic research and the encouragement of any attempts to apply the resultant knowledge to whatever problems are appropriate. The applications of operant conditioning concepts and techniques to innumerable behavioral problems by B. F. Skinner and his associates provide the most notable example of that approach in psychology.

Frankly, the defenders of basic research must accept some of the blame for the cry for more application in psychology. In Weinberg's analogy, there was constant activity, but there was agreement about what to do when opportunities arose. His team made field goals and Skinner finds remarkably varied uses for conditioning techniques. Others behave as if application will automatically flow if the journals only continue to print articles. Applied possibilities are beneath the dignity of serious men with the possible exception of the introductory portions of their grant proposals. The search for appropriate applications must be an active rather than a passive enterprise; the full development of a psychological technology will require the creative efforts of a large number of behavioral engineers. Deutsch (1969) notes:

> No guarantees can be given to those—from either the right or the left—who are demanding that social science be relevant. We can only guarantee that our efforts will be socially responsible, that our work will seek to be responsive to human concerns, and that we will be continuously concerned with fostering the application of psychological knowledge for the welfare of man [pp. 1091–1092].

Much of the preceding discussion espouses the view that applied and basic research are two somewhat different and laudable activities, each deserving of support, each requiring creativity, and each employing men of good will. Although agreement on that position would represent an improvement over the present atmosphere of criticism, there exist a more general problem and a more general solution which serve to place the basic–applied distinction in another perspective.

PARADIGM RESEARCH

It was suggested earlier that much research in the social-personality area is focused on the single experiment. Anyone reading one of our articles or listening to a paper presented at a convention would be convinced that he was in the presence of an active scientific enterprise. As the result of exposure to multiple articles or papers, however, it is not uncommon to hear expressions of puzzlement as to where all this might be leading. The possibility must be raised that much of our research, both basic and applied, may not be leading anywhere. Probably this is one of the reasons that considerable time is spent in suggesting solutions: let's get out of the laboratory; let's get back to the laboratory; what we need are basic facts; what we need is an inclusive theory; the solution lies in the physiological approach or in the multivariate approach or in the humanistic approach; etc. An additional panacea will be offered here.

Normal Science

In an incisive philosophical monograph, Kuhn (1962) has presented an intriguing description of the characteristics of science. His major interest was in the contrast between "normal" or "puzzle-solving" science and the occurrence of scientific revolutions. Our present concern lies in his depiction of the prerevolutionary stage of development. He sees the essential step in any scientific endeavor as the acquisition of a paradigm. By the term "paradigm" he means a specific body of research which is accepted by a group of scientists and which consists of specific procedures, measuring devices, empirical laws, and a specific theoretical superstructure. Without a paradigm, no field can progress. Kuhn (1962) indicates:

> In the absence of a paradigm or some candidate for paradigm, all of the facts that could possibly pertain to the development of a given science are likely to seem equally relevant. As a result, early fact-gathering is a far more nearly random activity than the one that subsequent scientific development makes familiar. Furthermore, in the absence of a reason for seeking some particular form of more recondite information, early fact-gathering is usually restricted to the wealth of data that lie ready to hand. The resulting pool of facts contains those accessible to casual observation and experiment . . . [p. 15].

This random fact-finding has been summarized by psychoanalyst Leslie Shaffer as embodying the wisdom of an ancient Patagonian proverb, "He who collects enough chamberpots will one day come to possess the Holy Grail." Kuhn (1962) describes the preparadigm state as "a condition in which all members practice science but in which their gross product scarcely resembles science at all [p. 100]." In addition, he notes that fields in the preparadigm stage of development are marked by frequent and deep debates over legitimate methods, problems, and standards of solution. As paradigms become established, time and energy are spent in developing them rather than on the question "What should we be doing?"

If the preparadigm stage consists primarily of debate among pre-scientists and random gathering of easily observable data, of what does paradigm research consist? Kuhn characterizes such research in terms of three types of activity: (*1*) attempts to increase the precision, reliability, and scope with which the facts are known; (*2*) comparison of the facts directly with predictions from the paradigm theory; and, most important of all (*3*) empirical research designed to articulate the paradigm theory and to reduce ambiguities. This latter work includes the determination of physical constants, the discovery of quantitative laws, and the attempt to devise ways to apply the paradigm to new areas of interest.

There are further characteristics to consider. Kuhn (1962) describes normal science as a puzzle-solving activity. The scientist no more seeks unexpected novelty than he seeks the solution to everyday problems:

> Bringing a normal research problem to a conclusion is achieving the anticipated in a new way, and it requires the solution of all sorts of complex instrumental, conceptual, and mathematical puzzles. The man who succeeds proves himself an expert puzzle-solver, and the challenge of the puzzle is an important part of what usually drives him on.
> . . . the really pressing problems, e.g., a cure for cancer or the design of a lasting peace, are often not puzzles at all, largely because they may not have any solution. Consider the jigsaw puzzle whose pieces are selected at random from each of two different puzzle boxes. Since that problem is likely to defy . . . even the most ingenious of men, it cannot serve as a test of skill in solution [pp. 36–37].

When the investigator becomes totally involved in the puzzle of a paradigm, he is free from concern with any and all phenomena. He is able to pursue selected phenomena in far greater detail, design special equipment for the task, and employ it more stubbornly and more systematically than was ever done before. This leads to a concentration on the subtlest and most obscure aspects of the natural phenomena that are under investigation. Communication becomes increasingly specialized and soon becomes unintelligible to anyone not in the particular speciality. Kuhn adds:

> The areas investigated by normal science are, of course, minuscule; the enterprise now under discussion has drastically restricted vision. But those restrictions, born from confidence in a paradigm, turn out to be essential to the development of science. By focusing attention upon a small range of relatively esoteric problems, the paradigm forces scientists to investigate some part of nature in a detail and depth that would otherwise be unimaginable [p. 24].

This description of science may sound tediously humdrum to those of us in psychology familiar with all-encompassing speculative "theories," the introduction of original methodology and novel procedures with each investigation, excitement over counterintuitive findings, and a pervasive orientation toward real life problems. It also sounds as if the critics are correct—basic research leads to more and more knowledge about less and less, and it results in few surprises. Nevertheless, "History suggests that the scientific enterprise has developed a uniquely powerful technique for producing surprises ... [Kuhn, 1962, p. 52]." How could that be?

> Without the special apparatus that is constructed mainly for anticipated functions, the results that lead ultimately to novelty could not occur. And even when the apparatus exists, novelty ordinarily emerges only for the man who, knowing *with precision* what he should expect, is able to recognize that something has gone wrong. Anomoly appears only against the background provided by the paradigm [p. 65].

How important is paradigm research for scientific advance? "Without commitment to a paradigm there could be no normal science. Furthermore, that commitment must extend to areas and to degrees of precision for which there is no full precedent [p. 99]."

Suggested Model for Conceptualizing Paradigmatic Research in Personality and Social Psychology

If paradigmatic research is characteristic of science and if a science of behavior is our goal, the next step is obvious. We should begin conducting paradigmatic research and be done with it. How might that be done? The schema presented below was formulated in bits and pieces as our attraction research progressed. It was not the roadmap for most of the research, because most of the research preceded or paralleled the map. It is not meant to represent the final word in structuring this or any other research. It does represent a way of thinking about research which may prove to be of some utility in the search for psychological paradigms.

Research and Theory as a Procedure for Making Sense out of the World. In Fig. 1–1 is a very general depiction of the function of scientific research and theory. Man is confronted by a threatening and confusing environment in which he is beset by discomfort, disease, natural disasters, and the seemingly infinite complexities of the behavior of other human beings. Any conceptual activity which results in bringing meaning out of chaos is both anxiety-reducing and potentially adaptive in an evolutionary sense. If the conceptual system also results in accurate prediction and control of the environment, its beneficial qualities are obvious. Oppenheimer (1956) describes this process of beginning with common sense observations, the necessity of then moving away from them, and the final step of returning to the common sense world:

> When we move from common sense into scientific things, we also move toward generality using analysis, using observation and, in the end, using experiment....
> We come from common sense; we work for a long time; then we give back to common sense refined, original, and strange notions, and enrich what men know and how they live [pp. 128–129].

All man's intellectual products may be seen as attempts to make sense out of his world and to achieve the means for predicting and controlling that world. Polanyi (1964) proposes that "Every interpretation of nature, whether scientific, nonscientific, or anti-scientific, is based on some intuitive conception of the general nature of things. . . . The premises of science on which all scientific teaching and research rest are beliefs held by scientists on the general nature of things [pp. 10–12]." Obvious examples of such

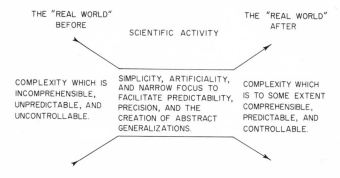

Fig. 1–1. Science as an intermediate activity between the complexity of experience and the same complexity brought at least partially under man's control.

products are religious beliefs, myths, political ideologies, folk sayings, and science. There are a number of similarities across these diverse systems. Each involves the creation of abstractions, a narrowing of focus to crucial elements, and a simplification of that which is originally complex. Strangely enough, this abstraction, narrowness, and simplification lead to greater generality in each instance. Lynes (1968) makes a similar point in a discussion of cartoonists; "This is not to say that the best cartoons are the most elaborate drawings of place and people. On the contrary it is the simplification of the complex by the deftest shorthand that evokes (as in the drawings of Steinberg) the most comprehensive view of the world [p. 23]."

In comparison to other systems devised to achieve understanding, science can be defended primarily on pragmatic grounds. That is, scientific conceptions have led to repeated instances of accurate prediction and valid application. We may not be happy with all of the technological fruits of science, but we cannot argue that science is ineffective. By comparison, the rain dance, human sacrifice, and the prayer wheel just didn't work out.

Outlines of a Paradigm

Conceptualizing and Establishing a Base Relationship. What are the first steps in moving from the complexity of everyday experience toward a scientific interest in a given phenomenon? One starting point is the perception of an antecedent–consequent relationship. The observation may be faulty or it may be a very rare occurrence or it may occur only under special conditions. It appears to the observer, nevertheless, that X results in Y. Further, it is a common human tendency to generalize from the $X \longrightarrow Y$ observation to other Xs and other Ys and to other situations than the one in which the original observation was made. A first scientific step would be to make deliberate observations to determine whether, in fact, that relationship can be objectively verified under careful and unbiased conditions and in various circumstances. Verification of observations is a midway step between the randomness of a preparadigm stage and the systematic concentration of research within a paradigm. The latter is underway when a decision is made to select the operations defining X and Y and to concentrate on establishing their relationship in detail and with precision.

In establishing a base relationship, the focus of interest is not on the everyday life observations which preceded the research. The operations are not artificial substitutes for something existing somewhere in real life. The operations and the network of empirical findings and theoretical constructs embodying them are the real life variables of the experimenter and theorist.

A base relationship in psychology most often consists of a stimulus variable and a response variable. The only requirement is that of an association between the two variables—an empirical relationship which may be expressed as a mathematical function. This base, by itself, is the first building block in the paradigm. All the subsequent activities within the paradigm may be seen as varied approaches to building an extended network of increasing generality.

Seeking Generality: Basic and Applied Research. In Fig. 1–2 is presented an organizational schema showing the kinds of research that can grow out of a base relationship. Each of the four categories of research will be described briefly.

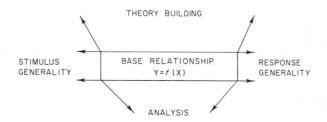

Fig. 1–2. A schematic model of paradigmatic research in personality and social psychology.

The horizontal portion of the figure describes research which is largely applied in orientation. The vertical portion of the figure describes basic research. The questions asked by the two kinds of research, the methodological issues raised, and the goals are those outlined earlier. One advantage of this conceptualization is that basic and applied research are seen as different activities, but in no way are they antithetical; that is, both are products of the same base relationship and each has implications for the other.

Analytic Research. One direction that research may take is an analysis of the elements constituting the base relationship. The goal is to isolate and to define more precisely the basic elements which are operating. In psychology, this type of research may be seen as directed toward the *identification of the stimulus* and the *isolation of the response*. Unless one has struggled directly with the problem, it is difficult to appreciate the extent to which even the seemingly most simple stimulus or response variable may turn out to be multifaceted. The identification of the basic elements, the separation of those that are relevant from those that are not, and the attaching of appropriate labels to them are each aspects of analytic research.

This concentration of nitpicking attention on the most minute and least obvious aspects of the variables under investigation tends to contribute directly to an increase in the meaningfulness, the precision, and the generality of the total conceptual structure.

Stimulus Generality. In the base relationship, the stimulus dimension is assumed to affect the response dimension on the basis of certain characteristics. When other stimulus dimensions are found to affect that same response dimension, information about the similarity of those different stimuli and about the essential components which influence the response are provided. For example, if varying amounts of food and water and electric shock each are able to bring about performance changes in a learning situation, we can surmise that these three quite different sets of stimuli share common properties. Hence, it is necessary to postulate a more general concept such as reinforcement to account for their similar effects.

Stimulus generality also involves the establishment of boundary conditions which limit or even alter the base relationship. A surprisingly common mistake is the assumption that an empirical law which fails to hold under any and all conditions is invalid, or at least imperfect. With respect to the base relationship for the attraction paradigm, one critic (Taylor, 1970) managed to make that mistake five times in one paragraph. Four of his points happen to be erroneous, but they would represent a curious view of science even if correct:

> In sum, Byrne's reference to the similarity–attraction relationship as a law is unwarranted because (a) crucial confounding variables (such as self-evaluation and cooperation–competition) have not been considered by Byrne and associates; (b) it has not been demonstrated that the similarity–attraction relationship is still linear if longitudinal measurement is employed; (c) the interdependence question has not been adequately resolved; (d) there is no evidence that the linear relationship (and its independence from various potentially confounding variables) is generalizable from the interpersonal-hypothetical design to real groups; ... and (e) the problem of intervening variables (in addition to tension) is still largely unexplored [pp. 109–110].

By way of comparison, note that reference to the law of gravity is unwarranted because it can be confounded (e.g., inside of a space capsule on a lunar trip), it has not been demonstrated to occur on Pluto, it is not clear to the casual observer whether an apple falls toward the earth or vice versa, there is evidence that the relationship does not hold in the real world (e.g., feathers in a wind storm), and the nature of gravitational force is not totally understood.

The investigation of stimulus generality, among other things, leads precisely to such applied problems as a specification of conditions that do and do not influence the relationship in various ways. The specification of boundary conditions and the identification of relevant variables are not generally viewed as activities that refute empirical laws.

Response Generality. Three somewhat different kinds of research are associated with the question of the generality of the response.

First, the stimulus variable of the base relationship is manipulated and its effects on additional response variables are determined. In part, because of the historical relationship with psychometric research, such investigations may be conceptualized as validational in that the construct validity of the original response measure is determined. As with all such research, one of the primary questions being asked is whether the label applied to the original response measure is a reasonable one in view of its relationship or lack of relationship with other response measures. That is, if one's operations are labelled Y, it is assumed that they will be found to covary with other operations labelled Y; if not, the label must be reconsidered.

Second, the generality of the base relationship may be sought in population samples quite different from the one originally used in establishing the relationship. A lawful function that holds only for the college sophomore suggests a quite different level of generality from a relationship that holds across groups different in age, education, and socioeconomic status. Similarly, cross-cultural replication of a relationship suggests a more general phenomenon than one limited to a single culture.

Third, a major source of the unexplained or unpredicted response variance (error variance) in the base relationship is usually attributed to "individual differences." That is, individuals who differ greatly in genetic characteristics or in a lifetime of learning experiences do not respond uniformly to a given stimulus. Such differences are comprised of variations in perceptions, abilities, expectancies, motives, attitudes, values, and other attributes. In lieu of ignoring such determinants, it is possible to subdivide samples into more homogeneous units on the basis of their responses to one or more personality measures. When the functional $S–R$ relationship is found to vary across different levels of a given personality dimension, we have additional evidence for the generality of the function and also increased accuracy of the prediction of the responses of specific individuals.

Theory Building. Each of the other types of research provides information concerning the generality of the base relationship and about the precise nature of the phenomena under investigation. At each step, also, the experimenter is faced with the necessity of attempting to make conceptual sense out of the proliferating empirical network. In answering the questions "Why?" and "How?" we turn to generalizations at a higher level of abstraction which are designed to clarify the multitude of individual relationships in terms of a relatively parsimonious set of basic principles.

The utility of theoretical formulations is determined by the extent to which they yield hypotheses which may be subjected to empirical test. Research directed at theory testing tends to lead the investigator to utilize experimental situations and operations far removed from the original base relationship. The theory as originally formulated and as subsequently modified is never verified for all times and seldom is definitively rejected:

> Few philosophers of science still seek absolute criteria for the verification of scientific theories. Noting that no theory can ever be exposed to all possible relevant tests, they ask not whether a theory has been verified but rather about its probability in the light of the evidence that actually exists [Kuhn, 1962, p. 144].

Thus, good theories are those that unify a large number of otherwise disparate findings under a common set of basic principles and generate new propositions which are open to verification.

With this general orienting framework, we shall turn to the study of attraction. An attempt will be made briefly to trace the history of the investigation of the determinants of attraction and then to present in some detail the results of a paradigmatic approach to the study of attraction. The organization of the remainder of this book follows the outline suggested in the present chapter. Chapters 2 and 14 represent the left and right portions of Fig. 1–1. The various segments of Fig. 1–2 are covered as follows: the base relationship in Chapter 3, analytic research in Chapter 4, stimulus generality in Chapters 5–7, response generality in Chapters 8–9, and theory construction in Chapters 10–13.

Chapter 2 / Similarity and Attraction: An Historical Perspective

Observations and generalizations about behavior did not begin with the advent of psychology as a formal discipline. Individuals noted regularities in the behavior of themselves and others, speculated about human nature, and suggested cause and effect relationships. Many such generalizations are preserved as sayings and proverbs which encompass the behavior in question. The survival of such formulations over time is in part a function of their predictive accuracy, though instances of long-lived errors and inconsistencies in folk wisdom are obviously numerous. Even so, if the same behavioral observation occurs in different cultures despite temporal, geographic, and linguistic variations, there is some reason to suspect that a valid psychological law may have been formulated, even though at a relatively low level of specificity and precision.

With interpersonal attraction as a potential research problem, one finds that observations concerning man's likes and dislikes, the basis of friendship, and the reasons for love and hate are painfully numerous and frequently contradictory. Could paradigm research possibly emerge from "absence makes the heart grow fonder," "love me, love my dog," "birds of a feather flock together," "out of sight, out of mind," "opposites attract," or "love is blind?" In a preparadigm period, there are no constraints and no guidelines. Each investigator tends simply to follow his interests and inclinations. All possible problems present equally reasonable targets of inquiry to be pursued in any imaginable manner. If a field is to progress from random research activity toward a paradigmatic science, it is imperative that interest become focused on a much narrower and more circumscribed problem.

In delineating a starting point for the research paradigm to be presented in the subsequent chapters, it may be helpful to trace the kind of original observations and generalizations which led to the initial empirical research on one possible determinant of attraction. Because the starting point of the present research endeavor was the relationship between attitude similarity–dissimilarity and attraction, the historical description will be limited to this single relationship. It seems likely, however, that any of a hundred conceivable alternative choices would have proven equally useful as a starting point for building a viable science dealing with attraction.

NATURALISTIC OBSERVATIONS AND GENERALIZATIONS

It should first be noted that the term "attitude" will be employed rather loosely in the coming chapters to denote an orientation along a positive–negative continuum with respect to any object or event. Thus, we may speak of our attitude concerning communism, the Democratic party, the concept of God, birth control pills, Richard M. Nixon, cigarette smoking, modern art, chess, miniskirts, or the Green Bay Packers. For our purposes, nothing would seem to be gained by drawing distinctions among attitudes, preferences, values, opinions, tastes, and related evaluational constructs.

The observation that an individual's stated attitudes influence the way in which others evaluate him is an ancient and apparently obvious one. A few scattered examples should serve to underline this point.

In the fourth century before Christ, Aristotle (translated 1932) indicated a number of antecedents of friendship as opposed to enmity. One such variable was attitude similarity–dissimilarity.

> And they are friends who have come to regard the same things as good and the same things as evil, they who are friends of the same people, and they who are enemies of the same people. . . .
> We like those who resemble us, and are engaged in the same pursuits. . . . We like those who desire the same things as we, if the case is such that we and they can share the things together . . . [pp. 103–105].

Approximately 2000 years later in seventeenth century Holland, Spinoza (translated 1951) described the origin and nature of the emotions and noted a related phenomenon. He also proposed that we are motivated to persuade others to adopt our own views:

> *If we conceive that anyone loves, desires, or hates anything which we ourselves love, desire, or hate, we shall thereupon regard the thing in question with more steadfast love, etc.*

> *On the contrary, if we think that anyone shrinks from something that we love, we shall*
> *undergo vacillation of soul.*
> ... it follows that everyone endeavors, as far as possible, to cause others to love what
> he himself loves, and to hate what he himself hates ... [p. 151].

Still another observer of the similarity–attraction relationship was Samuel Johnson (Boswell, republished 1963) in eighteenth century England. Johnson even suggested an underlying reason for the affect accompanying the discovery of disagreement, "being angry with one who controverts an opinion which you value, is a necessary consequence of the uneasiness which you feel. Every man who attacks my belief, diminishes in some degree my confidence in it, and therefore makes me uneasy [p. 267]."

At a broader level, one could make the case for the threatening quality of dissimilar beliefs by citing an array of endless centuries of persecution, rebellion, and warfare centering on disagreement concerning religious and political ideology. It is possible to conceptualize much of man's history as a series of efforts to establish the dominance of a given group's attitudinal system and to proselytize, banish, or destroy those who are dissimilar.

In any event, we note the antiquity and the ubiquity of observations concerning similarity and attraction. As was suggested earlier, objective verification procedures frequently serve to tarnish the shine of folk wisdom and armchair philosophy. That next step, the effort to operationalize the variables and to conduct systematic observations, constitutes the beginning of a formal scientific interest in the phenomenon. In the study of attraction, the intervening phase between everyday life observations and paradigm research began approximately 100 years ago.

SYSTEMATIC OBSERVATIONS: EMPIRICAL VERIFICATION OF THE
SIMILARITY–ATTRACTION RELATIONSHIP

In 1870 Sir Francis Galton touched on the problem of attraction and similarity in his study of "hereditary genius." He noted that at the time his work was first published, "the human mind was popularly thought to act independently of natural laws ... [Galton, republished 1952, p. vii]" and his aim was to show that behavioral differences are inherited in a lawful manner. Though he did not specifically deal with attitude variables, Galton discussed the marriage patterns of a group of eminent men and the 300 families which produced them, "(the findings) establish the existence of a tendency of (like to like) among intellectual men and women, and make it most probable, that the marriages of illustrious men with (equivalent) women ... are very common. On the other hand, there is no evidence of a strongly marked antagonistic taste [p. 315]."

Later quantification of these and additional data by Karl Pearson led to the same sort of conclusion that the bulk of the observed resemblance between spouses "is due to a direct, if quite unconscious, selection of like by like [Pearson & Lee, 1903, p. 375]."

The subsequent correlational studies of attraction and similarity essentially involved attempts to establish more firmly the validity and to extend more widely the generality of this formulation. With minor variations, these investigations have consisted of the identification of pairs of individuals who indicate mutual attraction (spouses, fiancées, sociometrically identified friends), assessment of these individuals on one or more attitudinal measures, and a statistical determination of the pairs' similarity. Often this similarity is evaluated not only in terms of departure from a theoretical base line of chance pairings ($r = .00$) but also by comparison with the similarity shown by random pairs or mutually antagonistic pairs from the same population. Over several decades in numerous samples on a wide variety of measures, the proposed similarity–attraction relationship has been subjected to repeated empirical tests.

Husband–Wife Similarity

The interest in family resemblances in the Galton tradition was evidenced by a number of studies in the early part of this century. One such investigation was conducted in 1905 by Heymans and Wiersma in Holland. Approximately 3000 Dutch physicians were asked to select a family and to respond to a series of questions about each member; over 400 cooperated. The questions dealt with personality characteristics, intellectual abilities, interests, and opinions. Schuster and Elderton (1906) obtained these data and computed a series of intrafamily correlations. The husband–wife correlations on the attitudinal items are shown in Table 2–1. Here we see the beginnings of what was to become a familiar and consistent empirical

TABLE 2–1
DUTCH HUSBAND–WIFE CORRELATIONS[a]

Characteristic	Correlation
Caring or not caring much for good eating and drinking	.42
Reading much or not	.11
Tendency toward drink	.36
Political opinions	.36
Religious feeling	.73

[a]Data from Schuster and Elderton, 1906, pp. 467–468.

generalization: husbands and wives tend to resemble one another in attitudinal characteristics.

The major thrust of the American studies of similarity as a correlate of positive interpersonal relationships came in the 1930s. For example, Schiller's (1932) research was described as an extension of Galton's work and was concerned with the analysis of factors entering into the establishment of marriage. The subjects were 46 married couples who were relatively homogeneous in age, education, occupation, socioeconomic status, and duration of marriage. A comparison group was formed by a random grouping of the subjects into male–female pairs. A portion of the resulting husband–wife correlations is presented in Table 2–2. These findings were seen as supportive of the notion of assortative mating through homogamy, at least with respect to such characteristics as opinions on current topics.

TABLE 2–2
HUSBAND–WIFE CORRELATIONS VERSUS
RANDOM MALE–FEMALE CORRELATIONS ON A SERIES
OF PHYSICAL AND PSYCHOLOGICAL CHARACTERISTICS[a]

Characteristic	Association of husband–wife pairs	Association of random pairs
Age	.69	.06
Height	.36	.10
Weight	.32	−.12
Arithmetic reasoning	.29	−.12
Information	.41	−.08
Opinions on current Topics	.65	.48
Political preference	.54	.50

[a]Data from Schiller, 1932.

Other data consistent with these general findings were soon reported by numerous researchers. For example, Kirkpatrick and Stone (1935) constructed a Belief Pattern Scale dealing with favorable versus unfavorable attitudes about religion. These scales were given to students at the University of Minnesota and to their parents. Significant parent–child correlations were found but more relevant to the present context was the husband–wife correlation of .56. In a theme to be repeated throughout this line of inquiry, the authors suggested, "There is a crumb of evidence for either assortative mating or attitudinal convergence of personality [Kirkpatrick & Stone, 1935, p. 582]." In a similar investigation, Morgan and Remmers (1935) also found parent–child and husband–wife pairs to be significantly correlated in their liberal–conservative attitudes toward statements of social, economic, political, educational, and religious policy. The husband–wife coefficient was .38. A third related study in the same year (A. McC. Hunt, 1935) utilized still a different kind of attitudinal content—the relative evaluation of a set of ideals. In the sample were 62 married couples, and the task was to rank order the importance of cheerfulness, cleanliness, cooperation, courage, courtesy, dependability, effectiveness, friendliness, good sportsmanship, honesty, initiative, obedience, openmindedness, respect, reverence, self-control, and thrift. Correlations for each husband–wife pair were obtained and the median value for the married couples was .48 (as compared to a median correlation of .25 for 62 random pairs). The author's superlatively cautious interpretation of the finding was that "This may or may not tend to prove that similarity of standards and ideals is sometimes one factor in the attraction of two young people to each other [A. McC. Hunt, 1935, p. 226]."

A somewhat more elaborate version of this kind of study was carried out by Schooley (1936). A sample of 80 married couples in Pennsylvania responded to a series of tests including measures of intellectual ability, personality traits, and visual acuity. Of interest here is her use of two Thurstone blanks measuring attitudes toward Communism and birth control and also the Allport-Vernon Scale of Values. Table 2–3 shows the husband–wife correlations for these variables. The findings are consistent and clear, namely, "Husbands and wives tend to marry persons similar to themselves in all of the characteristics measured by the present study [Schooley, 1936, p. 346]."

In one more study of intrafamily similarity from this era, Newcomb and Svehla (1937) administered Thurstone scales dealing with attitudes

TABLE 2–3
HUSBAND–WIFE CORRELATIONS ON
ATTITUDES AND VALUES

Variable	Correlation
Attitudes	
Communism	.60
Birth control	.58
Values	
Theoretical	.37
Economic	.25
Aesthetic	.23
Political	.45
Religious	.38

[a]After   Schooley,   1936,   p.   343, Table 1.

toward church, war, and Communism to members of almost 200 husband–wife pairs in Cleveland. The intraspouse similarities are shown by correlations of .76, .43, and .58 on the three topics. A smaller separate group of young husbands and wives yielded very similar coefficients ($r = .67, .53$, and .71) which at least suggests that similarity is not the result of an increasing convergence of attitudes over the course of a marriage.

In summary, then, the association between similarity and attraction has consistently been verified in the husband–wife studies.

Similarity between Friends

The study of attitude similarity between pairs of friends has led to results parallel to those involving married couples. Winslow (1937) suggested, "The bases for the establishment of the feeling of friendship between two persons are undoubtedly numerous. It may well be that an awareness of unanimity of opinion by two individuals fosters the establishment of friendship [p. 433]." The topics chosen for study were attitudes about Negroes, American foreign policy, current economic policy, religion, and government policies. The subjects were 86 general psychology students at Brooklyn College; each responded to the questionnaire and also gave it to a same-sex friend. When all of the items were scored along a liberal–conservative dimension, the friend pairs were found to correlate .24. For specific topics, the coefficients are shown in Table 2–4. Winslow concluded:

> The positive correlation found between friends' opinions, however, must indeed indicate that friends possess considerably more resemblance than could be expected by chance. But of course, the question is not answered as to whether the similarity is produced by the influence of the opinion of one upon the other in the friendship pair, or is really the basis in the first place for the establishment of the friendship [p. 441].

Richardson (1940) noted that "Informal observation suggests the hypothesis that resemblance in fundamental evaluative attitudes might be

TABLE 2–4

CORRELATIONS OF FRIEND PAIRS
ON ATTITUDE TOPICS[a]

Topic	Correlation
Foreign affairs	.16
Race	.44
Religion	.25
Economics	.11
Politics	.23

[a]Data from Winslow, 1937, p. 437.

characteristic of mutual friends [p. 303]." The degree of resemblance between friends versus the similarity of random pairs was determined on the Allport-Vernon Scale of Values. The subjects were drawn from a group of female students at the New Jersey College for Women and from a separate group of adult women. The findings are shown in Table 2–5. On the basis of these and other analyses, it was concluded that "community of values is a factor in friendships between women. This is more clearly demonstrated when the friends are mature women than when they are college students [Richardson, 1940, p. 309]."

TABLE 2–5

CORRELATIONS BETWEEN PAIRS OF FRIENDS
VERSUS RANDOM PAIRS ON VALUES[a]

Values	Undergraduate friends, 46 Pairs	Adult friends, 22 Pairs	Random undergraduates, 48 Pairs	Random adults, 21 Pairs
Theoretical	.21	.30	.06	−.33
Economic	.10	.36	−.06	−.13
Aesthetic	.26	.37	−.02	.02
Social	.15	.26	−.04	−.37
Political	.13	.01	−.18	−.09
Religious	.34	.45	−.08	−.21

[a]After Richardson, 1940, p. 307.

It should be pointed out that there are also a few negative findings in the literature. Each of these involves friends rather than marital partners and each could plausibly be explained away as a special case. For example, among 60 undergraduates, Vreeland and Corey (1935) found friends to be similar in social intelligence but not on the topics included in a public opinion scale. It was pointed out that the issues were not particularly relevant to the concerns of college students. Pintner, Forlano, and Freedman (1937) asked elementary school children to name their best friends in the classroom and found no evidence for attitude similarity between friends. That the choices were restricted to in-class friends may have been the reason for the lack of relationship. The investigators went to another elementary school and asked the children to name their best friends in or out of class. Under these conditions, the familiar friend–friend correlations appear in attitudes about art and music, in mental age, chronological age, and IQ. One other negative study (Reilly, Commins, & Stefic, 1960) indicated no evidence for friends' similarity on the Allport-Vernon scale, but it was pointed out that the subjects were all females in a Catholic college and, hence, represented a restricted range on the value dimensions.

In reviewing the husband–wife and friendship–pair similarity studies conducted between 1928 and 1939, Richardson (1939) concluded that attitudinal traits yielded the most consistent positive results. That same conclusion still holds true. On the type of topics which have been utilized in the various investigations, husbands and wives tend to resemble one another to a greater extent than would be expected by chance, and pairs of friends show the same tendency toward similarity. When one considers that these investigators each employed only a small number of attitude measures and that attraction is undoubtedly multidetermined, the fact that positive results are reported with great frequency in these real life studies is rather remarkable. It would appear that the basic notion of an association between attitude similarity and attraction is an accurate one.

EXTENDING THE SIMILARITY–ATTRACTION RELATIONSHIP

The series of correlational studies just described provide a relatively stable and consistent underpinning for further research on attraction. Such findings could be described as presenting the first of several identifiable decision points in the history of a research problem. How does one progress beyond the repetitive verification of an observed relationship? It is noticed that X and Y seem to be associated, these variables are operationalized in a variety of ways, and the observations are repeated in a systematic and objective way in several different samples. The original observation is verified and may be expressed in a quantified fashion. Anyone familiar with the field of psychology will not find it difficult to identify a multitude of behavioral findings both past and present which remain at just that point of progress. But, what else is there to do except move on to a different problem?

The general answer, as one might guess from the discussion in the previous chapter, is that paradigmatic science does not grow automatically out of a series of verifications of an infinite number of observed relationships. Progress involves a concentrated conceptual and empirical pursuit of a given phenomenon and not the random accretion of bits and pieces of low-level knowledge about multiple phenomena. The nature of the pursuit may take varied forms, and several different avenues have been explored in the study of attraction. One such avenue of progress involved remaining within the natural setting, retaining the correlational approach, and attempting to derive a somewhat more complicated hypothesis. We shall examine two such lines of research briefly.

Similarity and the Relative Success of the Relationship

Perhaps the earliest and certainly one of the most extensive of the investigations attempting to take an additional conceptual step was that conducted by Terman and Buttenweiser (1935a,b) at Stanford. They reasoned that if it were true that similarity results in mutual attraction, marital success should vary as a function of degree of similarity. For the first time, then, there was the intention of seeking a functional relationship rather than simply a factorial one.

A test designed to measure marital happiness was given to hundreds of married couples; the upper and lower thirds of this group (most and least happy) were selected for further study. Representing a still less successful point along the marital happiness dimension, a group of divorced couples also participated in the study.

From among these subjects, 100 couples in each group were equated for age, education, occupational status, and "environmental background." These 600 people were given the Strong Vocational Interest Blank and the Bernreuter Personality Inventory. On the variables measured by these instruments the correlations tended to be relatively low and not very promising for differentiating the couples with respect to marital success.

The authors suggested that "the evidence points consistently to the conclusion that such selection as takes place in these traits is in the direction of 'like' rather than 'unlike' matings [Terman & Buttenweiser, 1935a, p. 268]."

A more promising approach was to examine responses to each of the 545 items of the two tests with respect to husband–wife correlations across the three groups. From this array of coefficients, it is possible to identify those items for which the similarity of the most happy group is significantly different from that of either the unhappy or divorced group or both. Although the findings need to be cross-validated on additional samples, they at least represent a first step in seeking to use the general similarity effect to differentiate degrees of attraction. The 48 items yielding the best differentiation are presented in Table 2–6 as suggestive evidence of the kind of variables that might be pursued in future research.

The items deal with whether the respondent indicates that he feels positively or negatively about each activity, occupation, kind of person, or famous individual. The correlation coefficients reveal whether similarity, dissimilarity, or no relationship is characteristic of the group. For example, the happily married couples tend to be composed of pairs who both tend either to say that they avoid arguments or that they do not avoid arguments. The unhappy and divorced couples tend to be composed of pairs of which one member indicates a preference for avoiding arguments and the other

TABLE 2–6

HUSBAND–WIFE CORRELATIONS ON INDIVIDUAL
TEST ITEMS FOR HAPPY, UNHAPPY, AND DIVORCED COUPLES[a]

Item	Happy	Unhappy	Divorced
Avoid arguments?	.49	−.39	−.40
Life insurance salesman	.63	−.10	−.14
Teaching adults	.50	.08	−.23
Prefer a play to a dance?	.81	.35	.16
Dentist	.37	.09	−.38
Men who use perfume	.42	−.02	−.11
Are you usually considered indifferent to opposite sex?	.45	−.08	.04
Street car conductor versus motorman	.40	−.05	−.06
Definite salary versus commission	.43	−.10	.03
Easily discouraged when opinions of others differ from your own?	.64	.15	.25
Energetic people	.53	.02	.18
Like attention from acquaintances when ill?	.41	−.12	.09
Great variety versus similarity of work	.35	−.23	.08
J. J. Pershing, soldier	.44	.00	.08
Loan money to acquaintances	.30	−.10	−.10
Contributing to charity	.52	.16	.10
Looking at a collection of antique furniture	.44	−.02	.12
Willing to take chance alone in doubtful situation?	.40	.12	−.07
Quick-tempered people	.34	−.11	.03
Pessimists	.29	.12	−.30
Am quite sure of myself	.30	.10	−.16
Lack self-confidence?	.38	−.02	.04
Usually work better when praised?	.24	−.15	−.11
People who have done you favors	.40	.17	−.11
Prefer making hurried decisions alone?	.20	−.18	−.13
Meeting new situations	.32	−.03	−.06
Raising money for charity	.50	.18	.10
Teetotalers	.48	.41	−.17
Opportunity to understand how superior expects work to be done	.42	.14	−.02
Usually liven up the group on a dull day	.15	−.20	−.22
Pet canaries	.49	.02	.26
Regular hours of work	.25	−.10	−.10
Prefer to be alone at times of emotional stress?	.50	.03	.30
Criminal lawyer	.38	.13	−.04
Symphony concerts	.45	.34	−.13
Ever argue a point with respected older person?	.38	.15	−.05

TABLE 2–6 (Continued)

Item	Happy	Unhappy	Divorced
Chopping wood	.16	−.32	−.02
To be a president of a society	.25	.13	−.30
Want someone with you when you receive bad news?	.31	−.16	.14
Play your best even when opponent superior?	.22	−.06	−.14
Rather stand when late at meeting than take front seat?	.18	−.04	−.25
Often in a state of excitement?	.20	−.22	−.01
Operating machinery	.18	−.44	.16
People who borrow things	.23	.16	−.33
Thomas A. Edison	.44	.03	.21
Rancher	.46	.11	.19
Conservative people	.38	.23	−.08
Few intimate friends versus many acquaintances	.16	−.16	−.13

[a] Data from Terman and Buttenweiser, 1935b.

indicates a preference for not avoiding arguments. On the next item, the happily married spouses both tend to say that they would like or both dislike the occupation of life insurance salesman. The unhappy and divorced couples indicate neither similarity nor dissimilarity in attitudes about this occupation.*

In reading through this list of discriminating items, it is interesting to speculate as to why similarity and dissimilarity of particular attitudes might conceivably influence mutual attraction in a relationship. The reader might have noted that almost nothing has been said up to this point about why attitude similarity of any kind should influence attraction. That question will be taken up in the following chapters in some detail, and its omission here is simply a reflection of the atheoretical orientation which characterized almost all of these early correlational studies.

---

*There were also 11 items which indicated significant group differences in the opposite direction. In almost every instance, the happily married group showed no relationship whereas one or both of the other groups showed a positive relationship. Similarity tended to be associated with an unhappy relationship on the following items: Crossing a street to avoid meeting a person; being affected by praise or blame of many people; made discontented by discipline; accepting just criticism without getting sore; being an astronomer, an inventor, a landscape gardener, a librarian, an orchestra conductor, or a secret service man; and attitude toward talkative people.

Sequence of the Similarity–Attraction Relationship

A frequently noted problem of interpretation in the correlational investigations was the sequence of the similarity–attraction relationship. The usual proposal was that similarity elicited a positive response and, hence, led to the development of positive interpersonal relationships. It was equally possible, of course, that positive interpersonal relationships exerted pressures toward attitudinal congruence. It would clearly be of value to be able accurately to place the elements of this relationship in an antecedent–consequent framework. Within the naturalistic setting it would be possible to conduct a longitudinal investigation in which attitudes were assessed prior to friendship formation.

The work of Newcomb (1956, 1961) represents the apogee of the type of correlational study so far described and also, perhaps, a transition between an interest in spontaneous "real life" interaction and the controlled laboratory investigations of attraction.

For two separate 17-man samples of transfer students at the University of Michigan, Newcomb provided a rent-free semester in a cooperative housing unit in return for time spent each week serving as subjects. Two research assistants lived in the basement of the house throughout the study. In each sample, the students were strangers to one another when they arrived on the campus, and Newcomb's interest centered on the intragroup relationships which subsequently formed. Much of this research involved the testing of hypotheses related to Newcomb's theoretical system, but we shall defer a discussion of that issue for the present.

The research required up to 5 hours per week from each subject in responding to questionnaires, tests, and interviews. In the first year's sample, attraction was measured by a rank ordering of all the other subjects and also a division into like, neutral, and dislike categories. In the second year, there was the rank ordering plus a rating on a 100-point scale. Attraction responses were obtained weekly with few exceptions. Attitude measures included a rather wide range of issues such as university practices, racial and ethnic relations, religion, and sex. In the second year, the attitude items were more specific with items such as believing in a life after death, mathematics as a major, Eisenhower as president, and listening to classical music. The attitudes were measured first by mail, before the subjects came to Ann Arbor, and again at the end of the semester. A number of other measures were also obtained such as the Allport-Vernon-Lindzey Scale of Values and a series of questions concerning the perceptions of other subjects.

If attitude similarity is, in fact, a determinant rather than a consequent of attraction, similar attitudes are likely to influence attraction only after a period of interaction in which views could be expressed. Newcomb (1961) hypothesized, therefore, that, "as a function of increased acquaintance, actual agreement by pairs of persons is increasingly associated with degree of positive attraction of those persons toward each other [p. 71]."

No single issue would seem to be sufficiently important to account for a great deal of the variance in attraction responses for all subjects. With the total array of issues, it was possible to predict that the greater the number of agreements about important issues relative to the number of disagreements about important issues, the greater the mutual attraction. As hypothesized, agreement on these miscellaneous issues was found to be related to attraction late in the semester. Thus, preacquaintance agreement predicted who would like whom after a period of interaction, but it did not predict initial attraction. Here for the first time was evidence that attitude similarity precedes attraction and, hence, may be conceptualized as a determinant.

The most satisfactory attitude issue for data analysis consisted of attitudes concerning other house members. The index of agreement for each pair of subjects was the relationship between the attraction ranks given by the two of them to the other 15 students living in the house. The correlations between mutual pair attraction and the index of agreement are shown in Table 2–7. It may be seen that, as expected, the relationship between similarity and attraction rose from correlations near zero at the beginning of the acquaintance process to about $r = .50$ by the end of the semester.

TABLE 2–7
CORRELATIONS BETWEEN MUTUAL
PAIR ATTRACTION AND AGREEMENT
ABOUT OTHER STUDENTS[a]

Week	Year 1	Year 2
0	.13	.16
1	.18	.20
2	.43	.28
5	.48	.35
6	.42	.36
7	.54	.40
8	.55	.44
11	.52	.44
12	.50	.36
13	.48	.42
14	.41	.60
15	.50	.56

[a]After Newcomb, 1961, p. 75.

After a later reanalysis of these same data, Newcomb (1963) added:

> As group members interact with one another, each of them selects and processes information—about objects of common interest, about one another as objects of attraction—in such ways that the inconsistencies and conflicts involved in imbalanced relationships tend to be avoided.
>
> ...the consequence of reciprocal adaptation is a mutual relationship that is in fact maximally satisfying to both or all of them—that is, maximally within the limits of what is possible [p. 385].

EXPERIMENTAL APPROACH TO SIMILARITY–ATTRACTION: CANDIDATES FOR A RESEARCH PARADIGM

A further step in the research on attitudes and attraction involved the experimental approach and the transfer of interest from everyday life into the laboratory. This particular shift would seem to be characteristic of the beginnings of paradigm research in those fields where experimentation is possible. How does a paradigm come into being? What operations become the standard ones? What sort of pretheoretical assumptions can be helpful? There are no very explicit answers to these questions. A number of individuals independently began such research with a variety of operations and a variety of theories. Which of these various beginnings actually developed into a full-fledged paradigm or even a miniparadigm probably depended on a great many factors including research fertility, the interests and inclinations of particular investigators, luck, the Zeitgeist, and a host of fortuitous circumstances. We will examine the first steps in several of the possible starting points for the paradigmatic study of attitude similarity–dissimilarity and attraction.

It should be stressed that there is a considerable difference between the type of paradigm discussed by Kuhn and that which is to be discussed here. From an historical perspective, Kuhn was examining primarily some of the clearly significant and highly successful paradigms which have characterized astronomy, physics, and chemistry over the past few centuries. Within behavioral science, we must discuss paradigms from a quite different perspective. That is, in the first stages of moving away from preparadigm research we are able to point out a large number of possible candidates for paradigm for any given research problem. It is quite possible that none of the attraction research endeavors to be described will succeed in becoming the type of paradigm characteristic of the older sciences. What is absolutely necessary, however, is research activity conducted as if it represented an integral part of a well-established paradigm. "Without commitment to a paradigm, there could be no normal science [Kuhn, 1962, p. 99]." With reference to current personality and social psychology, it must be added that without a paradigm-like commitment, research is simply an intellectual exercise with little chance of progressing toward normal science.

As a representative sample of varying experimental approaches to a possible attraction paradigm, several types of attraction experiments will be examined.

Small-Group Research

A familiar setting for research in social psychology is the small group. For example, Schachter (1951) utilized such a design in order to investigate the consequences of deviation by a group member from the attitudes or opinions of the remainder of the group. Basically, there were a series of small groups in which bogus members behaved in specific ways in order to create a given degree of opinion similarity–dissimilarity. Attraction was measured by a rank ordering of group members by each subject.

A theory of communication processes, based in part on the type of attitudinal studies described in this chapter was developed by Festinger and his colleagues (Festinger & Thibaut, 1951; Festinger, Gerard, Hymovitch, Kelly, & Raven, 1952). The theory advanced to account for the empirical relationships rested on the premise, "Within any social group, pressures operate toward uniformity of attitude. The origins of such pressures are at least twofold: social reality and group locomotion [Schachter, 1951, p. 160]." This general proposition was further developed in terms of proposed functional relationships between the opinion difference separating a group and a deviate and the dependent variables of *pressure to change the deviate's opinion* (*Pch*) and also *dependence on the deviate's opinion as a reference point in establishing social reality* (*Dep*). These proposed relationships were further modified by the variables of group cohesiveness and the relevance of the issue to the group members. Fig. 2–1 shows the proposed interrelationships. The dependent variable of rejection (*Rej*) (i.e., the obverse of attraction) is a derived one which is given by the formula

$$Rej = Pch \times (1 - Dep).$$

Using this formula and the figure, one could predict relative degrees of rejection as a function of amount of opinion deviancy, level of group cohesiveness, and relevance of the issues.

In Schachter's experiment, each of 32 groups of male undergraduates was established as a club, and the experiment took place at the first club meeting. By means of instructional variations, eight groups were constituted as high in cohesiveness with a relevant issue, eight as low cohesive with a relevant issue, eight as high cohesive with an irrelevant issue, and eight as low cohesive with an irrelevant issue. Each group consisted of five to seven subjects plus three stooges who pretended to be regular club members.

At the first meeting, each member read a short version of the Johnny Rocco case after which the experimenter asked the group to discuss and decide the question, "What should be done with this kid?" Seven alternatives, ranging from love to punishment, served as a guide. Each subject was asked to announce his opinion among the seven alternatives, and the three stooges

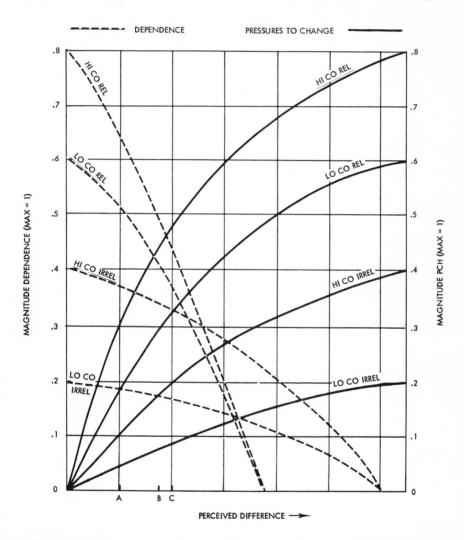

Fig. 2–1. Theoretical curves of the relationships among dependence, pressures to change, and cohesiveness, relevance, and perceived difference of opinion. LO = low; HI = high; CO = cohesiveness; REL = relevance; IRREL = irrelevance. (After Schachter, 1951, p. 196.)

responded last. Of the latter individuals, one chose an extremely deviant position but later changed to a modal position, one chose a deviant position from the beginning, and the third chose the modal opinion from the beginning. As a control, roles were rotated among the three confederates in different groups. The 45-minute discussion concentrated on thrashing out differences of opinion; halfway through and at the end each member again expressed his opinion. At this point sociometric questionnaires were filled out; subjects were asked to rank order their fellow group members.

The results were generally as predicted. The stooge who was the opinion deviate was the most rejected (lowest sociometric ranking) across groups and deviates were more rejected in high than in low cohesive groups. The predicted effects of issue relevance were not found in the rankings, but other data did support this prediction.

Emerson (1954) repeated the procedures of the Schachter experiment with high school students in the 10th, 11th, and 12th grades. Again, the deviate was the most rejected of the stooges, and he was rejected more in the high than in the low cohesive condition. As Emerson noted, these findings indicated that the laboratory techniques used by group dynamicists yield replicable data.

Pseudogroups

Within a relatively similar general paradigm, Berkowitz and Howard (1959) investigated some of the same variables plus group member interdependence and the personality variable of affiliation need (n Aff). It was proposed that pressure to change the deviate and, consequently, the rejection of a deviate who did not change would increase as group interdependence increased. Also, the greater the individual's affiliation need, the greater the amount of communication with the deviate and the more resistance to rejecting him.

The experimental setting was roughly parallel to that of Schachter. Four or five subjects of the same sex were brought together for a group task. Rather than Johnny Rocco, there was a case history outlining a labor–management dispute; the task was to predict the probable decision of a mediation board asked to settle the dispute. Prizes were to be awarded to the groups making the best prediction. There were 11 alternatives ranging from complete company blame to complete union blame. Opinions were to be given before and after a group discussion. Interdependence was manipulated by means of instructions, and n Aff was measured prior to the experimental sessions. Each subject sat in a separate cubicle and the information supposedly received from other group members was actually fictitious, having been prepared by the experimenters. Each subject was told that the other group members held opinions like their own or one step away; one group member, the deviate, was presented as four steps away. The 10-minute communication period was also experimentally controlled and consisted of the passage of notes; those received by each subject from those who agreed with his position were neutral whereas those from the deviate were an indication that he would not change his position. Then a questionnaire was given to assess attraction, "If you were to work on a similar problem again, to what extent would you want each of your present group members to be a member of your group?" The other group members were each rated on a 9-point scale.

It was found that the deviate was rated significantly more negatively than the other group members in the high interdependent condition by all subjects, but in the low interdependent condition the difference was significant only for the high n Aff subjects. The mean ratings are shown in Table 2–8.

TABLE 2–8

MEAN ATTRACTION RATINGS OF GROUP MEMBERS AGREEING AND DISAGREEING WITH SUBJECTS[a]

Group member	High interdependence condition			Low interdependence condition		
	High n Aff	Med. n Aff	Low n Aff	High n Aff	Med. n Aff	Low n Aff
Agreeing	7.39	7.79	7.75	6.80	6.41	6.60
Disagreeing	4.53	4.21	2.60	3.90	5.86	5.67

[a]After Berkowitz & Howard, 1959, p. 87.

Artificial Strangers

Still another approach to a research paradigm has been to present subjects with a stimulus such as a movie, a recording, or a sample of written material attributed to another subject. Attitudes, opinions, beliefs, or values can be presented in a controlled and consistent way, and the subjects' subsequent attraction responses obtained.

Jones and Daugherty (1959) were interested in the effects of similarity versus complementarity of personality variables and of values as represented by the Allport–Vernon–Lindzey scale and Christie's Mach IV scale. Tape-recorded interviews were made in which the experimenter interacted with two stimulus persons, one of whom was political in his beliefs and values, whereas the other was esthetically oriented. Two tapes were made in which order of presentation of the two orientations and the roles of the two stimulus persons were each reversed. Another variable was manipulated by means of instructions indicating that the subject should expect a competitive interaction, a cooperative interaction, or no interaction with the stranger. Attraction was measured by means of the subject's expressed preference between the two stimulus persons and also a 30-trait rating scale in which 15 favorable and 15 unfavorable adjectives were placed in a forced normal distribution to describe the stranger. It was found that the attraction ratings were positively though not significantly related to scores on the Allport–Vernon–Lindzey Political scale for the political stimulus person and negatively related for the esthetic stimulus person. The highest relationships were in the condition in which competitive interaction was anticipated. In the control condition there was a significant relationship between political values and preference for the political stimulus person, but this relationship did not hold in either interaction condition. With respect to political values:

> ...there is generally support for the similarity hypothesis. That is, the person who values political things in general, also values people who have a manifestly political orientation. When interaction was not anticipated, the higher a person's political values, the greater the tendency to "like" the political SP more than the esthetic SP... When a competitive interaction was anticipated, the positive attributes of the political SP became more salient to Ss with high political values, but while the "highs" flattered him more, they did not show any differential tendency to choose him in the interaction. Neither flattery nor preference related to political value score when a cooperative interaction was anticipated [Jones & Daugherty, 1959, p. 347].

Worchel and McCormick (1963) introduced Festinger's cognitive dissonance concept to account for response to the threat of attitudinal discrepancy. Dissonance reduction in such a situation could be brought about by changing one's beliefs, avoiding persons producing dissonance, seeking further validation of one's beliefs, or by rejecting the source of the dissonance. Among the proposed determinants of the specific mode of reduction taken were the person's certainty about the correctness of his beliefs and his self-ideal discrepancy. A group of 60 male subjects was divided into high, medium, and low thirds in terms of self-ideal discrepancy scores and assigned to one of two experimental conditions—agreement or disagreement. Individually, subjects were given a task in which they were to decide on one of two alternative solutions to a student problem and then indicate their degree of certainty about whether their choice was the better one. Then a second subject (a tape recording) gave his solution; the tape which the subject heard was a function of the experimental condition to which he was assigned and the solution he himself had chosen. Subjects were then asked to rate the stranger on a 5-point positive–

negative scale with respect to eight characteristics. It was found that the stranger was disliked significantly more when he had chosen a disagreeing solution than an agreeing one. Further, self-ideal discrepancy interacted with the experimental variable in that the low self-ideal discrepancy group showed the greatest reaction to agreement and disagreement. Also, the more uncertain the subjects were of their own opinion the more they liked an agreeing stranger and disliked a disagreeing stranger.

A paper and pencil presentation and manipulation of the stranger has been utilized by several experimenters. One of the first was A. J. Smith (1957, 1958, 1960) who worked within Heider's theoretical framework. In the first of these studies (A. J. Smith, 1957), each of 28 undergraduates was given the Allport–Vernon–Lindzey scale. Later in the semester they were given two partially completed scales (the subject's lowest value scale was left blank) which another student supposedly had filled out. One of the two scales was filled out exactly as the subject had done and one contained answers deviating from those of the subject. Subjects were told to study the booklets and develop an impression of what the person was like, then complete the test as they felt the other person would have done. An attraction measure was also given in which the stranger was rated on a 5-point scale in terms of the subject's willingness to work with him. Highly significant differences were found between the ratings of the similar and dissimilar stranger. Also, the blank scale filled out for the similar stranger was more like the subject's own than that filled out for the dissimilar stranger. In balance terms:

> ...we have confronted our subject with the situation $(p \ L \ x, \ o \ U \ x)$. That is to say, our subject has already answered an item on the Revised Allport-Vernon in a particular way and he perceives the hypothetical similar individual as having answered it in the same way. This generates a force in the direction $(p \ L \ o)$. As he examines each answer of the hypothetical similar individual he finds the same conditions exist $(p \ L \ x, \ o \ U \ x)$. Therefore, in each instance the tendency toward $(p \ L \ o)$ is strengthened and the final result would be expected to be $(p \ L \ o)$.
>
> When the subject examines the partially completed blank of the hypothetical dissimilar individual, the situation that exists is $(p \ L \ x, \ o{\sim} \ U \ x)$, or p likes x and o is not associated with x. The resolution of this disequilibrium could be accomplished by achieving the condition $(p{\sim} \ L \ o)$ which states that p does not like o. Again there is a tendency toward balance and a force in the direction of $(p{\sim} \ L \ o)$ arises [A. J. Smith, 1957, p. 258].

SELECTING A PARADIGM

Perhaps it should be reemphasized that the ultimate utility of any paradigm cannot be determined on an a priori basis. Of course, there are a few features of the proposed paradigms which might be considered in choosing a starting point—the uncontrolled stimulus variability inherent in the small-group method, the measurement limitations of a rank order procedure, the differential development of pretheoretical formulations across preparadigms, etc. Nevertheless, with continued refinement and extension, any of these approaches could easily serve as the basis for a program of basic research.

Another point, and one which is not terribly obvious, is the fact that whatever the general similarities among the experimental approaches just described, it is not reasonable to assume that they are part of the same potential paradigm. Even the Schachter and the Berkowitz–Howard approaches are only roughly parallel. They differ in terms of the nature of the stimulus presented to the subject, the amount of experimenter control over the stimulus, the topic about which opinions are elicited, and the way in which the dependent variable is measured. Because we have not agreed upon methodology and because the available data are limited, most of us pretend in writing journal articles that the findings of all such studies provide cumulative facts about the same problem. Thus, all reasonable sounding measures of attraction are treated as interchangeable as are all reasonable sounding operational definitions of similarity and dissimilarity. The fact is that the approaches cited above very likely represent different possible paradigms, both in theory and in methodology, and such differences will become increasingly manifest as the field progresses. A necessary, though hardly sufficient, condition for progress in research is consistency of operations across experiments. Different operations may or may not yield precisely the same results, but this is a matter for empirical determination rather than armchair assumption.

In any event, we can conclude that the common sense observation about a relationship between attitudinal similarity and attraction is sufficiently accurate and sufficiently general and sufficiently powerful to hold across a variety of situations, both in everyday life and in the laboratory and across a variety of operational definitions of the variables. Given a powerful and pervasive relationship, there is strong encouragement for suggesting that intensive research on this phenomenon within a single paradigm could prove to be a valuable endeavor. It is to one such line of research that we now turn our attention.

THE BASE RELATIONSHIP
AND ANALYTIC RESEARCH

Chapter 3 / Initiating Paradigm Research on Attitude Similarity–Dissimilarity and Attraction

It should be abundantly clear at this point that several different kinds of evidence indicate that interpersonal attraction is related to similarity and dissimilarity of attitudes. If, however, we wish to initiate a research paradigm, it is necessary to consider that apparent relationship as simply the starting point for a program of basic research.

The first investigation in this series necessarily set the pattern for much of what was to follow in the subsequent outpouring of attraction research. It should be noted that, although neither the present form nor the present scope of the endeavor was envisioned when the first experiment was planned in 1959, at least three underlying assumptions were present from the beginning. It may be helpful to note them briefly.

UNDERLYING ASSUMPTIONS

1. A meaningful and cumulative increase in knowledge is possible only if identical or equivalent operations serve as connecting links across experiments. Perhaps a simpler statement of the same proposition is that consistent results require consistent operations. This seemingly banal assumption is noted here in order to make explicit the necessity for consistency across experiments and to underline the existing state of inconsistency in many areas of behavioral research. If experiment A and experiment B are related only with respect to the words used to label the variables and not with respect to the actual stimuli and responses under investigation, A and B may, but very likely do not, have relevance to one another. Even if a rose is a rose is a rose, attraction is not necessarily attraction. And, similarity on one set of attitudes presented in a particular way is not necessarily the same as similarity on another set of attitudes presented in a different way.

In the research to be described, then, operations defining stimuli and responses were devised and then utilized in each of the subsequent experiments. Whenever new operations were introduced, the intention was to determine generality and not to assume it. In a field noted more for a curious delight in methodological innovation than for consistency, such concern with operational constancy is still somewhat of an anomaly. Some have misinterpreted the concern with methodological consistency to mean that innovation and elaboration are discouraged (Wright, 1971). In fact, the opposite is true so long as there are bridges connecting the old methods with the new (Byrne, in press).

2. *Theoretical constructs refer to the experimentally defined stimuli and responses rather than to the "real life" variables from which these operations were originally derived.* This assumption is closely related to the first one, but misunderstandings over this point occur with sufficient frequency that it may be helpful to anticipate them. The impetus for much of the research in the early phases of inquiry into any problem is likely to be naturalistic observation of phenomena. The relationship between similarity and attraction is a good example of this. But, when paradigmatic research is undertaken, it is characteristic to find a greater and greater disparity between the original phenomena of interest and that which is being investigated experimentally. Thus, as experimental control is extended and as measuring procedures are refined, and, as conceptual analysis is expanded, the focus of research inquiry often leads away from the uncontrolled complexities of the nonlaboratory world. This is not a tragedy to be deplored but an essential characteristic of basic research. As was discussed in Chapter 1, the possibility of applying research knowledge increases with such experimental isolation and theoretical development. In Chapter 14 some of the applied implications of attraction research will be made explicit. Application does not imply, though, that each time Y is found to be a function of X under highly specific conditions that variables resembling Y and X in natural settings should be related in the same way. Partly, this is because different stimuli and responses tend to be involved. Partly, it is because out there in the never-never land of everyday life, A and B and C and D and perhaps many other variables are also operating and hence may obscure or completely nullify the $Y–X$ relationship. As Farber (1964) notes, somewhat optimistically, "In any event, there is

universal agreement on one point: before one generalizes from observations of behavior in the laboratory to real-life situations, one had better consider very carefully the differences between the laboratory conditions and those in real life [p. 20]."

3. *In the initial stages of paradigm research, a preliminary theory is useful and perhaps essential in guiding and organizing experimental efforts.* It probably is not possible to conduct any kind of research in the absence of, at least, implicit notions about what is being studied and how one should proceed. For some, it is appealing to believe that one can conduct purely empirical research to obtain hard facts out of which a theory will grow. Such an approach most probably means that one's theoretical assumptions are simply not verbalized. In any event, there are a number of advantages in attempting to make explicit one's initial theoretical orientation.

A detailed description of attraction theory is reserved for a later section of this book; what follows is an outline of the tentative theory which guided this research effort from its inception.

> ... not all theories are paradigm theories. Both during pre-paradigm periods and during the crises that lead to large-scale changes of paradigm, scientists usually develop many speculative and unarticulated theories that can themselves point the way to discovery. Often, however, that discovery is not quite the one anticipated by the speculative and tentative hypothesis. Only as experiment and tentative theory are together articulated to a match does the discovery emerge and the theory become a paradigm [Kuhn, 1962, p. 61].

Beginning with the first experiment in this series (Byrne, 1961a), the theoretical underpinning of all of the research has been that attraction toward X is a function of the relative number of rewards and punishments associated with X.

The concept of reinforcement obviously suggests the possibility of a relationship between the attraction paradigm and learning theory. Clore (1966) notes:

> When the words *reinforcement model* are used they imply that the attributes and general inference rules of the model come from the experimental literature on reinforcement. The concept of reinforcement used to explain attraction is a model rather than a theory for at least two reasons. First, because reinforcement theory is a system with its own ideas and laws external to the attraction phenomenon. The attributes and meanings of this system are being transferred from their original realm, simple animal learning, to the previously unrelated data of interpersonal attraction. Secondly, a model rather than a theory is in use because we are not interested in altering learning theory with our data but rather in suggesting a theory of attraction. If our model does not fit we may certainly discard it, but we would not claim that learning theory had been shown to be in error. If the reinforcement model is worthwhile, one may expect it to play the role of midwife in the formulation of a genuine theory of attraction and in the generation of experimental situations that might not otherwise have been conceived [p. 12].

A. J. Lott (1966), in a similar vein, indicates that "By defining attraction toward persons in S–R terms we are able to place this concept within a large nomological net in which other concepts have already been linked, theoretically and empirically, and which provides a basis for derivations specific to the investigation of social behavior."

In the present line of research on attitude similarity and attraction, a reinforcement model has been employed along with speculations about some of the specific effects of attitude statements. The most general explanatory concept used to account for the effect of attitude similarity–dissimilarity on attraction is reward and punishment. When one individual receives positive reinforcement from another, positive affect is elicited and, through simple conditioning, becomes associated with the other individual. Subsequent evaluative responses directed toward the other individual will be positive. When one individual receives negative reinforcement from another, negative affect is elicited and becomes associated with the other individual. In this instance, subsequent evaluative responses directed toward that other individual will be negative. The relative amounts of reward and punishment associated with a given individual determine the strength and direction of attraction toward him.

Also, the effect of similar and dissimilar attitudes on attraction is interpreted as a special case of reward and punishment. Specifically, it is proposed that attitude statements are affect-arousing; the motive involved is the learned drive to be logical and to interpret correctly one's stimulus world.

With this very sketchy background, an attempt will be made to describe the development of the base relationship in the attitude–attraction paradigm.

DEVISING A METHODOLOGY

The basic methodology was utilized first in an experimental investigation which in many respects represented simply a further demonstration of the effect of attitude similarity–dissimilarity on attraction (Byrne, 1961a).

Procedure

What was sought as an initial empirical base was an experimental situation in which attitude similarity could be manipulated, as many as possible of the other determinants of attraction controlled, and attraction responses measured. As a means of eliminating the influence of variables such as physical attractiveness, accent, style, gestures, size, race, acting skills of stooges, a varient of the A. J. Smith (1957) approach was employed.

Subjects were told that they were taking part in a study of interpersonal judgment in which they would be given certain information about another individual and then asked to make several judgments concerning him. With minor modifications, the following instructions have been used in most of the parallel studies which were to follow:

> Earlier this semester, you filled out an attitude questionnaire called the Survey of Attitudes which dealt with a series of issues. One purpose was to learn something about student attitudes, but a second purpose was to determine the extent to which one person can form valid judgments about another person just by knowing a few of his attitudes. Last semester we carried out other studies of this sort. Students wrote down several sorts of information about themselves, their names were removed, and this information was given to other students. The task was to form an opinion about the stranger's intelligence, knowledge of current events, morality, and adjustment just on the basis of knowing a few bits of information about the person's past and present life. We found that students could guess these things with better than chance accuracy. So, this study is an extension of the previous one, and a major change has been introduced. Instead of information about the other person's life, you will be shown his or her attitudes on 26 specific issues. The background information was removed from each of these scales. Each of you will receive the attitude scale of another student. All I can guarantee is that this person is the same sex as yourself, to the best of our knowledge you do not know the person whose attitude scale you will receive, and it is not someone in the same psychology class as yourself. Please read the person's answers carefully and try to form an opinion about him or her. As soon as you have studied each of the attitudes, fill out the Interpersonal Judgment Scale and indicate your best guess as to this person's intelligence, knowledge of current events, morality, and adjustment. Also, indicate how much you think you would like this person if you met him and how much you think you would like to work with this person as partners in an experiment.

In the initial study, 34 college students were given a 26-item attitude scale early in the semester and then were assigned to one of two experimental groups. Half of the subjects were exposed to a stranger with attitudes like their own and half to a stranger with attitudes unlike their's. The stranger's scale could have been a genuine one drawn from a large pool to fit a particular subject as either like or unlike. It was more economical to construct an artificial stranger, and the situation for the subject is no different so long as the subject does not know that the experimenter filled out the stranger's scale. For each of the 17 subjects in the Similar Attitude group, an attitude scale was filled out in such a way that the "stranger" responded to all 26 of the issues exactly as the subject had done. In the dissimilar attitude group, each subject received a scale which was a mirror image of his own. For example, if the subject were strongly against integration and mildly in favor of smoking, the stranger was strongly in favor of integration and mildly against smoking. These bogus scales were filled out in a variety of styles (left- and right-handed check marks, Xs, large and small handwriting, etc.) and in a variety of colors in several media (fountain pen, ball point pen, pencil). The background information at the top of the first page was cut out with scissors, purportedly to preserve the anonymity of the student who had filled out the scale.

The Attitude Scale

On the basis of the numerous studies which had been carried out earlier, it was assumed that the specific content about which attitudes, beliefs, opinions, and values were expressed was not a crucial factor. In a pilot study, another group of undergraduates had been asked to list a series of issues which they and their acquaintances had discussed. Of the topics given, the 26 most frequently mentioned were converted into simple scales of the following type:

5. Belief in God (check one)
—I strongly believe that there is a God.
—I believe that there is a God.
—I feel that perhaps there is a God.
—I feel that perhaps there is no God.
—I believe that there is no God.
—I strongly believe that there is no God.

23. Political parties (check one)
—I am a strong supporter of the Democratic party.
—I prefer the Democratic party.
—I have a slight preference for the Democratic party.
—I have a slight preference for the Republican party.
—I prefer the Republican party.
—I am a strong supporter of the Republican party.

All of the attitude items used in this investigation as well as additional items used in subsequent investigations are shown in Appendix A.

The Attraction Measure

The measure of attraction consisted of two simple rating scales which essentially asked the two rather straightforward questions most frequently utilized in sociometric research. With respect to the stranger, each subject was asked to indicate whether he felt that he would like or dislike this person and whether he believed he would enjoy or dislike working with this person. These two variables are each measured on a 7-point scale. They are scored from 1 to 7 and then summed to yield the measure of attraction which ranges from 2 (most negative) to 14 (most positive). This two-item response measure has been found to have a split-half reliability of .85 (Byrne & Nelson, 1965a).

In order to disguise to some degree the major purpose of the experiment and to lend credence to the instructions concerning interpersonal judgment, the two attraction scales are embedded as the last two items in a 6-point Interpersonal Judgment Scale (IJS) which is reproduced in Appendix B. The first four items call for evaluations of the stranger's intelligence, knowledge of current events, morality, and adjustment. These four dimensions, incidentally, were based on intuitive speculations as to the way individuals repond to others who agree with them or who fail to do so. We shall return in a later chapter to these four scales and the effect of similarity–dissimilarity on them.

Results

The mean attraction response of the similar attitude group was 13.00 whereas that of the dissimilar attitude group was 4.41. This difference was a highly significant one. In fact, the most negative response in the similar attitude group was more positive than the most positive response in the dissimilar attitude group; the stimulus variable was sufficiently potent that there was no response overlap between the two conditions. The similarity–attraction hypothesis was once again confirmed, and our specific procedures and methods were shown to be effective for a laboratory recapitulation of the phenomenon. The only pertinence of this or any other single experiment is in its relationship to a conceptual system. A finding isolated from the context of a paradigm is scientifically meaningless, no matter whether it is clever or dull, whether the results are expected or unexpected and what the level of statistical significance might be. In the present instance, the experiment is of interest only because it turned out to be the first step in a particular paradigmatic approach to the study of attraction.

In attempting to establish a firm base relationship, the next research step was to attempt a more precise analysis of the stimulus-response sequence thus identified. One might say that the task was to specify more precisely and more accurately the stimulus to which subjects are responding.

DEVIANCY VERSUS DISSIMILARITY

As is usually the case, even a seemingly clear-cut finding such as the foregoing may be seen on further analysis to raise a number of questions. The first such problem to be considered was with respect to the nature of the stimulus dimension that was utilized.

Problem

In the previous investigation, one of the two stimulus conditions was labeled "similar attitudes" and the other "dissimilar attitudes." Because of an unanticipated methodological problem, however, this label remained open to question and, hence, the theoretical interpretation of the findings rested on a somewhat wobbly base. The problem was that the experimental subjects were remarkably homogeneous in responding to most of the attitude items. For example, almost all the subjects indicated that they believed in God, liked sports, and enjoyed science fiction. Since the majority of the items were answered with this type of uniformity, the stimulus properties of the resulting bogus stranger necessarily are ambiguous. A similar stranger not only agreed with the subject but also appeared to be a normal, average, conforming member of the Texas undergraduate culture. A dissimilar stranger, on the other hand, not only disagreed with the subject but also could be seen as a statistically abnormal individual whose viewpoint was extremely deviant in this culture. Thus, the stimulus for the differential attraction responses could have been similarity–dissimilarity of attitudes, conformity–deviancy, or some combination of these variables.

In order to identify the stimulus more explicitly, another investigation (Byrne, 1962) was undertaken in which the only attitudinal items employed were those that elicited heterogeneous views. On the basis of the responses of earlier subjects, the seven items of the 26-item scale on which there was the greatest diversity of opinion were arranged in a brief attitude scale. Now, a stranger could be made to express attitudes similar to or dissimilar from those of the subject without at the same time expressing either conforming or deviant beliefs. The specific topics were: undergraduates getting married; smoking; integration in public schools; drinking; money as a goal; the university grading system; and political parties.

Another major purpose of this investigation was to explore for the first time the functional relationship between similarity–dissimilarity and attraction. In the various experiments cited earlier, a factorial approach was followed uniformly. That is, there is an attempt to create similarity (as in the 26 similar, 0 dissimilar condition) and dissimilarity (as in the 0 similar, 26 dissimilar condition). It is then assumed that these two conditions represent points along a stimulus continuum and that intermediate points would yield intermediate attraction responses. With the seven-item attitude scale, it was feasible to present subjects with each possible variation in the number of similar and dissimilar attitudes expressed by a stranger and, thus, empirically to determine the effects of intermediate levels of similarity.

Procedure

The overall procedure followed that of the initial experiment. Each of 112 students was given the seven-item attitude scale and later presented with a scale supposedly filled out by a stranger who was to be evaluated on the IJS.

With respect to the bogus scales, a subject was assigned to one of eight experimental groups. Those in the first group were given a stranger who was similar to themselves on all seven issues (7–0). The next group received a stranger similar on six issues and dissimilar on one (6–1); the particular item which was dissimilar was varied randomly among the subjects in the condition. Each subsequent group, then, differed in the number of similar and dissimilar items on through the eighth group in which there was dissimilarity on all topics (0–7).

Results

The mean attraction responses of the eight experimental groups are shown in Table 3–1. Once again the experimental treatment was found to have a highly significant effect on attraction. The findings also provide evidence supporting the contention that the stimulus to which subjects respond should be labeled "similarity–dissimilarity." Further, a functional stimulus–response relationship may now be described. Rather than simply affirming that similarity and dissimilarity elicit different attraction responses, it is now possible to conceptualize the relationship as a continuous one in which the specific response to a stranger with a given set of attitudes could be predicted if the subject's own attitudes are known.

There are, nevertheless, still ambiguities concerning the stimulus. Further experimental analysis is required.

TABLE 3–1

FUNCTIONAL RELATIONSHIP BETWEEN
ATTITUDE SIMILARITY–DISSIMILARITY AND ATTRACTION[a]

Experimental condition	Mean attraction response
7 Similar, 0 dissimilar	12.15
6 Similar, 1 dissimilar	11.15
5 Similar, 2 dissimilar	11.43
4 Similar, 3 dissimilar	9.07
3 Similar, 4 dissimilar	8.69
2 Similar, 5 dissimilar	8.47
1 Similar, 6 dissimilar	7.71
0 Similar, 7 dissimilar	7.00

[a]Data from Byrne, 1962.

Proportion of Similar Attitudes

Problem

In the experiment just described, the eight experimental conditions in which attitudinal similarity was varied could be conceptualized as representing at least three different stimulus variables: number of similar attitudes, number of dissimilar attitudes, and the relationship between these two expressed as a ratio or a proportion. Each of these three stimuli varied across the experimental conditions, and the attraction responses could conceivably have been elicited by any one of them or by some combination of these stimuli.

Procedure

To resolve this question about the stimulus, Byrne and Nelson (1965a) provided an experimental design in which the number of similar and dissimilar attitudes as well as the ratio between them could each be varied independently. To do this, a series of attitude scales of different lengths was constructed. The 26 items already discussed plus additional items of similar format were utilized to build eight scales varying in length from 4 to 48 items. The scales were roughly matched as to the importance of the item topics and also as to the percentage of subjects responding in each direction on an item.

A total of 168 students filled out one of these attitude scales and went through the standard experimental procedure. Stranger similarity–dissimilarity was manipulated as shown in Table 3–2. It may be seen that if significant attraction differences were found across columns, they would be attributable to the number of similar attitudes expressed by the stranger. Significant row differences would be attributable to the proportion of similar attitudes. If the number of dissimilar attitudes was the crucial stimulus, there

TABLE 3–2
EXPERIMENTAL DESIGN: NUMBER OF ITEMS ON WHICH
THE STRANGER HELD SIMILAR–DISSIMILAR ATTITUDES[a]

Proportion of similar attitudes	No. of similar attitudes		
	4	8	16
1.00	4–0	8–0	16–0
.67	4–2	8–4	16–8
.50	4–4	8–8	16–16
.33	4–8	8–16	16–32

[a]After Byrne and Nelson, 1965a, Table 1, p. 660.

would be significant column differences (with means in the opposite direction from that expected for the number of similar attitudes), significant row differences, and most importantly a significant interaction between rows and columns.

Results

The means for these various experimental conditions are shown in Table 3–3. Both an inspection of the data in Table 3–3 and the statistical analysis indicate that the only significant effect is that of the *proportion* of similar attitudes. Thus, we gained a still clearer conception of the stimulus. Subjects appear to be responding not simply to the number of similar or dissimilar attitudes expressed by the stranger but to the *relative* number of the two types of attitudes, regardless of the total number of topics involved.

TABLE 3–3
MEANS OF ATTRACTION RESPONSES TOWARD
STRANGERS WITH VARYING NUMBERS AND VARYING
PROPORTIONS OF SIMILAR ATTITUDES[a]

Proportion of similar attitudes	No. of similar attitudes			
	4	8	16	Total
1.00	11.14	12.79	10.93	11.62
.67	10.79	9.36	9.50	9.88
.50	9.36	9.57	7.93	8.95
.33	8.14	6.64	6.57	7.12
Total	9.86	9.59	8.73	—

[a]After Byrne and Nelson, 1965a, Table 2, p. 660.

THE BASE RELATIONSHIP

At this point in our research effort, it became possible to describe the stimulus–response relationship with increased precision in mathematical form (Byrne & Nelson, 1965a). With the stimulus identified as proportion of similar attitudes, data from a variety of our investigations could be meaningfully combined even though attitude scales of various lengths had been used. Each of 790 subjects had been exposed to 1 of 11 proportions of similar attitudes attributed to a stranger and then had evaluated that stranger on the IJS. Plotting the relationship, as shown in Fig. 3–1, the mean attraction responses for the 11 stimulus values suggested a linear function. A straight-line function was fitted to the data, yielding the formula $Y = 5.44X + 6.62$.

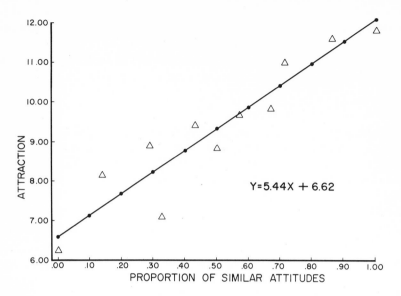

Fig. 3–1. Attraction toward a stranger as a linear function of proportion of similar attitudes. (After Byrne & Nelson, 1965a, p. 661.)

Thus, the relationship between attitude similarity–dissimilarity and attraction was now stated in terms of an empirical law, which enabled us to make specific predictions about attraction responses *within this type of experimental situation.*

It may be seen that the investigations proceeding from the initial factorial experiment toward the establishment of an *S–R* law involved analytic research directed toward an increasingly specific formulation of the stimulus. The following chapter contains a description of additional analytic experiments which serve further to identify the elements comprising the stimulus and, necessarily, to clarify and hence alter our conception of the stimulus. That is to say, there is no actual point at which the base relationship is solidly established for all times and the analytic research completed.

For the sake of exposition, however, the base relationship will be defined as that depicted in Fig. 3–1: attraction toward a stranger as a linear function of the proportion of similar attitudes expressed by that stranger. From this base, it will be shown how paradigm research can ramify in a surprising diversity of directions.

Chapter 4 / Analytic
Research on the Base Relationship

If we continue to focus attention on the base relationship, many possible complexities soon become obvious—even within this seemingly simple and unambiguous experimental situation. For example, what precisely are the stimulus attributes to which subjects are responding? Have we completed our analysis by identifying the stimulus as the relative number of similar and dissimilar attitudes or are there other stimulus elements to be discovered through a more detailed conceptual and empirical examination?

Before describing some of the directions in which analysis has proceeded, it might be noted that the question of analysis and the direction it takes may appear to be "purely empirical" and seemingly independent of theory. Only a thoroughgoing advocate of naive realism could believe that, however. On the contrary, it seems quite unlikely that proponents of different theoretical positions would be led to conduct the same kind of analytic experiments. For example, if the attitude–attraction relationship is seen as a complex social psychological situation in which individuals are striving to restore balance homeostatically or to reduce cognitive dissonance or to enhance self-esteem, subsequent research is not ordinarily directed toward identification of stimulus elements which contribute to response variance. In contrast, with the attitude–attraction relationship conceptualized as a stimulus–response sequence, the analysis of the stimulus into its component parts is a compatible research activity.

As a potentially useful theoretical analogue (and not as an experimentalist plot to dehumanize the warm throbbing flesh of real live people), we may conceptualize the experimental subject as more or less a complex stimulus-processing device. The attitude statements convey various bits of information and evoke several kinds of observed and unobserved responses. Those that we identify as attraction responses (consisting primarily of an evaluational component) vary as a function of the stimulus properties of the attitude material. The better we understand the elements of the stimulus which do or do not determine response variation, the more complete and more accurate is our theoretical description of the relationship. Though very little of our research has as yet been focused on an analysis of the response, such work represents another direction in which an analytic approach should eventually proceed. Various investigators have correctly stressed the importance of differentiating "attraction" into more specific response components such as friendship, general liking, romantic love, comradeship, sexual attraction, and parental love (Hogan & Mankin, 1970; Marlowe & Gergen, 1968; Rubin, 1970; Walster, 1970; Wright, 1969). It seems very likely that the antecedents of these various subcategories of attraction are not identical.

"EXTRANEOUS" DETERMINANTS OF ATTRACTION RESPONSES

Any investigator faces a problem when he applies a label to the operations with which he deals. The label applied to either the stimulus or the response may legitimately be questioned. One concern regarding the base relationship was to ascertain whether the phenomenon is best conceptualized as the effect of attitude similarity on attraction or as something else altogether, such as the effects of experimenter demands on the subject's acquiescence.

Experimenter Bias

Experimenter bias is one potential source of labelling error in attraction research. Rosenthal (1966) has shown that experimenters who are cognizant of an hypothesis tend to obtain results more favorable to that hypothesis than do unaware experimenters. It does not appear reasonable to propose that experimenter bias has any effect whatsoever on the results of attraction research. Many of the experiments have been conducted in a group setting with subjects from several different conditions present in each group simultaneously (e.g., Byrne, 1961a, 1962; Byrne & Nelson, 1965a). Additionally, the experimenter typically does not know the particular condition to which any given subject has been assigned. For the experimenter to bias the results under these conditions would require that he succeed in the impossible task of influencing different subjects in different directions at the same time even though he does not know in which direction any given subject must be influenced in order to provide support for the hypothesis. In some of the experiments (e.g., Byrne & Clore, 1966), the subject's experimental condition cannot be determined until after the experiment. To influence responses under these conditions, the experimenter must be biased, selective, and prescient. In the attraction experiments in which subjects are run individually (e.g., Byrne, Lamberth, Palmer, & London, 1969), the knowledgeable experimenter could influence the responses. It must be noted, however, that the responses obtained under these conditions are substantially the same as when the subjects are run in groups. It seems safe to conclude, therefore, that experimenter bias is not a stimulus variable in attraction research. Obviously, a badly designed attraction experiment might well involve experimenter bias as a major factor. The point is simply that the similarity–attraction function is not dependent on such bias.

Demand Characteristics

Another, and potentially more troublesome, source of labelling error for attraction research is the demand characteristics of the experimental setting (Orne, 1962). Specifically, Orne has called attention to the fact that subjects in an experiment have an investment in that particular experiment, and one of the consequences of this is that they want to be good subjects. If being a good subject means validating the experimenter's hypothesis and if it is possible to guess that hypothesis, then Orne argues that the results are a function of the demand characteristics of the situation and not of the experimental treatment.

The problem might best be conceptualized as an inquiry concerning the generality and applicability of experimental findings to nonexperimental settings. If demand characteristics were strongly operative only in the attraction laboratory, it is obvious that the stimulus to which subjects respond is not present in the "real world" and that generalization from one context to the other would be foredoomed. Actually, the generality of the similarity–attraction relationship is attested by the fact that the finding was originally established in real life situations. Presumably, the various friendships and marriages between attitudinally similar individuals did not develop in order to satisfy the demands of researchers who might happen along.

Despite the seeming confluence of laboratory and nonlaboratory attraction behavior, Orne's comments concerning demand characteristics merit further consideration. If demand characteristics are responsible for any portion of the response variance in attraction research, then it should be known to what extent we are studying the subject's ability to guess the similarity–attraction hypothesis plus his tendency to acquiesce. It is, of course, perfectly reasonable to study a subject's ability to guess hypotheses and/or his acquiescing tendencies. If so, the only error would be in labelling that behavior "interpersonal attraction."

Lamberth and Byrne (in press) conducted three experiments in an attempt to determine the role of demand characteristics in similarity–attraction research. In Experiment I, knowledge of the similarity–attraction hypothesis among subjects was investigated. One hundred and twenty-five subjects who had just participated in a standard attitude–attraction experiment were asked to state the experimenter's hypothesis; 76% were unable to verbalize any element of the hypothesis, and only 18% were able to answer the question correctly. In addition, the effect of similar attitudes on attraction did not differ for aware and unaware subjects. In Experiment II, the demand characteristics of the situation were manipulated. The similarity–attraction hypothesis was described to two groups of subjects, with one group asked to verify it and the other asked to do the exact opposite of the hypothesis. Two other groups were asked to guess the hypothesis with one group asked to verify it and the other to do the opposite. Analysis of variance indicated a significant effect of similarity, but the instructions had no effect on the subjects' attraction responses. In Experiment III, the two conditions in which subjects were asked to behave opposite to the hypothesis were replicated and two new groups introduced. A false hypothesis was described (i.e., opposites attract), with one group asked to support it and the other asked to do the opposite. Again, the only significant effect was attitude similarity.

The results of these investigations would seem to make a demand characteristics explanation of the similarity–attraction function untenable. Rather, the evidence is compatible with the proposition that the independent and dependent variables have been correctly labelled in attraction research.

DIFFERENTIAL IMPORTANCE OF ATTITUDINAL TOPICS

In the work described in the previous chapter, each attitude item was treated as an equally effective stimulus conveying information about similarity. Thus, the stranger's belief or lack of belief in God was treated no differently than his positive or negative reaction to Westerns. Actually, it was proposed that topic importance was likely to be a major determinant of an item's effect, but that differences in importance had been controlled by randomly assigning different topics as similar and dissimilar in each condition. The suggestion that importance is a crucial factor has been made by many other investigators. For example, Newcomb (1956) proposed that "The discovery of agreement between oneself and a new acquaintance regarding some matter of only casual interest will probably be less rewarding than the discovery of agreement concerning one's own pet prejudices [p. 578]." As a consequence of this assumption, Newcomb's (1961) index of agreement between two individuals is limited to topics of importance to both. In spite of the regularity with which topic importance tends to be included in such formulations, little systematic research had previously been directed toward this variable.

Scaling of Topic Importance

The first research step was to obtain judgments concerning the relative importance of the topics included on the attitude scales. In an unpublished study carried out by Mrs. Betsy Young, the original 26-item scale was expanded to 56 items (Appendix A) and presented to 138 undergraduates at the University of Texas. They were asked first to respond to the items in the usual way and then were instructed to rate each topic on a 4-point scale of importance. The topics are shown in Table 4–1 along with the mean rating obtained for each. These values are conceived as somewhat transitory because many specific ratings will undoubtedly be found to change over time and to vary in different subject samples.

Topic Importance and Attraction: Single Stranger Design

Method. On the basis of the importance ratings, Byrne and Nelson (1964) constructed four 14-item attitude scales ranging from the 14 least important items to the 14 most important ones. Each of 112 subjects filled out only *one* of these scales. Several weeks later they were recalled for an interpersonal judgment experiment with the usual instructions. Every subject was given the scale of one stranger who had responded to the same 14-item scale as he had done. The responses of the strangers were arranged to express either .00 or 1.00 similarity to those of the subject.

Results. The mean attraction responses are shown in Table 4–2. The proportion of similar attitudes exerted a highly significant effect on attraction, whereas topic importance did not even approach significance as a determinant of attraction. Subjects responded positively to a similar stranger and negatively to a dissimilar stranger regardless of the importance of the attitude topics.

TABLE 4–1
RELATIVE IMPORTANCE OF ATTITUDE TOPICS

Mean importance rating	Topics	Item No.
	14 Most important	
3.82	Belief in God	5
3.62	War	34
3.53	College education	43
3.46	American way of life	17
3.38	Premarital sex relations	19
3.35	Preparedness for war	27
3.33	Integration in public schools	10
3.31	Nuclear arms race	46
3.29	One true religion	25
3.26	Red China and the U.N.	31
3.16	Socialized Medicine	33
3.14	Divorce	48
3.11	Birth control	14
3.06	Professors and student needs	6
	14 Next to most important	
3.01	Acting on impulse	12
2.97	Money	21
2.95	Discipline of children	45
2.87	Family finances	53
2.86	Careers for women	55
2.85	Welfare legislation	28
2.79	Grades	22
2.77	Strict discipline	39
2.75	Draft	51
2.73	Financial help from parents	40
2.72	Undergraduate marriages	3
2.71	State income tax	35
2.68	Adjustment to stress	56
2.67	Group opinion	24
	14 Next to least important	
2.64	Women in today's society	52
2.60	Community bomb shelters	47
2.58	Necking and petting	8
2.57	Foreign language	42
2.55	Social aspects of college	13
2.50	Political parties	23
2.45	Drinking	16
2.40	Dating	30
2.25	Fresh air and exercise	44
2.15	A Catholic president	7
2.13	Creative work	29

TABLE 4–1 (Continued)

Mean importance rating	Topics	Item No.
1.99	Sports	18
1.98	Fraternities and sororities	1
1.93	Freshmen cars on campus	41
	14 least important	
1.92	Smoking	9
1.84	Dancing	50
1.78	Novels	32
1.51	Classical music	15
1.50	Modern art	54
1.47	Pets	37
1.35	Musical comedies	26
1.30	Tipping	36
1.29	Situation comedies	4
1.27	Foreign movies	38
1.26	Western movies and TV	2
1.25	Comedians who use satire	11
1.25	Gardening	49
1.24	Science fiction	20

Discussion. Since the effect of attitude similarity–dissimilarity on attraction was found to be independent of topic importance, should we conclude that Newcomb and others are incorrect in retaining that variable in their formulations? This is an example of a situation in which data do not correspond either to common sense or to theory. Although there is no reason to question the authenticity of the findings, it is reasonable to guess that the results may be attributable to certain aspects of the experimental design.

Two considerations argued against the premature rejection of topic importance as a variable. First, it seemed possible that the range of topic

TABLE 4–2

MEAN ATTRACTION RESPONSES FOR TWO LEVELS OF ATTITUDE SIMILARITY AND FOUR LEVELS OF TOPIC IMPORTANCE[a]

Proportion of similar attitudes	Topic importance			
	Least	Next to least	Next to most	Most
1.00	11.43	11.21	11.86	11.14
.00	6.36	5.79	7.71	5.71

[a]After Byrne and Nelson, 1964, p. 93.

importance utilized in this investigation was not sufficiently broad to elicit the hypothesized effect. It was proposed that the inclusion of more trivial items (such as attitudes toward cole slaw) and of more personally involving items (such as attitudes about the subject's sexual appeal) in the design would make it possible to demonstrate the effect of topic importance on attraction. Even with the present topics, however, it was difficult to believe that a stranger's attitude about dancing had as much effect as his attitude about war.

Second, it seemed possible that an adaptation effect obscured the operation of the importance variable. That is, each subject responded to only one stranger and, hence, did not compare strangers identical in proportion of attitudes to his own but with differences in topic importance across strangers. Had they been exposed to all four levels of importance, differential attraction might have resulted. This adaptation possibility was tested in the following investigation.

Topic Importance and Attraction: Multistranger Design

Byrne and Nelson (1965b) hypothesized that in a design utilizing a series of strangers with attitudes on topics of differential importance, similarity–dissimilarity and topic importance would each influence attraction.

Method. Again, the four 14-item attitude scales were employed. Each of 40 undergraduates filled out *all four* scales. Several weeks later, the interpersonal judgment experiment took place. The task was to examine four scales (each supposedly filled out by a different fellow student) and then evaluate the four strangers on the Interpersonal Judgment Scale (IJS). Half of the subjects were given four strangers who expressed 1.00 similarity; each stranger was represented by a different scale, one for each level of topic importance. The other 20 subjects responded to four strangers, each of whom represented .00 similarity on one of the four scales. The scales presented to each subject were made to appear as if filled out by four different individuals by means of using different colors of ink, various pencils, and different styles of check marks.

Each subject thus responded to four strangers who were either similar to or dissimilar from himself in attitudes, on topics representing four levels of importance.

Results. The mean attraction responses are shown in Table 4–3 for the topic importance and attitude similarity–dissimilarity variables. To our surprise, once again the only significant effect was that of attitude similarity. The subjects gave no evidence of responding differently to the four levels of topic importance.

TABLE 4–3

MEAN ATTRACTION RESPONSES FOR TWO LEVELS OF ATTITUDE SIMILARITY AND
FOUR LEVELS OF TOPIC IMPORTANCE[a]

Proportion of similar attitudes	Topic importance			
	Least	Next to least	Next to most	Most
1.00	10.25	9.80	10.20	10.85
.00	5.95	6.10	7.45	6.05

[a]After Byrne and Nelson, 1965b, p. 450.

Discussion. On the basis of the findings of this and the previous study, it would appear that the effect of attitude similarity–dissimilarity on attraction is not influenced by the importance of the attitudinal topics represented among the 56 items. Thus, the expression of similar attitudes elicits a positive response and the expression of dissimilar attitudes elicits a negative response whether the topic is a trivial one or an extremely important one.

The plausibility of the notion about topic importance, however, still induced us to suggest that the foregoing conclusion was possibly wrong in spite of two experiments to the contrary. By "wrong" it is only meant that topic importance may be ineffective under the special conditions of these two experimental designs. Conceivably in the multistranger design the subjects were responding not simply to the stranger's similarity or dissimilarity on the 14 items but also to his assumed similarity or dissimilarity on the remaining 42 items. If so, still a third type of research design would be required for an adequate test of the topic importance hypothesis.

If some subjects found that a given stranger was similar on unimportant topics and dissimilar on important ones, whereas other subjects responded to a stranger who was similar on important topics and dissimilar on unimportant ones, the effects of importance would be shown by differential attraction responses if proportion of similar responses were held constant.

Topic Importance and Attraction: Intrastranger Design

In the third investigation in this series, Byrne, London, and Griffitt (1968) tested the hypothesized importance effect by systematically varying the similar and dissimilar responses of each stranger with respect to whether they occurred on important or unimportant items. In addition, a second possible reason for the failure of the two previous experiments was explored. Topic importance, it will be remembered, was defined in each study in terms of the pooled judgments of a pilot sample as was summarized in Table 4–1. Any possible individual differences in importance ratings were simply ignored. If our subjects varied markedly from one another and/or from the pilot group in their notions of what was and was not important, the previous experiments would have been inadequate as tests of the importance hypothesis. In addition, in an early investigation in which importance had been self-defined (Byrne, 1961a), a significant importance effect had been found. In that study, subjects indicated their judgment as to the 13 least and 13 most important topics on a 26-item scale. With a stranger at .50 similarity, attraction was 8.47 when agreement was on the 13 most important items and 5.93 when agreement was on the 13 least important items. In any event, the present experiment utilized an intrastranger design in which importance was defined either by group judgments or by the individual subject himself.

Method. A group of 80 subjects was pretested on the 56-item attitude scale and later assigned to one of eight experimental conditions. In the pretesting session, each subject was also asked to divide the topics into four equal categories based on his judgment of the relative importance of the issues. For half of the group, topic importance was defined in terms of the four levels described in the two previous studies. For the other half, importance was defined for each subject on the basis of his own judgments given during pretesting.

The two levels of attitude similarity were .25 and .75; topic importance was manipulated by the choice of items on which the stranger was to be similar and dissimilar. Specifically, in the .75 condition, the 14 items of disagreement were either the 14 most important or the 14 least important ones. Analogously, in the .25 condition the 14 items of agreement were either the most or least important topics.

Results. The mean attraction responses for the various groups are shown in Table 4–4. In addition to the usual similarity effects, it may be seen that attraction is affected by importance when the similar and dissimilar attitudes attributed to a single stranger are systematically varied with respect to topic importance. With proportion held constant, similarity on important topics and dissimilarity on unimportant topics yields a more positive response than similarity on unimportant topics and dissimilarity on important ones. With an intrastranger design, then, differential topic importance is found to influence attraction responses.

The hypothesis of a greater effect of individually defined than of group–defined importance was not confirmed. It seems that with this series of topics in this population, agreement about the importance of issues is sufficiently high that the distinction is a negligible one.

TABLE 4–4

MEAN ATTRACTION RESPONSES TOWARD STRANGERS AT TWO LEVELS OF
ATTITUDE SIMILARITY WITH TWO LEVELS OF TOPIC IMPORTANCE FOR SIMILAR AND
DISSIMILAR ITEMS[a]

Proportion of similar attitudes	Similar items consist of more important topics than dissimilar items	Similar items consist of less important topics than dissimilar items
Topic importance based on group judgment		
.75	10.00	9.30
.25	6.90	5.20
Total	8.45	7.25
Topic importance based on individual's judgment		
.75	10.40	6.20
.25	6.30	6.00
Total	8.35	6.10

[a]After Byrne, London, and Griffitt, 1968, p. 303.

Discussion. It required three different experimental designs, but the importance hypothesis finally was provided with empirical support. The three studies together indicate that when all of the information about a stranger concerns a single level of importance, attitude similarity–dissimilarity on either important or trivial issues has the same effect. It is only when a single stranger expresses attitudes on more than one level that differential topic importance exerts an influence on attraction. A satisfactory explanation of this apparent inconsistency can best be given after one further experiment is described.

Topic Interest and Attraction: Intrastranger Design

At the University of Illinois, Clore and Baldridge (1968) attacked the same general problem from a slightly different viewpoint. They proposed that topic "interest" might prove to be a more viable differentiator of items than would topic "importance." It was suggested that "while most subjects would attest to the abstract importance of such issues as socialized medicine or racial integration, many might be personally uninterested in them [p. 341]." In addition, an intrastranger design was employed, and each individual's own judgment of interest was used rather than a group definition.

Method. The same 56-item attitude scale was given to 84 students along with a 4-point scale to measure each subject's interest in each issue. In the experimental session a week later, subjects were given a 12-item scale supposedly filled out by another student. Three levels of attitude similarity were represented: .25, .50, and .75. Within each similarity level, subjects received either agreements on interesting and disagreements on uninteresting topics or the reverse.

Results. The attraction means are presented in Table 4–5. As may be seen, their results exactly paralleled those of the final importance study. Using an intrastranger design, differential topic interest has the same kind of effect as differential topic importance. In spite of the logical distinction between the two concepts, the Illinois ratings of interest were found to correlate .80 with the Texas ratings of importance. Perhaps a more general concept such as topic impact should be used to encompass both dimensions.

TABLE 4–5

MEAN ATTRACTION RESPONSES TOWARD STRANGERS AT THREE LEVELS OF ATTITUDE SIMILARITY WITH TWO LEVELS OF TOPIC INTEREST FOR SIMILAR AND DISSIMILAR ITEMS[a]

Proportion of similar attitudes	Similar items consist of more interesting topics than dissimilar items	Similar items consist of less interesting topics than dissimilar items
.75	10.79	7.57
.50	9.43	5.43
.25	7.21	6.00

[a]After Clore and Baldridge, 1968, p. 341.

Differential Topic Impact

How can these various findings be incorporated within a single conceptual schema and how can the discrepancies between single stranger, multistranger, and intrastranger designs be reconciled? In addition, what implication does this series of studies have for the base relationship?

Weighted Proportion of Similar Attitudes. It will be recalled from the previous chapter that the base relationship was described as a linear function: $Y = mX + k$, in which Y is attraction, X is proportion of similar attitudes, and m and k are empirically derived constants. Since X is defined as $\Sigma S / [\Sigma(S + D)]$ with S and D representing similar and dissimilar attitudes, the total formula may be written

$$Y = m\left[\frac{\Sigma S}{\Sigma(S + D)}\right] + k$$

In order to be able to include items which affect attraction unequally within this formulation, Byrne and Rhamey (1965) proposed that each similar and dissimilar item be multiplied by a weighting coefficient corresponding to its reinforcement magnitude. Thus, the formula becomes

$$Y = m \left[\frac{\Sigma(S \times M)}{\Sigma(S \times M) + \Sigma(D \times M)} \right] + k$$

Attraction is described as a positive linear function of the sum of the weighted similar attitudes divided by the total number of weighted similar and dissimilar attitudes.

As Clore and Baldridge indicate, topic impact may be expressed in terms of differential weighting coefficients with more interesting and/or important topics being assigned a larger weight than less interesting and/or important topics. With their own data, they empirically established that a differential weighting of 3:1 between most and least interesting topics would yield a linear function as specified in the base relationship.

In order to include both the Byrne (1961a) data and the Byrne, *et al.* (1968) data with that of Clore and Baldridge (1968), we shall assume that their 3 to 1 ratio is correct and also that topics of intermediate impact will fall inbetween the other two. So, let topics of intermediate impact = 1, topics of high impact = 1.5, and topics of low impact = .5. With attitude scales of various lengths and with various impact levels in the three experiments, it may be helpful to examine Table 4–6 to see the way in which the weighted proportion of similar attitudes is obtained and the way in which this may differ from the regular, unweighted proportion.

It is now possible to plot attraction responses as a function of weighted proportion of similar attitudes, as shown in Fig. 4–1. Once again a linear function may be seen, and it is described by the formula $Y = 6.19X + 4.57$.

By way of contrast, examine Fig. 4–2 in which the unweighted proportion of similar attitudes appears along the X axis. There is no linear function and the prediction of Y from X would be poor indeed. By conceptualizing topic impact in terms of weighting coefficients, however, it is possible to retain the simple linear function and its predictive power. It might also be noted that the Clore and Baldridge weighting coefficients, derived in a sample of Illinois undergraduates, seem to be quite applicable to two independent samples of Texas undergraduates.

Homogeneous versus Heterogeneous Importance Levels. One seeming mystery remains. Why is it that differential topic impact was undetected in the two Byrne and Nelson (1964, 1965b) experiments? The answer was pointed out by Clore and Baldridge and simply involved the application of the Byrne–Rhamey formula. *The magnitude of a weighting coefficient has no*

TABLE 4-6

Obtaining the Weighted Proportion of Similar Attitudes for Items of Differential Impact

	No. of Attitudes	No. of similar (S) and dissimilar (D) attitudes — Impact: Low	Med.	High	Unweighted proportion, X =	Weighted proportion, X =
Byrne (1961a)	26	13D		13S	.50	$\dfrac{(13 \times 1.5)}{(13 \times 1.5) + (13 \times .5)} = .75$
	26	13S		13D	.50	$\dfrac{(13 \times .5)}{(13 \times .5) + (13 \times 1.5)} = .25$
Byrne, London, and Griffitt (1968)	56	14D	28S	14S	.75	$\dfrac{(14 \times 1.5) + (28 \times 1)}{(14 \times 1.5) + (28 \times 1) + (14 \times .5)} = .87$
	56	14S	28S	14D	.75	$\dfrac{(28 \times 1) + (14 \times .5)}{(28 \times 1) + (14 \times .5) + (14 \times 1.5)} = .62$
	56	14D	28D	14S	.25	$\dfrac{(14 \times 1.5)}{(14 \times 1.5) + (28 \times 1) + (14 \times .5)} = .38$
	56	14S	28D	14D	.25	$\dfrac{(14 \times .5)}{(14 \times .5) + (14 \times 1.5) + (28 \times 1)} = .12$
Clore and Baldridge (1968)	12	3D		9S	.75	$\dfrac{(9 \times 1.5)}{(9 \times 1.5) + (3 \times .5)} = .90$
	12	9S		3D	.75	$\dfrac{(9 \times .5)}{(9 \times .5) + (3 \times 1.5)} = .50$
	12	6D		6S	.50	$\dfrac{(6 \times 1.5)}{(6 \times 1.5) + (6 \times .5)} = .75$
	12	6S		6D	.50	$\dfrac{(6 \times .5)}{(6 \times .5) + (6 \times 1.5)} = .25$
	12	9D		3S	.25	$\dfrac{(3 \times 1.5)}{(3 \times 1.5) + (9 \times .5)} = .50$
	12	3S		9D	.25	$\dfrac{(3 \times .5)}{(3 \times .5) + (9 \times 1.5)} = .10$

effect on the resulting proportion unless differential weights are employed; otherwise, weighted proportion is equal to unweighted proportion. Therefore, attitudes of homogeneous high or low impact will have an identical effect on attraction. It is only when the stranger expresses opinions on items heterogeneous in impact that such a variable would be expected to influence

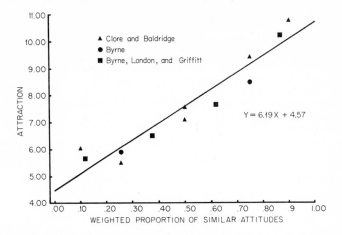

Fig. 4–1. Attraction toward a stranger as a linear function of weighted proportion of similar attitudes with weighting coefficients corresponding to levels of topic impact. (After Byrne, London, & Griffitt, 1968, p. 304.)

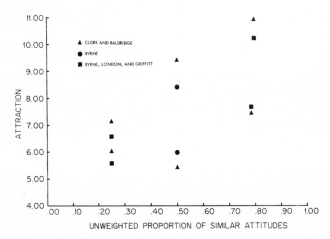

Fig. 4–2. Attraction toward a stranger as a function of unweighted proportion of similar attitudes with differential topic impact systematically associated with similar and dissimilar attitudes.

attraction. Clore and Baldridge, to demonstrate this proposition, went on to show that when items homogeneous in topic interest (either all high or all low) are used, subjects respond only to attitude similarity, and the interest variable has no effect on attraction.

A question might remain. What happens in the usual attitude and attraction study with heterogeneous topics randomly varying over the similar

TABLE 4–7

UNWEIGHTED AND WEIGHTED PROPORTIONS OF SIMILAR ATTITUDES WITH ITEMS
OF DIFFERENTIAL TOPIC IMPACT RANDOMLY DISTRIBUTED

No. of attitudes	No. of similar (S) and dissimilar (D) attitudes		Unweighted proportion, $X=$	Weighted proportion, $X=$
	Low impact	High impact		
12	2S 4D $\}$	2S 4D	.33	$\dfrac{(2 \times 1.5) + (2 \times .5)}{(2 \times 1.5) + (2 \times .5) + (4 \times 1.5) + (4 \times .5)} = .33$
12	3S 3D $\}$	3S 3D	.50	$\dfrac{(3 \times 1.5) + (3 \times .5)}{(3 \times 1.5) + (3 \times .5) + (3 \times 1.5) + (3 \times .5)} = .50$
12	4S 2D $\}$	4S 2D	.67	$\dfrac{(4 \times 1.5) + (4 \times .5)}{(4 \times 1.5) + (4 \times .5) + (2 \times 1.5) + (2 \times .5)} = .67$

and dissimilar items? The answer is again a simple one. Unless items of differential impact are systematically separated into similar and dissimilar, the weighted and unweighted proportions would remain the same and, hence, attraction would not be affected. To convince oneself of this truism, the reader might want to examine Table 4–7. In an experimental situation in which items were assigned randomly to be similar and dissimilar without regard to relative impact, the stimuli confronting a group of subjects would be expected to vary randomly about the values shown in columns two and three. As a consequence, the unweighted proportions would also vary, but their mean value would tend to equal the corresponding unweighted proportion. The effect of differential topic impact on attraction in such a situation, therefore, would be to increase the variance but not to affect the obtained attraction means.

In summary, this line of analytic research has resulted in the identification of another aspect of the stimulus in the base relationship to which subjects respond: topic impact. The impact variable is now included in an expanded attraction formula so that the lawful relationship between similarity and attraction has become more detailed and more precise. The goal of further analytic research would be to seek further precision through identification of additional elements in the relationship.

Topic Relevance

Galloway (1970) attempted to show that topics of differential relevance to the subject would have differential effects on attraction. The subjects were English Canadians in Quebec, whereas the simulated strangers were either French Canadians or English Canadians, and the attitude items were either relevant or irrelevant to French Canadian–English Canadian relations (matched for topic importance), and the similarity level was .25, .50, or .75 on a 12-item questionnaire. The stranger either agreed on relevant and disagreed on irrelevant issues or vice versa.

It was found that although the similarity variable significantly influenced attraction, neither ethnic group nor topic relevance yielded a significant effect. There was also an interaction between ethnic group and topic relevance, but in a surprising direction. The French Canadian stranger was liked less than the English Canadian if the issues agreed upon were relevant to the bicultural situation in Quebec, whereas the reverse held if agreement was on topics irrelevant to that situation.

In a *post hoc* analysis, Galloway suggested that (*1*) the subjects were almost all positive toward French Canadians, (*2*) agreement on relevant issues from the French Canadian stranger was expected and, hence, less important, and (*3*) agreement from other English Canadians on those topics was more important in that it added to their ingroup solidarity as a minority group in Quebec. It seems reasonable to suppose that topic relevance would have effects analogous to those of topic importance, but predictions about the direction of those effects may prove to be less straightforward.

RESPONSE DISCREPANCY ON THE ATTITUDE SCALE

Problem

With the attitudinal material used in the present paradigm, the definition of "similar" and "dissimilar" responses by a stranger could be specified in more than one way. Each item consists of a 6-point scale with 3 points representing varying strengths of opinion in one direction (e.g., pro Republican) and 3 points representing varying strengths of opinion in the other direction (e.g., pro Democrat). Similarity has been defined simply as any response on the same side of the neutral point as the subject's response, and dissimilarity as any response on the opposite side of the neutral point. In effect, each item has been treated as if it were a 2-point scale with mild, moderate, and strong feelings on a given side of an issue defined as equivalents. There was, therefore, some latitude in deciding which point on the scale to assign to the stranger's response.

In preparing a scale to represent the bogus stranger, several patterns of response simulation have been used. The various patterns can best be visualized by means of the information presented in Table 4–8. The original simulation pattern (identity–mirror) was one in which a stranger responded to each item exactly as the subject did or in exactly the opposite way. The major reasons for switching to the moderate discrepancy pattern in sub-

TABLE 4–8

DIFFERENT SIMULATION PATTERNS FOR SIMILAR (S) AND
DISSIMILAR (D) ITEM RESPONSES BY BOGUS STRANGER[a]

Subject's response	Identity-mirror		Moderate discrepancy		Constant discrepancy	
	S	D	S	D	S	D
1	1	6	2	5	2	4
2	2	5	3	4	1 or 3	5
3	3	4	2	5	2	6
4	4	3	5	2	5	1
5	5	2	4	3	4 or 6	2
6	6	1	5	2	5	3

[a]After Byrne, 1969, p. 55.

sequent research were (1) an attempt to disguise further the relationship
between the subject's own responses and those of the stranger and (2) a
decision to avoid the possible effects of extreme responses by a stranger
(the 1 and 6 points were never used). Nelson (1965) pointed out that one
result of using this second type of pattern was that a dissimilar response
varied from 2 to 4 scale points of discrepancy from that of the subject
whereas a similar response was always 1 scale point away. With the identity–
mirror pattern, similarity equals zero discrepancy, whereas dissimilarity
varies in discrepancy from 1 to 5 points. Nelson investigated the possible
effects of this differential discrepancy in his dissertation research. He
hypothesized that attraction is affected not only by agreement–disagreement but also by the amount of response discrepancy within the similar and
dissimilar categories.

Method

Nelson employed a 12-item attitude scale and followed the standard
procedures of attraction studies. From a large undergraduate subject pool,
80 subjects were drawn. In the experiment, subjects were asked to respond to
a stranger who was either similar (1.00 agreement) or dissimilar (.00 agreement) on all 12 items. There was also a manipulation of magnitude of
response discrepancy (small or large).

Results

The means of the attraction responses are shown in Table 4–9. As may
be seen, subjects are responsive to discrepancy as well as to similarity–
dissimilarity. If a subject is strongly committed to racial integration, for
example, he not only prefers integrationists to segregationists, he prefers

TABLE 4–9

MEAN ATTRACTION RESPONSES TOWARD SIMILAR AND
DISSIMILAR STRANGERS WITH LARGE AND
SMALL RESPONSE DISCREPANCY[a]

Similarity	Small discrepancy	Large discrepancy
1.00	11.50	10.10
.00	8.05	6.45

[a]Data from Nelson, 1965.

those strongly in favor (like himself) to those mildly in favor of integration. Here, then, is still another aspect of the stimulus to which subjects are responsive. Thus, "a simple agree–disagree dichotomy does not account for all the variance in attraction [Nelson, 1965, p. 35]."

Further Investigations of Discrepancy

Among the possibilities raised by Nelson in discussing his findings was that attraction toward X is basically "a negative linear function of the discrepancy of the attitudes of X from those of the subject [Nelson, 1965, p. 39]" or $A_x = -md_x + k$. On the basis of his data, he derived the specific formula as $Y = -.12X + 11.64$ as is depicted in Fig. 4–3. It was proposed that

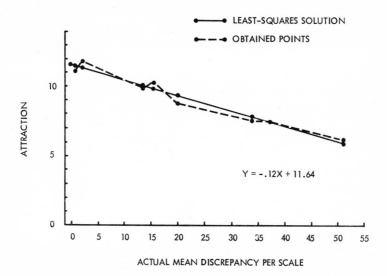

Fig. 4–3. Attraction toward a stranger as a linear function of mean response discrepancy per item. (After Nelson, 1965, p. 38.)

TABLE 4-10
MEAN DISCREPANCY PER ITEM FOR
NELSON'S FOUR EXPERIMENTAL CONDITIONS[a]

Similarity	Small discrepancy	Large discrepancy
1.00	.13	1.21
.00	2.24	3.68

[a] Data from Nelson, 1965.

the Byrne–Nelson formula is simply a special case of the discrepancy formula. He further raised the possibility that if discrepancy were held constant, attraction would not vary as a function of similar versus dissimilar attitude responses. The reason that this question could not be resolved by his data is shown in Table 4–10 in which the mean discrepancy per item of each of Nelson's groups is shown. It may be seen that the reported similarity differences as well as the discrepancy differences could quite possibly be a function of the discrepancy variable rather than the similarity–dissimilarity variable.

In order to test Nelson's hypothesis and, hence, to analyze further the stimuli to which subjects are responding, several studies were undertaken by Byrne, Clore, and Griffitt (1967), utilizing both old and new data.

Similarity–Dissimilarity with Discrepancy Controlled. In one experiment, 31 subjects were given a 56-item attitude scale and later presented with a stranger who expressed either 1.00 or .34 similarity. In place of one of the standard simulation patterns, the responses of the stranger were such that the mean discrepancy per item was maintained within the narrow range of 1.43 to 1.95. The mean discrepancy of the two experimental groups was almost perfectly matched (1.64 per item in the 1.00 condition and 1.63 per item in the .34 condition). Thus, if the similarity variable per se had no effect on attraction, the discrepancy formula would predict no differences in attraction responses for the two groups. If, however, the similarity variable influences attraction over and above the discrepancy effect, the groups would be found to yield differential attraction responses. The correctness of the latter proposition is shown by the obtained attraction responses of 9.24 for the 1.00 group and 5.21 for the .34 group.

A similar analysis was carried out on data previously gathered (Byrne & Clore, 1966) which involved 120 subjects who responded to a stranger's 12-item attitude scale. The discrepancy between each subject and the stranger to whom he responded was determined, and it was possible to divide the sample into three relatively homogeneous groups with respect

TABLE 4–11

MEAN ATTRACTION RESPONSE AT VARIOUS LEVELS OF
SIMILARITY WITH DISCREPANCY CONTROLLED

Discrepancy level	Proportion of similar attitudes		
	Low	Medium	High
1.92 to 2.58	5.23	8.46	—
1.58 to 1.83	5.86	7.54	9.33
.83 to 1.50	—	9.19	10.85

to discrepancy. Within each of these subgroups, it was again possible to determine the effect of similarity–dissimilarity on attraction. Responses at varying levels of similarity for each level of discrepancy are shown in Table 4–11. Within each level of discrepancy, attraction was significantly influenced by proportion of similar attitudes. It seems clear that the effect of attitude similarity–dissimilarity on attraction is not simply a function of the discrepancy variable. Nelson's demonstration of the effect of discrepancy on attraction is an indication of the operation of a stimulus variable *in addition to* similarity–dissimilarity rather than as *an alternative to* similarity. This suggests that attraction is a joint function of these two partially independent stimulus dimensions.

Combined Effects of Similarity–Dissimilarity and Discrepancy. In an effort to explore the joint-function possibility, data from two previous investigations (Byrne & Clore, 1966; Byrne & Griffitt, 1966a) were reanalyzed by means of a correlational approach. Each subject was considered with respect to proportion of similar attitudes expressed by the stranger, subject–stranger discrepancy, and the subject's attraction response. The two stimulus variables and the response variable were intercorrelated, and a multiple correlation coefficient determined between attraction and the two independent variables. These results are shown in Table 4–12.

The findings are relatively consistent across the six groups. Attraction is a positive function of similarity–dissimilarity and a negative function of discrepancy. With respect to the joint function, five of the six multiple *r*s indicate that a very small, though consistent, gain in predictive accuracy is achieved by considering both stimulus variables.

The findings dealing with discrepancy have two major possible implications. Methodologically, it has led to the adoption of the constant discrepancy simulation pattern shown in Table 4–8 which eliminates discrepancy differences among similar items and among dissimilar items and, hence,

TABLE 4–12
ATTRACTION (1) AS A JOINT FUNCTION
OF SIMILARITY–DISSIMILARITY (2)
AND DISCREPANCY (3)[a]

Group	r_{12}	r_{13}	$r_{1\cdot23}$
1, $N = 40$	.59	−.55	.61
2, $N = 40$	.46	−.34	.45
3, $N = 40$	.46	−.26	.47
4, $N = 95$	.23	−.23	.34
5, $N = 80$	.20	−.37	.38
6, $N = 97$	.42	−.53	.54

[a]After Byrne, Clore, and Griffitt, 1967, p. 398.

combines the effects of the two stimulus variables into a single effect. Conceptually, proportion of similar attitudes and discrepancy are seen to constitute two related but partially independent stimulus dimensions. It would seem that individuals are responding to extremely small degrees of discrepancy between themselves and the strangers as well as to the more gross variable of agreement versus disagreement. Similarity to self constitutes a crucial attribute in others not only with respect to positive or negative orientation toward a given attitudinal topic but also with respect to the specific degree of positiveness or negativeness.

This set of findings leads to an expansion of the base relationship to include an additional stimulus variable. Now, we are in a position to say that

$$Y = m_1 \left[\frac{\Sigma(S \times M)}{\Sigma(S \times M) + \Sigma(D \times M)} \right] - m_2 \left[\frac{\Sigma d}{I} \right] + k.$$

The new elements are d (subject–stranger response discrepancy on an item) and I (total number of items).

STRUCTURAL SIMILARITY

Tesser (to be published, 1971) at the University of Georgia has identified yet another component of the stimulus variable: structural similarity. He points out that there are internal relationships among a series of attitudes. It was suggested that a subject not only is able to keep a frequency count or become aware of the proportion of similar attitudes, but he is also able to determine whether the other person's attitudes are structured differently from his own.

As an example of the structural variable, Tesser (to be published) proposes:

> Consider two Os (O_1 and O_2) who have presented P with a sample of ten identical elements. Both Os agree with P on the evaluation of five elements and disagree on five elements. From P's point of view, elements 1 through 5 are related to one another but unrelated to elements 6 through 10, while elements 6 through 10 are related to one another. O_1 is similar to P on elements 1 through 5 and dissimilar on elements 6 through 10. O_2 is similar on elements 1, 3, 5, 7, and 9 and dissimilar on elements 2, 4, 6, 8, and 10.

It may be seen that attitude similarity is identical with respect to the two individuals (.50) but that O_1 is structurally similar to P, whereas O_2 is structurally dissimilar.

Tesser goes on to demonstrate that for interrelated items, structural similarity is associated with attitude similarity in a curvilinear function. That is, structural similarity will be greatest at either .00 or 1.00 attitudinal similarity, whereas structural dissimilarity is maximal at .50 attitudinal similarity. For unrelated items, structural similarity is not possible, so attraction is a linear function of proportion of similar attitudes. For interrelated items, attraction should be a curvilinear function of proportion of similar attitudes *if subjects are able to perceive structural similarity* and *if attraction is influenced by structural similarity.*

By constructing four-item attitude scales built of interrelated items and others built of uncorrelated items, Tesser (to be published) was able to test these propositions. Essentially, it was found that structural similarity was perceived to vary curvilinearly with attitude similarity among interrelated attitudes but not among independent attitudes. Attraction was found to be a linear function of attitude similarity on the independent items, whereas both linear and curvilinear trend components were found with the interrelated items.

In a second experiment (Tesser, 1971), structural and attitudinal similarity were manipulated independently and attraction was found to

TABLE 4–13
MEAN ATTRACTION RESPONSES
TOWARD STRANGERS DIFFERING IN
ATTITUDINAL AND STRUCTURAL
SIMILARITY[a]

Similarity	Low	High
Attitudinal	7.52	10.11
Structural	8.23	9.41

[a]Data from Tesser, 1971, p. 95.

vary as a function of each of these stimulus variables as is shown in Table 4–13. The structural similarity variable as perceived by the subjects was reflected by items on which the stranger was rated as more consistent, more predictable, and as looking at items in the same way as the subject under conditions of high structural similarity. Attitude similarity affected only the latter response.

Set Size

One to Six Items

The Byrne and Nelson (1965a) finding that number of attitude items (set size) has no effect on attraction is inconsistent with Anderson's (1967) finding that the number of adjectives influence the favorable–unfavorable responses in an impression formation task. Rosenblood (1970) proposed that the set size effect should be operative in the attraction situation.

In a within-subject design using 60 Ohio State undergraduates, Rosenblood presented subjects with sets of 1, 2, 3, 4, and 6 attitude items consistently similar to or dissimilar from the subject within sets in various orders across subjects. After examining each set of items, the subject rated the stranger on the IJS.

He found an interaction between similarity and set size. As number of attitude items increased, responses toward a similar stranger were increasingly positive and responses toward a dissimilar stranger were increasingly negative. Thus, the findings fit the Anderson model and were inconsistent with the Byrne and Nelson findings that subjects respond only to proportion and not to number of attitude items.

One possible explanation for the discrepancy is the effect of a within-subject design (Rosenblood, 1970) versus a between-subject design (Byrne & Nelson, 1965a). Rosenblood was able to provide between-subjects data by looking at only the first response of each of his subjects. Though the trend was still present, the significant set size effect disappeared in this analysis.*

A related explanation, and the one favored by Rosenblood, is that a set size effect occurs when set size is salient to the subject. Though an experiment designed to manipulate saliency was not entirely successful, he offered a modification of the attraction and impression-formation formulae to include the variables of set size and saliency of set size.

There is still another possible way to explain the discrepant findings. In the Byrne and Nelson experiment, the number of similar attitudes varied from 4 to 16, and number of dissimilar attitudes varied from 0 to 32.

---

*Further analysis yielded a significant effect for the personal feelings scale alone.

Rosenblood's range was from 1 to 6. It is conceivable that set size would affect attraction when only a small number of attitudes are involved but that past 4 or 5 items, number of attitudes becomes irrelevant as a variable.

Four to Sixteen Items

Gouaux and Lamberth (1970) varied the set size from 4 to 16 attitudes in a within-subjects design in an attempt to determine the effects of number of attitudes on attraction. With 38 Purdue undergraduates as subjects, the attitudes of three completely similar strangers (with 4, 8, and 16 attitude items) were examined. Interpersonal Judgment Scale responses were made toward each stranger before going on to the next stranger, as in Rosenblood's experiment. The order of presentation of the three different scale lengths was counterbalanced.

The mean attraction responses are shown in Table 4–14. Number of similar attitudes had no effect on attraction.*

Though it cannot be said that the set size question is entirely settled, it does seem that such an effect occurs only under relatively special circumstances.

TABLE 4–14
MEAN ATTRACTION RESPONSES AS A FUNCTION
OF SIMILAR ATTITUDES[a]

No. of similar attitudes:		
4	8	16
10.00	10.52	9.95

[a]After Gouaux and Lamberth, 1970, p. 338.

TEMPORAL VARIABLES

Stability of Attitude Items

When the subject's attitudes are measured at Time I and the stranger's attitudes are presented at Time II, any attitude change on the part of the subject during the interim results in differences between subject–stranger similarity as defined by the experimenter and as experienced by the subject.

---

*Half of the subjects served in a different condition in which the attitudes of all three strangers were presented and then all three were evaluated on the IJS. Here, a significant set size effect was found, but it was a somewhat puzzling one in that the means for 4, 8 and 16 attitudes were, respectively, 9.52, 11.10, and 10.84.

Prediction of the attraction response will obviously be adversely affected by unreliability of the stimulus dimension.

Both Nelson (1965) and Griffitt and Byrne (1970) investigated the test–retest reliability of 12 attitude items over a 2-week period with subjects at the University of Texas. The correlations ranged from .55 (dating in high school) to .95 (war). It may be seen that error variance can be reduced by employing the more stable attitudinal items or by reducing the time between the attitude measurement and the attraction experiment.

Griffitt and Byrne (1970) also found that proportion of similar attitudes between subject and stranger based on the attitude pretest correlated .37 with attraction. Proportion based on the attitude retest correlated .39 with attraction. It seems that the attitude items are sufficiently reliable that attitude change does not result in a significant decline in predictive accuracy over a 2-week period.

Stability of Attraction Response

When subjects are exposed to the attitudes of a stranger, attraction is generally assessed within a matter of minutes. Griffitt and Nelson (1970) raised the question of the extent to which this response persists over time in the absence of additional information concerning the stranger.

A group of 22 students at Kansas State University were exposed to the tape-recorded attitude responses of an anonymous same-sex stranger who was either .25 or .75 similar to the subject. Attraction was measured by the IJS. One week later, the subjects participated in an unrelated experiment on concept formation. Afterward, they were reminded of the earlier experiment and asked to evaluate the stranger again on the IJS.

As indicated in Table 4–15, the attraction response is quite stable; attraction at the two periods correlated .82. Further, the subjects were asked to fill out an attitude scale as the stranger had responded a week earlier. Proportion of similar attitudes as created by the experimenters

TABLE 4–15

MEAN ATTRACTION RESPONSES
AS A FUNCTION OF TIME OF ASSESSMENT
AND PROPORTION OF SIMILAR ATTITUDES[a]

Proportion of similar attitudes	Initial measurement	1 week later
.75	11.50	10.80
.25	8.83	8.67

[a]After Griffitt and Nelson, 1970, p. 120.

correlated .83 with proportion of similarity as remembered by the subjects a week later. Griffitt and Nelson (1970) noted:

> It is not contested, of course, that exposure to additional information concerning a target person is likely to alter systematically one's initial impression of the person. It is significant, however, that, in the absence of additional information, initial impressions are highly stable at least over the time period involved in the present experiment [p. 120].

SEQUENTIAL EFFECTS OF ATTITUDINAL STIMULI

In the research described up to this point, the several attitudes of a stranger have been presented as a unit to each subject; after examining the series of responses, he indicates his judgments about the stranger. We have analyzed several aspects of this stimulus, and the data suggest that attraction is a function of the weighted proportion of the attitudes which are in agreement with those of the subject, of the mean discrepancy per item between the responses of subject and stranger, of the structural similarity between the attitudes of subject and stranger, and, at times, of set size. The question now arises as to the possible effects of the order in which similar and dissimilar attitude statements occur within the stimulus unit. For example, if one learns that a stranger agrees with him about politics and then learns that he disagrees about religion, is attraction the same as when these bits of information are discovered in the reverse order? Possible sequence effects have been controlled by the process of randomizing the order of similar and dissimilar items across subjects within a given level of similarity. If, in fact, different sequences of similar–dissimilar attitude statements yield differential effects on attraction, not only would we gain more detailed knowledge of the stimulus in the basic paradigm relationship but we also would achieve greater accuracy in the prediction of the attraction response.

Background

A variable of continuing research interest outside of the attraction paradigm has been the sequence in which stimuli with positive and negative qualities are presented to a subject. Asch (1946) found that the initial descriptive adjectives in a list have the greatest influence on the resulting impression of the person being described; this primacy effect has been replicated in subsequent work (e.g., Anderson, 1965b; Anderson & Barrios, 1961; Anderson & Norman, 1964). Asch interpreted this finding in gestalt terms as a function of a directed impression radiating from the first portion of the sequence. A more quantitative and more convincing explanation, based on differential attention, has been offered by Anderson and Hubert

(1963). It was suggested that subjects pay a decreasing degree of attention to each item as the list progresses; hence the influence of any given adjective is a direct linear function of its ordinal position in the series. Supporting this proposition is the fact that primacy effects disappear when attention is controlled by informing subjects that they will be asked to recall the list afterward (Anderson & Hubert, 1963), by reducing the list to two adjectives (Anderson & Barrios, 1961), or by requiring the subject to respond after each item rather than simply at the end of the series (Stewart, 1965).

A second type of stimulus variable utilized in analogous investigations is that of positive or negative evaluations from the stimulus person directed toward the subject. In a series of interactions, the subject is evaluated or described by a stranger. In this situation, rather than primacy effects there are strong recency effects. This finding has been interpreted in terms of a contrast between the later communications and the expectancies built up by the early communications (Berkowitz, 1960a, b) and in terms of the gain or loss of self-esteem experienced by the subject in altering the stranger's evaluation during the course of their interactions (Aronson & Linder, 1965).

Similar and dissimilar attitude statements may be seen as a third type of positive and negative stimulus information concerning a stranger. The possible effects of the sequence of similarity–dissimilarity had not been investigated. On the basis of the adjective trait and the personal evaluation studies, it would follow that the order in which similar and dissimilar attitude statements are presented to the subject exerts an influence on the subsequent attraction responses. Unfortunately, the two lines of research lead to opposite predictions with respect to primacy versus recency effects. An experiment was undertaken, therefore, in an attempt to determine the effect of the sequential presentation of positive and negative attitudinal stimuli on attraction (Byrne & London, 1966).

Attitudes and Sequential Effects

Method. Following a model used in both an adjective trait investigation (Anderson & Barrios, 1961) and in a personal evaluation investigation (Aronson & Linder, 1965), four experimental conditions were established: similar (1.00), dissimilar (.00), similar–dissimilar (.50), and dissimilar–similar (.50).

The subjects consisted of 40 students who had taken a 56-item attitude scale at the beginning of the semester. They were randomly assigned to one of the four experimental conditions. For each subject, a special tape recording was prepared in which a student (the same sex as the subject) verbalized his or her response to each of the 56 attitude items. These responses were prearranged on the basis of the subject's own responses and the experimental condition to which he was assigned. In the similar condition, all of the responses were in agreement with those of the subject and in the dissimilar condition, all of the stranger's responses were in disagreement with those of the subject. In the similar–dissimilar condition, the following number of similar and dissimilar responses were given (in blocks of eight items): 8–0, 7–1, 6–2, 4–4, 2–6, 1–7, 0–8. Thus, the stranger's responses progressed from complete agreement to complete disagreement. In the dissimilar–similar condition, the pattern was simply reversed. The stranger expressed 28 similar and 28 dissimilar attitudes in each of the latter two conditions.

The subjects were given the usual instructions concerning interpersonal judgment and were told that the task was to determine how much one individual could learn about another on the basis of listening to a tape recording in which a stranger expressed his views. After hearing the recording, the subject evaluated the stranger on the IJS.

Results. The means of the attraction responses for the four experimental groups are shown in Table 4–16. There were highly significant differences among the groups. The critical comparison, however, is between the two .50 groups; the difference between them was not statistically significant.

TABLE 4–16
MEANS OF THE ATTRACTION RESPONSES
FOR THE FOUR EXPERIMENTAL CONDITIONS[a]

Condition	Mean
Similar (1.00)	11.90
Similar–dissimilar (.50)	8.20
Dissimilar–similar (.50)	7.30
Dissimilar (.00)	5.50

[a]Data from Byrne and London, 1966.

Thus, at this point it appears that subjects are not influenced by the sequence in which similar and dissimilar attitudes occur. The description of the base relationship need not, therefore, be altered to take account of sequential variables. Luckily, such conclusions are always made tentatively.

Continuous Responding and Sequential Effects

Byrne, Lamberth, Palmer, and London (1969) proposed that with primacy–recency effects inoperative in the attitude–attraction relationship, attraction at any point in the informational sequence should be a function of the proportion of similar attitudes in the total preceding series. An experiment was designed to demonstrate Anderson's (1965b) description of a continuous and systematic change in interpersonal responses as a function of specific stimulus information presented sequentially.

Three experimental conditions were established in which the overall proportion of attitude similarity was held constant at .50 while the sequence in which the similar and dissimilar attitudes occurred was varied. For each subject, a special tape recording was prepared in which another student (the same sex as the subject) purportedly verbalized his response to each of 24 attitude items. All subjects received 12 agreeing and 12 disagreeing attitude statements. In the similar–dissimilar ($S–D$) group, the following numbers of similar and dissimilar statements were given, in blocks of four: 4–0, 3–1, 2–2, 2–2, 1–3, 0–4. In the dissimilar–similar ($D–S$) condition, the pattern was reversed. Subjects in the "random" (R) condition received two similar and two dissimilar items in each block of four. The subjects were 30 undergraduates at the University of Texas. After hearing each statement, the subject was instructed to indicate his overall reaction toward the stranger by dropping a wooden token in the appropriate slot of the Interpersonal Judgment Apparatus (IJA) which is described in Chapter 9.

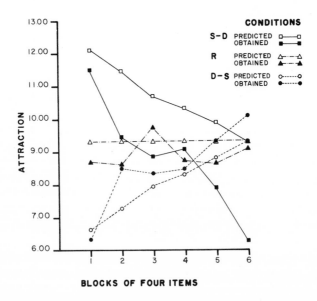

Fig. 4–4. Comparison of predicted and obtained attraction responses in a sequence of 24 similar and dissimilar attitude stimuli in three sequential arrangements. S, similar; D, dissimilar; R, random. (After Byrne, Lamberth, Palmer, & London, 1969, p. 72.)

An attempt was made to predict the responses in each condition at each point along the sequence of attitudinal stimuli using the Byrne–Nelson formula. In blocks of four items, the predicted and obtained responses are presented in Fig. 4–4. A visual inspection of the figure indicates clearly that the subject's responses do not correspond to the predicted values. At the time the final response was made, all groups had received .50 similar attitudes and should have been making identical attraction responses. The R group responded as expected, but the S–D and D–S groups each appeared to be overresponding to the later information in the series; that is, a recency effect was found.

The results of this experiment seem to be inconsistent with those of Byrne and London. How can the difference be explained? The primary dissimilarity between the two experiments was the way in which responses were made. In the Byrne–London experiment one attraction response was obtained after all of the stranger's attitudes had been received, whereas in the present experiment 24 attraction responses were obtained, one after each attitude statement was given. Could this difference in the nature of the response yield different sequential effects?

Interpolated Responses As a Source of Sequential Effects

The previous experiment was essentially repeated with a series of variations designed to test the hypothesis that recency sequential effects are directly related to the number of times an attraction response is interpolated within the sequence (Byrne *et al.*, 1969).

The attitude material was presented to the subjects in printed form by means of a slide projector. Each slide depicted one item of an attitude scale purportedly filled in by a stranger. The same three conditions of S–D, D–S, and R were employed.

The mode of responding was varied across three levels. The continuous responding group gave an attraction response after each attitude item (as in the previous experiment) for a total of 24 responses. The final responding group gave only one attraction response (as in the Byrne and London experiment) after all 24 attitudes had been presented. The intermediate responding group indicated attraction following the presentation of each set of four items for a total of six responses. Subjects were 90 Texas undergraduates.

The first question is whether the final responding group replicates the Byrne and London results in failing to demonstrate sequence effects. As may be seen in Table 4–17, with a final mode of responding, different sequences of similar and dissimilar attitudes once again show no effect on attraction. The intermediate and continuous groups, on the other hand, once again show recency effects as hypothesized.

TABLE 4-17

ATTRACTION RESPONSES TO THREE SEQUENCES
OF SIMILAR AND DISSIMILAR ATTITUDINAL STIMULI
WITH THREE MODES OF RESPONDING[a]

Response mode	Sequential conditions[b]		
	S–D	R	D–S
Continuous (blocks of 4 items)			
1–4	10.12	8.55	6.28
5–8	9.72	8.45	7.32
9–12	9.38	7.80	8.35
13–16	8.90	9.40	9.22
17–20	8.12	8.05	9.20
21–24	5.65	8.70	10.90
Intermediate (blocks of 4 items)			
1–4	10.40	8.20	6.00
5–8	9.50	8.90	6.60
9–12	9.20	8.20	7.30
13–16	8.00	7.30	7.70
17–20	7.20	6.70	8.00
21–24	5.40	7.80	9.60
Final 1–24	7.40	6.70	7.90

[a] After Byrne, Lamberth, Palmer, and London, 1969, p. 73.
[b] S = similar; D = dissimilar; R = random.

This experiment serves to resolve empirically the apparent inconsistency between the two previous sequential experiments. Recency effects
in the attitude–attraction relationship are obtained when a continuous
mode of responding is utilized, and such effects disappear when a final mode
of responding is used. The importance of the response mode is further
emphasized by the finding that intermediate responding yields intermediate recency effects.

With attraction measured only at the end of a sequence, subjects
respond to proportions of similar attitudes as may be seen in the two final
responding groups and in numerous previous investigations. Continuous
responding leads to quite different behavior than responding after a
series of items. This attempt to study the attraction process directly has
served to alter the process. Heisenberg's uncertainty principle is alive and
well in social psychology.

An examination of the item-by-item responses in the two continuous responding groups revealed a number of curious aspects. Responses following

a similar attitude were uniformly high and those following a dissimilar attitude were uniformly low, regardless of the proportion of similar attitudes preceding that item. An analogous situation might be the rapid fluctuations in popular esteem for a political leader presumably as a function of his most recent activity and not on the basis of the total array of activities constituting his career. It was suggested by Don Sachs (in a seminar) that the subjects were responding only to the proportion of similar attitudes presented since their last response. That is, in the continuous responding groups, all subjects responded to either .00 or 1.00 similarity on each trial. In the final responding condition, all subjects responded to .50 similarity. In the intermediate responding condition, a series of points along the similarity dimension are represented. When these data are plotted, the usual straight-line function between proportion of similar attitudes and attraction is found. The surprising thing, of course, is that subjects seemed to be ignoring all attitudinal stimuli and their own feeling about them prior to their last attraction response. It is possible that the act of making an evaluative response, whether positive or negative, somehow "neutralizes" or dissipates the implicit affect. Thus, on subsequent trials, the association of affect with the stranger begins all over again. Another experiment was designed to test this possibility.

Interpolated Implicit Responses

Byrne *et al.* (1969) proposed that when implicit affective responses are symbolized, either publicly or privately, there is a neutralization of the affect. With the sequential presentation of attitudinal stimuli, a recency effect should be obtained if the subjects are instructed to make *implicit* attraction responses after the presentation of each attitude followed by an explicit attraction response at the end of the sequence. That is, results obtained in a final responding condition with interpolated implicit attraction responses were expected to parallel those obtained in a continuous responding condition with interpolated explicit attraction responses.

The *D–S* and *S–D* conditions of the two previous experiments were replicated with one major difference. Instead of responding with a token dropped in the IJA after each attitude stimulus, subjects were asked to *think* about how they would respond after each item. No external response was made. Thus, in form, subjects were in the final responding condition but conceptually they were in the continuous responding condition. Subjects were 20 Texas undergraduates.

The mean attraction response for the *S–D* group was 7.90, whereas that for the *D–S* group was 10.60. The hypothesis was confirmed.

Conclusions

The present series of experiments has shown that sequential effects occur in the attitude–attraction relationship when subjects make evaluative responses during the sequence. Further, these responses need not involve physical activity as with the IJA or a public commitment in the presence of the experimenter; interpolated responses result in recency effects even when made covertly in response to instructions to do so. A recent experiment at Syracuse University by Blank and Arensen (1971) using a very different design, provides striking confirmation of the effect of interpolated attraction responses and the irrelevance of attitude material presented prior to such responses.

An extrapolation from these findings leads to the speculation that the adjective-impression situation and the usual attitude–attraction situation do not yield recency effects because subjects do not ordinarily make any formal evaluational response until asked to do so at the end of the sequence. Further, the interaction situation is sufficiently impactful that subjects spontaneously make implicit attraction responses toward the stranger even when there are no instructions to do so. Thus, subjects are able to hear a list of descriptive adjectives or a series of attitudinal statements without necessarily symbolizing how positively or negatively they feel. When a peer indicates that the subject is stupid or likable or boring or interesting, on the other hand, subjects spontaneously symbolize their attraction response toward the person. If so, the recency effects of the interaction studies are a function of situationally demanded continuous responding and not a function of thwarted expectancies or of gain and loss of self-esteem.

In addition to a clarification of the variables determining the presence and absence of sequential effects in the attitude–attraction relationship, the present experiments also led us to an unexpected and intriguing problem. It appears that the attraction response is not only a sensitive index of the affect aroused by a stimulus or series of stimuli but that the affect is neutralized by the overt or covert symbolization of feelings. Additional evidence for such a neutralization effect is provided by Hodges and Byrne (1971) who found that subjects who were allowed to express their feelings on an adjective check list immediately after seeing a stranger's attitudes no longer were differentially attracted to similar and dissimilar strangers.

One final point of interest involves the way in which subjects respond to a series of stimuli. With respect to impression formation, Anderson (1962) suggested a simple averaging model: "It was as though the subject assigned a value to each single adjective and, when presented with a set of adjectives, gave the mean of the corresponding values as his response [p. 818]." The fact that subjects respond to the proportion of similar attitudes expressed by a stranger has led to a similar model for attraction. Continuous and intermediate modes of responding appear to interfere with such a process. If, however, all of the responses made during the sequence are averaged by the experimenter, the mean responses are essentially the same across response modes and across sequential conditions. That is, the kind of subjective averaging hypothesized to occur as an unobserved intervening process in the usual attraction experiment can be duplicated by taking a series of responses made toward a stranger and actually computing their average. This result would seem to constitute indirect support for the model.

For the moment, these findings bring the analytic research on the attitude–attraction relationship up to date. As was indicated earlier, one can seldom consider analysis to be completed. It is anticipated that additional elements in the relationship will continue to be identified and that the resulting description of the attitude–attraction function will continue to grow in complexity and in precision.

STIMULUS GENERALITY

Chapter 5 / **Stimulus Generality:**
I. **Attitudes and Opinions**

Research directed toward establishing the limits of stimulus generality extending from the base relationship has been of sufficient quantity and variety that it is necessary to divide its presentation among three chapters. All of these investigations are relevant to the question of the extent to which the base relationship between attitude similarity and attraction is dependent on the use of the particular stimuli which chanced to be employed in the initial studies. That is, our research has used a specific body of attitudes, measured in a specific way, presented to subjects in a specific standard fashion with a given set of instructions. In the following series of experiments, various changes in the stimulus have been systematically introduced in order to determine the effect, if any, of such changes on the attraction response. In the present chapter, research is described in which attitude content is altered minimally while varying the mode in which the attitudes are presented to subjects.

Research of this variety has three somewhat different implications. First, and most obviously, such research may be viewed as methodological or merely methodological, depending on one's system of values. For those working within a given paradigm, additional knowledge concerning methods is always useful and sometimes vital to the success of ongoing research efforts. Second, and not nearly so obviously, research on stimulus generality may be seen as analytical experimentation of direct theoretical relevance. Such research constitutes a further effort in the attempt correctly to identify the stimulus to which subjects are responding and, hence, to verify or sub-stantiate a basic construct in the theory. Third, and even less obviously, a detailed investigation of stimulus generality is a necessary prerequisite to the possibility of application and an integral step in moving toward the development of a technology in any field. One cannot successfully leap from the insularity of the experimental laboratory to the distant complexity of the outside world; a bridge must be laboriously built.

VARYING THE STIMULUS MODE

Audio and Audiovisual Expressions of Attitudes

The use of mimeographed scales both to measure the attitudes of the subjects and later to present the attitudes of the bogus strangers proved to be an effective and efficient means of manipulating the attitudinal information. Nevertheless, if we are correct in conceptualizing the stimulus in the base relationship as *similarity and dissimilarity of attitudes*, the attitude–attraction function should remain the same even if the attitudes of the stranger were communicated to the subject in a greatly different fashion. Clearly, the generality and meaning of the base relationship would be severely limited if attraction were a linear function of attitude similarity only in those instances in which attitudes were indicated on a mimeographed sheet of paper.

In several experimental investigations of interpersonal attraction outside of the paradigm, the stimulus person has been presented in a variety of forms. For example, as described in Chapter 2, subjects have been asked to respond to another individual who is actually a stooge (Schachter, 1951), who is depicted in a specially prepared motion picture (Altrocchi, 1959), and whose voice has been recorded on tape (Jones, 1965). The possible influence of mode of presentation on any single measure of attraction or on the functional relationship between similarity and attraction had not been investigated, however. It seemed possible, for example, that as the number of available cues (e.g., voice quality, attractiveness, accent) increases, the prediction of attraction on the basis of attitude similarity becomes progressively less accurate.

In the initial experiment directed at this question (Byrne & Clore, 1966), the effects of three different stimulus modes were compared: mimeographed scale, tape recording, and a color movie with sound track.

Method. One hundred and twenty students were asked to fill out a 12-item attitude scale and immediately afterward were exposed to the attitudes of a same-sex stranger. One-third of the subjects read the stranger's responses on an attitude scale, one-third listened to a recording in which the stranger indicated his or her attitudes, and one-third viewed an 8-mm color sound movie of the stranger giving his or her opinions. Each subject responded to only one stranger in one stimulus condition presenting one set of attitudes. For each condition, however, there was a male and a female stranger, each of whom had prepared responses with both a standard A and a standard B pattern. The A and B patterns were mirror images, so that, for different subjects, a particular stranger in a particular condition had expressed all possible views on the topics. This methodology, by the way, was labeled the "standard stranger technique."

Results. The similarity between any given subject and the stranger to whom he was exposed could vary from .00 to 1.00 similarity, depending on his attitudes and those expressed by the A or B stranger. The actual variation was found to range from .08 to .83 similarity. Subjects were divided approximately evenly into four groups in terms of the similarity dimension, and an analysis of variance was carried out. As usual, attitude similarity was found to have a highly significant effect on attraction, but the three

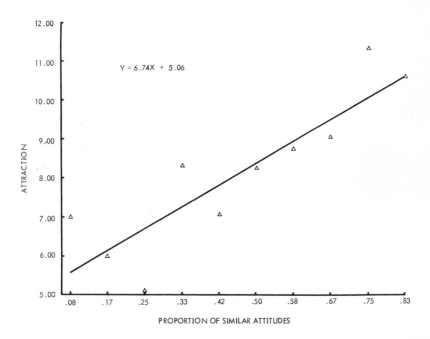

Fig. 5–1. Attraction toward a stranger as a linear function of proportion of similar attitudes with movie, tape recording, and mimeograph conditions combined. (After Byrne & Clore, 1966, p. 240.)

stimulus modes did not differ from one another nor was there an interaction effect. Subjects appeared to be responding to attitude similarity regardless of the form in which attitudes were presented.

Data for all 120 subjects were combined, and the attraction responses were plotted as a function of proportion of similar attitudes expressed by the stranger. The least squares method yielded a straight-line function with the formula $Y = 6.74X + 5.06$, as shown in Fig. 5–1. Thus, the linear relationship between similarity of attitudes and attraction was found to hold across quite divergent stimulus modes. Subsequent work has shown, not surprisingly, that a videotape presentation yields comparable results (Hodges & Byrne, in press; Mueller, 1969; Peterson, 1969). The law of attraction is not bound to paper and pencil strangers.

Face-to-Face Interaction

As a further extension of the research just described, it would be expected that the expression of attitudes by a stranger in a face-to-face interaction would affect attraction in the same way as in the various non-interactive situations.

Despite the type of evidence documented in Chapter 2, several considerations led McWhirter and Jecker (1967) to test the hypothesis that the impact of similarity is stronger when a real stimulus person is present that when his attitudes are presented on a mimeographed sheet.

Method. In the portion of their experiment relevant to the present topic, McWhirter and Jecker used 90 subjects. Half of these individuals were exposed to a "mythical stranger." That is, they were asked to evaluate a stranger on the basis of his responses to a seven-item attitude scale. These scales had been prepared by the experimenters to express similarity on either 2, 4, or 6 of the items. The remainder of the subjects were exposed to a "real stranger" (a confederate). After filling out attitude scales, each of the two individuals was asked to read his answers aloud, with the subject responding first. The confederate simply agreed with the subject on the appropriate number of items according to a prearranged schedule.

Among the subsequent measures given to 48 of the subjects were the two attraction items from the Interpersonal Judgment Scale (IJS).*

---

*Attraction was found to correlate .87 with the inferred attraction measure which was discussed in the article; hence, the two measures will be treated as equivalent here. The actual attraction means were not reported in the article or in the original study (McWhirter, 1966) and were not available from the authors.

Results. It was found that under each condition, attraction was significantly influenced by proportion of similar attitudes but not by the stimulus mode nor by the interaction. In fact, the paper and pencil stranger and the real stranger elicited almost identical responses, as may be seen in Table 5–1.

TABLE 5–1

MEANS OF INFERRED ATTRACTION RESPONSES
TOWARD REAL AND MYTHICAL STRANGERS
AT THREE LEVELS OF SIMILARITY[a]

	Proportion of similar attitudes		
Stranger	.29	.57	.85
Mythical	5.90	8.90	11.30
Real	6.50	8.10	11.50
Total	6.20	8.50	11.20

[a] After McWhirter and Jecker, 1967, p. 226.

A Positive Face-to-Face Effect. Even though the similarity–attraction relationship is the same whether or not the stranger is physically present, findings indicating one additional effect should be noted. Unless the stranger disagrees on a number of topics or is otherwise unpleasant to the subject, there seems to be a tendency to respond more positively to strangers who are physically present than to those not present. Elevated attraction means may be noted in several face-to-face investigations to be discussed in subsequent chapters (e.g., Griffitt & Guay, 1969; McDonald, 1962; Wiener, 1969).

In one experiment (Bloom, 1968), the possibility of meeting the stranger was specifically manipulated as part of the research design. The subjects were 54 male high-school students. An eight-item attitude scale was used, and each subject was exposed to a stranger representing .12 similarity. Approximately half of the subjects was informed that they would be meeting the stranger the following week, whereas the other half was given the standard instructions. The mean attraction response of the former group was 8.03 which was significantly higher than the 6.28 mean of the latter group. Whether this effect stems from the subject's reluctance to give extremely negative ratings because he suspects the recipient may have access to his responses or whether there is an actual increase in positiveness toward a stranger with whom one has interacted or will interact is still an open question. Further, it should be noted that this effect sometimes is not in evidence (as in the McWhirter and Jecker study just described).

In an attempt simply to find a type of reinforcement which would clearly be of greater magnitude than that represented by attitudinal agreement, Byrne and Rhamey (1965) selected a new informational stimulus, namely, personal evaluations. There is considerable support for the proposition that the motive to maintain and enhance one's self-concept is a powerful one. Thus, when an individual receives positive or negative evaluations of himself from another person, it seems safe to assume that rewards and punishments of a relatively large magnitude are being administered.

Even if the self is simply conceptualized as another possible topic about which attitudes may differ, this particular topic should be of much greater importance to each of us than impersonal ones such as politics. For the vast majority of subjects, positive and negative evaluations would constitute, respectively, attitudes similar to and dissimilar from his own. Even though subjects prefer correct to incorrect evaluations of themselves, it is also consistently found that positive evaluations are preferred to negative ones (Berscheid & Walster, 1970; Deutsch & Solomon, 1959; Dickoff, 1961). When the evaluated characteristic has components of social desirability and when the subject's standing on the characteristic is at all ambiguous, the differential effects of positive and negative evaluations should be even greater.

The general hypothesis, then, was that positive and negative evaluations concerning personal attributes are powerful determinants of attraction toward the evaluator and that such evaluations exert a greater effect on attraction than does similarity–dissimilarity of attitudes with respect to impersonal topics.

Personal Evaluations: Paper and Pencil

Method. Attitudes about impersonal topics were measured in the usual manner, using a 12-item attitude scale. The 180 subjects who took this scale were assigned on a random basis to one of four groups varying in the proportion of similar attitudes held by the stranger (1.00, .67, .33, and .00) and to one of three groups varying in the stranger's evaluation of the subject's personal attributes (positive, negative, and a control group without evaluations). About a week after the attitude measurement, the subjects were seen in small groups for the experiment and given the standard instructions concerning an interpersonal judgment situation.

For the subjects in the positive and negative evaluation conditions, the following additional information was also provided before they were given the stranger's attitude scale:

The attitude scale which you filled out, with all background information (including your name) removed, was given to another student who was asked to give these judgments about you. We thought it might be interesting for you to know how he or she judged you and if this additional information would affect the accuracy of your judgments about him.

Each of you will receive the attitude scale of one of these people and that person's opinion of you. For both the attitude scale and the judgment scale, the background information has, of course, been removed. As far as I know, you do not know this person, he or she is the same sex as yourself, and is not in your psychology class.

First, look over his or her judgments about you on the Interpersonal Judgment Scale, and then read the answers to the attitude items carefully and try to form an opinion of this person from this information.

The subjects in the positive evaluation group were informed, by means of a spurious IJS, that the stranger considered them to be very much above average in intelligence, very much above average in knowledge of current events, moral, well adjusted, and as someone who would be liked very much and with whom he would very much enjoy working. Those in the negative evaluation group were informed that the stranger considered them to be below average in intelligence, slightly below average in knowledge of current events, immoral to a slight degree, maladjusted to a slight degree, and as someone who would be disliked very much and with whom he would very much dislike working.

Results. The means of the attraction responses are given in Table 5–2. Analysis of variance indicated that each independent variable and the interaction between them exerted a highly significant effect on attraction.

Even though the evaluation conditions influenced attraction, this does not test the hypothesis specifically. Each of the six items of information about personal attributes was conceptualized as a positive or negative reinforcement as was each of the 12 attitude items dealing with impersonal topics. Thus, each subject in the two evaluation conditions was exposed

TABLE 5–2

MEAN ATTRACTION RESPONSES TOWARD STRANGERS WITH VARYING PROPORTIONS OF SIMILAR ATTITUDES AND VARYING TYPES OF EVALUATIONS OF SUBJECT[a]

Proportion of similar attitudes	Evaluation conditions			
	Positive	Negative	Control	Total
1.00	13.13	8.40	12.60	11.38
.67	13.00	5.87	12.00	10.29
.33	10.73	4.87	7.53	7.71
.00	10.33	3.47	6.27	6.69
	11.80	5.65	9.60	—

[a] After Byrne and Rhamey, 1965, p. 886.

to 18 reinforcements, and each subject in the control condition received 12 reinforcements. Using the Byrne–Nelson formula, the authors found that the attraction responses obtained in the control condition did not differ from those predicted by the formula. In the other two conditions, however, there was a significant departure from the predicted values. The obtained attraction responses were higher than predicted in the positive evaluation condition and lower than predicted in the negative evaluation condition. This is, of course, what would be expected if the hypothesis of differential effect were correct; thus, the hypothesis was confirmed.

Discussion. Why should personal evaluations have a greater influence on attraction than attitude statements? In common sense terms, one *is more concerned* with what another person thinks of him than with what that person thinks of the Democratic Party. With respect to our theory of attraction, personal evaluations must *arouse greater affect* than do attitude statements. Further, because such stimuli are assumed to have reinforcement properties, personal evaluations must constitute *greater magnitude of reinforcement* than do attitude statements.

How can concepts such as differential concern, affect, and reinforcement magnitude be best represented in the attraction formula? Our solution was to add a weighting factor to designate magnitude of effect. This innovation proved to be a useful modification of the formula defining the base relationship. Assuming that various stimuli of varying strengths would be found in future research, the authors proposed that the attraction law be rewritten

$$A_x = m \left[\frac{\Sigma(PR_x \times M)}{\Sigma(PR_x \times M) + \Sigma(NR_x \times M)} \right] + k$$

or attraction toward X is a positive linear function of the sum of the weighted positive reinforcements (Number $\times$ Magnitude) associated with X divided by the total number of weighted positive and negative reinforcements associated with X.

Ideally, a procedure will be found for obtaining weighting coefficients in some manner independent of their effect on the dependent variable. Until such a methodology is devised, it is necessary to work backward from the data in order to arrive at a *post hoc* approximation. It should be noted that this is not simply a tautological undertaking because, once weighting coefficients are established for given stimuli, they should prove applicable among new subjects and in new situations. The initial task is to find a weighting coefficient that yields a linear function with the data at hand. Byrne and Rhamey used a simple trial-and-error method to arrive at weighting coefficients which by inspection provided the best fit for a linear function. A more sophisticated procedure was introduced later by Clore and Bald-ridge (1968). Several alternate weights are assigned and, for each possibility, correlation coefficients are computed between weighted proportion of pos-itive reinforcements and attraction. The weights yielding the highest correlation are then accepted as correct. By using either method, it is found that a straight line can be attained for the Byrne-Rhamey data by weighting the evaluation items on a 3 to 1 basis compared with the attitude items. The recomputation of proportions based on this weighting is shown in Table 5–3. Attraction was plotted as a function of these weighted proportions, as shown in Fig. 5–2, and a straight-line function was fitted to the data by the least squares method. It is obvious by inspection that the curve fits the data very closely. The solution yielded the formula $Y = 10.17X + 3.64$.

TABLE 5–3

PROPORTION OF POSITIVE REINFORCEMENTS BASED ON
WEIGHTED COMBINATIONS OF EVALUATION ITEMS
$(M = 3)$ AND ATTITUDE ITEMS $(M = 1)^a$

Proportion of similar attitudes	Evaluation conditions	
	Positive $(18 +, 0 -)$	Negative $(0 +, 18 -)$
1.00 (12 +, 0 −)	1.00	.40
.67 (8 +, 4 −)	.87	.27
.33 (4 +, 8 −)	.73	.13
.00 (0 +, 12 −)	.60	.00

[a]After Byrne and Rhamey, 1965, p. 888.

PERSONAL EVALUATIONS: FACE-TO-FACE INTERACTION

Aronson and Worchel. Presumably as an alternative to reinforcement theory, it was proposed by Aronson and Worchel (1966) that the effect of attitude similarity on interpersonal attraction is based entirely on the subject's implicit assumption that someone who shares his attitudes would like him. Even though the Byrne-Rhamey experiment had already shown that both attitude similarity and personal evaluations affect attraction, Aronson and Worchel dismissed that finding as an artifact limited to a "noninteractive" experimental design. That suggestion appears to in-corporate a painfully familiar belief that behavior must be studied in complex interpersonal situations and, the corollary notion, that responses

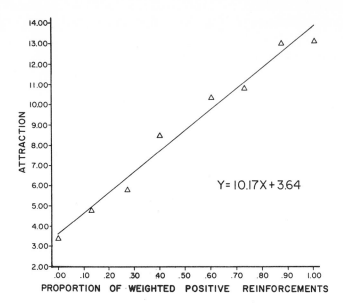

Fig. 5–2. Attraction toward a stranger as a linear function of proportion of positive reinforcements based on a weighted combination of evaluation items and attitudinal items. (After Byrne & Rhamey, 1965, p. 888.)

elicited by verbal material are qualitatively different from responses elicited by the behavior of other human beings who are physically present. They predicted that "after a face-to-face interaction, if O likes P, P will like O; the similarity or dissimilarity of O's attitudes to P's attitudes will have a negligible effect [p. 157]."

Aronson and Worchel's (1966) procedure involved the interaction of a subject with a stooge who expressed either similar or dissimilar attitudes followed by an exchange of messages in which the stooge indicated either liking or disliking for the subject. Then, attraction toward the stooge was ascertained. They reported a significant main effect for the evaluation variable, whereas "Neither the effect of similarity nor the interaction approaches significance [p. 158]." They suggested that the effects reported by Byrne and Rhamey must be limited to a noninteractive situation. Without additional research, it might reasonably have been concluded that there is little continuity between the kind of behavior studied within the attraction paradigm and that which occurs in real life interactions. There has, however, been additional research.

Byrne and Griffitt. In a follow-up article, Byrne and Griffitt (1966b) suggested that the Aronson and Worchel study potentially could have been of value as an exploration of the generality of the attraction paradigm. The study would have provided such an extension if the investigators had simply repeated the Byrne and Rhamey experiment with one alteration, namely, a face-to-face interaction. In fact, they altered the attitude variable as well. They used only a seven-item attitude scale, and either two or five similar items constituted the attitude dimension, whereas the original study used a 12-item scale with similarity ranging from .00 to 1.00. With a new stimulus context and a restricted range of the attitude similarity variable, it obviously becomes difficult to evaluate the meaningfulness of their findings. It must also be noted that though the relevant F ratio for similarity was not reported in their article, a reanalysis of their data indicated an F of 3.66 which is significant of the .06 level. Thus, contrary to their published report, the main effect for similarity actually approaches significance very closely. The arguments against accepting the Aronson and Worchel conclusions seemed compelling, but rather than leave the issue in a slightly ambiguous state, Byrne and Griffitt (1966b) applied a touch of gilt to the lilly by replicating the Aronson-Worchel experiment with a somewhat more extended range of attitude similarity–dissimilarity.

The subjects were 30 male undergraduates. The procedure was the same as that Aronson and Worchel had used. The subject and stooge each filled out a seven-item attitude scale. Each then read their own responses aloud, with the subject responding first each time. By a pre-arranged schedule, the stooge either expressed similar views on all items or dissimilar views on all items. The subject and stooge were then asked to write a few sentences regarding their reaction to the experiment; these messages were then exchanged, and the subject received one of the Aronson-Worchel communications in which like or dislike was expressed. The subject and stooge were then asked to evaluate each other on the IJS.

The means of the attraction responses are shown in Table 5–4. Analysis

TABLE 5–4

MEAN ATTRACTION RESPONSES TOWARD CONFEDERATE
AS A FUNCTION OF ATTITUDE SIMILARITY AND
EXPRESSED LIKING TOWARD SUBJECT[a]

Proportion of similar attitudes	Evaluation conditions	
	Positive	Negative
1.00	12.30	7.86
.00	10.40	5.62

[a]After Byrne and Griffitt, 1966b, p. 295.

of variance indicated that both the like–dislike variable and the similarity–
dissimilarity variable yielded highly significant effects, just as in the Byrne-
Rhamey experiment.

Discussion. It appears, then, that the results of all three investigations
are quite consistent in showing (*1*) the powerful effect of interpersonal
evaluations on attraction and (*2*) the less powerful but clearly significant
effect of attitude similarity–dissimilarity on attraction when combined
with evaluations, even in a face-to-face interaction.

The latter two studies also provided an opportunity for cross-validat-
ing the weighting coefficients tentatively proposed in the Byrne and Rhamey
experiment. Each subject received from the stooge seven units of attitudinal
information and four units of evaluational information (enjoyed working
with him, profound, interesting, well-informed or did not enjoy working
with him, shallow, uninteresting, not well-informed). Each of the latter
statements was assigned a weight of 3 and each attitude item a weight of 1.
Attraction was plotted as a function of proportion of weighted positive

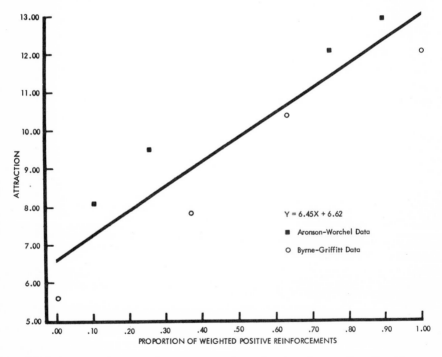

Fig. 5–3. Attraction toward a stooge as a linear function of proportion of positive reinforcements based on a weighted combination of evaluation statements and attitudinal
items. (After Byrne & Griffitt, 1966b, p. 296.)

reinforcements as shown in Fig. 5–3. A straight-line function was fitted to the data by the least squares method, yielding the formula $Y = 6.45X + 6.62$. Though the constants in the function differ from the Byrne-Rhamey ones, it is quite clear that the results in a face-to-face situation correspond remarkably well to the noninteractive findings.

Personal Evaluations in the Absence of Additional Information

In the discussion of research on topic importance in Chapter 4, it was pointed out that differential importance was irrelevant when items of homogeneous weights are employed or when there are conditions of .00 or 1.00 similarity or, as a more general statement, in any situation in which the weights of the positive and negative reinforcements are equal. These propositions could be deduced from the Byrne-Rhamey formula (though it took some of us an uncomfortably long while to do so), and they have been empirically confirmed.

Clore and Baldridge (1970) extended the above reasoning to the study of personal evaluations. Even though there is ample evidence that personal evaluations have a greater effect on attraction than do attitude statements, the model indicates that personal evaluations presented alone would have the same effect as attitude material presented alone.

Method. A group of 48 students at the University of Illinois responded to a 24-item attitude survey. In the experimental session, half responded to the attitudes of a stranger who was either .00 or 1.00 similar to themselves. The other half received no attitudinal information but was told that the stranger had evaluated them on the basis of their attitudes; these subjects then were shown an IJS which indicated either a positive or a negative reaction as in the Byrne-Rhamey experiment. All subjects rated the stranger on the IJS.

Results. The mean attraction responses for the four groups are shown in Table 5–5. Analysis of variance indicated that the only significant effect was that of .00 conditions versus 1.00 conditions, as hypothesized. The authors (Clore & Baldridge, 1970) note:

> Consistent with the model, the attitudes and the evaluations both influence attraction and to the same extent. If the model is correct, the absence of an effect is due to the presentation of the personal evaluations alone and the attitudes alone, with no opportunity for the differently weighted items to be juxtaposed. [p. 180]

Discussion. As a further demonstration of the model's effectiveness, the authors also successfully replicated a portion of the Byrne-Rhamey study in which the differential effect of personal evaluations and attitudes was once again shown.

TABLE 5–5

MEAN ATTRACTION RESPONSES FOR HOMOGENEOUS
ATTITUDINAL AND EVALUATIONAL GROUPS RECEIVING
EITHER POSITIVE OR NEGATIVE INFORMATION[a]

Type of information	Proportion of positive information		
	.00	1.00	Total
Attitudinal only	5.50	11.25	8.38
Evaluational only	5.75	12.25	9.00
Total	5.63	11.75	—

[a]After Clore and Baldridge, 1970, p. 180.

Using the previously established weights of 3:1 for evaluations–attitudes, they plotted the data from both experiments in terms of attraction as a function of weighted positive reinforcements and obtained the familiar straight-line function; the specific formula was $Y = 5.75X + 5.61$. Finally, they employed Grant's (1962) method to test the fit between obtained responses and those predicted by the Byrne-Rhamey model. The test was run for their two experiments, for the Aronson and Worchel (1966) and Byrne and Griffitt (1966b) experiments, and for the original Byrne and Rhamey (1965) data. In each instance, for five experiments involving 30 data points and 406 subjects, deviations from the model were found to be nonsignificant, whereas correspondence with the model was highly significant.

Attitudinal Similarity versus Evaluational Congruency

Dutton's (1969) dissertation research at the University of Toronto also dealt with the general problem of the combined effects of similarity and evaluation. He created experimental conditions in which the subject believed that she had presented arguments supporting a given opinion either well or poorly and in which the position was actually her own or the opposite of her own. After the presentation, the subject received information from four confederates as to whether or not she agreed with the subject and as to how well the subject had presented the arguments. It was arranged that two confederates agreed with the position and two disagreed; one of each of these pairs said that the subject had argued well and one said that she had argued poorly. Subsequently, the subject's attraction toward each confederate was ascertained.

It was found that when subjects were presenting their own positions on the issue, attraction was influenced primarily by agreement on the issue (attitude similarity) and only secondarily by agreement about how well she had argued (evaluational congruency). When the subject was presenting an opinion opposite to her own, the relative effect of the two variables on attraction was reversed.

Dutton concluded that the differential weights of attitude similarity and evaluational congruency were dependent on the subject's goals in a specific situation.

OTHER DETERMINANTS OF SIMILARITY EFFECTS

Judgment Similarity

Mascaro (1970) suggested that the effects of judgment similarity should be like those of attitude similarity. In two experiments (Mascaro, 1970; Mascaro & Lopez, 1970), judgment similarity was manipulated. The following are some examples of items used:

The average number of schools destroyed by the Viet Cong in South Vietnam during the period from 1958 to 1960 was about

(a) 26 per month

(b) 16 per month

A Stanford University home economist has estimated that the average American spends about

(a) 37 minutes of his day eating

(b) 89 minutes of his day eating

In each experiment, judgment similarity was found to have a significant influence on attraction, as hypothesized.

Opinion Similarity

When subjects are found to respond to attitude similarity–dissimilarity, they are presumed to be reacting to the stranger's congruency or incongruency with respect to their own well-established positions on a variety of issues. What if the issues were relatively transitory opinions about the probable attitudes of others? For example, what if the question were not whether the stranger himself prefers the Republican or Democratic party but whether he agrees or disagrees with the subject about the political preferences of the majority of students? It could be argued that such questions might function as attitudes (and perhaps relatively trivial ones at that) only in a context in which the opinion could not be confirmed by factual information. If, however, the subject knew that an accurate answer is available, there should be little reward value in an agreement with oneself by an equally uninformed stranger and little threat represented by a disagreement expressed by such a stranger.

In an unpublished study, the author and Griffitt administered a special 12-item opinion scale to 94 Texas undergraduates. The format and content were drawn from the attitude scales but the wording took the form "Most students believe that racial integration in public schools is a mistake and are very much against it." They were asked in each instance simply to indicate their opinion about the attitudes held by most students.

The experimental session several weeks later involved the standard interpersonal judgment instructions plus information relevant to the possibility of verifying the opinions expressed by the subject himself and by the stranger. Subjects in the No Information group were told that it is almost impossible to find out the opinions of all 24,000 students at the University, that no adequate methods have been worked out to sample such attitudes, and that there is, therefore, no way to know for sure whether one's opinions about student attitudes are correct or incorrect. The Delayed Information group was told that an attitude study was in progress and that the results would be distributed to them before the end of the semester. The Information group was told that a large-scale study had just been completed and that the results would be given to them during the experimental session.

The opinion scale of each stranger was constructed such that he held opinions similar to those of the subject on .33 or 1.00 of the items.

TABLE 5–6

ATTRACTION RESPONSES TOWARD STRANGERS
DIFFERING IN PROPORTION OF SIMILAR OPINIONS

Availability of information about correctness of opinions	Proportion of similar opinions		
	.33	1.00	Total
No Information	8.47	10.50	9.39
Delayed information	8.29	11.22	9.80
Information	7.69	11.20	9.57
Total	8.19	11.00	—

The mean attraction responses are shown in Table 5–6. Analysis of variance indicated that the only significant effect was that of proportion of similar opinions. There is even a trend for the reverse of the hypothesis— the greatest similarity effect occurred in the Information condition, and the least similarity effect occurred in the No Information condition. Thus, the proposed effects of information availability were not confirmed, and the experiment only served to demonstrate once again that attraction is a function of similarity. There is a slight increase in stimulus generality in that the similarity involves opinions about the attitudes of others rather than attitude similarity itself.

Basis of the Stranger's Attitudes

Batchelor and Tesser (in press) proposed that individuals would respond not only to the attitudes expressed by another person but also to the reason as to why he holds that attitude. Thus, the attitude stimulus increases in complexity if it involves not only positive or negative feelings about a topic but also the basis for those feelings. Some bases would be expected to be more socially desirable than others. Therefore, the effect of attitude similarity should combine with the effect of attitude base in determining attraction.

The authors defined the following four attitudinal bases in order of social desirability:

Value Expressive. Individuals have characteristic values which serve to help them know who they are and what they are. This attitude is internalized by the person as an end, not as a means to achieving some environmental reward.

Need for Cognition. People are uncomfortable with situations and things which are ambiguous, chaotic, and unpredictable. By maintaining this particular attitude this person is better able to understand and predict the events in his world so that he can behave effectively.

Utilitarian. This person holds this attitude because it facilitates his attainment of some objective. He holds this attitude as a means of achieving a practical end—maximizing gains and minimizing losses.

Ego-Defensive. This person holds this attitude as a way of defending himself against recognizing, or becoming aware of, the fact that he harbors unwelcome thoughts, feelings, or impulses.

The subjects were 40 undergraduates at the University of Georgia. In one portion of the experiment, subjects responded to eight strangers with all possible combinations of similarity versus dissimilarity and the four attitude bases.

In Table 5–7 are shown the mean attraction responses toward similar and dissimilar strangers identified as having different bases for their attitudes. It was found that attraction was influenced by both attitude similarity and attitude base.

It could be concluded that in any situation in which the basis of another individual's attitudes is expressed or in which it may be inferred, the effect of attitudes on attraction will be a joint function of similarity and base.

TABLE 5-7
MEAN ATTRACTION RESPONSES
AS A FUNCTION OF ATTITUDE SIMILARITY
AND ATTITUDE BASE[a]

Attitude Base	Attitude similarity	
	Dissimilar	Similar
Value expressive	8.03	11.03
Need for cognition	7.85	10.33
Utilitarian	5.40	8.25
Ego-defensive	5.85	7.25

[a]Data from Batchelor and Tesser, in press.

GENERAL STATEMENTS EMBODYING ATTITUDES

In experiments concerned with the effect of stimulus mode, the attitude material was deliberately maintained in the same form as when an attitude scale constituted the stimulus. The strangers simply verbalized the appropriate words from the scale item. In spite of this experimental precaution, there is no reason to suspect that the attitude statements expressed by the stranger must necessarily be phrased in the words of the attitude scale item. If subjects are in fact responding to the attitudinal content of a statement, the effects of "I prefer the Republican party," "The Republican party is best," "Republican philosophy is superior to Democratic philosophy," "The Republican party tends to nominate better candidates than does the Democratic party," and "Nixon is preferable to Humphrey" should be indistinguishable. Once again, the generality of the attitude–attraction relationship would be increased by the confirmation of that proposition.

Written Statements with Attitudinal Content

Byrne, Young, and Griffitt (1966) tested the effects on attraction not only of attitudinal statements but also of neutral statements of fact. For reasons which will be discussed in Chapter 12 statements of fact were conceptualized as constituting instances of consensual validation about noncontroversial topics but with a lower magnitude of effect than similar attitude statements. It was, therefore, hypothesized that (a) neutral statements of fact have a positive effect on attraction and (b) the positive effect of neutral statements is less than that of similar attitude statements.

Method. A 12-item attitude scale was administered to a pool of several hundred students enrolled in an introductory psychology class at the University of Texas. From this group, 98 subjects (45 males, 53 females) were drawn and assigned randomly to one of six experimental groups. The subjects were later seen in small groups. They were informed that students in another class had been given a list of the same 12 topics which were included in the attitude scale and then asked to write a sentence expressing the first thoughts that occurred to them concerning each topic. The subjects were supposed to read the 12 sentences written by one of these other students, form an impression about him or her, and then evaluate this other person.

The sentences written by the stranger were bogus ones prepared by the experimenters, consisting of handwritten copies of three types of statements (see Appendix C). For example, one item of the attitude scale asks the subject to indicate whether or not he believes in God. The three statements relevant to this item were "There is definitely a God," "There is no God," and "Most modern religions are monotheistic." There is thus a statement in agreement with the subject's position, a statement in disagreement, and a neutral statement of fact.

The proportion of similar (S), neutral (N), and dissimilar (D) statements was varied across the six experimental groups. One third of the subjects received only similar and neutral statements (four similar and eight neutral or eight similar and four neutral), one-third received only similar and dissimilar statements (four similar and eight dissimilar or eight similar and four dissimilar), and one-third received only neutral and dissimilar statements (four neutral and eight dissimilar or eight neutral and four dissimilar). Thus, attraction should be influenced by the number of relatively positive and relatively negative (or relatively less positive) reinforcements (8–4 more positive than 4–8) and by the relative magnitude of the positive reinforcements represented by the similar and neutral statements (S–N more positive than S–D more positive than N–D). The strangers were evaluated on the IJS.

Results. The means of the attraction responses for the six conditions are presented in Table 5–8. Analysis of variance indicated that both hypotheses were confirmed.

Since neutral statements were found to have less effect on attraction than the attitude statements, their weighting coefficients must be less. Tentatively, the neutral statements were assigned a weighting coefficient of .5 and the attitude statements 1. Utilizing these coefficients, the six experimental groups reduce to five different conditions with respect to proportion of weighted positive reinforcement as shown in Table 5–9. Attraction

TABLE 5–8
MEANS OF ATTRACTION RESPONSES
TOWARD STRANGERS ON ,THE
BASIS OF WRITTEN STATEMENTS[a]

Type of sentences	No. of relatively positive and negative sentences		
	4–8	8–4	Total
Similar–neutral	9.41	11.29	10.35
Similar–dissimilar	6.93	8.93	7.93
Neutral–dissimilar	6.11	7.44	6.78
Total	7.49	9.20	—

[a] After Byrne, Young and Griffitt, 1966, p. 273.

TABLE 5–9
PROPORTION OF WEIGHTED POSITIVE REINFORCEMENTS[a]

Type of sentences	No. of relatively positive and negative sentences	
	4–8	8–4
Similar–neutral	$\frac{8}{8+0} = 1.00$	$\frac{10}{10+0} = 1.00$
Similar–dissimilar	$\frac{4}{4+8} = .33$	$\frac{8}{8+4} = .67$
Neutral–Dissimilar	$\frac{2}{2+8} = .20$	$\frac{4}{4+4} = .50$

[a] After Byrne, Young, and Griffitt, 1966, p. 274.

was plotted as a function of these weighted proportions (see Fig. 5–4). A straight-line function was fitted to the data by the least squares method, yielding the formula $Y = 5.36X + 5.06$. The curve obviously fits the data quite closely.

It would seem that the linear relationship between proportion of similar attitudes and attraction is unaffected by the form in which the attitudes are expressed.

Oral Statements with Attitudinal Content in Face-to-Face Interaction

Even though attraction is found to vary in the expected way when the attitude statements take a general form, there, nevertheless, remains a considerable gap between the highly controlled laboratory situation in the

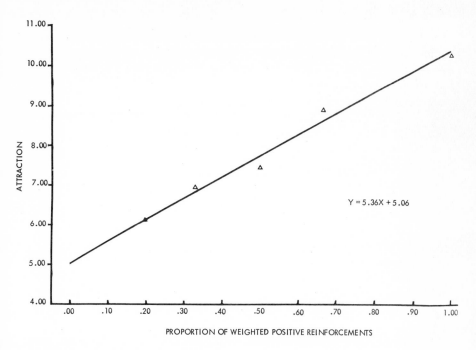

Fig. 5–4. Attraction toward a stranger as a linear function of proportion of weighted positive reinforcements. (After Byrne, Young, and Griffitt, 1966, p. 274.)

experiment just reported and a conversation about a given topic between two individuals. Research by Brewer and Brewer (1968) provides the needed link between those two situations.

Method. As part of a multifaceted investigation, 623 subjects were given a 20-item attitude scale concerned with the topic of capital punishment. A total of 216 high- and low-scoring individuals were selected for the experiment in order to have subjects strongly for or strongly against capital punishment. Two-person groups were established with all pairs being of the same sex. Half of the groups consisted of individuals selected for attitude similarity in that they each had high or each had low scores on the scale. The other groups were made up of dissimilar pairs with individuals scoring on opposite ends of the scale. The task was to discuss the topic of capital punishment for a 20-minute period. The number of statements made by each participant was recorded as well as its relation to capital punishment: pro, con, or neutral. After the interaction, attraction toward the partner was measured.

Results. For each subject, proportion of agreeing statements received from the partner was computed. That is, the number of capital punishment statements in agreement with the subject's views was divided by the total number of capital punishment statements. The average correlation across all of the conditions between proportion of agreeing statements and attraction was .62, which is statistically significant.

It may be seen that this experiment provides what is probably the most difficult test and the most striking evidence yet reported for the generality of the law of attraction as originally established in a controlled experimental situation. Here, two individuals are freely interacting and expressing their genuine opinions according to no prearranged schedule or sequence. When the statements are classified as to content and the resulting figures expressed as proportion of similar attitudes, the familiar similarity–attraction relationship is shown to be operating even in this complex interpersonal interaction. It's enough to make you believe in science.

In conclusion, we have seen that the effect of attitude similarity on attraction has been extended from the paper and pencil manipulation of attitudes to attitudinal material presented on tape recordings, in movies, on videotape, and in face-to-face interactions. Personal evaluations of the subject are found to influence attraction with weights approximately 3 times as great as those of attitude items, whether the manipulation is by means of paper and pencil or in face-to-face encounters. The weights of other kinds of evaluational congruency probably depend on situationally specific determinants. Attraction is also influenced by similarity of relatively transitory opinions and by the basis on which a stranger's attitudes are held. Finally, the expression of the attitude content may vary within relatively wide limits, including the expression of genuine attitudes in a conversation, without changing the similarity–attraction relationship.

Chapter 6 / **Stimulus Generality:**
II. Effect of Overt Stimulus Characteristics

The reinforcement formulation states that attraction toward X is a function of the rewards and punishments associated with X. Such association occurs during interpersonal interactions which range from confrontations between real individuals expressing their true opinions to one another as in the Brewer and Brewer study to the interaction between a subject and a bogus stranger who is represented by his purported responses on an attitude scale. How, then, is it possible to account for indications of differential attraction between strangers who meet for the first time? Here, there have been no past interactions during which reinforcements could have occurred. In these first-impression situations, individuals are presumably responding to the overt stimulus properties of other individuals in terms of their beliefs about the meaning of those properties. In some instances, attraction is based on generalization from reinforcements in previous interactions with others who possessed the same or similar stimulus properties. More frequently, attraction in such situations is a function of the individual's expectancies concerning the behavioral consequents of overt stimulus variables. Thus, when individuals are initially attracted to or repulsed by strangers who are overweight, have a Southern accent, wear a beard, or belong to a minority group, the response is a function of learned expectancies which occasionally are based on past experiences with overtly similar individuals.

Previous research has shown that attraction is affected by variables such as quality of clothing (Hoult, 1954; Lefkowitz, Blake, & Mouton, 1955) and vocal attractiveness (Lerner, 1965). In the experimental investigation of attraction, the possible effects of the stimulus attributes of the target person have generally been controlled by having the same confederate play different roles across conditions or by the use of written material to eliminate such observable variables altogether. In this chapter, several overt stimulus characteristics are brought back into the attraction situation one by one in order to determine their effects.

Prestige or Status of Stranger

In almost all of the experimental research on attraction, the stimulus person is identified as a member of the subject's peer group. Presumably, peers constitute a major source of consensual validation and invalidation through the expression of attitudes and beliefs. In interactions with non-peers, the prestige of the individual expressing similar or dissimilar attitudes would seem to be a likely candidate as a potentially important parameter of the attitude–attraction relationship. A number of sociometric studies have reported a positive relationship between prestige as defined by socio-economic status and number of friendship choices received within a group (Bonney, 1944; Grossman & Wrighter, 1948; Loomis & Proctor, 1950; Lundberg, 1937). Similarly, prestige or status as defined by military rank has been found to be positively correlated with number of sociometric choices received (Kipnis, 1957; Masling, Greer, & Gilmore, 1955).

On the basis of these prestige findings, Byrne, Griffitt, and Golightly (1966) formulated two equally plausible alternative hypotheses concerning prestige influences in the attitude–attraction paradigm. First, it was hypo-thesized that the prestige of a stranger has a positive effect on attraction toward him, in addition to the effects of attitude similarity–dissimilarity. Thus, one might expect that similar attitudes expressed by a high prestige stranger would elicit a more positive attraction response than similar attit-udes expressed by a stranger of medium prestige who, in turn, should elicit a more positive response than a low prestige stranger. Analogously, dis-similar attitudes would elicit the most negative response when expressed by a low prestige stranger and the least negative response when expressed by a high prestige stranger.

A second line of reasoning led to a somewhat different hypothesis. If similar and dissimilar attitude statements constitute consensual validation and invalidation, it would seem that the incentive value of such statements would vary with the authoritativeness of the source. Thus, similar attitudes from an individual of high prestige should have the greatest positive value, whereas dissimilar attitudes expressed by the same individual should have the greatest negative impact. At the other end of the prestige dimension, neither similarity nor dissimilarity from a low-status stranger would be expected to have much effect because that particular source is not of great value as a validator or a great threat as an invalidator. Given this reasoning, it was hypothesized that the effect of differential attitude similarity–dissimilarity on attraction is greatest with high prestige strangers and least with low prestige strangers. That is, an interaction effect was predicted.

Two parallel investigations were conducted in order to test these alternate hypotheses.

Occupational Prestige

Method. In a pilot study, 49 occupational descriptions were presented to 30 students with instructions to rate each on a 7-point scale on the basis of prestige. The scale ranged from 7 or "very high prestige" to 1 or "no prestige at all." Based on these ratings, three occupations were selected as representing three levels of prestige with little variability among the judges. The three occupations were janitor (mean = 1.67, SD = .79), electrician (mean = 3.93, SD = .57), and physicist (mean = 6.20, SD = .60).

In the experiment itself, subjects were 85 male introductory psychology students at the University of Texas. They were given a 12-item attitude scale dealing with a variety of issues. The subjects were then assigned to one of two experimental conditions in which the proportion of similar attitudes held by a stranger was either .17 or .83 and to one of three experimental conditions in which the prestige of the stranger's occupation was varied (janitor, electrician, physicist).

Several weeks later, the usual interpersonal judgment experiment took place. The major difference introduced was that the attitude scales had supposedly been administered not only to students but to a wide variety to university employees, including faculty members, office workers, and men working at various skilled and unskilled jobs on the campus. The occupation of each subject's "stranger" was indicated on a typed information card accompanying the attitude scale.

Results. The means of the attraction responses toward a stranger relatively similar to or dissimilar from the subject in attitudes and identified in terms of occupation are shown in Table 6–1. Attitude similarity–dissimilarity was once again found to have a highly significant effect on attraction. Neither the prestige variable nor the interaction between prestige and attitude similarity–dissimilarity influenced attraction. Thus, neither of the alternate hypotheses was supported by the results of this experiment.

TABLE 6–1
MEANS OF ATTRACTION RESPONSES TOWARD
INDIVIDUALS DIFFERING IN PROPORTION OF
SIMILAR ATTITUDES AND IN OCCUPATIONAL PRESTIGE[a]

Proportion of similar attitudes	Prestige level			
	Low (Janitor)	Medium (Electrician)	High (Physicist)	Total
.83	10.20	10.80	10.21	10.41
.17	7.84	9.17	7.88	8.24
Total	9.11	10.07	8.97	—

[a]After Byrne, Griffitt, and Golightly, 1966, p. 438.

It seemed possible that these subjects had somehow ignored or discounted the information concerning the occupation of the stranger, and, hence, our manipulation had simply failed. To test the success of the manipulation, responses to one of the buffer items of the Interpersonal Judgment Scale (IJS) (estimated intelligence of the stranger) were analyzed. It was found that the mean estimated intelligence was highest for the physicist and lowest for the janitor with differences among the three means significant at the .001 level. Apparently the subjects were aware of the occupational level of the strangers, and they responded both differentially and appropriately to them in estimating intellectual ability. Nevertheless, attraction was not influenced by prestige level.

Before discussing this finding, the parallel experiment will be described.

Military Rank

Method. The subjects were 55 male sophomore and junior members of the Cadet Corps at Texas A & M University. Military training in this organization is required during the freshman and sophomore years and is optional during the junior and senior years. At graduation, corps members receive a reserve commission in the U.S. Army. The hierarchical organization of a military unit makes it possible to define prestige in terms of rank. In order to create three levels of prestige or status for the stranger, low status was defined as characteristic of freshmen members of the Cadet Corps, medium status as the same rank as that of the subject, and high status as senior cadet officers.

Other than the use of military rank to identify the strangers, the second experiment was essentially a replication of the first.

TABLE 6–2
MEANS OF ATTRACTION RESPONSES TOWARD
INDIVIDUALS DIFFERING IN PROPORTION OF
SIMILAR ATTITUDES AND IN MILITARY RANK[a]

Proportion of similar attitudes	Rank			
	Low	Medium	High	Total
.83	8.56	10.33	9.89	9.59
.17	6.22	6.00	6.20	6.14
Total	7.39	8.17	7.95	—

[a]After Byrne, Griffitt, and Golightly, 1966, p. 439.

Results. The means of the attraction responses are shown in Table 6–2. As in the first experiment, attitude similarity–dissimilarity influenced attraction at the .001 level, whereas neither military rank nor the interaction between rank and similarity yielded significant effects. Again, the hypotheses were not confirmed.

Discussion. There seemed to be one fairly plausible explanation for the lack of prestige effects. It has been suggested by Asch (1948) and supported by several investigators (e.g., Cole, 1954; Lewis, 1941) that in many of the "prestige-suggestion" experiments, subjects find themselves in ambiguous situations in which a response is required. With only limited cues available, they simply utilize what is provided and hence are "influenced by prestige" in that prestige is the major source of information. When additional cues are added, however, the effect of prestige is negligible. With sufficient information, individuals need not rely on vague assumptions or stereotypes; instead they use the actual information. Thus, in the two prestige studies just discussed, the general effects of prestige factors on attraction were absent because the subjects were able to respond to the stranger on the basis of his attitudes and beliefs.

If this proposition is correct, attraction would be a function of prestige only in situations devoid of additional information.

Occupational Prestige with and without Attitudinal Information

If prestige were found to influence attraction in the absence of attitude information, it would become important to seek an explanation of this process. One possibility is that prestige is simply associated with a wide variety of cues (e.g., money, fame, intelligence, success, power) such that low prestige has many negative and high prestige many positive implications.

A somewhat different explanation of a prestige effect is that a prestige–attraction relationship is mediated by assumptions about similarity of attitudes. Thus, prestige cues ⟶ assumptions about attitudes ⟶ attraction. The latter formulation is appealing in that it suggests the way in which various determinants of attraction may be related to attitudinal variables and it also suggests why the addition of actual attitudinal information serves to negate prestige effects.

Bond, Byrne, and Diamond (1968) attempted to test the hypothesis that prestige is a determinant of attraction when information is limited and to ascertain whether assumed similarity mediates the proposed prestige–attraction relationship. It was hypothesized that (a) in the absence of additional information, attraction toward a stranger is a positive function of his occupational prestige and (b) differential attraction toward low and high prestige strangers is a function of differential assumed attitudinal similarity between strangers and subjects.

Method. The subjects were 139 students (93 males, 46 females) enrolled in the introductory psychology course at Stanford University. Early in the quarter, a 56-item attitude scale was administered, and several weeks later the experimental portion of the investigation was conducted in a series of small groups.

Eight different conditions were created. In order to test the first hypothesis, two conditions were arranged in which the information about the stranger concerned one of two occupational levels (bus driver or physician); no attitudinal information was included. Two conditions consisted of attitudinal information only (.20 or .80 similarity). Four conditions constituted a partial replication of the Byrne. Griffitt, and Golightly (1966) experiment; subjects responded to one of the two levels of occupational prestige plus one of the two levels of attitude similarity.

The subjects were told:

A number of research investigations in recent years have been designed to determine the extent to which one person can form valid judgments about another person just by knowing a small amount of information about him. These studies involved obtaining the attitudes on different issues from various occupational groups. In addition, for individuals within each of these occupational groups, biographical information was gathered.

In this study, we are interested in seeing how accurately you can estimate the attitudes held by these individuals on the basis of limited information about them. To assist you in forming your impression, you will be given some of the collected information about the other person. We would like you to read over this information as carefully as possible, exactly in the order presented.

For the group receiving occupational information, the following paragraph was included:

The subject about whom you are to form an impression is a 30-yr.-old physician (bus driver) working in Palo Alto where he lives. He was married at age 26 and has one son aged two. Both his parents are alive, residing in San Francisco.

For the groups receiving attitudinal information, a 10-item scale purportedly filled out by the stranger was also presented. In the condition receiving both occupational and attitudinal data, the order of presentation was counterbalanced

In addition to attraction, a measure of assumed similarity of attitudes was obtained. The assumed similarity measure consisted of a 10-item blank attitude scale on which the subject was to predict the stranger's responses. Assumed similarity was scored if a predicted response fell on the same side of the neutral point as the subject's own original response to the item, and dissimilarity was scored if the predicted response was on the opposite side of the neutral point.

Results. The means of the attraction responses in the eight conditions are shown in Table 6–3. When occupational information is presented alone, prestige influences attraction as was hypothesized with the subjects responding more positively to the physician than to the bus driver. A comparison of the two attitude conditions simply reaffirms that attitudinal information

TABLE 6–3

MEAN ATTRACTION RESPONSES TOWARD STRANGERS
IDENTIFIED ON OCCUPATIONAL INFORMATION, ATTITUDINAL
INFORMATION, OR COMBINED INFORMATION[a]

Type of information	Response		
Occupational only			
Bus driver	8.53		
Physician	10.20		
Attitudinal only			
Similarity .20	5.60		
Similarity .80	10.20		

Combined	Proportion of similar attitudes:		
	.20	.80	Total
Physician	6.95	9.90	8.42
Bus driver	6.95	9.00	7.98
Total	6.95	9.45	—

[a]After Bond, Byrne, and Diamond, 1968, p. 1170.

alone also affects attraction. For the combined conditions, proportion of similar attitudes was found to have a significant effect, whereas the influence of occupational prestige and the interaction were negligible. Thus, in a new subject population and with different specific occupations representing the prestige levels, it was once again found that prestige level does not affect attraction when attitude information is also presented.

The second hypothesis was tested by means of a correlational approach. If attraction is a function of assumed similarity, the two response variables should be positively correlated. For the entire group, the correlation was .32 which supports the hypothesis. When the subjects are subdivided, however, a somewhat different picture emerges. For subjects who received only attitudinal information about the stranger, the correlation between attraction and assumed similarity was .52. For those who received both types of information, the correlation was .29. In the comparison which is most important for testing the hypothesis (those receiving only occupational information), the relationship was only a nonsignificant .13. Therefore, there appears to be good reason to question the generality of the relationship between assumed similarity and attraction and no reason at all to believe that response to occupational prestige is a function of assumed similarity.

It was further reasoned, however, that if attraction is mediated by assumed similarity, those groups asked to project attitudes prior to evaluating the stranger should show higher assumed similarity–attraction correlations than those groups asked to evaluate prior to projecting. The projection task would make their similarity–dissimilarity with the stranger more pronounced, thus tightening the assumed similarity–attraction relationship. For those asked to project first, the correlation between the assumed similarity and attraction measures was .43. For those asked for their attraction response first, the correlation was a nonsignificant .18.

Discussion. The effects of prestige on attraction which are apparent when no other information is available disappear or are completely dominated by the effects of attitude similarity when the two types of information are presented together.

The plausible explanation that differential attraction to different prestige levels is based on assumed similarity received equivocal support. On the one hand, there is some indication that assumed similarity of attitudes is associated with liking only to the extent that other attitudinal information is provided. On the other hand, the assumed similarity–attraction relationship is considerably strengthened when the subjects are provided with an anchorage point for their attraction by projecting the stranger's attitudes prior to evaluating him.

SEX AND PHYSICAL ATTRACTIVENESS

It would seem safe to propose that in our society, physical attractiveness is a positively valued attribute. That is, both males and females would prefer to be attractive rather than unattractive, to have attractive friends, to marry an attractive spouse, and to produce attractive offspring. Such concerns seem both arbitrary and petty in the abstract, but they are obviously of considerable personal import in the concrete world of dating, television commercials, and cosmetic surgery. What relevant research data are there?

In a study conducted at the University of Texas in 1921, Perrin found a rank order correlation of .60 between liking and physical attractiveness. Two unpublished studies conducted at Amherst (Megargee, 1956; M. J. Taylor, 1956) dealt with the stratification of the student body in terms of social status. With 45 men in the class of 1956, Taylor obtained ratings which placed them in one of four status categories, and he then compared this categorization with independent ratings of such characteristics as physical attractiveness. His findings indicate a strong positive relationship much like that reported by Perrin. Taylor concludes "The most reliable dimension which is associated with social status is that of looks. Of all the criteria, this has the most consistently low variation. Moreover, there is a strong positive relationship between status and ratings of good looks."

Megargee went on to investigate the extent to which the students were aware of the role of variables such as looks in their judgments. He found no relationship between the criteria that the students verbalized as indicators of social status and the criteria identified by Taylor. In any event, these correlational findings are quite consistent in suggesting the relationship between physical attractiveness and the positiveness of response from peers.

A field study by Walster, Aronson, Abrahams, and Rottman (1966) yields additional supportive data. Couples at the University of Minnesota were randomly paired with one another at a 'computer dance.' Four judges unobtrusively rated the physical attractiveness of each of 752 freshmen subjects as they purchased tickets for the dance. During intermission, the subjects filled out a questionnaire in which they evaluated their dates. As in the earlier Texas and Amherst studies, popularity (self-rated) was significantly correlated with physical attractiveness (rated by the judges). More importantly, it was found that regardless of the subject's own attractiveness, the largest determinant of liking for one's partner ($r = .31$ for female subjects and .39 for male subjects) was the attractiveness of the partner. Using the subject's own rating of the date's physical attractiveness, liking was correlated .78 with attractiveness for male subjects and .69 for female subjects.

Within the present research paradigm, Byrne, London, and Reeves

(1968) investigated the effect of physical attractiveness on interpersonal attraction under laboratory conditions. Given the findings of previous investigators and the proposed reward value attached to physical attractiveness, it was hypothesized that (*a*) interpersonal attraction is greater toward an attractive than toward an unattractive stranger. The possible differences between same-sex and opposite-sex attraction presents additional problems. For one, the correlational sociometric studies of attraction which have dealt with this variable have tended to indicate that within-sex attraction exceeds cross-sex attraction (e.g., Bjerstedt, 1958; Faunce & Beegle, 1948). Nevertheless, in a college-age population, expectancies concerning the reinforcement value of a stranger of the opposite sex should be greater than expectancies about a stranger of the same sex. In addition, the hypothesized effect of physical attractiveness should be greater with opposite sex than with same sex strangers. It was, therefore, further hypothesized that (*b*) attraction is greater toward an opposite sex stranger than toward one of the same sex, and (*c*) the effects of physical attractiveness and sex are interactive.

Response to Photographs of Strangers

Method. In order to obtain sets of photographs of males and females representing two levels of attractiveness, it was necessary to carry out a preliminary scaling procedure. Glossy prints of college yearbook photographs of 84 males and 84 females were used as a stimulus pool. The judges consisted of 30 male and 24 female introductory psychology students drawn from the same population as the experimental subjects.

Each judge was given the pile of photographs of one sex at a time with instructions to sort them with respect to physical attractiveness. A forced normal distribution of nine intervals was employed with the following frequencies required: 1, 3, 9, 18, 22, 18, 9, 3, 1. Pile No. 1 was labeled as the least attractive, No. 9 as the most attractive, and No. 5 as neutral.

From the resulting distribution of judgments, photographs were selected for experimental use if they met the following criteria: above 6.2. or below 3.5 in mean attractiveness rating, a standard deviation of 1.5 or less, and a nonsignificant difference between the mean ratings made by the male and female judges. A total of 13 male photographs and 15 female photographs met these criteria. For the four sets of pictures, the mean ratings are 6.66 for the attractive males, 6.70 for the attractive females, 3.10 for the unattractive males, and 2.97 for the unattractive females.

For the experiment itself, 89 introductory psychology students (47 males, 42 females) served as subjects. The study was described as part of a project dealing with interpersonal judgment. Each subject was given a sheet of blank paper on which a Xerox reproduction of one of the yearbook photographs was mounted. Subjects were instructed to examine the picture carefully and to attempt to form an evaluative opinion of the person.

Each subject responded to only one stranger. The three independent variables were sex of subject, sex of stranger, and attractiveness of stranger.

Results. The means of the attraction responses are shown in Table 6–4. The only hypothesis to receive support was that dealing with physical attractiveness. Thus, for both sexes, interpersonal attraction is positively influenced by physical attractiveness, and (with the possible exception of males responding to males) the sex of the stranger is of negligible importance.

TABLE 6–4
MEAN ATTRACTION RESPONSES
TOWARD STRANGERS DIFFERING IN PHYSICAL ATTRACTIVENESS[a]

| | Subjects | | | |
| | Male | | Female | |
Strangers	Unattractive	Attractive	Unattractive	Attractive
Male	9.77	9.46	9.10	10.40
Female	8.82	10.80	9.55	11.82

After Byrne, London, and Reeves, 1968, p. 263.

Response to Photographs plus Attitudes

On the basis of the previous experiment, Byrne, London, & Reeves (1968) hypothesized that attraction toward a stranger is a joint function of attitude similarity–dissimilarity and physical attractiveness. In view of the results just described, neither the sex of the subject nor the sex of the stranger was expected to influence this relationship.

Method. The same general procedures were followed as in the experiment with the photographs alone. The four independent variables were sex of subject, sex of stranger, attractiveness of stranger, and attitude similarity–dissimilarity. The subjects were 205 introductory psychology students (103 males, 102 females) at the University of Texas.

The only procedural difference was in the attitude variable provided by responses to a 12-item scale. The scales of simulated strangers were prepared which expressed either similarity on ten issues and dissimilarity on two or the reverse. To each scale was attached a picture of either a male or a female who was either physically attractive or unattractive.

TABLE 6–5

MEAN ATTRACTION RESPONSES
TOWARD STRANGERS DIFFERING IN PHYSICAL ATTRACTIVENESS
AND EXPRESSING SIMILAR AND DISSIMILAR ATTITUDES[a]

| | Proportion of similar responses | | | |
| | .17 | | .83 | |
Strangers	Unattractive	Attractive	Unattractive	Attractive
	Male subjects			
Male	6.92	8.50	9.71	10.15
Female	7.25	8.50	9.21	10.54
	Female subjects			
Male	6.69	6.46	10.33	11.64
Female	7.33	7.92	10.42	11.00

[a]After Byrne, London, and Reeves, 1968, p. 265.

Results. Table 6–5 presents the means of the attraction responses. The only significant effects were the stranger's attractiveness and the similarity of the stranger's attitudes to those of the subject. Thus, each of those variables when studied in isolation is found to influence attraction; when they are combined, the independent effects of each are still evident.

It might be of interest to note the effect of these variables on responses to the four buffer items of the IJS. All four variables (Intelligence, knowledge of current events, morality, and adjustment) were found to be influenced by attitude similarity–dissimilarity. Physical attractiveness, however, exerted an effect only on judgments of intelligence and morality and only through an interaction with the sex of the stranger. Specifically, attractive male strangers were seen as less intelligent and less moral, whereas attractive female strangers were seen as more intelligent and more moral when compared with their unattractive counterparts. Apparently, there exist some sexual stereotypes associated with physical attractiveness.

Discussion. The generality of the similarity–attraction relationship is further extended by the finding that it is not influenced by the sex of the stranger to whom agreeing or disagreeing attitudes are attributed. Thus, the utilization of same-sex strangers in experiments would appear to be a needless control. Responsiveness to attitude similarity–dissimilarity of opposite-sex strangers also provides evidence that the present series of experimental investigations is consistent with the correlational studies of husband–wife similarity which were summarized in Chapter 2. It should be noted, however, that under the special circumstances in which the stranger is of the opposite sex and gives a negative evaluation of the subject, females respond more negatively to such a stranger than do males (Ervin, 1967).

Physical attractiveness, on the other hand, does exert an influence on interpersonal attraction for subjects of each sex toward strangers of either sex. Clearly, the proposition that members of our culture attach meaning to physical attractiveness is supported. Since both attractiveness and similarity are found to influence attraction, it should again be possible to examine more precisely the way in which physical attractiveness may be considered as simply an additional element of stimulus information. Knowing only that attractiveness is conceptualized as positive information and unattractiveness as negative, a series of arbitrary trials yields $+4$ and -4 as satisfactory weighting coefficients for the present stimulus materials. If these values are added to the attitudinal information and the resulting weighted proportion of positive reinforcements substituted in the Byrne–Nelson formula, then the results are as shown in Table 6–6. The correspondence between the predicted and obtained values once again suggests the utility of this approach in dealing with determinants of attraction, provided that it proves possible to cross-validate the weighting coefficients.

TABLE 6–6

PREDICTED AND OBTAINED ATTRACTION VALUES
WITH ATTRACTIVENESS INFORMATION ASSIGNED
POSITIVE AND NEGATIVE WEIGHTS[a]

Condition	Weighted proportion of positive reinforcements	Predicted attraction responses	Obtained attraction responses
Similar–attractive	.88	11.41	10.83
Similar–unattractive	.62	9.99	9.92
Dissimilar–attractive	.38	8.69	7.84
Dissimilar–unattractive	.12	7.27	7.05

[a]Data from Byrne, London, and Reeves, 1968.

Other Research on Attractiveness

The pervasiveness of the effects of physical attractiveness have been demonstrated repeatedly in a series of additional laboratory investigations. For example, McWhirter (1969) in his dissertation research at Texas Tech University combined photographs of girls in bathing suits with information about attitudes. Again, both the attractiveness and similarity variables influenced attraction, and sex of subject was irrelevant. The subjects were also rated for their own attractiveness, and McWhirter found that the most attractive subjects gave the most positive responses to the strangers. An interaction revealed that for attractive subjects the influence of similarity decreases as stranger attractiveness increases, whereas for unattractive subjects the influence of agreement increases as stranger attractiveness increases. Moss (1969) conducted similar dissertation research at Kansas State University. Male subjects were asked to rate a series of eight photographed females on the IJS and to rank them in terms of who would be asked for a date. The more attractive the girl, the greater the attraction and the higher she was ranked, though this tendency is greatest for the most attractive subjects. In fact, the least attractive subjects were most positive toward the girls in the middle of the attractiveness dimension. Moss interpreted these responses as strategies aimed at maximizing success in the dating situation.

On the other hand, Brown and Eng (1970) in a study at the University of British Columbia manipulated similarity, race of the stranger (Oriental and Caucasian), and physical attractiveness. They found significant effects only for the first two variables (strangers who were similar and/or Chinese were preferred). They attributed the failure of the attractiveness variable to the difficulty subjects experienced in rating the Chinese photographs and to the somewhat out-of-date hair styles of the individuals in the photographs. Another possibility is that of cultural differences between Canada and the United States in the value placed upon physical attractiveness.

Finally, in those situations in which attractiveness is found to affect attraction, A. G. Miller (1970) provides data that suggest that attractiveness serves as a cue to differential expectancies about the individual's personality characteristics. The more attractive the stranger in a photograph, the more he or she was rated as curious rather than indifferent, complex rather than simple, perceptive rather than insensitive, confident rather than unsure, assertive rather than submissive, happy rather than sad, active rather than passive, amiable rather than aloof, humorous rather than serious, pleasure-seeking rather than self-controlled, outspoken rather than reserved, and flexible rather than rigid. With such expectancies operating, it is little wonder that attractive strangers are preferred and that blonds (attractive ones, anyway) have more fun.

Physical Attractiveness in Face-to-Face Interaction

The establishment of continuity between laboratory findings and the complexities of the nonlaboratory world is a primary goal of the stimulus generality investigations. The way in which physical attractiveness influences evaluative behavior in an interactive situation would be expected to parallel that reported in the laboratory situation.

Method. In an investigation of computer dating to be reported in greater detail in Chapter 14, Byrne, Ervin, and Lamberth (1970) arranged for 44 couples who were similar or dissimilar on a 50-item scale to meet and interact in a 30-minute coke date on the campus. Among the data obtained were ratings of each subject's physical attractiveness by the experimenter and also by the subject's date. The correlation between the experimenter's ratings and the date's rating for female subjects was .34 and for male subjects .56. Both coefficients are significant, but there is far from perfect agreement between experimenter and dates about attractiveness. As in the Walster *et al.* (1966) study, we would expect a greater effect of physical attractiveness as rated by the subject than as rated by the experimenter.

After the brief date, the subjects were separated and asked to fill out a special IJS (See Appendix D) which included additional 7-point items about whether the other person would be liked or disliked as a date, enjoyed or disliked as a spouse, and whether he or she was sexually attractive or sexually unattractive.

Results. The results from this dating situation are remarkably like those in the laboratory. For subjects of both sexes, there was a significant relationship between proportion of similar responses on the pretest and attraction (for males, $r = .30$ and for females, $r = .33$). And, for both sexes, there was a significant relationship between physical attractiveness (as rated by the date) and attraction (for males, $r = .37$ and for females, $r = .65$). The best prediction of attraction is obtained by combining both stimulus variables. The multiple correlation coefficient between attraction and similarity plus physical attractiveness for males was .47 and for females .69.

TABLE 6–7

PROPORTION OF SIMILAR RESPONSES
AND PHYSICAL ATTRACTIVENESS AS PREDICTORS
OF SEXUALLY ORIENTED INTERPERSONAL EVALUATIONS[a]

Variable	Male subjects		Female subjects	
	Physical attractiveness of date	Proportion of similar responses	Physical attractiveness of date	Proportion of similar responses
Dating	.67	.26	.59	.23
Marriage	.59	.20	.61	.21
Sexuality	.77	.17	.69	.00

[a]Data from Byrne, Ervin, and Lamberth, 1970.

When we move from the attraction response to the more sexually oriented concerns of dating, marriage, and sexual attractiveness, physical attractiveness is a highly significant correlate of all three variables for both sexes. The correlations are shown in Table 6–7. It seems that students of both sexes are strikingly similar in placing a heavy emphasis on physical attractiveness in considering dates, marriage, and sex. Although each of these variables is positively related to the attraction measure, they are, nevertheless, differentiated from attraction with respect to the relative influence of similarity and physical attractiveness.

EMOTIONAL DISTURBANCE

As might have been noted from time to time by the discerning reader, the effect of similarity on attraction is not assumed to result from any magical qualities inherent in similarity. Rather, similarity is rewarding and dissimilarity punishing because of the meaning of such stimulus qualities to most individuals in a wide variety of situations. As we examine the effects of similarity to individuals outside of the subject's peer group, the meaning of similarity and its relevance to the subject would be expected to change. Our manipulation of the stranger's prestige was an example of an unsuccessful attempt to find a differential effect beyond the peer group. With a better choice of attributes for the stranger, however, it should be possible to mitigate and conceivably even reverse the similarity effect.

The Novak and Lerner Experiment

Novak and Lerner (1968) proposed a motive which could operate to make similarity unpleasant or even threatening—we need to believe that there is an appropriate fit between our behavior and what fate deals out in rewards and punishments.

> If people were not able to believe they could get what they want and avoid what they dislike by performing certain appropriate acts, they would be anxious, and, in the extreme, incapacitated. Because of the importance of this belief, the person is continually vulnerable to objective evidence that fate can be capricious and beyond one's efforts. This vulnerability becomes important in situations where the person is confronted with someone who has been seriously harmed through no apparent fault of his own—for example, someone with a severe physical or emotional handicap. The presence of such a person may elicit the threatening thought, "Can this also happen to me?" The person would prefer to believe that such a terrible fate can occur only to someone who has deserved it by virtue of having committed some undesirable act ... or because of an inherent personal failing ... —in any case, someone unlike himself [pp. 147–148].

Selecting emotional disturbance as the unpleasant handicap, the authors proposed that similarity under these conditions should be negatively reinforcing and dissimilarity positively reinforcing.

Method. The subjects were 96 Kentucky undergraduates. Subjects reported in pairs and in separate rooms. They were asked to fill out an attitude questionnaire. Afterward, these questionnaires were supposedly exchanged, but each subject actually received material prepared by the experimenter. In the similar condition, 20 of the 26 Survey of Attitudes items were prepared as similar to those of the subject or as dissimilar. On a 10-item experiences and aspirations questionnaire, similarity and dissimilarity were also manipulated. Each subject also received a personal data sheet with such background information as age, year in school, etc., plus an "other information" question which was either filled out "None" or with a paragraph indicating that the person had had a nervous breakdown leading to hospitalization the previous fall, was presently seeing a psychiatrist, and was feeling "shaky" at the moment.

The dependent variables included the IJS.

TABLE 6–8

MEAN ATTRACTION RESPONSES
TOWARD SIMILAR AND DISSIMILAR STRANGERS
IDENTIFIED AS NORMAL OR EMOTIONALLY DISTURBED[a]

Stranger	Dissimilar	Similar
Normal	7.50	11.04
Emotionally disturbed	8.20	9.67

[a]Novak and Lerner, personal communication, 1969.

Results. The mean attraction responses* are shown in Table 6–8. It was clear that the usual similarity effect which is found with the normal stranger is modified when the stranger is described as emotionally disturbed. There is still a preference for the similar stranger, but the attraction response is less positive than in the parallel normal condition; even more interesting is the slightly less negative rating of the dissimilar disturbed stranger.

*It should be noted that Novak and Lerner were particularly interested in whether the subject would choose to approach or avoid the partner. Their predicted reversal regarding this variable was obtained in that subjects tend to want to avoid the dissimilar normal partner and the similar disturbed partner.

Thus, Novak and Lerner were successful in creating stimulus characteristics that mitigated the similarity effect.* What are the implications of that finding for the attraction paradigm?

Predicting Attraction in a Novel Situation

From the viewpoint of a reinforcement model, the prediction of attraction responses is a matter of applying general theoretical principles to the specifics of a given situation. The Byrne–Rhamey formula may be seen as embodying a major tenet of this theoretical approach. There is considerable predictive utility in viewing attraction in terms of the formula $Y = 5.44X + 6.62$ in which Y is attraction as measured by the IJS and X is the weighted proportion of positive reinforcements. One of the more utilitarian features of such a theoretical statement is that a large number of diverse and seemingly special elements may be reduced to a small number of theoretical constructs. If the goal of science is conceptualized as the prediction of a maximal number of phenomena from a minimal number of principles, clearly the attraction formula is a step toward a science of attraction.

One point is sometimes a source of confusion. General principles may be applied to any situation in which the relevant stimulus and response components are known. For example, if it has been established that a stimulus has specific reinforcing properties, learning principles allow us to predict the effects of that stimulus on an instrumental response. One view of the task of behavioral science is the formulation of such principles and the identification of such properties. What happens, however, when one decides to investigate the effects of a new stimulus—emotional disturbance of a stranger for example? According to Aronson (1970), it is with respect to novel stimuli that reinforcement theory proves to be of little use in that there can be no *a priori* predictions. It may come as a surprise, but all formal theories are useless in the sense that Aronson means. No science can predict in the absence of information about the properties of the independent and dependent variables—necromancy maybe, but not science.

If we assume that the law of attraction has some utility and if we wish to apply it in a novel situation, two alternatives are open. First, we may use various procedures to determine the relevant properties of the new variables. Analogously, it is a prerequisite that we measure weight or temperature or brightness or whatever before general principles of the physical sciences are of any predictive value in various situations. We shall eventually need to develop appropriate measuring devices to assess the reinforcement

---

*In a more recent investigation (Lerner & Agar, to be published), the identification of the stranger as a dope addict had effects parallel to those reported here for emotional disturbance. Our reinforcement analysis would be the same for both manipulations.

magnitude of the stimuli in attraction research. Second, we may approach a novel situation subjectively and attempt to predict via experience and empathy and insight what the effects might be. This was essentially the cognitively oriented approach of Novak and Lerner. Without the needed measuring devices, this second approach is our only avenue to a novel situation.

Conceptualizing the Mitigating Effects of Emotional Disturbance

At the simplest and least abstract level, it could be said that the emotional adjustment of the stranger (as operationally defined) constitutes a boundary condition within which the similarity–attraction function is altered. It has been said that such a finding limits the generality of the similarity effect. In the same way, altitude "limits the generality" of the relationship between temperature and the boiling point of a substance. In any event, it would be possible empirically to establish an infinite number of specific instances in which the attraction formula would necessarily be altered in order to predict accurately in each new situation. Further, each new finding could be interpreted in a cognitive fashion with respect to the meaning of the stimulus situation from the subject's point of view, using common sense examples, anecdotes, and analogies.

At the same time, it is equally reasonable to attempt to reduce the variables to more basic and less qualitative abstractions in order to increase the generality of our descriptions. It is here that the formal theoretical framework is of critical importance in increasing both the scope and the precision of our predictions. If one assumes that attraction is a simple linear function of positive and negative stimulus elements, any attraction effect can be explained by analyzing the stimulus context in those terms.

In the Novak and Lerner experiment, the two normal stranger conditions should obviously be like the usual conditions in our attraction research. A different problem is posed by their emotionally disturbed conditions. If the model is correct, information that the stranger is emotionally disturbed must involve additional elements in the stimulus complex. A general positive effect of new stimuli or a general negative effect can readily be explained in terms of an increase in the number and/or magnitude of the positive or negative reinforcements associated with X. An interactive effect is slightly more complicated, and Palmer (1969) was the first to deal with it successfully. Given his finding of an interaction between attitude similarity and information about the competence of a stranger, he simply assumed that a stranger's competence involves both positive and negative qualities for the subject. The way in which this accounts for an interaction will become clear shortly.

Following Palmer's example, we shall assume that emotional disturbance in others has both positive and negative stimulus qualities and, hence, elicits both positive and negative affect. Besides the mathematical necessity for this assumption, the same idea can be justified in cognitively oriented common sense terms. An emotionally disturbed person in our culture is interesting, pitiable, and amusing and at the same time is frightening, disgusting, and upsetting. Both aspects of our attitudes about mental illness are frequently depicted on television, in movies, and in our humor. With respect to the attitudinal material, no special assumptions are required. All of the Novak and Lerner subjects received 26 units of attitude information (20+ and 6− or the reverse) and 10 units of questionnaire information (8+ and 2− or the reverse). In addition, those receiving the paragraph indicating emotional disturbance were exposed to an unknown quantity of positive and negative affective stimulation. By working backward from a curve-fitting process in one of the cells (disturbed–similar), it was found that the assignment of the tentative values of 11 +, 22 − to the stimulus resulted in the obtained mean matching that predicted by the Byrne–Nelson formula. That is, finding that the stranger had had a nervous breakdown, had been hospitalized, was seeing a psychiatrist, and feels shaky was equivalent to having him agree with the subject on 11 topics and disagree on 22 topics. With respect to all three stimulus elements, the resulting values to be inserted in the attraction formula are shown in Table 6–9.

The quantities presented in Table 6–9 were then used to determine the weighted proportion of positive reinforcements received by subjects in each

TABLE 6–9

UNITS OF POSITIVE AND NEGATIVE REINFORCEMENTS
IN THE NOVAK AND LERNER EXPERIMENT[a]

	Attitudes			
	Dissimilar		Similar	
Emotional condition	+	−	+	−
Normal				
Attitude scale	6	20	20	6
Questionnaire	2	8	8	2
Other information	0	0	0	0
Proportion of positive reinforcements	.22		.78	
Disturbed				
Attitude scale	6	20	20	6
Questionnaire	2	8	8	2
Other information	11	22	11	22
Proportion of positive reinforcements	.28		.57	

[a]After Byrne and Lamberth, in press.

TABLE 6–10
PREDICTED AND OBTAINED ATTRACTION RESPONSES
IN THE NOVAK AND LERNER EXPERIMENT[a]

Condition	Weighted proportion of positive reinforcements	Predicted attraction response	Obtained attraction response
Normal–similar	.78	10.86	11.04
Disturbed–similar	.57	9.72	9.67
Disturbed–dissimilar	.28	8.14	8.20
Normal–dissimilar	.22	7.82	7.50

[a]After Byrne and Lamberth, in press.

condition of the experiment. The resulting values were substituted in the attraction formula, and the outcome may be seen in Table 6–10. The close correspondence between the predicted and obtained values is occasion only for muted celebration. The two normal conditions simply indicate that an attraction formula derived in a sample of Texas undergraduates is an accurate predictor of the responses of a sample of Kentucky undergraduates. The new reinforcement values were derived in the disturbed–similar condition, so the nearly identical values for predicted and obtained means are obviously only a testament to our arithmetic skills. The sole test of the *post hoc* values is provided via cross-validation in the disturbed–dissimilar condition in which values derived in a different condition clearly lead to an accurate prediction of the attraction response.

This little exercise has shown, then, that the Novak and Lerner data can be conceptualized in more than one way. More importantly, it suggests the strength of the reinforcement approach in reducing varied and complex stimuli to a few basic constructs which have transituational generality and which may be treated in simple mathematical equations. It would be of much greater importance if it were possible to utilize these concepts to make novel predictions in a different situation. Byrne and Lamberth (in press) were, without undue modesty, able to accomplish that feat.

Eliminating and Duplicating the Emotionally Disturbed Effect

If the overall model is correct, it follows that the appropriate manipulations of the number and/or strengths of the positive and negative reinforcers present in the situation could result in the nullification of the effect of the stranger's emotional disturbance or in the creation of that same "mitigating" effect by quite different stimuli. The predictions made at this point depend entirely on the attributes of the theoretical model and on reinforcement values established in previous research.

Eliminating the Emotionally Disturbed Effect. If information about another person's emotional disturbance has a quantitative rather than a qualitative effect on attraction, it may be seen that the addition of other quantities to the stimulus complex could serve to alter that effect in any desired manner. Our strategy was to replicate the Novak and Lerner normal condition and then to recreate their disturbed condition with one change. That change was the addition of a sufficient number of attitudes attributed to the stranger to make the proportion of positive reinforcements approximately equal in the normal and disturbed conditions. In Table 6–11 it can be seen how this goal was accomplished. The hypotheses are clear-cut. If emotional disturbance represents a special condition that necessarily mitigates the similarity–attraction effect, an interaction will be found. If emotional disturbance represents an established set of specific positive and negative elements (e.g., 11 +, 22 −), there will be only a main effect for attitude similarity which is actually a main effect for proportion of positive reinforcements.

TABEL 6–11
ELIMINATING THE EMOTIONALLY DISTURBED EFFECT[a]

Emotional condition	Attitudes			
	Dissimilar		Similar	
	+	−	+	−
Normal				
Attitude scale	6	20	20	6
Questionnaire	2	8	8	2
Other information	0	0	0	0
Proportion of positive reinforcements	.22		.78	
Disturbed				
Attitude scale	4	52	52	4
Questionnaire	2	8	8	2
Other information	11	22	11	22
Proportion of positive reinforcements	.17		.72	

[a]After Byrne and Lamberth, in press.

The experiment was conducted using 38 Purdue undergraduates as subjects, and the Novak and Lerner procedures were employed. The only alteration was the use of a 56-item attitude scale in the disturbed condition rather than a 26-item scale.

The results are shown in Table 6–12. The only significant effect was for the similarity variable as predicted by the reinforcement model.

Duplicating the Emotionally Disturbed Effect. The second experiment approached the same theoretical issue from the opposite direction. If the

TABLE 6–12

MEAN ATTRACTION RESPONSES TOWARD SIMILAR AND
DISSIMILAR STRANGERS IDENTIFIED AS NORMAL OR EMOTIONALLY
DISTURBED WITH ATTITUDES ELIMINATING THE
EMOTIONALLY DISTURBED EFFECT[a]

Emotional condition	Attitudes		
	Dissimilar	Similar	Total
Normal	8.10	11.90	10.00
Disturbed (+ 56 attitudes)	7.89	10.67	9.28
Total	7.99	11.28	—

[a]After Byrne and Lamberth, in press.

information about another person's emotional disturbance has a quantitative rather than qualitative effect on attraction, that same effect should be attainable by the addition of the appropriate number of positive and negative elements to the stimulus complex—even though the added elements have no relationship to emotional disturbance. The strategy here was to replicate the Novak and Lerner disturbed condition and then to recreate their normal condition with one change. That change is the addition of other positive and negative reinforcements approximately equal to the $11+$, $22-$ values attributed to emotional disturbance. The new material consisted of personal evaluations of the subject by the stranger, an item of information which, as we have seen in Chapter 5, has a weight of 3 ($3+$ for a positive evaluation and $3-$ for a negative evaluation). If a stranger expressed four positive evaluations of the subject ($4 \times 3 = 12$) and seven negative evaluations ($7 \times 3 = 21$), the resulting reinforcements theoretically approximate those attributed to emotional disturbance. Table 6–13 indicates how the conditions were created. Again the hypotheses are straightforward. If emotional disturbance represents a special condition that necessarily mitigates the similarity–attraction effect, an interaction will be found. If emotional disturbance represents an established set of specific positive and negative elements ($11+$, $22-$), the evaluation information will have approximately the same effect ($12+$, $21-$), and there will be only a main effect for similarity. Again, this main effect is actually the proportion of positive reinforcements.

The second experiment used 40 Purdue undergraduates as subjects and again employed the Novak and Lerner procedures. In the evaluation conditions, the Byrne–Rhamey (1965) methodology was utilized in which the subject is given feedback concerning the stranger's evaluation of him. In this instance, each subject received four positive and seven negative

TABLE 6–13
DUPLICATING THE EMOTIONALLY DISTURBED EFFECT[a]

	Attitudes			
	Dissimilar		Similar	
Emotional condition	+	−	+	−
Normal				
Attitude scale	6	20	20	6
Questionnaire	2	8	8	2
Other information	0	0	0	0
Evaluations	12	21	12	21
Proportion of positive reinforcements	.29		.58	
Disturbed				
Attitude scale	6	20	20	6
Questionnaire	2	8	8	2
Other information	11	22	11	22
Proportion of positive reinforcements	.28		.57	

[a]After Byrne and Lamberth, in press.

evaluations on a special 11-item IJS. Beyond the original six IJS items, the ratings dealt with the subject's desirability as a roommate, physical attractiveness, interestingness, open-mindedness, and whether he would make one feel at ease.

The results are shown in Table 6–14. Once again, as predicted by the reinforcement model, the only significant effect was for similarity. The objection might be raised that mixed evaluations could be interpreted by the subject as indicative of emotional disturbance, pushing us back to a qualitative rather than a quantitative interpretation of the results. The evidence does not support this notion. On the adjustment item of the IJS, the stranger

TABLE 6–14
MEAN ATTRACTION RESPONSES TOWARD SIMILAR
AND DISSIMILAR STRANGERS IDENTIFIED AS NORMAL
OR EMOTIONALLY DISTURBED WITH EVALUATIONS DUPLICATING
THE EMOTIONALLY DISTURBED EFFECT[a]

	Attitudes		
Emotional condition	Dissimilar	Similar	Total
Normal (+ evaluations)	7.20	9.70	8.45
Disturbed	7.80	9.70	8.75
Total	7.50	9.70	—

[a]After Byrne and Lamberth, in press.

with mixed evaluations was rated as better adjusted (4.70) than was the emotionally disturbed stranger (3.60). Even though the two kinds of information had identical effects on attraction, they were quite distinguishable with respect to adjustment.

Further Implications of the Model

The attraction formula allows us to predict that the responses of the subjects in the eight conditions of the two Byrne and Lamberth experiments should yield a linear function; further, the specific mean responses of each condition are predicted. Trend analysis indicates that the overall linear trend is significant; thus, the hypothesis concerning the function was confirmed. The relationship is depicted graphically in Fig. 6–1. Furthermore, Grant's (1962) technique was used to test the fit between the predicted and obtained responses. It was found that the obtained data did not deviate significantly from the model and, conversely, the correspondence between data and model was highly significant. The overall performance of the model was one of remarkable accuracy. Let it be emphasized that these various analyses of the data are not intended and should not be interpreted as demonstrations of the superiority of a reinforcement theory over a cognitive theory. Rather, they show the utility of a formal quantitative theory over

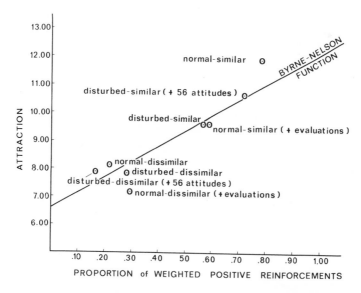

Fig. 6–1. Attraction as a linear function of proportion of weighted positive reinforcements, regardless of the stranger's normality or emotional disturbance. (After Byrne & Lamberth, in press.)

an informal qualitative one and the advantages of using each approach at the appropriate point in investigating new variables.

The moral of the story is that neither the cognitive nor the reinforcement approach has a monopoly on truth and that each can be extremely valuable when used as conceptual tools and not as chauvinistic banners.

Rychlak (1968) describes a dimension of meaning which he labels as dialectical (including the cognitive approach) and demonstrative (including the reinforcement approach). He refutes the argument that one of the poles of the dimension is good and the other bad. Rather, he sees the necessity for mixing the two strategies of theorizing and concludes:

> This historical bifurcation speaks out to proclaim that meanings, facts, ideas, hunches, and so on, vacillate between the poles of doubt and certainty, denotative clarity and connotative implication, creative error and creative accuracy, and so on. These are different ways of expressing the same thing—i.e., that knowledge grows as meanings change and as evidence is brought to bear. Our dimension is unresolvable because in its essentials it describes what *must take place* for meaning to advance. Its import is that it charges each of us with the responsibility of not overlooking his left hand while he turns the knobs of science with his right. A complete explication of our data cannot be found *only* in one end of this dimension of meaning. We must avoid thinking in terms of only one side, and cross over whenever and wherever it is possible to do so. The more crossing the better, for such journeys to the other side will serve to educate us and raise our level of meaningful understanding.
> ... though dialectic may be basic to man's free use of reason, it is a demonstrative tactic which brings him the ultimate fruit of that creative intellect. Only in this way can he acquire a lasting body of knowledge. Those who would stay exclusively on the side of dialectic must end their theoretical days in sophistry. We want open systems in psychology, opened by dialectic to be sure, but also brought to points of reference for experimentation in demonstrative fashion. They may then be opened once again by a dialectical tactic, and so forth [pp. 457–458].

It is proposed that the demands of science require both the formal theoretical systems characteristic of reinforcement theory and the intuitive understanding characteristic of cognitive theory. It is as difficult to imagine a science beginning with mathematical equations as it is to imagine a science terminating with artistic descriptions.

RACE

Before getting into the specific research in which racial membership is treated as simply another overt stimulus characteristic, an overview of a closely related line of research provides a useful perspective.

Belief Prejudice or Racial Prejudice

Rokeach, Smith, and Evans (1960), from Michigan State University, made the novel proposal that what is commonly labelled as racial prejudice is actually reducible to prejudice concerning beliefs and attitudes. It was suggested that bigotries arise in response to real or imagined areas of disagreement rather than to race, nationality, etc. Specifically, they hypothesized that "*insofar as psychological processes are involved*, belief is more important than ethnic or racial membership as a determinant of social discrimination [p. 135]." In one experimental test of this proposition, subjects were given descriptions of abstract individuals and asked to respond to each on a 9-point scale ranging from "I *can't* see myself being friends with such a person" to "I can *very easily* see myself being friends with such a person." The following are some examples:

A white person who believes in God.
A Negro who believes in God.
A white person who is an atheist.
A Negro who is an atheist.

Similar combinations were made with respect to attitudes about socialized medicine, Communism, labor unions, desegregation, interracial fraternities and sororities, racial equality, and racially open housing. Subjects were assessed as to their own attitudes about each topic and then asked to respond to the abstract stranger. It was found that the great majority of the subjects preferred blacks who agree with them to whites who disagree, and the difference in responding to blacks and whites was small compared to the difference in responding to those who agree and disagree.

A similar study with Jewish children led to the conclusion that subjects prefer as friends those who agree with them far more than those who disagree, regardless of race or ethnic group; with beliefs held constant, there is a small preference for one's own ethnic and racial group.

Triandis (1961), in a study at the University of Illinois, objected to the Rokeach *et al.* conclusions in that their dependent variable was limited to friendship choices, whereas their conclusions dealt more broadly with prejudice. Triandis proposed that a social distance response measure (items representing a 100-point scale) would yield different results.

He presented 112 subjects with 16 stimulus persons such as the following:

White, same philosophy, same religion, bank manager.
Different philosophy, white, bank manager, same religion.
Same philosophy, Negro, coal miner, same religion.

For each of the four variables (race, philosophy, religion, occupation), two levels were represented. Analysis of the data indicated that all four variables significantly affected social distance, but that race had the greatest effect of all. He concluded (Triandis, 1961) that "Rokeach's magnificent attempt at subsuming all the data under one simple notion succeeded only because of the design of his study. Had he considered something more than friendship he would not have obtained his results [p. 186].''

Rokeach (1961) countered with the judgment that Triandis' method was inappropriate and, hence, his conclusion faulty. Not only had Triandis changed the dependent variable, but he altered the independent variable as well. Rokeach et al. (1960) had used quite concrete content in describing the stimulus persons (believes in God, atheist) whereas Triandis had used quite abstract descriptions. "The belief variable pitted against race is vague, abstract, overintellectual, and complicated; hence weak! [Rokeach, 1961, p. 187].''

In a subsequent study, Triandis, Loh, and Levin (1966) made still another change in the independent variable. With the stimulus person represented both on photographic slides and a tape recording, he was either black or white, either well dressed or poorly dressed, either for or against integrated housing, and either spoke excellent or ungrammatical English.

It was found that the social distance variable was influenced significantly by the race and grammar variables but not by belief or dress. A friendship measure was significantly influenced by race, dress, and grammar but not by belief. Noting the findings of this and other studies (e.g., Triandis & Davis, 1965), Triandis et al. (1966) pointed out that different dependent variables (admiration of ideas, willingness to marry, acceptance as an intimate friend, exclusion from one's neighborhood, etc.) are distinct and are each influenced by different stimulus variables.

Another study in this general series was reported by Rokeach and Mezei (1966) with a change in both the independent and dependent variables. Briefly, subjects engaged in a group discussion covering one of five topics. The other four members of the group were confederates—an agreeing and a disagreeing white; an agreeing and a disagreeing black. Afterward, each subject was asked to select two of the group members to join him for coffee. In a parallel study, black and white applicants for a mental hospital job waited to be interviewed along with four other applicants who were confederates. With respect to the problem of working with mental patients, the four confederates again divided along racial and opinion lines. Afterward, subjects were asked to name the two members with whom they wished to work.

In analyzing both sets of data, it was found that 7 times as many individuals chose two who agreed with him regardless of race as chose two who were of his own race regardless of belief.

These and other findings led again to the conclusion that similarity of belief was a more important variable than similarity of race and that "the importance of racial attitudes per se as determinants of racial discrimination have been greatly over-estimated and the importance of congruence of beliefs correspondingly underestimated [p. 171].''

In a study at Kent State University, Hendrick, Bixenstine, and Hawkins (1971) suggested that the problem was essentially one of scaling the strength of the manipulation of the two independent variables. They created an interaction situation in which two whites and two blacks discussed an issue on video tape. It was felt that the tape insured a strong manipulation of the racial variable in that both blacks and whites were visually present throughout the discussion. The belief variable was also strong in that the issue was the war in Vietnam. Subjects viewed the taped discussion in which one member of each racial group took the prowar and one the antiwar position. Afterward, the subjects rated the four discussants. In this situation, there were few effects for race but very strong effects for belief similarity.

Stein, Hardyck, and Smith (1965), at the University of California (Berkeley), suggested that the inconsistent findings with respect to race and belief were largely a function of the methods used. Their stimulus persons were presented to teen-age subjects by means of the attitude simulation technique utilized in the attraction paradigm. Each subject was asked to respond to four strangers—two like him in values and two unlike him; two black and two white. As dependent variables, they used a 5-point rating scale of friendliness and a social distance scale patterned after that of Triandis.

With the friendliness variable, belief congruence was found to account for much more of the variance than the variable of race, but both variables were significant. On the total social distance scale, the results were identical to these. On an item basis, however, race and belief were differentially influential—race was significant only with respect to "invite home to dinner," "live in same apartment house," and "date my sister (brother)."

The authors suggest that "a belief effect is strong on all the items, whereas a race effect occurs on items that appear to involve publicly visible relationships that are 'sensitive' or controversial by prevailing cultural standards [Stein *et al.*, 1965, p. 288]." Thus, the discrepant results in the various studies were a function of the amount of information provided about the stimulus person and the type of response elicited from the subject. A later replication and extension by Stein (1966) provided additional support for this conclusion.

This brief set of interrelated investigations provide further evidence that different operations lead to different conclusions. Perhaps it is not necessary to belabor that point. Research findings are of greatest value within a particular paradigm, and attention must be focused on the particular operations used in a given experiment rather than on the real life variables to which these operations may or may not be directly relevant.

Race, Prejudice, and Expectancies

With the kinds of overt stimulus characteristics discussed earlier in this chapter, a general effect was hypothesized to hold across all subjects. That is, the expectancies aroused by prestige or physical attractiveness or emotional disturbance were assumed to be general ones. There are other stimulus characteristics, such as race, which one would guess to be associated with quite different expectancies for different individuals. Since there are known to be wide individual differences in racial prejudice, it would be necessary to take this fact into account in predicting the effects of racial membership on expectancies and, hence, on attraction.

Measuring Antiblack Prejudice. In the series of investigations to be described, a single measure of prejudice was employed. The desegregation scale was constructed by Kelly, Ferson, and Holtzman (1958) and later published by Holtzman and Young (1966). From a pool of 200 statements dealing with attitudes toward blacks the best 76 items were selected for further refinement. The final scale is made up of the 26 items on which there was the least disagreement among the subjects. These items represent approximately equal points along the dimension of favorableness toward the Negro race. The following are a few items and their median values on an 11-point scale:

10.59   The prospect of intermarriage is repulsive to me.
8.94   Negroes living in a white neighborhood lower the standards of cleanliness.
7.75   Admitting Negroes to white schools would not work because most Negroes do not have the necessary background to keep up with white students.
4.30   The Negro race will eventually reach the cultural and intellectual level of white people.
3.42   I would not object to participating in school athletics with Negroes.
2.18   I would not object to dancing with a good Negro dancer.
1.15   The best way to solve the race problem is to encourage intermarriage so that there will eventually be only one race.
        [Holtzman & Young, 1966, pp. 31–32]

The 26 items are embedded in a questionnaire, and subjects are asked to indicate degree of agreement with each. Items are scored from 0 to 4, and high scores indicate relatively antiblack attitudes. Total scores range from 0 to 104.

Expectancies and Prejudice. Byrne and Andres (1964) proposed that those individuals high in antiblack prejudice, as measured by instruments such as the desegregation scale, expect negative reinforcements from a stranger identified as a black, whereas individuals low in prejudice expect positive reinforcements from such a stranger. It was hypothesized that the ratio of positive-to-negative reinforcements expected as a consequence of black–white interactions is greater for low prejudice than for high prejudice individuals.

A group of 70 white students in the introductory psychology course at the University of Texas was given the desegregation scale. From the pool of subjects, 19 high prejudice (scores of 43 to 95) and 20 low prejudice (scores of 8 to 32) individuals were selected to take part in the investigation.

In order to ascertain expectancies with respect to the consequences of interactions between whites and blacks, a Test of Social Perception was constructed. The 39 subjects were asked to read about a series of hypothetical social situations, imagine themselves involved in each situation, and make several judgments about them. After the presentation of each situation, the subjects were asked to suggest the most probable pleasant and unpleasant consequences and to predict the behavior of others. The six black–white situations were as follows:

1. You have been assigned a room in a university dormitory. To your surprise, your roommate is a Negro. Assume that you do not change rooms or roommates for a semester.

2. One of your close friends marries a Negro girl. You and several of your friends are invited to a party given by this couple at their home. Assume that you attend the party.

3. You, your spouse, and your three children move into a new house in a very nice residential area. A Negro couple with three children buys the house next door to yours. Assume that you and your new neighbors do not move.

4. In a high school gym class, your daughter is assigned a locker next to a Negro girl. Assume that the locker assignments are not changed.

5. At a university social function, a well-dressed Negro male student asks a white coed if she will dance with him. Assume that she accepts.

6. You are the mayor of a small Midwestern community. You receive a letter from a well-known Negro group wishing to hold a convention in your city.

For comparison purposes, two other types of interaction were included:

7. You have been assigned a room in a university dormitory. To your surprise, your roommate is a heroin addict. Assume that you do not change rooms or roommates for a semester.

8. One of your close friends marries an English girl. You and several of your friends are invited to a party given by this couple at their home. Assume that you attend the party.

Expectancy was independently scored by two judges who were unaware of the subjects' Desegregation Scale scores. For each black – white item of the Social Perception Test, the response was evaluated as expressing positive or negative reinforcements for which the black individual or other whites were responsible and which occurred as consequences of the black–white interaction. On this basis, interaction with a black could conceivably be expected to result in any combination of the following four consequences:

PN: Positive reinforcement from the Negro (learning at first hand about someone different from oneself, simply enjoying him or her as a friend, dancing with a good dancer).

NN: Negative reinforcement from the Negro (Negro would act "pushy" about himself and the Negro cause, Negro will smell or be otherwise personally offensive, Negro is hostile or dangerous).

POW: Positive reinforcement from other whites (others will admire the individual's courage, the fact that he stood up for his or her convictions, family would encourage the person to do as he or she thinks is right).

NOW: Negative reinforcement from other whites (friends would reject or ostracize the individual, friends or even strangers would create unpleasant incidents; family would strongly disapprove and take steps to alter the situation).

No scoring category was assigned more than once per situation. Each subject received four scores consisting of the total number of times each of the four categories occurred across the six situations.

To obtain relative positive–negative expectancies, the negative scores were subtracted from the positive scores for each subject separately for black and white expectancies and for the total. (A constant was added to eliminate negative numbers.) The means for these various scores are shown in Table 6–15.

When high and low prejudice groups were compared, significant differences were obtained with respect to the total scores and the Negro score; the "other white" difference was not quite significant.

When analogous scores were assigned to expectancies concerning the heroin addict and the English bride, the high and low prejudice groups

TABLE 6–15
POSITIVE VERSUS NEGATIVE EXPECTANCIES
CONCERNING BLACK–WHITE INTERACTIONS
FOR HIGH AND LOW PREJUDICE SUBJECTS[a]

Reinforcement expectancies[b]	High prejudice	Low prejudice
Total expectancies (PN + POW) − (NN + NOW)	3.21	6.85
Expectancies about Negroes (PN) − (NN)	2.58	5.20
Expectancies about other whites (POW) − (NOW)	1.63	2.65

[a]After Byrne and Andres, 1964, p. 443.
[b]PN—positive reinforcement from the Negro; POW—positive reinforcement from other whites; NN—negative reinforcement from the Negro; NOW—negative reinforcement from other whites.

were found not to differ on either. There is no evidence, then, that those who differ with respect to attitudes about blacks differ in their expectancies about interactions with nonblacks.

The results, then, tend to confirm the general proposition that individuals high in antiblack prejudice express expectancies of fewer positive relative to negative reinforcements as a consequence of black–white interactions than do individuals low in prejudice. The way in which interacial attitudes and differential expectancies may be learned has been succinctly described by Bernice Lott:

> It is not too big a step to assume that if children can learn to prefer the color yellow, for example, over the colors green and black as a result of the type of training given them in this investigation, they can also, as a result of similar training, learn to prefer people called Englishmen over those called Poles and Italians, even though they have had no differential reward and punishment experience with any of those three national groups. The essential requirement for this learning is that individuals should learn to attach the same labels to the word "Englishman" as to stimuli with which they have rewarding experience, and to attach the same labels to the words "Pole" or "Italian" as to stimuli with which they have had neutral or punishing experience [Eismar 1955, p. 325].

Race, Prejudice, and Attraction

It is perhaps less than startling to propose that individuals who obtain high scores on a measure of antiblack prejudice and who express negative expectancies concerning the consequences of black–white interaction will not be attracted to a black stranger in our experimental paradigm. Nevertheless, it was essential to obtain empirical verification of this proposition and to have such data as a base line for subsequent experimental work. Wong (1961) conducted a preliminary investigation for this purpose.

Method. With 73 University of Texas undergraduates as subjects, Wong divided them into high and low prejudice subgroups on the basis of scores on the desegregation scale. In the experimental session, they were asked to make judgments about strangers based on the minimal background data provided on an information card. The only relevant variable on the card was race, which was indicated as "white" for half of the subjects and as "Negro" for the other half.

Results. The means of the attraction responses are given in Table 6–16. It may be seen that those individuals high in prejudice were less attracted to a black stranger than to a white stranger. Further, they responded more negatively to a black stranger than did low prejudice subjects.

TABLE 6–16
MEAN ATTRACTION RESPONSES OF HIGH
AND LOW PREJUDICE SUBJECTS TOWARD
STRANGERS IDENTIFIED AS WHITE
AND BLACK[a]

Prejudice	White stranger	Black stranger
High	10.35	8.22
Low	9.58	11.21

[a]Data from Wong, 1961.

Race, Prejudice, and Assumed Dissimilarity of Attitudes

Both the balance theory of Heider (1958) and the strain toward symmetry formulations of Newcomb (1953) would predict that an individual who dislikes blacks should assume that they hold attitudes dissimilar from himself. In Newcomb's terminology, if *A* (highly prejudiced subject) has negative feelings toward *B* (black stranger) and positive feelings toward *X* (e.g., classical music), symmetry can be obtained by *A* if he assumes that *B* dislikes classical music. Similarly, if a subject low in prejudice has positive feelings toward a black stranger and positive feelings toward science fiction, he achieves symmetry by assuming that the black stranger also likes science fiction.

On the basis of such reasoning, Byrne and Wong (1962) hypothesized that individuals high in prejudice assume a greater degree of attitude dissimilarity between themselves and a black stranger than between themselves and a white stranger, whereas individuals low in prejudice do not assume differential dissimilarity on the basis of race.

Method. A group of 54 introductory psychology students at the University of Texas was given the desegregation scale. They were divided into subgroups of 24 high prejudice (scores of 48 to 82) and 30 low prejudice (scores of 8 to 43).

Several weeks later in the experimental session, they were told that the study involved personality judgments on the basis of physical appearance. The subjects were asked to study carefully the photograph of another college student and then to fill out an attitude survey as they believed the depicted student had done.

The photographs were of the college yearbook variety. Half were of blacks and half of whites. Strangers and subjects were matched by sex. Guesses about the stranger's attitudes were made on the 26-item attitude scale.

Results. The scoring was on the basis of the number of attitudes out of the 26 on which the subject assumed dissimilarity in terms of direction of opinion (opposite side of the neutral point). One point was assigned for each item on which the stranger was guessed to be of an opposing view; dissimilarity could range from 0 to 26.

TABLE 6–17

MEANS OF ASSUMED DISSIMILARITY SCORES
OF HIGH AND LOW PREJUDICE SUBJECTS
JUDGING WHITES AND BLACKS[a]

Prejudice	White stranger	Black stranger
High	7.08	9.83
Low	6.67	7.53

[a]After Byrne and Wong, 1962, p. 247.

In Table 6–17 the means of the assumed dissimilarity scores are shown. The variable of race was found to affect assumed dissimilarity for pre-judiced subjects. High prejudice subjects assumed greater dissimilarity between themselves and a black stranger than between themselves and a white stranger. They also assumed greater dissimilarity between themselves and a black than did the low prejudice subjects. For low prejudice subjects, the assumed dissimilarity scores for whites and blacks did not differ significantly.

Discussion. Alternative interpretations of these findings might be considered. It is possible, for example, that the assumed dissimilarity is in terms of stereotypes held by the high prejudice subjects. The reported differences might simply reflect differences in the extent to which the two groups of subjects accept and express stereotyped beliefs about blacks. On each of the 26 items, high and low prejudice subjects were compared with respect to the attitudes they ascribed to the depicted blacks. Not one of the 26 items yielded significant differences. Rather than generally held stereotypes, there seem to be individually assumed dissimilarities. For example, in the high prejudice group, seven subjects indicated that they were in favor of smoking; of these, four guessed that the black in the photograph was against it. Of the five high prejudice subjects who were against smoking, three assumed that the black favored it. Although the 15 low prejudice subjects were similar to the high prejudice ones in their own diverse attitudes about smoking, only four of them assumed that the black in the photograph disagreed with them.

Still another possibility was that the dissimilarity assumed by the high prejudice students was the result of realistic evaluations on their part. Perhaps their attitudes on the various issues actually are more different from blacks than are the attitudes of low prejudice subjects. That is, rather than prejudice leading to assumed dissimilarity, it is possible that actual dissimilarity leads to prejudice. Even though the previous analysis would argue against this possibility, a group of 27 black students and 27 white students were given the attitude scale. Then, the attitude scales of the high and low prejudice subjects from the experiment were paired randomly with the scales filled out by these white and black strangers. There was little variation in the actual dissimilarity of attitudes of randomly matched strangers on the basis of race or racial prejudice. Thus, one of the concomitants of racial prejudice seems to be an unwarranted assumption of dissimilarity with respect to members of the target group.

Race, Prejudice, and the Effect of Attitude Similarity–Dissimilarity

The studies of prejudice within the paradigm indicate that individuals high in prejudice express negative expectancies concerning blacks, indicate less attraction toward a black than toward a white stranger, and assume greater dissimilarity between themselves and an unknown black than between themselves and an unknown white. What would happen, though, if this symmetry were disturbed by confronting a highly prejudiced subject with information indicating a high degree of similarity of attitudes between himself and a black? And, what happens when a subject low in prejudice is confronted by a black with attitudes dissimilar from his own? If we conceptualize the black race as a stimulus characteristic which conveys negative information to some of our subjects, how do those individuals combine the attitudinal and racial information? The belief versus race studies do not provide us with an answer because of their array of operations and because they largely ignored individual differences in prejudice.

Attitude similarity, race, and racial prejudice were investigated by Byrne and Wong (1962). It seemed reasonable in the light of our knowledge at the time to expect that either prejudice or attitude similarity or neither might predominate in determining attraction.

Method. The subjects were 120 introductory psychology students. These individuals represented the high prejudice (scores of 48 to 95) and the low prejudice (scores of 9 to 47) extremes from a group of 166 students who had taken the desegregation scale and the 26-item attitude scale.

Several weeks later they took part in the attraction experiment in which each subject responded to the attitude scale of a stranger who was either similar on all 26 issues or dissimilar on all 26 and who was identified as either white or Negro on the background information at the top of the scale.

TABLE 6–18

MEAN ATTRACTION RESPONSES OF HIGH AND LOW
PREJUDICE SUBJECTS TOWARD WHITES AND BLACKS
WITH SIMILAR AND DISSIMILAR ATTITUDES[a]

| Prejudice | Proportion of similar attitudes: | | | |
| | .00 | | 1.00 | |
	White	Black	White	Black
High	4.93	5.73	12.40	11.13
Low	4.87	6.47	13.07	12.27

[a]Data from Byrne and Wong, 1962.

Results. Table 6–18 contains the means of the attraction responses given in each condition. The most surprising finding was that regardless of the prejudice of the subject or the race of the stranger, similarity of attitudes resulted in positive responses whereas dissimilarity of attitudes resulted in negative responses.

Race, Prejudice, and the Similarity–Attraction Function

On the basis of the reinforcement formulation, it would be assumed that as a high prejudice subject reads through an attitude questionnaire in which a black stranger expresses views similar to his own on 26 assorted items, the experience is that of receiving 26 rewards. As a consequence, at least for a limited time period and with respect to one particular black, the high prejudice subjects indicate that they like the black stranger and would enjoy working with him. Byrne and McGraw (1964) followed up that experiment with an attempt to determine the required proportion of rewards in a black–white interaction necessary to evoke positive responses from high prejudice whites toward black strangers. From our current perspective, it may be seen that Byrne and McGraw were on a fool's errand. At that point in time, however, the Byrne–Nelson function and the Byrne-Rhamey modification were as yet unborn. It was, therefore, somewhat naively hypothesized that interpersonal attraction toward a stranger varies directly with the proportion of similar attitudes which he expresses, regardless of the stranger's race or the subject's prejudice.

Method. From a pool of approximately 900 students who had taken the desegregation scale, 320 subjects were selected for the experiment. There were 160 high prejudice subjects (scores of 47 to 90) and 160 low prejudice subjects (scores of 5 to 44). Each subject was also given a seven-item attitude scale.

Each of the prejudice groups was divided into eight subgroups with respect to the proportion of similar attitudes expressed by a stranger. In the experimental session, each subject received the attitude scale of a stranger with proportion of similar attitudes at one of the eight possible levels ranging from .00 to 1.00 similarity. To each scale was attached a yearbook photograph, supposedly of the person who filled out the scale. Each subject was given only one photograph, but a large series of different photographs was used across the total group of subjects. Half were of blacks and half of whites, with subject and stranger matched for sex.

TABLE 6–19

MEAN ATTRACTION RESPONSES OF HIGH AND LOW
PREJUDICE SUBJECTS TOWARD BLACK AND WHITE
STRANGERS WITH VARYING PROPORTIONS
OF SIMILAR ATTITUDES[a]

Proportion of similar attitudes	Low prejudice		High prejudice	
	White	Black	White	Black
1.00	13.20	11.00	11.20	9.10
.86	12.10	11.80	11.70	8.90
.71	10.80	11.20	10.60	6.70
.57	9.80	10.40	10.60	8.60
.43	10.30	10.60	9.70	9.10
.29	9.60	9.10	8.80	9.00
.14	8.10	9.30	8.90	9.60
.00	8.10	8.90	8.60	7.20

[a] Data from Byrne and McGraw, 1964.

Results. Table 6–19 gives the means of the attraction responses for each subgroup. The most crucial finding is that in this experiment, high prejudice subjects responded to a black stranger on the basis of race and made little differentiation among blacks on the basis of similarity of attitudes.

Discussion. Inability to replicate a finding is always a source of concern. The possibility was raised that the earlier results were simply chance findings. It was also conceivable that the discrepancy resulted from a minor methodological difference in the two investigations. In the previous study, the race of the stranger was indicated on the bogus protocol by the word "Negro" or "white." In the Byrne and McGraw study, in order to enhance the realism of the stranger, race was additionally indicated by means of a small yearbook photograph. It seemed plausible that more cues to negative interracial expectancies are evoked by a photograph of a black than by the word "Negro." If so, the use of photographs might serve to mitigate the powerful effects of attitude similarity. In order to explore these two possibilities, a second experiment was undertaken (Byrne & McGraw, 1964).

Chance Findings versus Mitigation by Photographs

Method. Three levels of attitude similarity were employed with two of these (26 similar, 0 dissimilar; 0 similar, 26 dissimilar) exactly as in the Byrne and Wong investigation. The third condition was .50 similarity (13 similar, 13 dissimilar). All of the strangers were identified as blacks. A photograph was attached to the attitude protocols of half of the strangers; on the other half, race was indicated in writing.

From a group of 350 students, 60 high prejudice (scores of 50 to 87) and 60 low prejudice (scores of 5 to 43) subjects were drawn.

TABLE 6–20

MEAN ATTRACTION RESPONSES OF HIGH AND LOW PREJUDICE
SUBJECTS TOWARD BLACKS WITH VARYING PROPORTIONS OF
SIMILAR ATTITUDES WITH AND WITHOUT PHOTOGRAPHS[a]

Proportion of similar attitudes	Low prejudice subjects		High prejudice subjects	
	Photo	No photo	Photo	No photo
1.00	11.40	12.00	10.00	9.70
.50	10.10	8.40	7.60	6.10
.00	7.20	6.10	6.10	4.50

[a]Data from Byrne and McGraw, 1964.

Results. The means of the attraction responses are given in Table 6–20. There were significant effects for the prejudice variable, the attitude similarity variable, and for the photograph variable. The latter finding, unexpectedly, was that more positive responses were elicited from subjects in the photograph condition.

Discussion. In part, it was shown that the Byrne and Wong findings could be replicated. Proportion of similar attitudes influenced attraction toward black strangers from subjects scoring at both extremes of the desegregation scale; in addition, low prejudice individuals tended to respond more positively to black strangers than did high prejudice individuals. The reason for the photograph effect was not obvious at the time, but the later studies on physical attractiveness offered a clue. Perhaps displaying a well intentioned bit of reverse racism, the experimenters had systematically eliminated the less attractive photographs. The photograph effect would seem simply to be the now familiar physical attractiveness effect.

It can be seen that the two reasons suggested for the discrepancy between the Byrne–Wong results and the first Byrne–McGraw results were not supported by the data. Why, then, was there no relationship between attitude similarity and attraction toward black strangers among high prejudice subjects in the first Byrne–McGraw experiment? In the context of the present chapter, the answer may readily suggest itself, but let us return to that question after describing two more prejudice studies.

Prejudice, Emotional Arousal, and Sex

The prejudice experiments described so far have involved same-sex black strangers. Picher (1966) extended the scope of these investigations to include the opposite sex. He pointed out the strong taboos on interracial sex (especially for the ingroup female with the outgroup male) and the folklore concerning the hypersexuality of the outgroup members, including the anatomical superiority of the outgroup male. For example, Dollard (1949) observed that:

> ... Rape and the wish to commit it seem to be constantly posited by the white caste as features of the Negro psychology.
> ... One theory is that there actually is a considerable attraction between white women and Negro men, that the white men are unconsciously aware of this attraction but dare not call up the intolerable idea, and that, as a result, they are jealous lest their women should make sexual contacts with the virile (in their stereotype) Negro men; consciously the whole matter is charged off to the sexual aggressiveness of the Negro men and in this way the complicity of the white women is avoided.

Combining the reinforcement approach with the sexual speculations, Picher proposed that high prejudice white females have a higher expectancy of negative sexual reinforcements (molestation, rape, etc.) from a black male than do low prejudice white females. Therefore, females high in prejudice should not only respond negatively to blacks, but more negatively to black males than to black females. In addition, if the individual were in a stage of heightened sexuality, these differences should be intensified.

Method. A pool of over 500 Texas undergraduates was given the desegregation scale and the third most prejudiced (scores of 46 to 104) and least prejudiced (scores of 8 to 34) were selected as potential subjects. The final number of individuals run was 171. An eight-item attitude scale was also given to each subject.

Half of the subjects were asked to read four sexually arousing literary passages, and half were asked to read neutral passages. In the experiment, attitude similarity was held constant at .50. To each attitude scale was attached a picture of the alleged strangers; these were a series of glossy yearbook proofs from black coeducational colleges in Texas. Each had been previously rated by a group of white subjects as physically attractive.

TABLE 6–21

MEAN ATTRACTION RESPONSES OF HIGH AND LOW PREJUDICE
SUBJECTS UNDER SEXUALLY AROUSING AND NEUTRAL CONDITIONS
TOWARD BLACK STRANGERS[a]

Condition	Low prejudice subjects		High prejudice subjects	
	Black male	Black female	Black male	Black female
Females				
Sexually aroused	10.82	11.19	9.10	7.20
Neutral	9.90	11.18	8.60	8.46
Males				
Sexually aroused	10.64	9.46	8.90	4.46
Neutral	9.46	9.10	7.91	7.91

[a] Data from Picher, 1966.

Results. The mean attraction responses* are presented in Table 6–21. One clear-cut finding is the expected difference between high and low prejudice subjects. The unexpected finding, however, was that the high prejudice individuals of both sexes respond more negatively to a black female stranger when sexually aroused. This reaction is not in the least evident among the low prejudice subjects. In fact, their responses to the black stranger appear to be unrelated to the sex arousal manipulation and they tend to prefer a black stranger of their own sex to one of the opposite sex.

Discussion. Contrary to Picher's hypothesis, the high prejudice students respond as if they are more threatened by a black female than by a black male under sexually arousing conditions. There is even a slight tendency to like a black male better when sexually aroused than under neutral conditions. Any attempt to explain these findings requires a radically new formulation, and one does not readily suggest itself. At the very least, it should be emphasized that sex arousal in combination with the sex of a black

---

*Picher analyzed Items 5 and 6 of the IJS separately because he found (using the Byrne–McGraw data) that the correlation between the two items is greater for low prejudice than for high prejudice subjects when the stranger is a black. The difference increases when a photograph is used.

stranger has quite striking effects on those high in prejudice. It should also be noted that under normal conditions, the sex of a black stranger has little effect on the attraction responses of either group of white subjects. In addition, the effect of sex arousal on response to white strangers requires further investigation. Brehm and Behar (1966) found that subjects who believed themselves to be physiologically aroused preferred to be with members of the same sex in contrast to nonaroused controls who preferred the opposite sex.

Positive and Negative Evaluations of the Subject by a Black Stranger

A final experiment in this series (Byrne & Ervin, 1969) was conducted specifically to determine whether response to a black by high prejudice subjects is determined in the same mechanical way as has been found with other variables investigated within the paradigm. That is, does the information "Negro" have a specific negative weight for high prejudice individuals which can be balanced or overpowered in predictable ways by appropriate positive weights from other stimulus sources such as similar attitudes and/or positive evaluations? If so, it should be possible to nullify or enhance the negative effects of racial prejudice simply by manipulating the appropriate stimuli.

Method. Again, the desegregation scale was used to select high (scores of 37 to 85) and low (scores of 2 to 36) prejudice subjects at the University of Texas. A group of 176 individuals served as subjects.

On a 40-item attitude scale, conditions of .20, .50, and .80 similarity were created. In addition, the Byrne–Rhamey procedure was used to create positive and negative evaluation conditions in which the subject was informed of the stranger's purported evaluations of himself on the IJS; a nonevaluational neutral condition was also employed.

All of the strangers were identified as blacks by means of a photograph attached to the attitude scale.

Results. The results are shown in Table 6–22. Analysis indicated that the low prejudice subjects respond more positively than those high in prejudice, that similar strangers are liked better than dissimilar ones, and that positively evaluating strangers are liked better than negatively evaluating ones.

Discussion. In view of a number of studies already described, the findings here, as expected, do not seem astonishing. Rather, it was shown that each of the three independent variables can be combined in a more complex situation to yield predictable effects.

It is, of course, possible to become much more precise than simply

TABLE 6–22

MEAN ATTRACTION RESPONSES TOWARD BLACKS BY
HIGH AND LOW PREJUDICE SUBJECTS WITH THREE
LEVELS OF ATTITUDE SIMILARITY UNDER THREE
PERSONAL EVALUATION CONDITIONS[a]

Proportion of similar attitudes	Evaluation conditions		
	Negative	Neutral	Positive
High prejudice subjects			
.80	5.30	8.75	11.54
.50	7.00	7.13	11.56
.20	5.36	5.38	11.00
Low prejudice subjects			
.80	8.80	10.63	12.10
.50	9.00	10.60	11.00
.20	6.30	7.90	10.82

[a] After Byrne and Ervin, 1969, p. 400.

stating that the variables may be combined. One approach, taken by Byrne and Ervin (1969) was to utilize a multiple correlation analysis across the entire series of prejudice studies with attraction as a function of proportion of similar attitudes, scores on the desegregation scale, personal evaluations, and physical attractiveness of the stranger in the photograph. The resulting multiple correlation coefficient is .84 which indicates that about 70% of the response variance is attributable to these four independent variables.

A related approach is that of considering each element of stimulus information in terms of positive and negative reinforcement properties, establishing appropriate weighting coefficients, and substituting the resulting weighted proportions of positive reinforcements in the Byrne–Nelson formula. As usual, similar attitudes will each be considered as $+1$ and negative attitudes as -1; positive evaluations as $+3$ and negative evaluations as -3. Only attractive photographs were used, and these had previously been set as equal to $+4$. For low prejudice subjects, the information that the stranger is a black has no effect and, hence, will be given no reinforcement weight. For high prejudice individuals, the information that the stranger is a black is negative information, and a trial of several alternative weights on the second Byrne–McGraw experiment indicated that -11 was a satisfactory value. The least amount of data was available for the very special condition of Picher's in which high prejudice subjects in a sexually arousing condition responded to a black female. The extremely negative response here indicates a large negative weight and the value of -50 was tentatively assigned. Then, all of the data involving black strangers from all of the prejudice–attraction studies employing one or more of the above variables were combined according to the weighting scheme. Thus, 687 subjects from five independent experiments were included in the analysis. Subjects who received the same proportion of weighted positive reinforcement (even if from different stimulus sources) would, of course, be predicted to give the same attraction response and, hence, were combined. In Fig. 6–2 the obtained responses (plotted separately for high and low prejudice subjects) are shown in relation to the responses predicted by the Byrne–Nelson function. To this somewhat biased observer, the correspondence seems clear.

It may be obvious, but perhaps should be emphasized that this way of conceptualizing the data makes it plain why the prejudice variable did not seem very influential in the Byrne–Wong experiment but was overwhelming in the first Byrne–McGraw experiment. If the effect of the information

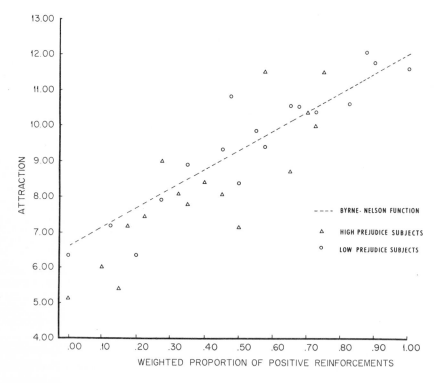

Fig. 6–2. Attraction of high and low prejudice subjects toward a black stranger as a function of weighted proportion of positive reinforcements, combining the effects of attitude similarity–dissimilarity, positive and negative evaluations, physical attractiveness, race and racial prejudice, and sex arousal.

"Negro" equals the effect of eleven disagreements, the 26 similar attitudes of Byrne–Wong are relatively influential. A high prejudice subject receives .70 positive reinforcements and would be predicted to respond quite positively at 10.43; the actual response was 11.13. On the other hand, the seven-item attitude scale of the first Byrne–McGraw study plus an attractive photograph was somewhat overshadowed by the −11 value of the stranger's race. Here, in the complete similarity condition the proportion of positive reinforcements is .50, the predicted response is 9.34, and the actual response was 9.10. The surprising differences in attraction responses in the 1.00 attitude similarity conditions of the two experiments turns out to be not at all surprising once we know a little more about the way these variables operate.

In conclusion, attraction has been found to vary as a function of several different kinds of stimulus information attributed to a stranger, including prestige or status (though attitude information can eliminate the effect), physical attractiveness, emotional disturbance, and race. All such effects are attributed to positive and negative stimulus properties of specific weights which can be determined empirically. The transituational generality of these stimulus properties and the predictable way in which they combine in determining attraction has been variously demonstrated.

Chapter 7 / Stimulus Generality:
III. Nonattitudinal Similarity

Prior to a discussion of the effects of similarity not involving attitudes, a point must be made concerning what has been labelled by others as "the similarity hypothesis." As has been pointed out previously in a different context, the paradigm does not rest on a similarity hypothesis. The relationship between attitude similarity and attraction is a low-level empirical law. It does not constitute either a moral or a theoretical imperative; it simply describes the way subjects from a specific population are found to respond under specified conditions. The basic principle which is proposed is the relationship between positive reinforcement and attraction. The fact that human beings respond to similar attitudes as positive reinforcements does not result from some perverse whim of the author nor does it necessarily even meet with his approval.

When we move to stimuli other than attitudes, there is no theoretical reason to assume that similarity will play the same role as in the attitudinal realm. If anyone asks whether similarity of personality or of economic status or of ability would be expected to have a positive effect on attraction, one must counter with an inquiry as to whether such similarity is rewarding. Intuitively, it would seem likely that some kinds of similarity are rewarding, some punishing, and still others a matter of indifference. If research indicates that most kinds of similarity do, in fact, turn out to be rewarding, the responsibility lies with our subjects and not with attraction theory. Festinger is not at fault either, but he has provided a theoretical rationale for expecting a similarity effect. In his theory of social comparison processes (Festinger, 1954), it is hypothesized that "To the extent that objective, non-social means are not available, people evaluate their opinions and abilities by comparison respectively with the opinions and abilities of others [p. 118]." He goes on to suggest that "A person will be less attracted to situations where others are very divergent from him than to situations where others are close to him for both abilities and opinions [p. 123]." It follows that, under ordinary circumstances, individuals will prefer others similar to themselves.

There is some empirical support for the hypothesis that attraction is a function of similarity of abilities (Zander & Havelin, 1960), emotional states (Zimbardo & Formica, 1963), and even amount of paint consumption (Brock, 1965). From our theoretical framework, such findings suggest that, with other variables held constant, the behavior of another individual is positively reinforcing to the extent that it is similar to one's own behavior. It may be that behavioral similarity to self, whether involving attitudes or values or abilities or emotional responses or tastes or adjustive responses or worries or need hierarchies or whatever, provides evidence that one is functioning in a logical and meaningful manner; similarity makes one's interpersonal environment more predictable and understandable.

Personality Similarity: Defense Mechanisms

On the basis of the general reasoning just presented, the law of attraction should be applicable to personality similarity, at least within the delimited laboratory setting. It was hypothesized by Byrne, Griffitt, and Stefaniak (1967) that attraction toward another individual is a positive linear function of the proportion of that individual's personality characteristics which are similar to the characteristics of the subject.

There has been a considerable amount of previous research dealing with the problem of personality similarity, and it is necessary to examine this literature briefly in order to place the present work in context.

Previous Research on Personality Similarity

Controversy has characterized theoretical speculations concerning the nature of the relationship between personality similarity and attraction. It has been proposed that attraction is facilitated by either similarity, complementarity, or both (e.g., Levinger, 1964). The theoretical differences remain unresolved because the research findings have been sufficiently inconsistent to provide support for the similarity hypothesis (Banta & Hetherington, 1963; Izard, 1960a,b; Maisonneuve, 1954; Mehlman, 1962; Miller,

Campbell, Twedt, & O'Connell, 1966; Murstein, 1961), for the complementarity hypothesis (Cohen, 1956; Kerckhoff & Davis, 1962; Rychlak, 1965; Winch, Ktsanes, & Ktsanes, 1955), and for some combination of the two (Becker, 1964; Secord & Backman, 1964).

There are additional findings which give only partial support to the similarity hypothesis in that similarity is positively associated with attraction only under limited conditions, or only in specific groups, or with respect to only a few variables (Bonney, 1946; Bowerman & Day, 1956; Izard, 1963; Katz, Glucksberg, & Krauss, 1960; Rosenfeld & Jackson, 1965; Van Dyne, 1940). In addition, a number of investigators have simply found no relationship between personality similarity and attraction (Corsini, 1956; Gordon, 1957; Hoffman, 1958; Hoffman & Maier, 1966; Katz, Cohen, & Castiglione, 1963; Pintner, Forlano, & Freedman, 1937; Reilly, Commins, & Stefic, 1960; Thorpe, 1955).

A familiar and lamentable reason for this kind of empirical inconsistency is that among personality and social psychologists, almost every investigation represents an exploration in procedural novelty. That is, different investigators employ different independent and dependent variables in situations of varying complexity in which a seemingly limitless array of parameters must be operative.

Over and above the problem of methodological variety, however, are two basic flaws which make it literally impossible to determine the effect of personality similarity on attraction with the two research designs that have been employed. In one approach, existing "real life" attraction pairs (e.g., friends, fiancées, spouses) are selected and assessed with respect to one or more personality variables. Then, the scores of the series of pairs are correlated. In the second approach, the personality measure or measures are obtained, and then previously unacquainted subjects are selected on the basis of test scores and placed in a situation requiring some degree of interaction. Thus, similar and dissimilar pairs or groups are created, and their interpersonal responses are assessed following the interaction. Two insurmountable difficulties are inherent in either approach.

First, attraction responses are known to be multidetermined. For example, attraction varies as a function of such determinants as propinquity, the reinforcing properties of the situation, attitude similarity–dissimilarity, perceived similarity, physical attractiveness, race, and emotional disturbance. In the previous investigations of personality similarity, all such variables plus an unknown number of as yet unidentified variables are potentially operative but are not consistently controlled. Further, personality similarity itself is defined in terms of similarity on one or at best a small subgroup of personality variables so that similarity along all other personality dimensions is also not controlled. The situation, then, is one in which the effect of a very limited number of independent variables on attraction is determined in a context where 1---*n* uncontrolled independent variables are operating. Only if the variable under investigation were of sufficient strength to override all other independent variables or if a sufficient number of the other independent variables happened to covary with it or if the other variables were accidentally controlled through randomization would the hypothesized relationship be observed. The lack of consistency in the findings suggests that these special circumstances do not occur regularly. It should be noted that the research designs under discussion are perfectly suitable for answering the limited question concerning the role of similarity along a given personality dimension in a specific uncontrolled situation. Those designs are inappropriate, however, for answering the prototypic question concerning the effect of personality similarity on attraction. The solution lies either in employing a multivariate methodology in the uncontrolled situation or in moving to a traditional experimental situation in which extraneous variables are controlled.

Even if the multitude of stimulus variables are brought under experimental control (e.g., Altrocchi, 1959), a second difficulty remains in studying personality similarity. The relationship between scores on a personality measure and behavior in an interpersonal situation is crucial. Presumably, personality variables influence attraction only to the extent that they are reflected in overt behavior in a given situation; it is the behavioral stimuli to which the subjects are responding rather than to a nonobservable personality construct. But, the relationship between scores on a personality test and behavior in various everyday life encounters or behavior in a semicontrolled laboratory situation is for the most part either negligible or unknown (Mischel, 1968). To borrow a phrase, the correlations range from slim to none. In any given instance, it seems safe to bet that a 1:1 relationship does not hold. Thus, one is in the position of defining personality similarity in terms of Behavior A (responses to the test) and determining its effect on attraction in a situation involving Behavior B (responses in the interaction) with little or no correspondence between Behaviors A and B. It is, therefore, necessary to identify the stimulus to which subjects are expected to respond. One must move from an interest in similarity of personality to an interest in similarity of specific personality characteristics.

It follows from this analysis that an appropriate test of the proposed relationship between personality similarity and attraction requires an experimental design in which (*a*) the independent variable is manipulated while the additional stimulus determinants are controlled and (*b*) there is a known relationship between the personality-relevant behavior of the subject and the personality-relevant behavior of the person to whom he responds. It also follows that any single such investigation cannot be interpreted as indicating the relationship between other personality characteristics and attraction nor the relationship that might be found in quite different situational contexts. Overgeneralization may be hazardous to your conceptual health.

Repression–Sensitization: Similarity and Attraction

The first personality dimension to be investigated using the design just described was that of repression–sensitization—a behavioral continuum involving characteristic responses to anxiety-evoking stimuli. At one extreme are behaviors such as denial, avoidance, and repression, whereas at the other extreme are behaviors such as intellectualization, approach, and sensitization. Much of the research on this personality dimension has been reviewed elsewhere (Byrne, 1964b).

To investigate personality similarity with respect to repression–sensitization or any other dimension, either of two behavioral samples might be employed. First, one could determine the characteristic responses of a subject in a series of quite specific situations and then expose him to the behavior of a stranger in those same situations. Second, the subject's behavior could consist of those specific test responses that indicate his position on the dimension, and the observed behavior of the stranger could consist of the latter's responses to the same instrument. The second approach was used by Byrne *et al.* (1967).

Method. The personality dimension was measured by means of the repression–sensitization (R-S) scale (Byrne, Barry, & Nelson, 1963). A special version of this test was constructed for the attraction experiment using only the 127 cross-validated scorable items. In order to facilitate the association between item content and the stranger's responses, answers were made directly on the test booklet with checks in T and F boxes to the left of each item rather than on an IBM answer sheet. The sampled behavioral domain of both subject and stranger thus consisted of 127 responses to the same set of test items. Examples are "Once in a while I think of things too bad to talk about"; "I have very few quarrels with members of my family"; "I am happy most of the time"; "At times I feel like picking a fist fight with someone."

The modified R-S scale was administered to approximately 450 male and female students enrolled in a section of the introductory psychology course at the University of Texas. On the basis of scores obtained on the test, three groups of subjects were selected: 48 sensitizers, 54 neutrals, and 49 repressers.

In the experimental session, subjects were given the usual interpersonal judgment instructions.

Within each of the three repression–sensitization groups, subjects were assigned to one of three experimental conditions, consisting of three levels of subject–stranger similarity in responding to the R-S scale. In the .20 condition, subjects received a test on which the stranger responded exactly as the subject did to 25 items and exactly the opposite to 102 items. In the .50 condition, there were 64 similar and 63 dissimilar responses. In the .80 condition, there were 102 similar and 25 dissimilar ones. Within each condition, a different random pattern of specific items of similarity and dissimilarity was devised for each subject; for example, in the .20 condition each subject responded to a stranger like himself on 25 items, but the actual items comprising the 25 were different for each subject.

TABLE 7–1

MEAN ATTRACTION RESPONSES OF REPRESSERS, NEUTRALS, AND SENSITIZERS TOWARD STRANGERS DIFFERING IN PROPORTION OF SIMILAR RESPONSES TO THE REPRESSION–SENSITIZATION (R-S) SCALE[a]

R-S scale level of subjects	Proportion of similar responses made by strangers			
	.20	.50	.80	Total
Repressers	5.06	7.50	8.67	6.96
Neutrals	6.24	8.37	10.33	8.35
Sensitizers	7.22	8.94	10.00	8.58
Total	6.17	8.29	9.70	—

[a]After Byrne, Griffitt, and Stefaniak, 1967, p. 86.

Results. The means of the attraction responses for the three personality groups in the three experimental conditions are given in Table 7–1. There was a highly significant effect attributable to differences in the proportion of similar responses to the personality items. The analysis also indicated unexpected personality differences in that repressers gave the most negative attraction responses and sensitizers the most positive ones.

Discussion. With respect to the repression–sensitization dimension and within the limits of the present research design, the evidence clearly supported the notion of a linear relationship between personality similarity and attraction.

The other significant finding created a problem. The most obvious explanation is that of personality differences in responding to similarity and dissimilarity. If the dissimilar responses of the stranger represent some degree of threat to the subject, the findings are consistent with other represser–sensitizer differences which have been found in that repressers are made hostile by situations evoking anxiety in sensitizers. A second experiment (reported in Chapter 8) explored this possibility by exposing repressers, neutrals, and sensitizers to three levels of attitude similarity. Here, the usual effect of attitude similarity was found, but differences in repression–sensitization were unrelated to the response differences. Thus, the represser–sensitizer differences in the personality similarity experiment do not appear to be attributable to personality differences in responding to such stimuli. How, then, can the differences be explained?

There was an additional source of variance in the stimuli presented to the subjects which has not yet been discussed. It was noted above that different random patterns of items were prepared for each subject within a given level of similarity. With such a procedure, the repression–sensitization score of each "stranger" varies widely within each cell. The difference between the variables "proportion of similar responses" and "score discrepancy" and the fact that they are independent can best be understood by examining the example shown in Table 7–2. With a hypothetical 10-item personality test, the scoring key is used to obtain scores for a subject and

TABLE 7–2

AN EXAMPLE OF VARIATIONS IN SCORE DISCREPANCY WITH PROPORTION OF
SIMILAR RESPONSES HELD CONSTANT

Item	Scoring key	Subject	Stranger 1	Stranger 2	Stranger 3
1	T	T	T	F	T
2	F	T	T	F	F
3	F	F	T	T	F
4	T	F	F	F	T
5	F	T	T	F	F
6	T	T	F	T	F
7	T	F	F	F	T
8	F	F	T	T	F
9	T	T	F	T	T
10	F	F	T	F	F
Score		6	1	5	9

Subject and stranger 1
  Proportion of similar responses = .50
  Score discrepancy = −5
Subject and stranger 2
  Proportion of similar responses = .50
  Score discrepancy = −1
Subject and stranger 3
  Proportion of similar responses = .50
  Score discrepancy = +3

three different strangers. In this example, proportion of similar responses remains constant at .50 whereas score discrepancy varies from -5 to $+3$. It seemed possible that (a) the discrepancy between subject and stranger on the repression–sensitization dimension might fortuitously have been different for repressers, neutrals, and sensitizers, and (b) this discrepancy might influence attraction in addition to the effects of proportion of similar item responses.

The absolute R-S scale discrepancy score (difference between subject's score and his stranger's score) was determined for each subject. It was found that the mean for repressers was 47.59, for neutrals 21.24, and for sensitizers 10.94. Analysis of variance indicated that these differences are highly significant. Thus, the first proposition was confirmed: the discrepancy differences parallel the represser–sensitizer differences. This suggests the possibility that the findings with respect to personality differences were artifactual.

To test the effect of discrepancy on attraction, a correlational analysis was employed. For the total group of 151 students, the subject–stranger discrepancy score correlated $-.52$ with attraction. To discount the confounding effects of experimental conditions, correlations were also obtained separately within each condition, yielding coefficients of $-.39$ in the .20 condition, $-.28$ in the .50 condition, and $-.34$ in the .80 condition, each of which is significant. It seems that subjects were responding to R-S scale score discrepancy as well as to proportion of similar responses. The two stimulus variables are not completely independent because discrepancy tends to decrease as proportion of similar items increases ($r = -.56$).

Nevertheless, each stimulus dimension does influence attraction even with the other dimension controlled. The correlation between proportion of similar items and attraction with R-S scale score discrepancy partialled out is .33, and the correlation between R-S scale score discrepancy and attraction with proportion of similar items partialled out is $-.33$. In order to provide more conclusive evidence that it is subject–stranger discrepancy rather than subject repression–sensitization which accounts for the apparent personality differences, it was necessary to use double partial correlations. The relationship between R-S scale score discrepancy and attraction with both proportion of similar items and subject's R-S scale score held constant is a significant one ($r = .20$), whereas the analogous relationship between subject's R-S scale score and attraction is not significantly different from zero ($r = .11$).

The situation, then, is one in which the dependent variable is affected by two independent variables, one of which was varied as part of the experimental design and one of which was accidentally manipulated. It is possible, therefore, to conceptualize attraction as a function of both variables, each of which represents a different aspect of personality similarity. One way of describing this relationship is by means of a multiple-correlation coefficient which is found to equal .59.

Returning to the problem of accounting for represser–sensitizer differences in attraction, it would seem that they may be explained simply in terms of group differences in discrepancy scores. This can be demonstrated rather convincingly by predicting each subject's attraction response on the basis of a multiple-regression equation ($Y = -.04X_1 + 3.88X_2 + 7.16$). In Table 7–3, the attraction responses as predicted by this equation are presented along with the obtained attraction responses. The obviously close correspondence is confirmed by the fact that the mean difference between predicted and obtained responses was found to be $-.004$.

TABLE 7–3

COMPARISON OF MEAN PREDICTED AND OBTAINED ATTRACTION RESPONSES ON THE BASIS OF BOTH PROPORTION OF SIMILAR ITEM RESPONSES AND SUBJECT–STRANGER DISCREPANCY[a]

R-S scale[b] level of subjects	Proportion of similar responses					
	.20		.50		.80	
	Predicted	Obtained	Predicted	Obtained	Predicted	Obtained
Repressers	4.96	5.06	7.22	7.50	9.60	8.67
Neutrals	6.61	6.24	8.16	8.37	9.96	10.33
Sensitizers	7.23	7.22	8.74	8.94	10.08	10.00

[a]After Byrne, Griffitt, and Stefaniak, 1967, p. 88.
[b]Repression–sensitization scale.

The methodological approach employed here confirmed the proposed relationship between personality similarity and attraction and led to the finding that subjects are surprisingly sensitive to the similarity cues presented by the stranger. They respond not only to specific response similarity but also to similarity at a more abstract or generalized level, that is, to the personality dimension itself. Attraction is responsive to variation in both stimulus dimensions, and the nature of the relationship is entirely consistent with the findings in the attitude studies.

Repression–Sensitization: Similarity and Awareness of Similarity

Individuals respond to similarity of personality characteristics, but to what extent are they aware of doing so? Are subjects able to verbalize the degree of similarity between themselves and the stranger? A related question is the extent to which the similarity–attraction relationship is dependent upon accuracy of perception. The awareness variable was first investigated by Byrne and Griffitt (1969).

Method. The overall design involved the selection of subjects representing various levels along the repression–sensitization dimension and later the presentation to each subject of a stranger's responses to a short version of the personality measure. These responses were prepared such that three levels of subject–stranger similarity were represented. The dependent variables consisted of attraction and two measures of each subject's awareness of the degree of similarity between stranger and self.

The modified R-S scale was administered to over 400 male and female undergraduates. Selection of subjects was based on the same criteria for defining the personality groups as in the previous study. The three levels of subject–stranger similarity of responses were again .20, .50, and .80.

The experimental session involved instructions to read the stranger's responses to half of the R-S scale and to evaluate him or her on the Interpersonal Judgment Scale (IJS). As measures of awareness, two somewhat different approaches were used. The first and more direct scale, verbalized similarity, required the subject to estimate the proportion of items to which the stranger had responded exactly as he did. The scale ranged from .00 to 1.00 with increments of .05. The second and more indirect measure of awareness, projected similarity, required the subject to fill out the remaining half of the R-S scale as he believed the stranger had done. Similarity here was defined as the proportion of items on this prediction scale that the stranger was guessed to have answered the same as the subject had done. Thus, awareness is defined in terms of a comparison between proportion of similar responses created by the experimenter and the proportion perceived by the subject measured either directly in terms of verbalized similarity or indirectly by the projected similarity task.

Results. The means of the attraction responses are shown in Table 7–4. The only variable significantly influencing attraction was the proportion of similar responses.

The unexpected finding of the previous study that score discrepancy affected attraction was also replicated; discrepancy correlates $-.34$ with attraction. When the multiple regression equation derived in the other study is applied to the present data, the mean difference between predicted and obtained attraction responses is found to be less than 1. The correlation between predicted and obtained responses is .51.

Among the other findings was the positive effect of similarity on ratings of intelligence. In addition, adjustment ratings yielded an interaction effect; for repressers and neutrals similarity to self was positively related to ratings of adjustment, whereas for sensitizers the reverse was true.

TABLE 7–4

MEAN ATTRACTION RESPONSES OF REPRESSERS,
NEUTRALS, AND SENSITIZERS TOWARD STRANGERS
DIFFERING IN PROPORTION OF SIMILAR RESPONSES TO
REPRESSION–SENSITIZATION SCALE[a]

Levels of subjects on R-S scale	Proportion of similar responses			
	.20	.50	.80	Total
Repressers	6.50	8.40	9.70	8.20
Neutrals	7.00	8.90	10.60	8.83
Sensitizers	7.10	8.90	9.90	8.63
Total	6.87	8.73	10.07	—

[a]After Byrne and Griffitt, 1969, p. 181.

TABLE 7–5

MEAN VERBALIZED SIMILARITY RESPONSES[a]

Level of subjects on R-S scale[b]	Proportion of similar responses			
	.20	.50	.80	Total
Repressers	.22	.38	.64	.41
Neutrals	.46	.51	.60	.53
Sensitizers	.43	.61	.72	.58
Total	.37	.50	.66	—

[a]After Byrne and Griffitt, 1969, p. 182.
[b]Repression–sensitization scale.

TABLE 7–6

MEAN PROJECTED SIMILARITY RESPONSES[a]

Level of subjects on R-S scale[b]	Proportion of similar responses			
	.20	.50	.80	Total
Repressers	.35	.55	.76	.55
Neutrals	.50	.59	.70	.59
Sensitizers	.52	.61	.72	.62
Total	.46	.58	.73	—

[a]After Byrne and Griffitt, 1969, p. 182.
[b]Repression–sensitization scale.

Awareness. The two measures of awareness were relatively consistent in their indication of subjects' perceptions of the stranger's similarity. The means of these two response measures are reported in Tables 7–5 and 7–6. Both measures were significantly affected by the experimental manipulation of similarity. As actual similarity increased, perceived similarity increased. In addition, as R-S scale scores increased, perceived similarity increased.

The question of the role of awareness in responding to similarity–dissimilarity was then examined. When verbalized similarity is held constant, the relationship between proportion of similar responses and attraction remains a significant one (r 12.3 $=$ .29). Further, when the effects of both types of perceived similarity are eliminated simultaneously by a double partial correlation technique, there is still a relationship between the stimulus conditions and the subject's attraction responses (r 12.34 $=$ .29).

The question can also be approached in the opposite way. That is, even though perceived similarity is not an essential component of the personality similarity effect, is attraction influenced by it? It was found that verbalized similarity is related to attraction even with proportion of similar responses held constant (r 12.3 $=$ .30) but that projected similarity is minimally related to attraction when proportion of similar responses is partialled out (r 12.3 $=$ .18). It appears, then, that awareness of stimulus conditions contributes to the usual similarity–attraction relationship, but that awareness is not a necessary component of that relationship. Response to personality similarity does not seem to require the accurate perception of similarity.

A somewhat different question involves the subject's accuracy in perceiving the stimulus conditions and the effect of accuracy on the similarity–attraction relationship. On the basis of absolute discrepancy between the proportion of similar responses created by the experimenter and the subject's perception of the similarity, the sample was divided approximately at the median on each set of awareness scores into the most and least accurate subgroups; their mean attraction responses were almost identical.

Discussion. Once again it was shown that individuals are quite responsive to indications of similarity and dissimilarity of personality characteristics. Perhaps of greater importance is the finding that this response may occur independently of accurate verbalizations concerning self-stranger similarity. What is suggested is a relatively automatic mechanism whereby the affective response to the stimulus person is determined by the series of cues associated with that person. Perceived similarity does not serve as a primary mediating factor but is simply another response variable which is in part determined by the external stimulus conditions.

Altogether, these findings lead to the proposition that attraction in this kind of experimental situation is a function of a series of partially independent determinants. Two stimulus variables (proportion of similar responses and score discrepancy) and two response variables (verbalized similarity and projected similarity) are associated with attraction. It is possible to use a multiple function to predict attraction responses (r 1.2345 = .60). It might be noted that prediction based on the two stimulus variables alone (r 1.23 = .55) is almost as accurate as when all four variables serve as predictors.

PERSONALITY SIMILARITY: SELF-DESCRIPTIONS

Following the same kind of reasoning which led to the repression–sensitization experiments, Griffitt (1966) proposed a relationship between similarity of self-concept and interpersonal attraction.

Self-Concept

In the first of these investigations, Griffitt hypothesized that attraction is a positive function of similarity of self-concept.

Method. To 265 introductory psychology students at the University of Texas, Worchel's (1957) Self Activity Inventory was administered. This scale consists of 42 statements describing various kinds of behaviors and reactions to which the subject responds on a 5-point scale indicating the degree to which the activity is like him (self-concept) and on a 5-point scale indicating the degree to which the activity is the way he would like to be (ideal self-concept). On the basis of self-ideal discrepancy scores, a group of 25 high discrepancy and 23 low discrepancy individuals were selected for the experiment.

Several weeks later, each subject was asked to evaluate an anonymous stranger on the basis of his or her responses to the Self Activity Inventory. In all cases Griffitt provided complete similarity on the ideal self-responses and manipulated only the self-descriptions. Half of the subjects received a self-scale which had been filled out exactly like their own. The other half received a scale with .33 of the self-responses similar to their own and the remainder dissimilar. The dissimilar self-items were discrepant from those of the subject either 2 points in a positive (desirable) direction on all 28 dissimilar items or 2 points in a negative (undesirable) direction on all 28 dissimilar items.

Results. The mean attraction responses are given in Table 7–7. The only significant effect was that of proportion of similar self-concept statements. A comparison within the .33 group of the subjects with +2 discrepancies versus those with −2 discrepancies indicated no significant difference in attraction. Thus, subject–stranger dissimilarity leads to less

TABLE 7–7

MEAN ATTRACTION RESPONSES OF HIGH AND
LOW SELF-IDEAL DISCREPANCY SUBJECTS
RESPONDING TO TWO LEVELS OF SIMILARITY
TO SELF[a]

Self-ideal discrepancy	Proportion of items similar to self-concept		
	.33	1.00	Total
High	9.15	10.75	9.92
Low	8.33	12.54	10.35
Total	8.76	11.61	—

[a]After Griffitt, 1966, p. 583.

positive responses whether the stranger differs in expressing a more effectual or a more ineffectual self-concept than that of the subject.

Discussion. Griffitt proposed that proportion of similar self-responses could be inserted in the Byrne–Nelson formula. In the 1.00 condition, the formula predicts an attraction response of 12.06; the obtained mean of 11.61 does not differ significantly from the predicted one. In the .33 condition, the obtained mean of 8.76 does not differ significantly from the predicted response of 8.42. Griffitt (1966) notes "Thus, the attraction formula derived from investigations of attitude similarity yields accurate predictions in both conditions involving information concerning personality similarity [p.584]."

Self-Concept and Ideal Self-Concept

In subsequent work, Griffitt (1969b) went on to investigate the effects of both similarity in self-concept and in ideal self-concept. He hypothesized that attraction is a positive function of both types of similarity.

Method. Two experiments were carried out, each using the basic methodology of the previous study. In the first, two levels of similarity between subject's self-concept and stranger's self-concept were created. In the second, there were two levels of similarity between the subject's ideal self-concept and the stranger's self-concept. Again, the Self Activity Inventory was administered, high and low self-ideal discrepancy subjects were selected, and the bogus strangers were evaluated on the IJS. Forty subjects were employed in each experiment.

In the first experiment, half of the subjects judged a stranger whose self-description was like their own self-description on .20 of the items, like their ideal-self description on .40 of the items, and dissimilar from both self and ideal-self on .40 of the items. The other half of the subjects judged a stranger whose self-description was like their own self-description on .80 of the items and like their ideal self-description on .40 of the items. Thus, similarity to ideal self was .40 for both groups while similarity to self was varied (.20 and .80).

In the second experiment, half of the subjects judged a stranger whose self-description was similar to their own ideal self-description on .20 of the items, similar to their own self-description on .40 of the items, and dissimilar from both on .40 of the items. The remaining subjects judged a stranger whose self-description was similar to their own ideal self-description on .80 of the items and similar to their own self-description on .40 of the items. Here, similarity to self was held constant at .40 for both groups while similarity to ideal self was varied (.20 and .80).

Results. The attraction responses in the two experiments are given in Tables 7–8 and 7–9. In each instance, the only significant effect was the manipulation of similarity. Attraction was found to be influenced both by similarity of self to self and by similarity of self to ideal self.

Discussion. Griffitt (1967) went on to consider both types of manipulation simultaneously. He decided to examine the combined effect by determining a total self and ideal-self similarity for each condition. For each subject, some of the items were similar to self only, some similar to ideal self only, some similar to both self and ideal self, and some similar to neither. With each item of the first three types considered as a positive reinforcement and each item of the fourth type considered as a negative reinforcement, a total proportion of positive reinforcements was computed for each subject by dividing the number of positive reinforcement items by the total number of items. These total proportions are given in Table 7–10 along with the attraction responses which are predicted by the Byrne–Nelson formula and the attraction responses actually obtained. The predicted and obtained values did not differ statistically. These relationships are depicted graphically in Fig. 7–1.

Griffitt (1967) concludes:

> It is clear that, although differences in similarity to self as well as differences in similarity to ideal self yield differential attraction responses, the most precise predictions may be made when both similarity to self and similarity to ideal are expressed as a single stimulus dimension of total proportion of similarity [p. 38].

Self-Esteem

Guthwin (1970) approached the problem of personality similarity from the viewpoint of self theory and proposed that if self-acceptance is derived

TABLE 7–8

MEAN ATTRACTION RESPONSES OF HIGH AND
LOW SELF-IDEAL DISCREPANCY SUBJECTS
RESPONDING TO STRANGERS VARYING IN
SIMILARITY TO SELF WITH SIMILARITY TO
IDEAL SELF HELD CONSTANT[a]

Self-ideal discrepancy	Proportion of items similar to self-concept		
	.20	.80	Total
High	9.00	11.30	10.15
Low	9.70	11.30	10.50
Total	9.35	11.30	—

[a]After Griffitt, 1969b, p. 141.

TABLE 7–9

MEAN ATTRACTION RESPONSES OF HIGH AND
LOW SELF-IDEAL DISCREPANCY SUBJECTS
RESPONDING TO STRANGERS VARYING IN
SIMILARITY TO IDEAL SELF WITH SIMILARITY TO
SELF HELD CONSTANT[a]

Self-ideal discrepancy	Proportion of items similar to ideal self-concept		
	.20	.80	Total
High	8.80	11.10	9.95
Low	8.30	10.70	9.50
Total	8.55	10.90	—

[a]After Griffitt, 1969b, p. 143.

TABLE 7–10

TOTAL PROPORTION OF POSITIVE REINFORCEMENTS ON SELF-DESCRIPTION SCALE IN
RELATION TO PREDICTED AND OBTAINED ATTRACTION RESPONSES

Experimental condition	Total proportion of positive reinforcement	Predicted attraction response	Obtained attraction response
I, .20 Self, .40 Ideal	.40	8.80	9.35
I, .80 Self, .40 Ideal	.86	11.30	11.30
II, .40 Self, .20 Ideal	.40	8.80	8.55
II, .40 Self, .80 Ideal	.88	11.40	10.90

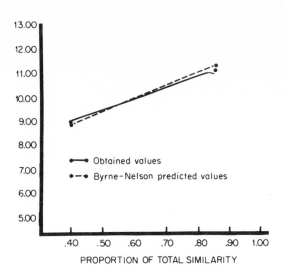

Fig. 7–1. Attraction as a function of total proportion of similarity to self and ideal self. (After Griffitt, 1967, p. 39.)

largely from the reflected appraisal of others, it should also reflect the individual's expectations about his reception in social situations. These expectations, in turn, should influence the acceptance of or attraction toward others.

From a group of 101 undergraduates who had taken a measure of self-esteem (Jackson, 1967), three groups were selected to represent high, medium, and low levels of self-esteem. In the experimental session, they were given information about four same-sex students. There were 12 self-attitude items for each stranger, purportedly selected by each individual as the items best characterizing him or her. The items actually represented .00, .33, .66, and 1.00 similarity to the subject on the measure of self-esteem. Each stranger was rated on the IJS. Afterward, each subject was asked to estimate how much he would expect each stranger to like him and to enjoy working with him.

Guthwin found that proportion of similar self-statements influenced both attraction and expectation of attraction, whereas the different levels of self-esteem had no effect on either dependent variable. Thus, the hypothesized relationship between self-esteem and acceptance of others or expected acceptance by others was not confirmed. There was, however, an additional finding of interest. At .00 similarity, the subject expected to be liked more than he liked the stranger. At 1.00 similarity, the subject expected to be liked less than he liked the stranger.

PERSONALITY SIMILARITY: MASCULINITY–FEMININITY

Despite the sparsity of data supporting the operation of personality complementarity, the idea of opposites attracting is an appealing one. At the very least, some personality variables should show such an effect. Three of the likeliest candidates for complementarity would seem to be masculinity–femininity, dominance–submissiveness, and sadism–masochism. The third of these variables still remains outside of the paradigm, but studies dealing with the first two offer scant encouragement to the proponents of complementarity.

In an unpublished investigation, Haywood (1965) studied two aspects of masculinity–femininity as determinants of attraction toward the opposite sex.

Proportion of Similar Responses

It seems logical that attraction toward the opposite sex would be greatest to those least like oneself in masculinity–femininity. Nevertheless, Haywood pointed out that studies by Lundy (1956, 1958) suggested that personality similarity holds even in this instance. Lundy had male and female subjects fill out the masculinity–femininity (M–F) scale of the Minnesota Multiphasic Personality Inventory (MMPI) for self, ideal self, and then for positive and negative sociometric choices of the same and opposite sexes. It was found that a liked person of either sex is perceived as more like oneself in masculinity–femininity than is a disliked person. Haywood attempted to encompass that relationship within the present attraction paradigm and also to extend it. He approached the problem in terms of proportion of similar responses to the M–F scale and also in terms of the dimension itself via score discrepancy with proportion of similar responses held constant. Only one investigation is involved, but for reasons of clarity it is reported here as two studies.

Method. The subjects were 24 male and 24 female undergraduates at the University of Texas. Each subject filled out the 60-item M–F scale of the MMPI. This scale includes such questions as "I like mechanics magazines," "I would like to be a florist," "I like to cook," and "I very much like hunting." Two weeks later, each subject received the simulated M–F scales of four strangers of the opposite sex (order of presentation counterbalanced) along with the usual instructions.

Two of the strangers were designed so as to have the same M–F score as the subject, but they differed in proportion of responses similar to those of the subject. One expressed .80 similarity and the other 1.00 similarity. The strangers were evaluated on the IJS to which three items were added: dating,

TABLE 7–11
MEAN ATTRACTION AND HETEROSEXUAL ATTRACTION RESPONSES
TOWARD OPPOSITE-SEX STRANGERS AT TWO LEVELS OF RESPONSE
SIMILARITY ON THE MASCULINITY–FEMININITY SCALE

	Attraction; proportion of similar responses		Heterosexual attraction; proportion of similar responses	
Subjects	.80	1.00	.80	1.00
Males	8.63	12.00	11.58	16.46
Females	8.92	11.54	10.75	14.29
Total	8.77	11.77	11.17	15.38

marriage, and sexual attraction. These three scales were summed to yield a measure of heterosexual attraction.

Results. Table 7–11 indicates the mean attraction responses and the mean heterosexual attraction responses for the two conditions. It may be seen that proportion of similar responses influences both the regular attraction measure and Haywood's new measure. In addition, there is a sex difference on the heterosexual items with females indicating less attraction than males. Thus, even with opposite-sex strangers on items concerned with masculine and feminine interests, subjects prefer strangers like themselves.

Response to Masculinity–Femininity

The second portion of Haywood's investigation dealt with response to level of masculinity–femininity, with proportion of similar responses held constant. The question is whether or not individuals respond differentially to opposite-sex strangers who differ in masculinity–femininity in comparison with the subject's own masculinity–femininity.

Method. The other two opposite-sex strangers were simulated in such a way that there was .80 similarity in terms of responses to the M–F scale, but one of the strangers was 12 points more masculine than the subject and the other was 12 points more feminine than the subject.

Results. Because of differential scoring for males and females. "Higher M–F" in Table 7–12 means 12 points more masculine for male subjects and 12 points more feminine for female subjects. Similarly, "Lower M–F" means 12 points more feminine for male subjects and 12 points more masculine for female subjects. Table 7–12 presents the attraction responses for these two new conditions along with the .80 condition (same M–F score as subject) already reported. Again, both dependent variables suggest that subjects

TABLE 7–12

MEAN ATTRACTION AND HETEROSEXUAL ATTRACTION RESPONSES TOWARD
OPPOSITE-SEX STRANGERS WITH HIGHER, EQUAL, AND LOWER MASCULINITY–
FEMININITY SCALE SCORES

Subjects	Attraction			Heterosexual attraction		
	Lower	Same	Higher	Lower	Same	Higher
Male	8.21	8.63	9.63	11.63	11.58	12.42
Female	8.46	8.92	9.58	10.08	10.75	10.83
Total	8.33	8.77	9.58	10.85	11.17	11.63

are responsive to the stranger's position on the personality dimension in relation to their own position. It will be noted that all of these means are lower than for the 1.00 condition; the most positive response is toward an opposite-sex stranger exactly like oneself. The most unusual finding here, however, was that, with proportion controlled, male subjects are most positive toward a female stranger more masculine than themselves, whereas female subjects are most positive toward a male stranger more feminine than themselves. In fact, this progression from lower to same to higher masculinity–femininity yields a significant linear trend.

Discussion. Given these unexpected and as yet unreplicated findings, it is well to be tentative in interpreting them. Haywood (1965) suggests one possibility:

> Males favor females with higher masculinity scores. This holds for judgments of the females' intelligence, knowledge of current events, morality, adjustment, liking, and desirability as a working partner. Females also prefer males with higher femininity scores than their own positions. These results are not directly suggested by the studies of attitude similarity but do correspond to the process of ascribing characteristics to same and opposite sex strangers described by Lundy (1958). Attitude investigations lead us to believe that subjects will give the most positive evaluation to strangers with similar M–F scores. Why do we, however, respond with preferential evaluations and acceptance of others who have more M–F characteristics typical for our own sex than we have ourselves? One possibility is that when we evaluate individuals who differ in M–F scores, there is a greater expectation of responses typical of our own sex, because these are the ones that had a greater frequency of occurrence in the past. When our expectancies are not rewarded with agreement, we react with negativism which is one way of reducing dissonance. Another way of saying this is that boys are not familiar with the typical attitudes of girls, and therefore, base their judgments on expectations of familiar masculine responses. This line of reasoning modifies attraction theory based on attitude studies and Festinger's theory of social comparison processes. Instead of being attracted to others who have similar personality traits, subjects display positive evaluations toward others who display familiar or expected personality traits [p. 35].

PERSONALITY SIMILARITY: DOMINANCE–SUBMISSIVENESS

It might be well to emphasize that a complementarity effect would be quite compatible with a reinforcement model. Dominance–submissiveness provides a good example of the possibility. Complementary need satisfaction has been proposed in that a submissive person satisfies the dominant person's need to dominate and vice versa. Leary (1957) has taken a theoretical position along this line and contends that the most stable relationships will be formed between persons who are different (complementary) on this dimension. The primary empirical support for the complementarity hypothesis has come from a study by Winch *et al.* (1955) in which the findings suggested that "receptive" individuals tend to have "assertive" spouses. Subsequent research has generally revealed inconsistent and weak relationships on such relevant traits as dominance, deference, succorance, and abasement among friends, fiancés, and spouses (Cohen, 1956; Katz *et al.*, 1960, 1963; Kerckhoff & Davis, 1962; Rychlak, 1965).

Only by utilizing an equivalent-behavior design with a personality variable such as dominance–submission is it possible to provide a clear confrontation between the similarity and complementarity hypotheses. An experiment by Palmer and Byrne (1970) was designed to provide that test.

Experiment I

Procedure. Subjects were defined as dominant or submissive on the basis of their scores on the Interpersonal Checklist (ICL) (Leary, 1957). In a later session, they were asked to examine the responses of dominant and submissive persons on the ICL and to evaluate them.

Approximately 360 introductory psychology students at the University of Texas were given the ICL. This instrument is a 128-item adjective checklist designed to measure two personality dimensions: dominance–submissiveness and love–hate. The dominant group consisted of 21 males and 21 females, whereas the submissive group consisted of 25 males and 25 females.

In the experimental session, subjects examined the ICL responses of four strangers, but only two of these (one dominant and one submissive) are relevant here. Each stranger was identified as a member of the opposite sex.

Results. The mean attraction responses given by the dominant and submissive subjects to the two strangers are presented in Table 7–13. Analysis revealed a significant interaction, with the direction indicating support for the similarity hypothesis. There is also a significantly more positive response to dominant than to submissive strangers, though this is greatest for dominant subjects.

TABLE 7–13

MEAN ATTRACTION RESPONSES OF DOMINANT AND SUBMISSIVE
SUBJECTS TOWARD DOMINANT AND SUBMISSIVE STRANGERS[a]

Subject	Stranger		
	Submissive	Dominant	Total
Dominant	7.23	10.93	9.08
Submissive	7.80	9.66	8.73
Total	7.54	10.24	—

[a]After Palmer and Byrne, 1970, p. 110.

A further analysis with additional subjects indicated that males responded more favorably than females to the submissive stranger and females responded more favorably than males to the dominant stranger.

Experiment II

In order to assess the stability of the findings of Experiment I, a replication was attempted. The procedure was the same. The dominant group consisted of 10 males and 10 females, and the submissive group was composed of 12 individuals of each sex.

Results. The mean attraction responses are shown in Table 7–14. The interaction is again significant, and again the dominant stranger elicited more positive responses than the submissive stranger. The findings of Experiment I were thus replicated.

TABLE 7–14

MEAN ATTRACTION RESPONSES OF DOMINANT AND SUBMISSIVE
SUBJECTS TOWARD DOMINANT AND SUBMISSIVE STRANGERS
(REPLICATION)[a]

Subject	Stranger		
	Submissive	Dominant	Total
Dominant	7.30	10.95	9.13
Submissive	8.71	10.08	9.40
Total	8.07	10.48	—

[a]After Palmer and Byrne, 1970, p. 111.

Discussion

These two experiments provide a modicum of support for the proposition that people similar to each other with respect to dominance–submissiveness are more attracted to each other than are individuals dissimilar on this dimension.

Despite the fact that submissive subjects found the dominant stranger to be more attractive than the submissive stranger, it would be very misleading to interpret this finding as evidence for a "complementarity effect." This particular result can be attributed entirely to the greater attractiveness of the dominant stranger across all subjects. The crucial variable in comparing the similarity and complementarity hypotheses is the relative attractiveness of the strangers *relative to the dominance levels of the subjects.*

One of the more striking findings to emerge from both experiments was the large difference in attraction responses toward the dominant and submissive strangers. From the standpoint of reinforcement theory, it is not immediately apparent why dominant and submissive persons should have differential reinforcing properties. Edwards (1957) had subjects rate each item on the ICL for social desirability on 9-point scales. It was found that the mean rating of items in the dominant stranger's profile is 6.04 in contrast to that of 5.04 for those in the profile of the submissive stranger. It seems possible that our findings indicate that persons are most attracted to others who conform more closely to cultural norms of desirable behavior. Either such individuals are intrinsically more rewarding or association with such persons may bring rewards in the form of approval from the larger society which defines these norms. Consistent with this interpretation is the finding of the present investigation that the dominant male and submissive female stranger each received higher ratings than did their respective counterparts. In Western society, at least prior to the Women's Liberation Movement, dominance has generally been considered to be the masculine role, and submissiveness the feminine role.

In order to avoid undue overgeneralization from a specific experimental finding and also to dampen the astonishment of those who discover that an alteration in conditions usually leads to an alteration in results, a few words of caution will be included. First, the generality of the similarity–attraction relationship for dominance may obviously be restricted by the role relationships of the individuals involved. For example, complementarity on dominance and submissiveness may be facilitative of interpersonal interaction in a decision-making situation but have a stultifying effect in a casual social encounter. Likewise, the present results based on opposite-sex strangers may or may not hold for same-sex strangers. Second, and most generally, different contexts often yield different stimulus–response relationships. Even though similarity leads to attraction in the type of experimental situation used here, it does not invariably follow that similarity leads to the most congenial relationships under quite different circumstances. For example, Bermann and Miller (1967) found that, although student nurses preferred as roommates peers who were similar to themselves on dominance, the most stable relationships existed among roommates who are complementary on dominance. For behavioral laws to demonstrate generality and predictive power rather than suffer from overgeneralization and inaccuracy, it is essential to emphasize specificity of detail at each step in the theory-building process. Therefore, it may be seen that an issue such as similarity versus complementarity is meaningful only as a guide to research in the relatively early stages of development of a field of inquiry.

Personality Similarity: Introversion–Extroversion

Hendrick and Brown (in press) pointed out the difficulty we have experienced in discovering a set of conditions under which a positive similarity–attraction relationship does not hold and the interest there would be in establishing such conditions. For one thing, boundary conditions can have implications for competing theoretical explanations. They suggest that extroversion-introversion as measured by the Maudsley Personality Inventory might be expected to play a role in setting boundary conditions. In a study using the *Q*-sort technique, they had previously found that extroverts view both themselves and their ideal selves as extroverted. For introverts, however, the ideal self also was extroverted. This discovery raised the possibility that in responding to the introversion–extroversion of a stranger, extroverts would show the usual similarity effect, whereas introverts would prefer dissimilar (extroverted) strangers.

Subjects took a modified version of the Maudsley test and extreme scorers were selected to form introversive and extroversive subgroups. Two simulated strangers were prepared for each subject, one extroverted and one introverted, and the strangers were rated on a variety of scales.

On the measure of liking, the hypotheses were partially supported. Extroverts showed the usual similarity effect. Introverts did not significantly differentiate similar and dissimilar strangers, and there was actually a trend toward a reversal effect.

The findings were interpreted in reinforcement terms in that extroverted behavior is more socially desirable among college students than is introverted behavior.

ABILITY SIMILARITY: INTELLIGENCE

Intellectual ability lies at the borderline between personality variables and individual differences in skills and achievement. Festinger's social comparison theory would lead us to expect that similarity in intellectual ability would result in attraction. In addition, numerous studies indicate that in the United States the IQ scores of pairs of spouses tend to correlate about .50. Perhaps to a greater extent than with personality variables, it is unclear as to the way in which differences in intelligence are expressed in specific behaviors and, hence, perceived by others. As a first step in seeking an answer to that question, London (1967) conducted two experiments dealing with intellectual similarity and attraction.

He pointed out that with ability variables, there is both the possible effect of similarity as a reinforcement and the desire to do better. Thus, both factors might contribute to the effect of ability information on attraction. London sought to create (1) a situation in which social desirability was not dominant, predicting a similarity effect, and (2) a situation emphasizing social desirability, predicting a positive response to those of high ability regardless of subject–stranger similarity.

Intellectual Similarity: Responses to Army General Classification Test

Method. The Army General Classification Test (AGCT) was administered to 40 elementary psychology students at the University of Texas. This is a group test with multiple choice answers. The subjects were assured that the test had nothing to do with the military service and that the results would not in any way be made known to the University or any of the armed services. On the basis of the test scores, the subjects were divided at the median into high and low intelligence groups. Each of these two groups was further divided into those individuals receiving a stranger's responses corresponding with their own on 1.00 of the items and those receiving a stranger's responses .33 similar to their own.

In the experimental session, several weeks later, the subjects received a set of instructions, an AGCT test booklet with an answer sheet filled out by the stranger, and an IJS.

Results. The mean attraction responses are shown in Table 7–15. The effect of similarity of intelligence test responses is highly significant, whereas neither the intelligence of the subject nor the interaction approached significance.

As a check on the subjects' perceptions of the stranger's intelligence, a correlation was run between the number of questions the stranger answered correctly on the AGCT and the subject's rating of the stranger's intelligence. The coefficient was .75. Thus, these individuals were able to respond with

TABLE 7–15
MEAN ATTRACTION RESPONSES FOR HIGH- AND
LOW-INTELLIGENCE SUBJECTS RESPONDING TO
TWO LEVELS OF SIMILARITY OF AGCT
RESPONSES[a,b]

Subject's Intelligence	Proportion of similar responses	
	.33	1.00
High	5.50	11.44
Low	6.50	11.00

[a]After London, 1967, p. 9.
[b]AGCT—Army General Classification Test.

reasonable accuracy as to the meaning of the stranger's performance on the test, but their attraction was determined only by similarity.

Intellectual Similarity: Intelligence Test Scores

Method. In London's (1967) second experiment, the aim was to create conditions in which social desirability was dominant. The subjects were 40 introductory statistics students who had been pretested on the AGCT. They were divided at the median into high- and low-intelligence subgroups. Instead of receiving an answer sheet purportedly filled out by a stranger, they were given the intelligence score of a stranger with half being given a high score and half a low score. The subjects were not told how well they themselves had done.

Results. The mean attraction responses are shown in Table 7–16. As hypothesized, those strangers to whom high-intelligence test scores were assigned were liked significantly better than those assigned low scores. In addition, the low-intelligence subjects responded more positively to the low-intelligence strangers than did the high-intelligence subjects.

Discussion. London suggested that the positive response to strangers with high intelligence results from the general acceptance in our culture of the idea that intelligence is a highly valued attribute. Thus, we are more attracted to those described as highly intelligent. The difference in response to the low-intelligence stranger could be attributed to the additional influence of a similarity effect. London (1967) concludes, "If an ability is put into a social desirability framework, the unidirectional drive upward is more important and people are highly attracted to those of high ability. When it is not, then similarity to self is more important and people are more highly attracted to those of equal ability [p. 21]."

TABLE 7-16

MEAN ATTRACTION RESPONSES OF HIGH- AND
LOW-INTELLIGENCE SUBJECTS RESPONDING TO
TWO LEVELS OF INTELLIGENCE SCORES[a]

Subject's Intelligence	Stranger's intelligence score	
	Low	High
High	7.70	10.50
Low	9.83	11.22

[a]After London, 1967, p. 11.

Intellectual Similarity: Responses to Vocabulary Test

Reagor and Clore (1970) manipulated subject–stranger similarity on vocabulary test responses in order to test Festinger's hypothesis. They noted that Zander and Havelin (1960) had previously conducted an ability comparison experiment in which three-man groups were made to appear either capable, mediocre, or incapable in putting together a puzzle within a given time limit. Among other findings, it was reported that higher ratings were given to strangers of apparently similar competence, even for subjects in the incapable group. Reagor and Clore pointed out that in the Zander and Havelin design, similarity is confounded with group membership. Strangers who were similar in ability were in the subject's own trio, whereas dissimilar strangers were in different groups. Therefore, the effects attributed to similarity–dissimilarity of competence could have been due to the ingroup–outgroup distinction.

Their experiment, run independently of and approximately at the same time as the London experiment, utilized subjects in individual tasks. In addition, cues to the objective goodness of performance were minimized by the extreme difficulty of the task.

Method. The subjects were 80 introductory psychology students at the University of Illinois. They responded to a vocabulary test and later were asked to make judgments about a stranger who had responded similarly or dissimilarly on that test.

The Verbal Competence Test was constructed by administering a pool of forced-choice word-definition items to a pilot group. The final items were selected on the basis of maximal difficulty. There were 24 items which were defined correctly by less than 50% of the subjects, and the alternatives were reduced to the two that had been chosen most often. Some sample items are listed here:

—1.	HIRSUTE	A) hateful	B) hairy
—4.	LISSOM	A) slim	B) limber
—13.	FLAG	A) to signal	B) to fail in vigor

Instructions emphasized that a good command of the English language is a must for success in college. Subjects were told that the words had been selected for their difficulty but that previously successful students had reported that, by carefully examining each definition, they could arrive at a "best bet" for each item.

Results. The mean attraction responses of the .17 similar group was 8.30, whereas that of the .83 similar group was 10.60. The difference is a highly significant one. In addition, the similar stranger was rated as more intelligent than the dissimilar one. It was also shown that the actual ability of the subjects on the vocabulary test was unrelated to their rating of the stranger.

Discussion. These three experiments add further support to the generality of the similarity effect and confirm once again the utility of Festinger's social comparison theory.

Economic Similarity–Dissimilarity

There are sociometric data which suggest that friendship choices within a group tend to be between members of the same general socio-economic status (Bonney, 1946; Dahlke, 1953; Longmore, 1948; Lundberg & Beazley, 1948; Lundberg & Steele, 1938). There are, of course, a variety of ways to explain such findings besides a causal relationship between economic similarity and attraction. Festinger (1954), however, provides a framework for explaining such a relationship. He has suggested:

> The segmentation into groups which are relatively alike with respect to abilities also gives rise to status in a society. And it seems clear that when such status distinctions are firmly maintained, it is not only members of the higher status who maintain them. It is also important to the members of the lower status to maintain them for it is in this way that they can relatively ignore the differences and compare themselves with their own group. Comparisons with members of a different status group, either higher or lower, may sometimes be made on a phantasy level, but very rarely in reality [p. 136].

In order to manipulate economic similarity in a controlled laboratory setting and to obtain attraction data directly comparable to that obtained in attitude studies, Byrne, Clore, and Worchel (1966) undertook the following investigation. With the same general experimental methodology as in the attitude studies, subjects were asked to evaluate a stranger about whom information concerning both attitudes and economic status was provided. It was hypothesized that attraction is a positive function of similarity of economic status.

Method

The subjects were 24 male and 24 female students enrolled in several sections of a required sophomore history course at the University of Texas. In their classrooms the subjects were given a scale dealing with their economic level and also an attitude scale. A week later each subject was instructed to examine both an economic and an attitude scale supposedly filled out by another student and to evaluate him.

Economic Level. In order to build realistic economic items, a pilot study was carried out, using 30 undergraduates. In response to open-ended questions, the students were asked to indicate their monthly spending money, entertainment expenses, clothing expenses, and the number of several specific items of clothing which they owned. On the basis of these data, four-item scales for males and females were constructed; on each item, subjects could indicate his or her own economic standing on a 9-point scale ranging from "very much less than average" to "very much more than average." The items were

1. The average University of Texas undergraduate male (female) spends about $26 ($19) per month on entertainment. I spend:
2. The average University of Texas undergraduate male (female) has about $43 ($40) per month of spending money besides food, rent, and other such necessities. I have:
3. The average male (female) at Texas spends $8 ($20) per month on clothes. I spend:
4. The average male (female) at Texas has 3 sport coats and 3 suits (7 pairs of high heeled shoes and 4 cocktail dresses). I have:

Attitudes. After filling out the economic level items, the subjects responded to a four-item attitude scale. The items were selected on the basis of yielding approximately 50–50 opinion splits among previous subjects. They dealt with the university grading system, undergraduate marriages, strict disciplining of children, and sex differences in adjusting to stress.

Experimental Session. The subjects were divided into three experimental groups of 16 subjects each. On the basis of their responses to the four economic items, subjects were divided at the midpoint of the economic score into high and low groups. In Condition L–H, subjects of relatively low economic level were asked to evaluate high economic level strangers; in condition H–L, subjects of relatively high economic level were asked to evaluate low economic level strangers. The difference between each subject and his dissimilar stranger was a constant total of 15 scale points on the economic items. A third condition (L–L, H–H) consisted of both low and high economic level subjects who were presented with strangers similar to themselves in economic level. For all subjects, the bogus stranger's responses to the attitude items are made to agree with 50% of the subject's opinions.

The standard instructions were given, and strangers were evaluated on the IJS. In addition, subjects indicated on a 4-point scale the extent to which they would prefer to have the amount of spending money the stranger had or the amount they themselves had.

Results

The means of the attraction responses are shown in Table 7–17. It may be seen that the attraction responses are most positive toward a stranger of similar economic status and least positive toward a stranger of dissimilar economic status.

On the relative-preference item, the H–L subjects indicated a preference for their own economic status, whereas the L–H subjects would prefer the economic standing of the stranger. Thus, the manipulation of the stranger's economic standing in relation to that of the subjects' was apparently successful.

TABLE 7–17

MEAN ATTRACTION RESPONSES
TOWARD STRANGERS OF SIMILAR
AND DISSIMILAR ECONOMIC
LEVEL[a]

Experimental conditions[b]		
L–H	H–L	L–L, H–H
8.50	7.62	10.12

[a]Data from Byrne, Clore, and Worchel, 1966.

[b]L–H, subjects of relatively low economic level evaluating high economic strangers; H–L, subjects of relatively high economic level evaluating low economic strangers; L–L, H–H, low and high economic level subjects evaluating strangers similar to themselves in economic level.

Discussion

The next question was whether the law of attraction holds with respect to the economic similarity–dissimilarity variable. Each subject received eight units of information concerning a stranger, four dealing with attitudes and four dealing with economic status. It was assumed that similarity to the subject in either instance constitutes a unit of positive reinforcement and dissimilarity a unit of negative reinforcement. The proportion of positive reinforcements received by the L–L, H–H group is .75 (two similar attitudes, four units of economic similarity, and two dissimilar attitudes) which would yield an expected attraction response of 10.70. The difference between this predicted response and the obtained mean of 10.12 is not significant. For the other two groups the proportion of positive reinforcements is .25 which would indicate an expected attraction response of 7.98 for each. Neither of the obtained means (8.50 and 7.62) differ significantly from the predicted mean. Thus, the attraction formula derived from attitude investigations yields accurate predictions of response to attitude plus economic information.

BEHAVIORAL SIMILARITY

A final aspect of nonattitudinal similarity is represented by Huffman's (1969) studies of similarity–dissimilarity of overt behaviors. He points out that a number of individuals have suggested the conceptual division of attitudes into three components: cognition, affect, and action. Though this division had not been taken into account in previous attraction research, Huffman proposed that similarity of action attitudes (those primarily concerned with behavior) influences attraction in the same manner as do affect and belief attitudes.

Behavioral Similarity or Attitudinal Similarity

Method. In the first of these studies, the subjects were asked to examine either an attitude or behavior questionnaire reportedly filled out by an anonymous student. Each subject received a questionnaire that agreed with his own responses on two, four, or six of the seven items. The behavioral questionnaire was composed of seven questions concerning behavior in cooperative activities with others (See Appendix E). Each question is followed by two behavioral alternatives. The subject indicates his choice and the degree of preference.

All subjects had responded to both types of questionnaires, but in the experimental session, each received only an attitudinal scale or a behavioral scale.

Results. The mean attraction responses to various levels of behavioral or attitudinal similarity are shown in Table 7–18. The only significant effect was that of similarity. Neither the type of information nor the interaction between similarity and type of information was found to affect attraction. The responses here did not differ from those predicted by the Byrne–Nelson formula.

Behavioral Similarity and Attitudinal Similarity

Huffman reasoned that the two types of information could be combined in a simple fashion and the effect on attraction be predicted on the basis of the total array of information.

Method. The only difference in experimental design from the previous experiment was that subjects in the experimental session examined both sets of questionnaires supposedly filled out by the stranger before evaluating him. The similarity of the stranger to the subject was varied independently on the two scales, resulting in nine possible combinations of attitudinal and behavioral similarity. Each subject was exposed to one of these combinations.

Results. The mean attraction responses are shown in Table 7–19. In contrast to the first experiment, only attitude similarity was found to have a significant effect on attraction. This finding suggests that behavioral similarity is instrumental in the development of affective relationships only in the absence of supplementary attitudinal cues. The findings with respect to prestige or status may be remembered as parallel to these.

Discussion. Huffman suggested that his second experiment raised more questions than it answered. Not only was the expected additive effect not obtained but attitude items retained their potency as predictors of attraction, whereas behavioral items lost all influence in the combined condition.

TABLE 7–18

MEAN ATTRACTION RESPONSES TOWARD INDIVIDUALS
DIFFERING IN PROPORTION OF SIMILAR ATTITUDES
OR SIMILAR BEHAVIORS[a]

	Proportion of similarity		
	.29	.57	.86
Behaviors	8.70	8.30	10.90
Attitudes	7.50	9.30	10.60

[a]After Huffman, 1969, p. 36.

TABLE 7–19
MEAN ATTRACTION RESPONSES FOR THREE LEVELS OF
ATTITUDINAL AND OF BEHAVIORAL SIMILARITY[a]

Proportion of similar attitudes	Proportion of similar behaviors		
	.29	.57	.86
.86	9.10	10.50	10.90
.57	8.20	9.60	8.80
.29	7.10	7.20	8.20

[a]After Huffman, 1969, p. 38.

One possible source of the unexpected finding was the fact that the behavioral items dealt with a limited and specific situation—behavior in a small decision-making group. The attitudes, in contrast, dealt with a wide variety of topics. It seemed possible that the range of information supplied about the stranger served to differentiate the effect of the two types of items rather than differentiation based simply on attitudes versus behavior. Previous analytic research had not dealt with that particular variable. A third experiment explored this question.

Behaviors and Attitudes: Range of Topics

Method. Two new types of items were prepared. Items were written representing behavior in a variety of situations (see Appendix F), whereas attitudinal items were chosen to represent a homogeneous topic (see Appendix G). The new materials were presented either separately or combined.

Results. The mean attraction responses for these new conditions are presented in Table 7–20. With the narrow attitudes and broad behaviors presented as the only type of information, there is once again a similarity effect. The only new finding is that the narrow attitude statements elicit less positive attraction responses than do broad behaviors, narrow behaviors, or broad attitudes. When the narrow attitudes and broad behaviors are presented as combined information, it is found that both types of similarity influence attraction. Thus, the finding in the second experiment in this series that behavioral similarity loses its effectiveness when combined with attitudinal information was shown to be a function of the narrowness of that behavioral information and not a function of behavioral content per se.

Discussion. Besides showing the effects of behavioral similarity on attraction and the importance of topic range as an additional stimulus

TABLE 7–20

MEAN ATTRACTION RESPONSES TOWARD STRANGERS
ON THE BASIS OF NARROW ATTITUDINAL INFORMATION
AND/OR BROAD BEHAVIORAL INFORMATION[a]

A. Narrow attitudes or broad behaviors

	Proportion of similar responses		
	.29	.57	.86
Narrow attitudes	6.30	6.50	9.80
Broad behaviors	8.10	10.60	10.10

B. Narrow attitudes and broad behaviors

Proportion of similar attitudes	Proportion of similar behaviors		
	.29	.57	.86
.86	7.80	9.00	9.80
.57	6.40	6.90	8.70
.29	5.80	6.60	8.20

[a]Data from Huffman, 1969.

determinant, Huffman went on to plot his data and reported one further finding. The slope of the similarity–attraction function was greater for the two combined information conditions than for the four independent information conditions. He proposed that it was possible that the combined information sets arouse more affect than do the independent sets. A second possibility, because of the greater difference at the dissimilar end of the continuum than at the similar end, is that unfavorable responses to the stranger are inhibited by limited information. Huffman (1969) suggests, "as the amount of dissimilar information increases, the subject feels greater justification in expressing unfavorable opinions toward the stranger. Positive responses, on the other hand, may be freely expressed with or without extensive justification [pp. 34–35]."

As someone once noted, further research is needed.

RESPONSE GENERALITY

Chapter 8 / **Response Generality: I. Subject Variables**

In attempting to seek generality beyond the specific conditions of the base relationship, stimulus generality is only one area of concern. On the response side, it is necessary to examine the extent to which the obtained relationship may be generalized to different classes of individuals and the extent to which other response measures of attraction yield results comparable to those obtained with one specific paper and pencil measure.

The present chapter deals with the generality of the response in various groups of individuals. Two specific questions have received attention. (1) Is the base relationship generalizable beyond the rather narrow and specific undergraduate population from which the initial samples of subjects were drawn? (2) Are there individual differences in responding to similar and dissimilar attitudes which are predictable on the basis of personality measures?

BEYOND THE COLLEGE SOPHOMORE: SAMPLING OTHER POPULATIONS

It is a truism that personality and social psychologists, among others, tend to build laws of behavior based on the responses of college sophomores. The reason is not difficult to ascertain. College students, much like laboratory animals, are close at hand and at least periodically under our control. Thus, subjects are either coerced (participation as subjects serve a course requirement) or seduced (participation earns bonus points or approbation) into the experimental setting. When experimenters look beyond this group, the difficulties involved in conducting research increase dramatically. If other captive groups are sought, negotiations must be undertaken with noncollege administrators to promote the activity. Research space must be obtained. Materials must be transported to new sites. Procedures must be adapted to the abilities and interests of quite diverse groups. It would seem that the effort involved in conducting research beyond the barricades of academe is sufficiently great that it is most likely to be undertaken only with respect to phenomena well established with our usual groups of subjects. The similarity–attraction relationship seems to meet that criterion.

The first concern about generality was the extent to which our findings were limited not only to college students but to the undergraduate population of the University of Texas. Because this was the source of subjects in all of our initial experiments, there was no way to be certain that the relationship was generalizable beyond the Texas population. As research within the paradigm expanded in subsequent years, it was gratifying, therefore, to find that subjects at Texas were prototypical, at least with respect to similarity–attraction, of students at British Columbia (Brown & Eng, 1970), Cooke County Junior College (Scott, 1969), Embry-Riddle Aeronautical Institute (Mascaro & Lopez, 1970), Florida (Mascaro, 1970), Georgia (Batchelor & Tesser, in press; Tesser, to be published, 1971), Hawaii (Griffitt, 1968a,b, 1969a; Griffitt & Guay, 1969), Illinois (Clore & Baldridge, 1968, 1970; Clore & Gormly, 1969; Gormly & Clore, 1969; Reagor & Clore, 1970; Stapert & Clore, 1969), Illinois, Chicago Circle (Moss, 1970), Iowa State (Sherman, 1969), Kansas State (Griffitt, 1970, 1971; Griffitt & Jackson, 1970, to be published; Griffitt & Nelson, 1970, Griffitt & Veitch, 1971), Kent State (Hendrick, Bixenstine, & Hawkins, 1971; Hendrick & Page, 1970; Hendrick & Taylor, 1971), Kentucky (Novak & Lerner, 1968), McGill (Galloway, 1970), Northern Illinois (Kaplan & Olczak, 1970; Olczak, 1969), Ohio State (Rosenblood, 1970), Purdue (Byrne & Lamberth, in press; Ettinger, 1967; Ettinger, Nowicki, & Nelson, 1970; Gouaux & Lamberth, 1970; Gouaux, Lamberth, & Friedrich, to be published; Hodges & Byrne, 1971; Meadow, 1971; Mitchell, 1970; Nowicki, 1969; Smith, Meadow, & Sisk, 1970), South Carolina (Baron, 1970a, 1971; Baron & Kepner, 1970), Stanford (Bond, Byrne, & Diamond, 1968; Byrne, Bond, & Diamond, 1969; Griffitt, Byrne, & Bond, 1971; Tornatzky & Geiwitz, 1968), Syracuse (Blank & Arenson, 1971), Texas A&M (Byrne, Griffitt, & Golightly, 1966), Washington (Smith & Jeffery, 1970), and Western Ontario (Guthwin, 1970; Reitz & Robinson, 1969).

Given evidence of generality among American and Canadian college students, we are still limited to a narrow population of subjects. That is, the various college samples consist of relatively young, relatively well adjusted, relatively bright individuals representing predominantly a white middle-class culture. It would be fairly easy to make a case for the proposition that the tendency to respond positively to attitude similarity and negatively to attitude dissimilarity constitutes a special behavior characteristic, observable only in these restricted samples. If so, the findings reported so far in this book would be of less interest as general behavioral phenomena than if they should be found to be representative of a broader segment of the general population.

Children and Adolescents

One of the first explorations of the noncollegiate generality of the law of attraction was carried out by Byrne and Griffitt (1966a). It was suggested that opinions, beliefs, values, and attitudes are acquired throughout the developmental period. It seemed plausible to propose a steady increase throughout childhood of the extent to which attitudes are sufficiently well formulated for agreement and disagreement to affect attraction. It was, therefore, hypothesized that the linear relationship between attitudes and attraction develops gradually throughout childhood and assumes its final form in adolescence.

Method. The subjects were 272 primary and secondary public school children of both sexes enrolled in Grades 4 through 12 inclusively. The age range was from 9 to 20 years. The standard stranger technique was used with an eight-item attitude scale. For the fourth to ninth graders, the topics were poetry, relative intelligence of boys and girls, sports, studying, summer camp, brothers and sisters, trips with parents, and comic books. For the three older grades, the topics were smoking cigarettes, reading books and magazines, strict rules, studying, religion, brothers and sisters, racial integration, and comic books.

The subjects were told that other students in other schools had filled out the attitude scales, and they would have a chance to look at the answers of one of these students who was of their same sex and in the same grade. Evaluations were made on a special version of the Interpersonal Judgment Scale (IJS) (See Appendix H).

Results. The data were first examined by individual grade levels in order to ascertain whether or not there were any obvious trends in the similarity–attraction function across age levels; none were found. Therefore, in order to facilitate analysis, the attitude similarity variable was trichotomized and the age variable dichotomized as shown in Table 8–1.

TABLE 8–1

MEAN ATTRACTION RESPONSES OF SUBJECTS REPRESENTING TWO AGE LEVELS
TOWARD STRANGERS DIFFERING IN PROPORTION OF SIMILAR ATTITUDES[a]

Grade level	Proportion of similar attitudes			
	Low (.12–.38)	Medium (.50)	High (.62–.88)	Total
Older (8th–12th)	6.80	7.90	9.29	8.07
Younger (4th–8th)	8.39	8.76	10.06	9.12
Total	7.60	8.33	9.68	—

[a]After Byrne and Griffitt, 1966a, p. 700.

There was once again a highly significant effect for attitude similarity. There was also a significant age effect in that the younger children tend to give more positive responses than the older ones. For all of the subjects, a straight line function was fitted to the data by the least squares method, and the solution yielded the formula $Y = 7.03X + 5.16$, as shown in Fig. 8–1. The relationship depicted is obviously very close to the Byrne–Clore function.

Thus, the hypothesized generality of the law of attraction was confirmed, but the hypothesized differences in the function across age levels were not found.

Discussion. The failure to find a different similarity–attraction function at different ages was somewhat surprising. It would appear that the similarity–attraction relationship is as strongly operative by 9 years of age as it is in adulthood. It is hoped that in future research, the developmental sequence can be traced by extending the attraction research to still younger children.

It was proposed that (Byrne & Griffitt, 1966a) "as soon as a child acquires a sufficient mastery of the language to hold and to express opinions, beliefs, values, and attitudes, he responds to agreement by others as positively reinforcing and disagreement by others as negatively reinforcing [p. 702]."

Female Clerical Workers

As part of a larger study, Krauss (1966) administered a 20-item attitude scale to 160 female clerical employees of the Bell Telephone Laboratories. Shortly afterward, each subject received a scale supposedly filled out by a fellow worker. The bogus scales conformed to either a 17–3 or a 3–17 similar–dissimilar pattern. Using the methodology of the present paradigm,

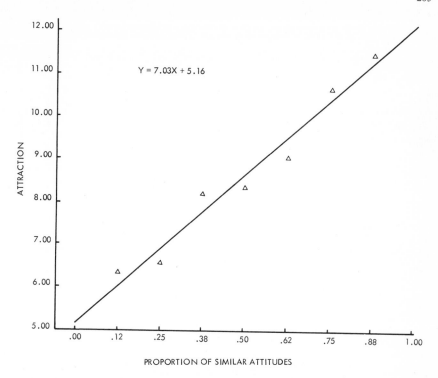

Fig. 8–1. Attraction toward a stranger as a linear function of proportion of similar attitudes among elementary and secondary school students in Grades 4 through 12. (After Byrne & Griffitt, 1966a, p. 701.)

Krauss then asked each subject to evaluate the other individual on the IJS.

Although mean attraction responses were not reported, analysis of variance indicated highly significant attraction differences. It might be noted that these office workers also responded differentially to similar and dissimilar partners on the other items of the IJS.

Hospitalized Male Patients

Byrne, Griffitt, Hudgins, and Reeves (1969) pursued the similarity–attraction relationship in additional nonstudent samples.

Method. The subjects consisted of three distinct groups of male hospital patients who could be characterized as older and less well-educated individuals representing a lower socioeconomic level than had previously been utilized in the experimental study of attraction. Specifically, the three groups

were 13 surgical patients at the John Sealy Hospital of the University of
Texas Medical Branch in Galveston, 29 alcoholic patients at the Austin
State Hospital, and 42 schizophrenic patients at the Austin State Hospital.
In age, the subjects ranged from 15 to 71 with medians of 23, 43, and 45 in
the three groups. Educational levels ranged from the third grade through
college graduation with a high school diploma as the median. Almost all of
the subjects were employed in either skilled or unskilled laboring jobs.
Approximately one-quarter of the subjects were blacks.

In small groups, each subject was first given an eight-item attitude
scale. Immediately afterward, while the subjects were engaged in a neutral
activity, a bogus attitude scale was prepared for each subject such that the
responses were in agreement with their own on none, four, or all eight of
the items. Each subject received one of these bogus scales and was told that
it contained the responses of another patient in the same hospital.

Results. The means of the attraction responses of the three groups are
shown in Table 8–2. Once again, the effect of attitude similarity on attraction
was confirmed.

TABLE 8–2

MEAN ATTRACTION RESPONSES OF SURGICAL,
ALCOHOLIC, AND SCHIZOPHRENIC PATIENTS TO
THREE LEVELS OF ATTITUDE SIMILARITY[a]

Group	Proportion of similar attitudes		
	.00	.50	1.00
Surgical patients	5.00	7.60	10.75
Alcoholic patients	6.10	7.56	10.00
Schizophrenic patients	8.35	9.79	11.64

[a]After Byrne, Griffitt, Hudgins, and Reeves, 1969, p. 157.

Job Corps Trainees

In a population as yet relatively untapped by behavioral research, the
generality of the attitude–attraction function was also explored among
members of the Job Corps Training Program (Byrne *et al.*, 1969).

Method. The subjects were 82 trainees at the Gary Job Corps Training
Center in San Marcos, Texas. In age they ranged from 16 to 22 (median =
18.5) and in educational attainment from 6th to the 12th grade (median =
9th). Approximately 44% of the sample consisted of Anglo-Americans, 36%
of blacks, and 15% of Latin-Americans and American Indians.

The attitude scale contained 12 items. Immediately after taking the scale, the subjects were given the interpersonal judgment instructions and another attitude scale, purportedly filled out by another job corpsman. Each subject actually received one of two random "standard stranger" scales.

Results. To facilitate analysis, the subjects were divided into three levels of attitude similarity. As expected, proportion of similar attitudes was found to exert a significant influence on attraction.

A comparison was made of the responses of these subjects and the responses predicted by the Byrne–Clore formula. The difference was not significant. Once again, the formula derived in a sample of college students was found to predict the attraction responses of a quite different sample of subjects.

Because this particular group contained relatively large proportions of minority group members, it was decided to explore possible ethnic differences in the attitude–attraction function. A stimulus–response correlational analysis was employed. For the total sample, the correlation between proportion of similar attitudes held by the stranger and attraction responses was found to be .27. In the ethnic comparison, this correlation was −.07 for Anglo-Americans, .46 for blacks, and .34 for the Latin-American and Indian group.

The surprising finding, of course, is that there was no relationship between attitude similarity and attraction for the Anglo-Americans, the group that had furnished the majority of the subjects in previous research. It was assumed that some other variable, such as level of educational attainment, must be operating differentially across these three groups of trainees. In support of this possibility, it was found that the black trainees had the highest mean educational level (9.88) and the Anglo-Americans the lowest (9.07) of the three groups, and this difference was a significant one. On the basis of this finding, the sample was rearranged by educational level, ignoring ethnic membership. As hypothesized, attitude similarity was significantly correlated ($r = .45$) with attraction among the best educated trainees (10th–12th grades), whereas the correlation ($r = .13$) was not significant among the trainees with the lowest educational attainment (6th–8th grades). Since it has already been found that children in the 6th–8th grades respond to attitude similarity, the findings with the least-educated job corps trainees suggest these early school dropouts represent a special group in terms of factors such as intellectual ability and reading skills. It may be that such individuals do not respond to similar and dissimilar attitudes with differential attraction, but it seems more likely that they simply were unable to understand the instructions or to read the attitude scale and the IJS.

Discussion. It seems clear that the law of attraction is a phenomenon generalizable beyond the college student. In samples unlike college undergraduates in age, education, socioeconomic level, intelligence, and adjustment, not only does a linear function hold between the two variables, but the specific responses of the subjects are predictable on the basis of a formula derived on college students. The tendency to make a positive response to a stranger who expresses attitudes similar to one's own and a negative response to one who expresses dissimilar attitudes is obviously relatively general in the population. These relationships are shown graphically in Fig. 8–2.

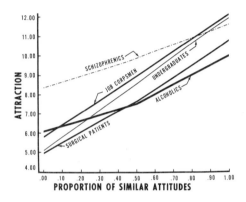

Fig. 8–2. Attraction as a function of proportion of similar attitudes among surgical, alcoholic, and schizophrenic patients, job corps trainees, and college undergraduates. (After Byrne, Griffitt, Hudgins, & Reeves, 1969, p. 161.)

Cross-Cultural Comparisons

In building general theories of human behavior, we most often do not know whether we are dealing with universal laws or with something which is culture-specific. For example, the observation of a latency period in preadolescence could be interesting either as a peculiar characteristic of middle-class Viennese at the turn of the century or as a general characteristic in the psychological development of man; it is, nevertheless, essential that we know which it is. Whiting (1968) states the general problem, "Since most social-psychological studies are done within the framework of western European culture, one never can be certain the discovered relationships are valid for all mankind or whether they are an artifact of some limitation or special circumstance of the culture in which they have been discovered [p. 694]."

It would seem, then, that cross-cultural experimentation should provide essential information concerning the generality of any lawful relationship identified in a single culture. Certainly the linear function linking proportion of similar attitudes expressed by a stranger and attraction toward that stranger is one of the most firmly established such relationships in social psychology. All of the subjects in the experiments described so far were residents of the United States or of Canada. A question to be answered is whether the response to attitude similarity–dissimilarity represents a general characteristic of mankind. Only cross-cultural research can determine whether the similarity–attraction relationship is to be pursued as the unique outcome of North American cultural factors or as a common behavioral manifestation in diverse cultures. Byrne, Gouaux, Griffitt, Lamberth, Murakawa, Prasad, Prasad, and Ramirez (in press) undertook such an investigation.

For comparison purposes, subject samples were drawn from Asia and North America from two nations with highly developed economies (Japan and the United States) and from two nations with less developed economies (India and Mexico). A portion of the United States sample consisted of Chinese Americans and Japanese Americans in Hawaii, representing a midway point between the two continents both geographically and culturally.

Method. The subjects were 506 students at various educational levels in four nations.

Hawaii. Undergraduates with an age range of 17 to 23 at the University of Hawaii of Chinese ($N = 30$) and Japanese ($N = 65$) descent served as subjects.

India. A total of 104 undergraduate and postgraduate students at the University of Patna in Bihar, India, participated in the experiment. Their ages ranged from 16 to 38. Approximately 85% of the sample were Hindus, and the rest were Moslems with the exception of one Christian.

Japan. The males were 48 undergraduate and graduate engineering students at Osaka City University, with an age range of 20 to 25. The females were 66 preschool education students at the St. Agnes' College for Girls in Kyoto, between 19 and 22 years of age.

Mexico. The youngest subjects, aged 14–16, were the 76 students at Escuela Secundaria Federal de Cd. Miguel Aleman in the state of Tamaulipas.

Texas. The subjects were 117 undergraduates enrolled in an introductory course in personality at the University of Texas.

The standard stranger technique was used. Subjects, run in groups, were given a survey of attitudes consisting of 15 items and then a scale purportedly filled out by another student like themselves.

The attitude scales, instructions, and attraction measure were prepared in English (for Hawaii, India, and Texas) and in Japanese and Spanish, with a few minor changes across groups to clarify the meaning of specific topics.

Results. In order to facilitate analysis of the data, the subjects were divided approximately into thirds on the basis of the similarity condition in which they fell. The mean similarity stimulus values for the three groups were .34, .54, and .71. The mean attraction responses are shown in Table 8–3.

TABLE 8–3

MEAN ATTRACTION RESPONSE TOWARD STRANGERS
AT THREE LEVELS OF ATTITUDE SIMILARITY
IN EACH OF FIVE CROSS-CULTURAL SAMPLES[a]

	Proportion of similar responses			
Cultural groups	.00–.40	.47–.60	.67–1.00	Total
Hawaii	7.03	8.27	8.46	7.92
India	7.19	8.34	9.40	8.31
Japan	6.27	6.94	7.53	6.91
Mexico	7.31	8.55	9.11	8.32
Texas	6.00	7.33	7.38	6.90
Total	6.76	7.89	8.37	—

[a]After Byrne, Gouaux, Griffitt, Lamberth, Murakawa, Prasad, Prasad, and Ramirez, in press.

There was a significant overall similarity effect and a sample effect. The similarity effect plus the lack of an interaction indicates that the similarity–attraction function has generality across quite different cultural groups. The sample differences do not indicate differences in the general nature of the function but rather in the overall level of attraction responses; subjects in Japan and Texas gave the most negative responses, and those in India and Mexico gave the most positive responses.

Responses to the other scales of the IJS were also analyzed. The effect of similarity was significant with respect to all four evaluations. The greater the stranger's similarity to the subject, the more positively he was evaluated on intelligence, knowledge of current events, morality, and adjustment. In none of the five samples was there a significant sex difference in attraction responses.

Discussion. For the first time, the law of attraction had been shown to be independent of the cultural context in which it was originally established. Although, obviously it cannot be claimed that complete universality has been demonstrated, it has been established that the effect of attitude similarity on attraction is not narrowly bound by nationality, race, or language.

These cross-cultural findings provide a broad base from which to investigate the origins of the positive response to similar attitudes and the negative response to dissimilar attitudes. Sears (1961) has suggested, "To the extent that there are universal characteristics of people as biological organisms and universal characteristics of environment, to that extent there are likely to be transcultural properties of behavior [p. 448]." One supposition is that the response to attitudes is based on common learning experiences which stress the desirability of being logical and correct in perceiving the world as others do.

Intensive study of the development of this reaction tendency may provide not only a more detailed knowledge of its specific antecedents, but it may also provide the possibility of learning about tolerance for disagreement. If research can identify cultures, subcultures, or even families in which the similarity–attraction function does not operate, the antecedents of tolerance may be identified. It might even be possible to avoid responding to honest disagreements about Vietnam, campus demonstrations, economics, or racial problems with the fury and fright of small children.

INDIVIDUAL DIFFERENCES
IN THE SIMILARITY–ATTRACTION RELATIONSHIP

One of the most obvious and most frequently encountered observations concerning the similarity–attraction relationship is that individuals must vary in their tendencies to dislike dissimilar others and/or to like similar others. For example, males and females might be expected to differ in their response to attitude similarity; no consistent sex differences are reported, however. An adequate presentation of the rationale of the search for personality trait measures that mediate stimulus–response relationships (Byrne, 1966) and the difficulties encountered in adhering to that approach (Mischel, 1968) requires more space than is possible here. The findings to be presented are, however, relevant to both issues.

The similarity–attraction relationship provides a particularly intriguing situation in which to examine the phenomenon of individual differences. The relationship is, as may be crushingly clear even to the casual reader, exceedingly stable and consistent. Thus, when Wiener (1970) conducted a series of experiments in which 291 subjects were exposed to the attitudes

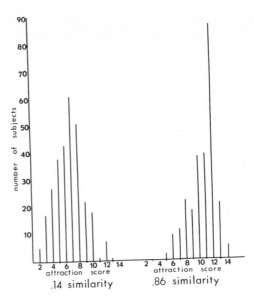

Fig. 8–3. Individual differences in responding to a similar and to a dissimilar stranger. (Figure provided by Dr. Daniel J. Wiener.)

of a .14 similar stranger and 252 subjects were exposed to the attitudes of a .86 similar stranger, the resulting attraction responses could be predicted on the basis of the Byrne–Nelson formula. The predicted means of 7.38 and 11.30 are impressively close to those obtained by Wiener (6.66 and 10.62). The variance about those means is not, however, zero. As may be seen in Fig. 8–3, a few individuals disliked the .14 stranger more than the formula predicts, whereas others liked the .86 stranger more than the formula predicts. Of greater interest is the fact that a very few individuals in the .14 condition liked the stranger very much, and a few in the .86 condition disliked the stranger very much. As Cronbach (1957) has suggested, experimentalists are content to cast such individual variation into the outer darkness of error variance and to strive to reduce such variance in subsequent experiments. This reaction is not shared by all in that "The correlational psychologist is in love with just those variables the experimenter left home to forget [p. 674]." A number of us at the golden mean between experimentalists and correlationalists have attempted repeatedly to bring the "error variance" within the predictive framework of the attraction paradigm by means of a search for relevant personality traits.

The search for predictable individual differences within attraction experiments has proven to be the most frustrating and difficult area into which attraction research has been extended. Not only have perfectly reasonable personality variables failed to show any relationship to attraction responses but those variables for which positive results are obtained often show no effect in subsequent experiments or only in seemingly random subsequent experiments. Because of the plethora of negative findings and of somewhat "mushy" findings, the following section will not present in great detail the reasoning behind each personality variable's inclusion in attraction research nor the explanations for each nonsignificant finding. Rather, the aim is to document the variety of personality variables which have been the subject of successful and unsuccessful experimentation within the attraction paradigm.

Authoritarianism and Dogmatism

Authoritarianism and Attitude Similarity–Dissimilarity. Included in the authoritarian syndrome are a number of characteristics that suggest that those high on the California F Scale are relatively rigid and dogmatic with respect to the opinions and beliefs that they hold and are relatively insecure about (and threatened by) the possibility of being incorrect. It would be expected, therefore, that various attitudes held by authoritarian individuals are rigidly structured into dichotomies of right and wrong, truth and falsehood, proper and improper. Further, disagreement on the part of others about various topics should create an ambiguous and threatening situation that the authoritarian would be expected to resolve by strongly rejecting the holder of dissident opinions. On the other hand, individuals low in authoritarianism should be much more flexible in the attitudes they hold, more tolerant of and less threatened by the possibility of being incorrect, and less likely to reject another individual because he expresses dissimilar opinions.

On the basis of these propositions, Byrne (1965) hypothesized that, as the proportion of a stranger's dissimilar attitudes increases, high authoritarians respond to him more negatively than do low authoritarians.

The California F Scale (Adorno, Frenkel-Brunswik, Levinson, & Sanford, 1950) was given to several sections of introductory psychology students. From the total pool of subjects, 80 authoritarians and 80 equalitarians were selected. A different experimenter administered a seven-item attitude scale to the original pool of subjects.

In the experimental session, each subject was given the attitude scale of a stranger who had responded at one of eight different levels of similarity, ranging from .00 to 1.00.

The mean attraction responses are shown in Table 8–4. The main effect of attitude similarity was significant, but neither authoritarianism nor

TABLE 8–4

MEANS OF ATTRACTION RESPONSES OF AUTHORITARIANS
AND EQUALITARIANS TO STRANGERS DIFFERING IN
PROPORTION OF SIMILAR ATTITUDES[a]

Proportion of similar attitudes	Equalitarians	Authoritarians
1.00	11.70	12.70
.86	11.90	11.90
.71	10.30	11.10
.57	9.70	10.70
.43	10.80	9.20
.29	8.80	9.60
.14	7.80	9.20
.00	7.70	9.00

[a]After Byrne, 1965, p. 253.

the interaction between similarity and authoritarianism reached significance.

One possibility that was raised in explaining the absence of authoritarian–equalitarian differences was that such reactions are elicited only in connection with topics that are relevant to authoritarian ideology. That is, dissimilarity of the beliefs of others may be overly threatening to those high in authoritarianism only in areas involving antidemocratic beliefs and correlates of antidemocratic beliefs.

If this proposition were true, two hypotheses follow. First, the seven attitudes utilized in this particular study should be uncorrelated with the F scale. For the 160 subjects, correlations were computed between their scores on the F scale and their responses to each of the attitude items; the seven coefficients ranged from −.15 to .11, none of which is significant. Second, a replication of the F scale experiment, in which each of the seven attitudes were known to be related to authoritarianism, would be expected to yield the originally hypothesized results. This second hypothesis was then tested by Sheffield and Byrne (1967).

Authoritarianism and Response to Similarity–Dissimilarity on Authoritarian-Relevant Attitudes. Prior to the main investigation, a 14-item attitude scale was constructed such that opinions on each issue were hypothesized to be relevant to authoritarianism. This scale and the California F Scale were administered to 125 introductory psychology students at the University of Texas.

Of the 14 new attitude items, 9 were found to correlate significantly with the F scale. There was a positive relationship between the subjects' authoritarian score and endorsement of statements indicating that they would enjoy serving in the armed forces, that they dislike reading novels concerned with sexual behavior, that the United States is ahead of Russia in the race for outer space, that Communism is a greater danger to the world than Fascism, that it is worthwhile to attend church every week, that they are against intermarriage between Jews and Gentiles, that they dislike comedians who make fun of our political leaders, that they are in favor of the establishment of community fallout shelters, and that they favor strict disciplining of children. Attitudes concerning socialized medicine, rugged individualism, flouridating of drinking water, the inferiority of blacks, and the admission of immigrants to this country were unrelated to scores on the F scale.

The F scale was administered to several sections of introductory psychology students, and the new seven-item attitude scale (outer space and fallout shelters were omitted) was administered at the same time. From this pool of subjects, three subgroups of 40 subjects each of authoritarians, neutrals, and equalitarians were drawn.

Several weeks later, the subjects took part in the interpersonal evaluation procedure. Four levels of attitude similarity were created.

Results. The mean attraction responses for the three levels of authoritarianism and four levels of attitude similarity are shown in Table 8–5. As in the previous investigation, there was a highly significant effect for the similarity–dissimilarity variable, but only nonsignificant effects for authoritarianism and for the interaction.

It was suggested that perhaps the F scale does not adequately measure those specific attributes that would predispose an individual to overreact to attitude similarity–dissimilarity. The F scale measures so many other

TABLE 8–5

MEAN ATTRACTION RESPONSES OF
HIGH, MEDIUM, AND LOW AUTHORITARIANS
TO STRANGERS DIFFERING IN PROPORTION
OF SIMILAR RESPONSES TO AUTHORITARIAN-RELEVANT ISSUES[a]

Proportion of similar attitudes	Equalitarians	Neutrals	Authoritarians
.86	10.90	11.90	11.90
.57	10.30	9.20	9.30
.29	7.30	7.20	7.80
.00	7.50	5.70	6.10

[a]After Sheffield and Byrne, 1967, p. 121.

characteristics of the authoritarian syndrome that perhaps it does not distinguish differences in rigidity of belief systems or differential tolerance for dissimilarity of beliefs, opinions, and attitudes. It was pointed out that the dogmatism scale of Rokeach (1960) was designed to measure the tendency toward closed versus open minds. Rokeach proposed that the more closed a person's mind, the more he should evaluate others according to the agreement or disagreement of their beliefs with respect to his own. It was proposed, therefore, that a replication of the authoritarian experiments, using the dogmatism scale rather than the F scale to categorize subjects, would yield the predicted interaction.

Dogmatism and Response to Attitude Similarity–Dissimilarity. Baskett (1966), following the proposals of Sheffield and Byrne, tested the hypothesized effects of dogmatism on the attitude–attraction function.

A total of 85 introductory psychology students responded to Rokeach's dogmatism scale and a 12-item attitude scale. Immediately afterward, they were presented with one of two standard bogus attitude scales, purportedly filled out by a stranger, and were asked to evaluate him on the IJS. The subjects were divided at the median on the dogmatism variable into high and low subgroups.

The mean attraction responses are shown in Table 8–6. There were significant similarity and dogmatism effects, but the hypothesized interaction was just short of reaching significance at the .05 level.

Thus, Baskett was able to demonstrate a significant effect for the dogmatism variable. The general relationship originally hypothesized for authoritarianism was finally substantiated with respect to this more specialized measure of rigidity and closed-mindedness.

Because the interaction only approached significance, however, Baskett decided to replicate the investigation with more clear-cut points on the

TABLE 8–6

MEAN ATTRACTION RESPONSES OF HIGH AND
LOW DOGMATIC SUBJECTS RESPONDING TO
STRANGERS WITH VARYING PROPORTIONS OF
SIMILAR ATTITUDES (TEXAS STUDENTS)[a]

	Proportion of similar attitudes		
Dogmatism	Low	Medium	High
High	5.38	7.52	11.66
Low	6.16	8.67	10.75

[a]After Baskett, 1966, p. 10.

similarity dimension. High and low dogmatic subjects were presented with strangers who were similar to themselves on either .15 or .85 of a group of 20 attitude items. In this second experiment, neither dogmatism nor the interaction reached significance. The two most plausible explanations for this inconsistency are either (*1*) there is actually no dogmatism effect and the first experiment represented chance findings or (*2*) the effect holds only in the middle range of attitude similarity and is washed out by either very high or very low proportions of similar attitudes. This latter possibility seems reasonable because in Baskett's first experiment, the standard stranger methodology leads to the majority of strangers falling in the middle ranges of similarity. Baskett hypothesized that it is the ambiguity represented by the moderate levels of similarity which leads to greater rejection by the highly dogmatic subjects.

Further data are obviously required to resolve these inconsistencies. In any event, it is clear that authoritarianism and dogmatism are not powerful mediators of the attitude–attraction relationship.

Dogmatism at Illinois. A third dogmatism experiment was conducted by Gormly and Clore (1969). From a pool of 240 undergraduates at the University of Illinois, 96 subjects were drawn on the basis of extreme scores on Rokeach's dogmatism scale. The attraction experiment involved a stranger who was similar on either eight out of ten issues or on two of ten issues.

The results are shown in Table 8–7. The similarity–dogmatism interaction is almost significant ($p < .07$) as is the high-low dogmatism difference in the .20 similarity condition. As the authors suggest "The negative findings of Baskett's data and of the data presented here strongly suggest that the

TABLE 8–7

MEAN ATTRACTION RESPONSES OF
HIGH AND LOW DOGMATIC SUBJECTS
RESPONDING TO SIMILAR AND
DISSIMILAR STRANGERS (ILLINOIS
STUDENTS)[a]

Dogmatism	Proportion of similar attitudes	
	.20	.80
High	6.00	10.75
Low	7.50	10.34

[a]Data from Gormly and Clore, 1969, p. 11.

Dogmatism Scale can not reliably predict differences in attraction ratings as a function of attitude similarity and dissimilarity [Gormly & Clore, 1969, p. 13]."

Repression–Sensitization

In the personality similarity experiment reported in Chapter 7, Byrne, Griffitt, and Stefaniak (1967) initially found a difference among repressers, neutrals, and sensitizers in their attraction responses toward strangers of varying degrees of similarity in responding to the repression–sensitization scale. Specifically, the repressers responded more negatively than the other two groups at each level of similarity. If these results were, in fact, an indication of personality differences in responding to similarity–dissimilarity, the same effect should be found in responding to similar and dissimilar attitudes.

The R-S scale was administered to over 400 male and female students in introductory psychology. On the basis of their test scores, 49 sensitizers, 51 neutrals, and 49 repressers were selected as subjects.

At another class session, a 12-item attitude scale was administered. Subjects in each personality group were randomly assigned to one of three experimental conditions varying in proportion of similar attitudes attributed to a bogus stranger: .00, .50, and 1.00. The experimental session consisted of the standard instructions and measurement of attraction.

The means of the attraction responses are presented in Table 8–8. There was the usual highly significant similarity–dissimilarity effect, but neither the personality variable nor the interaction significantly affected attraction.

This finding, as has been discussed earlier, led to a reexamination of the earlier represser–sensitizer differences. Even in the personality similarity

TABLE 8–8
MEAN ATTRACTION RESPONSES OF REPRESSERS,
NEUTRALS, AND SENSITIZERS TOWARD STRANGERS
DIFFERING IN PROPORTION OF SIMILAR ATTITUDES[a]

R-S[b] level of subjects	Proportion of similar attitudes			
	.00	.50	1.00	Total
Repressers	6.47	8.00	11.62	8.65
Neutrals	6.61	9.13	11.89	9.22
Sensitizers	5.14	8.05	12.20	8.49
Total	6.14	8.35	11.90	—

[a]After Byrne, Griffitt, and Stefaniak, 1967, p. 87.
[b]Repression–sensitization.

situation, represser–sensitizer differences disappeared when the discrepancy variable was taken into account. Thus, individual differences in the similarity–attraction relationship do not appear to be a function of differences along the dimension of repression–sensitization.

Self-Ideal Discrepancy

Response to Similar and Dissimilar Self-Descriptions. In three experiments on personality similarity by Griffitt (1966, 1969b) which were discussed in Chapter 7, individual differences in self-ideal discrepancy were hypothesized to influence attraction responses toward strangers relatively similar and dissimilar in responses to a measure of self-concept. Similarity effects were found, but there was no support for the hypothesized effect of self-ideal discrepancy. In addition, Guthwin (1970) reported no effects for different levels of self-esteem. There are, however, two other experiments which should be noted.

Response to Positively and Negatively Described Strangers. Griffitt (1967) conducted an experiment in which the stranger was represented only by varying proportions of positive and negative descriptive adjectives and in which subjects had been selected on the basis of high or low self-ideal discrepancy. He hypothesized that attraction would be a function of the positiveness of the adjective description and that the positiveness–attraction relationship would be stronger for the low self-ideal discrepancy subjects than for those high in self-ideal discrepancy. Extreme scorers on Worchel's (1957) Self Activity Inventory served as subjects. The adjectives were taken from Anderson's (1964) list. Strangers in the positive condition were described as responsible, reasonable, tactful, patient, and amusing. Those in the negative condition were ill-mannered, abusive, irresponsible, boastful, and careless. The results are shown in Table 8–9. Adjective differences

TABLE 8–9

MEAN ATTRACTION RESPONSES TOWARD
POSITIVELY AND NEGATIVELY DESCRIBED
STRANGERS BY SUBJECTS WITH HIGH AND
LOW SELF-IDEAL DISCREPANCY[a]

Self-ideal discrepancy of subject	Stranger's description	
	Negative	Positive
High	5.40	12.90
Low	3.70	11.50

[a]After Griffitt, 1967, p. 34.

yielded the expected effect, but instead of the hypothesized interaction, it was found that the self-concept measure yielded a significant main effect. Not only were positively described strangers liked better, but subjects high in self-ideal discrepancy responded more positively to both types of stranger. Griffitt suggested that a replication was needed in that the personality similarity experiments had not found a self-ideal discrepancy effect.

Response to Attitudinally Similar and Dissimilar Strangers. Hendrick and Page (1970) utilized a *Q* sort as the measure of self-esteem and a 19-item attitude scale dealing with such issues as civil rights demonstrations, the Vietnam war, drug use, and sex standards. On each attitude item, only two response alternatives were possible. Each subject was asked to respond to three stimulus persons who represented .10, .50, and .90 proportions of similar attitudes. Subjects were divided into three levels on the self-esteem variable.

On the measure of liking, there was a highly significant similarity effect, no effect for self-esteem, and an interaction that only approached significance. The latter finding, supported more strongly by other response measures, was attributable to the tendency of the moderate self-esteem subjects to respond less negatively to the dissimilar stranger than either the high or low self-esteem groups. The authors (Hendrick & Page, 1970) suggest, "If moderate self-esteem subjects are better adjusted . . . than either high or low self-esteem subjects, they should be better able to tolerate conflicting opinions different from their own. The result would be less rejection of dissimilar persons (p. 599)."

As with dogmatism, if these findings prove to be replicable ones, they suggest at best a very small and highly restricted role for self-esteem differences in moderating the similarity–attraction relationship.

Cognitive Complexity

By extrapolating from previous research and theory, Baskett (1968) hypothesized that the slope of the similarity–attraction function would be steeper for cognitively simple than for cognitively complex individuals. The personality variable was measured with a modified version of Bieri's Rep Test. From a pool of 364 students, those scoring highest and lowest in complexity were selected for the experiment.

The stranger's responses to a 24-item attitude scale were prepared to represent .20, .50, or .80 similarity. The results are depicted in Table 8–10. The only significant effect was that of attitude similarity–dissimilarity. Thus, one more personality variable was found to be irrelevant in the similarity–attraction relationship.

TABLE 8–10

MEAN ATTRACTION RESPONSES OF COGNITIVELY
SIMPLE AND COMPLEX INDIVIDUALS TOWARD
STRANGERS VARYING IN PROPORTION OF
SIMILAR ATTITUDES[a]

Cognitive Complexity of subjects	Proportion of similar attitudes		
	.20	.50	.80
Complex	6.16	8.00	10.40
Simple	6.72	6.94	9.44

[a]Data from Baskett, 1968, p. 19.

Anxiety

Test anxiety. Two anxiety measures have been used in the attempt to predict individual differences in the attraction situation. Reagor and Clore (1970) in the experiment discussed in Chapter 7 manipulated similarity of vocabulary test responses and investigated differences on the Mandler-Sarason (1952) Test Anxiety Questionnaire. Contrary to their prediction, there was a tendency for the high anxiety subjects to respond less negatively toward the dissimilar stranger and less positively toward the similar stranger than the low anxiety subjects. The means are shown in Table 8–11. In explanation, it was suggested that those high in test anxiety place less confidence in their ability to make any accurate judgments about others than do those low in test anxiety.

Manifest Anxiety Scale. Sachs (1969) employed the Manifest Anxiety Scale (MAS) (J. A. Taylor, 1953). First, it should be pointed out that the MAS has been found to correlate in the .40s and .50s with the Mandler-Sarason scale by several investigators (Byrne, 1966) and .91 with the R-S

TABLE 8–11

MEAN ATTRACTION RESPONSES OF HIGH AND
LOW TEST ANXIETY SUBJECTS TOWARD SIMILAR
AND DISSIMILAR STRANGERS[a]

Test anxiety questionnaire	Proportion of similar responses	
	.17	.83
High anxiety	8.60	10.10
Low anxiety	8.00	11.10

[a]After Reagor and Clore, 1970, p. 219.

TABLE 8–12

MEAN ATTRACTION RESPONSES OF HIGH
AND LOW MANIFEST ANXIETY INDIVIDUALS
TOWARD SIMILAR AND DISSIMILAR STRANGERS[a]

Manifest anxiety scale	Proportion of similar attitudes	
	.00	1.00
High anxiety	6.60	11.65
Low anxiety	6.04	10.87

[a]Data from Sachs, 1969, p. 14.

scale (Joy, 1963). Since repression–sensitization has been found to be un-related to the attraction response and test anxiety is found to yield a weak interaction effect in the similarity–attraction function, to predict an effect for manifest anxiety requires the help of a Quija board. The results, sum-marized in Table 8–12, provide one more example of the excitement gene-rated by personality variables in attraction research. It was found that the high anxiety individuals responded significantly more positively toward similar and dissimilar strangers than did low anxiety individuals. Thus, anxiety and anxiety-correlated measures have been found to yield a positive main effect, an interaction effect, and no effect.

Need for Approval

For a number of reasons, the Marlowe–Crowne Social Desirability Scale (M–C scale) (Crowne & Marlowe, 1964) would seem to be a likely predictor of attraction responses within the present paradigm. Conceptual-ized as a measure of need for approval, this trait is one which would logically be related to interpersonal behavior. Several studies have employed this variable and again the outcome is a mixed bag.

Response to Strangers with Expectations of Meeting or Not Meeting. Bloom (1968) exposed 54 male high-school students to the attitudes of a stranger, and all subjects received a .88 similar stranger. Half of the subjects were led to expect a meeting with the stranger and half were not; half had obtained high scores on the M–C scale, and half low scores. The attraction results are shown in Table 8–13. Need for approval yielded a significant interaction with the experimental manipulation. The primary effect here was the lower attraction responses of the low need for approval individuals in the nonmeet condition. Bloom suggested that high approval motivation serves to inhibit negative attraction responses.

TABLE 8–13

MEAN ATTRACTION RESPONSES OF HIGH AND
LOW MARLOWE-CROWNE SCALE SUBJECTS IN
MEET AND NONMEET CONDITIONS[a]

Marlowe-Crowne Social Desiribility Scale	Experimental conditions	
	Nonmeet	Meet
High	7.15	8.21
Low	5.53	7.83

[a]After Bloom, 1968, p. 12.

Response to Similarity and Dissimilarity of Need for Approval. Nowicki (1969)* manipulated similarity of responses on the M–C scale with .50 and .75 similar strangers for subjects with high and low scores on the M–C scale. In addition to a highly significant similarity effect, there was a weak main effect of need for approval on attraction. Those with high scores responded more positively than did those with middle or low scores and thus, added support to the Bloom findings.

Response to Attitude Similarity and to Personal Evaluations. In a further study of this variable (Ettinger, 1967; Ettinger, Nowicki, & Nelson, 1970), subjects differing in M–C scale scores were placed in an attitude similarity experiment (.00, .50, and 1.00 similarity) and in an evaluation experiment (.00, .50, or 1.00 positive evaluations). There was no M–C effect in the attitude similarity task (unlike the two previous studies), but those high in need for approval were more positive toward the stranger than were those medium or low in need for approval in the personal evaluation task ($p < .05$).

Mueller (1969), in an experiment to be described in Chapter 9, manipulated both attitude similarity and personal evaluations. For the 80 subjects in her experiment, attraction responses correlated .04 with scores on the M–C scale.

In a very extensive and most determined pursuit of a significant relationship between attraction and need for approval, Wiener (1970) conducted a series of similarity–attraction experiments and measured the 543 subjects on the M–C scale. Attraction responses were found to correlate a convincing .00 with need for approval scores. In addition, he

---

*In this and the following study, the attraction measure was altered by adding a third item. Though this three-item scale is highly correlated with the usual two-item scale, the means are not directly comparable to those reported throughout this book and hence will be omitted here.

found nonsignificant correlations between attraction and scores on the Edwards Social Desirability Scale, the D-30 Depression Scale, the test anxiety questionnaire, and the dominance, submission, love, and hate dimensions of Leary's Interpersonal Checklist. One cannot prove the null hypothesis, but one may come to have great respect for it.

Thus, in a repetition of a now familiar theme, need for approval has been found to be unrelated to attraction, to be positively related, and to be positively related only under special circumstances.

Affiliative Needs and Fears

The last group of individual differences variables to be considered here would also seem to be the most obvious predictor of attraction responses. Need for affiliation (*n* Affiliation or *n* Aff) is defined as concern for establishing, maintaining, or restoring a positive affective relationship with others. Fear of failure in social situations involves anxiety, concern with the evaluations of others, and, at the extreme limits, avoidance of social–evaluative interactions. A number of arguments suggest that these constructs should be maximally useful as predictors because of their specific relevance to the attraction situation (Mischel, 1968).

Projective Measure of n Affiliation. Various studies have indicated that affiliation need is positively related to approval-seeking behavior as rated by peers (Atkinson, Heyns, & Veroff, 1954), self-ratings of popularity (French & Chadwick, 1956), and the frequency with which telephone calls are made and letters written (Lansing & Heyns, 1959). On the basis of such findings, two investigations (Byrne, 1961b, 1962)* were conducted. The initial proposal was that as *n* Affiliation increased, positive response to other people would increase. In a situation separate from the attraction experiments, the Atkinson (1958) procedure for measuring affiliation need was used. Subjects responded to four pictures presented on slides with brief stories which were later scored for *n* Aff. In the experimental session, the attitudes of strangers were presented at one of eight levels of similarity ranging from .00 to 1.00. The resulting attraction responses are shown in Table 8–14. Analysis indicates a significant similarity effect, a significant affiliation need effect, and a significant interaction.

The nature of these differences can best be seen in Fig. 8–4. One point of interest is that if the various levels of affiliation need are ignored, the usual similarity–attraction function is found. A second point of interest is that individuals high in affiliation need tend to respond to a stranger more

---

*The data for these two investigations have been combined in the present report.

TABLE 8–14

MEAN ATTRACTION RESPONSES OF INDIVIDUALS LOW, MEDIUM,
AND HIGH IN AFFILIATION NEED TOWARD STRANGERS AT
VARIOUS LEVELS OF ATTITUDE SIMILARITY

Need for affiliation	Proportion of similar attitudes				
	.00	.14–.29	.43–.57	.71–.86	1.00
High	6.60	10.10	9.11	11.80	11.85
Medium	5.48	7.30	9.80	11.75	11.21
Low	7.85	7.62	7.67	10.33	11.15

positively than do those low in affiliation need, except at the lowest levels
of similarity. The low *n* Aff individuals, in fact, seem indifferent to the
stranger except at relatively high levels of similarity. The most unusual group
is composed of medium *n* Aff individuals who respond like the high group
at the upper levels of similarity and then give the most negative responses
at the lower levels of similarity. It was proposed that high *n* Aff indicated
primarily an approach motive and positive attitudes toward others, that low
n Aff indicated an avoidance motive and negative or indifferent attitudes

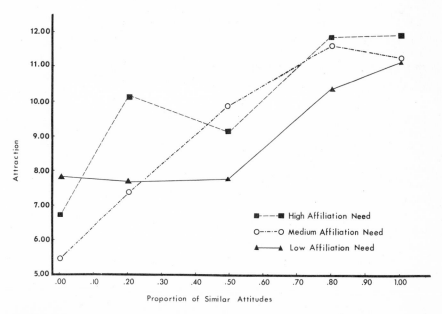

Fig. 8–4. The relationship between proportion of similar attitudes and attraction,
plotted separately for individuals low, medium, and high in need for affiliation.

toward others, and that medium n Aff indicated conflicted individuals who desired to affiliate but strongly feared rejection. Subsequent investigations by Byrne, McDonald, and Mikawa (1963) and by Hamilton (1964) added support to this formulation.

Birth order. Another intriguing bit of support for the importance of affiliation need is Nowicki's (1969) finding that subjects who were first-born in their family responded more positively than did middle- or last-borns. Schachter's (1959) formulation of the relationship between birth order and affiliation need suggests that this is an important confirmation of the n Aff findings.

Response to Positive and Negative Ratings. Before the shouts of "Eureka!" get out of hand, however, the usual negative results with an individual differences variable must be reported. McDonald (1962), in an experiment to be described in Chapter 11, manipulated the positiveness of ratings received from strangers and also obtained a need for affiliation measure on each subject in the manner described above. He found no relationship between n Aff and attraction.

Social Avoidance and Distress Scale. Watson and Friend (1969) defined social-evaluative anxiety as "the experience of distress, discomfort, fear, anxiety, etc., in social situations; as the deliberate avoidance of social situations; and finally as a fear of receiving negative evaluations from others [p. 448]." They built scales to measure both social avoidance and distress (SAD) and fear of negative evaluation. The SAD scale has been employed with consistent results in two attraction experiments. The scale consists of items such as:

I usually feel calm and comfortable at social occasions. (F)
I try to avoid talking to people unless I know them well. (T)
Being introduced to people makes me tense and nervous. (T)
I try to avoid formal social occasions. (T)

R. E. Smith (1970) proposed that an individual high in social anxiety would be strongly motivated to avoid social disapproval and that similar and dissimilar attitudes would have greater reinforcement magnitude for them than for individuals low in social anxiety. It was predicted that individuals with high scores on the SAD scale would be more positive toward agreeing strangers and more negative toward disagreeing strangers than would individuals with low scores on the SAD scale. Subjects at the University of Washington who represented high and low thirds of the SAD distribution were exposed to strangers who were .08 or .92 similar on a 24-item attitude scale. The results, shown in Table 8–15, clearly supported Smith's hypothesis in that the high SAD subjects showed the greatest similarity–attraction effect. Further analysis indicated that the personality

TABLE 8–15

MEAN ATTRACTION RESPONSES OF
INDIVIDUALS HIGH AND LOW IN
SOCIAL AVOIDANCE AND DISTRESS
(SAD) TOWARD SIMILAR AND
DISSIMILAR STRANGERS (UNIVERSITY
OF WASHINGTON)[a]

	Proportion of similar attitudes	
SAD	.08	.92
High	4.37	11.39
Low	6.06	10.87

[a]Data from R. E. Smith, 1970.

variable yielded significant differences only in the dissimilar condition. Thus, the socially anxious person was found to respond more negatively to disagreeing attitude statements than the socially nonanxious person.

Gouaux, Lamberth, and Friedrich (to be published) administered the SAD to 111 Purdue students and divided them into high, medium, and low subgroups. The subjects were later given the 24-item attitude scale of a stranger who was either .17 or .83 similar. The results are shown in Table 8–16. As in the Smith experiment, the personality variable yields effects solely in the dissimilar condition. Not only are the high and low SAD groups strikingly similar to those of Smith, but the medium SAD group falls neatly between the two extreme groups. In correlational terms, SAD scores and attraction responses correlate −.33.

TABLE 8–16

MEAN ATTRACTION RESPONSES OF
INDIVIDUALS HIGH AND LOW IN
SOCIAL AVOIDANCE AND DISTRESS (SAD)
TOWARD SIMILAR AND DISSIMILAR
STRANGERS (PURDUE UNIVERSITY)[a]

	Proportion of similar attitudes	
SAD	.17	.83
High	5.70	9.87
Low	8.00	10.95

[a]Data from Gouaux, Lamberth, and Friedrich, to be published.

Although it is perhaps premature to celebrate the identification of personality variables that should be given a secure home within the attraction paradigm, it appears that need for affiliation and social avoidance and distress may play precisely that role. Considering the rather dismal array of nonsuccess with authoritarianism, dogmatism, repression–sensitization, self-ideal discrepancy, cognitive complexity, test anxiety, manifest anxiety, and need for approval, it is somewhat gratifying to find that individual differences in responding to attitude similarity may be in part predictable. It would seem that success depended on the utilization of personality measures dealing with behavior closely related to that which occurs in the attraction situation.

Chapter 9 / **Response Generality: II. Other Responses**

One of the most important and least understood aspects of the attraction paradigm has been the decision to concentrate on a single response variable as an initial research strategy. That decision was not made because of a conviction that we had discovered the best of all possible indices of attraction. The decision was not made because we lacked the inventiveness to conceive of any alternative measures. The decision was not made because we felt that there is only one way in which interpersonal attraction can be expressed or that attraction must necessarily be limited to a simple, unidimensional concept. Because each of those incorrect assumptions has been expressed by one or more observers, a word or two of explanation would perhaps prove helpful.

The measurement of any response variable presents us with two somewhat conflicting requirements. On the one hand, the operation chosen to define a behavior represents a partially arbitrary compromise between a theoretical construct and pragmatism. Once the decision is made by a particular investigator, progress is dependent upon operational consistency in subsequent investigations. Misplaced creativity in devising new and different measures of the same construct for each new experiment can only bring empirical and conceptual chaos. A conflicting demand, however, arises from the fact that we do not have standard, accepted behavioral measures analogous to measures of time, temperature, or distance. When a given operation is labelled "aggression" or "dependency" or "dominance," we still must inquire about its validity. Thus, a reasonable research strategy would seem to be one that involves operational consistency tempered by periodic exploration of the meaning of the operation.

Though the problem in the present context may be seen as one concerning the "validity" of the attraction measure, the definition of that issue is not always clear:

> It seems possible to conceptualize sociometric measures in such a way that one purports to measure nothing more than verbal choice behavior, which is manifestly true, and therefore requires no further demonstration of validity. Measures of interpersonal attraction assess a response or series of responses that are ordinarily conceptualized as dependent variables. Thus, it is as meaningful to discuss the validity of sociometric choices or attraction ratings as it is to discuss the validity of running speed in a straight alley runway, the validity of lever pressing in a Skinner box, or the validity of a series of paired-associate words on a memory drum. All such techniques permit the quantification of some aspect of a class of responses. They are useful to the extent that lawful relationships can be established between such response variables and other variables. If such relationships are established, the response measures are of obvious interest in their own right and the question of their validity is a minor one [Lindzey & Byrne, 1968, p. 480].

The response to the two attraction items of the Interpersonal Judgment Scale (IJS) is not conceptualized as either an imperfect substitute for everyday life attraction or as an inadequate index of the subject's "real" though unobservable feelings of attraction. Rather, the IJS operation defining attraction constitutes the dependent variable which our research is designed to explicate. This may seem to be a niggling distinction, but a great deal of confusion has centered around just such questions (Byrne, 1964a).

Lindzey and Byrne (1968) go on to consider the problem of criterion-related validity:

> Failure to observe substantial relations between verbal behavior on the sociometric measure and physical behavior in another situation . . . is not necessarily an indictment of the validity of the assessment device (or of the validity of the behavioral measure). For example, if one defines prejudice toward minority groups in terms of the extent to which an individual selectively chooses or avoids members of various minority groups, it would not necessarily be an indication of the invalidity of this measure of prejudice to show that it did not correspond closely to prejudice as measured by one of the paper-and-pencil attitude scales. Both sets of responses are undoubtedly determined by a series of antecedents, and not necessarily the same antecedents. . . .
> The same consideration applies to differences between choice behavior as revealed in sociometric measures and overt choice behavior as revealed in an observational study. There are many determinants or conditions which influence overt behavior (e.g., physical constraints, social obligations, perceived likelihood of reciprocation, estimation of the social acceptability of a given choice) that do not have the same effect on verbal choice behavior, and vice versa. Nevertheless, the relationship between the two types of behavior is of interest [pp. 481–482].

It may be seen, then, that any relationship or lack of relationship between the attraction response and other responses elicited concurrently by the same stimulus variables may be an interesting research question. The concern is not with the psychometric evaluation of a measuring device but with establishing the generality of a construct.

What, then, do we know of the generality of attraction as measured by the IJS?

ALTERNATIVE VERBAL MEASURES OF ATTRACTION

Although attraction obviously could be measured in an almost infinite number of different ways, the equivalence and, hence, the interchangeability of any two such measures cannot be assumed in the absence of empirical evidence. To the extent that different verbal indices of interpersonal reactions are found to be related, the meaning of each is broadened. Data are available on four alternative paper and pencil response measures.

Social Distance Scale

As part of his dissertation research, Schwartz (1966) obtained IJS attraction responses and responses to a social distance scale concerning feelings about a stranger from 109 high-school students. The social distance scale (Table 9–1) consisted of 10 items dealing with social interactions of varying degrees of closeness. A total social distance score was obtained by summing the number of "yes" responses. The two measures of attraction correlated .67 for the 47 male subjects and .66 for the 62 female subjects. Thus, a substantial correlation is found between the IJS measure of attraction and this index of social distance.

Willingness to Expend Effort for Another Person

At the University of Georgia, Abraham Tesser and Mo Kian conducted an experiment which dealt with attraction and reinforcement theory. With respect to our immediate interests, however, they also extended the response measure by giving the IJS items and six "obstacle" items. The latter dealt with the extent to which an individual is willing to expend effort in different situations in order to help someone. Presumably, as attraction toward another individual increases, the amount of trouble which one is willing to undergo on his behalf should also increase.

The 42 undergraduates in their experiment responded to both verbal measures of attraction. The obstacle items and the correlation between each and the IJS attraction measure are given in Table 9–2. The two

TABLE 9–1
SOCIAL DISTANCE SCALE[a]

I think I would be willing:
Yes No
—— ——to invite this person home to dinner
—— ——to go to a party to which this person was invited
—— ——to go to the same school with this person
—— ——to have this person as a member of my social group or club
—— ——to live in the same apartment house with this person and his family
—— ——to sit next to this person in a class or meeting
—— ——to work on a committee at school with this person
—— ——to have this person as a close personal friend
—— ——to have this person as a substitute teacher
—— ——to have this person as an assistant to my teacher

[a]After Schwartz, 1966, p. 117.

TABLE 9–2
CORRELATIONS BETWEEN TESSER AND KIAN OBSTACLE ITEMS AND INTERPERSONAL
JUDGMENT SCALE ATTRACTION RESPONSE[a]

Obstacle item
    If this person were to be arrested for a traffic violation,
——A. I would make every effort to bail him out.
——B. I would visit him in jail.
——C. I would send him a letter of concern.
——D. I would let him take care of his own problem.
Correlations = .61 and .60

    Assume this person is going to be married in San Francisco in the middle of the school
year. Under this condition,
——A. I would try to get to San Francisco for the wedding.
——B. I would send him a gift and a telegram of congratulation.
——C. I would send him a card.
——D. I would ignore the wedding.
Correlations = .60 and .56

    If this person needed money for his education, I would be willing to help him up to
——A. 50% of my monthly allowance.
——B. 20% of my monthly allowance.
——C. 10% of my monthly allowance.
——D. none of my monthly allowance.
Correlations = .49 and .28.

    Assume that you are trying to form a social club among your friends at school. After a
few of you have gotten the club started, this person applies for membership. Most of your
friends seem to be against the admission of this person. Under this condition,
——A. I would say that if they were going to automatically rule out this person I wouldn't
        want to be in the club.
——B. I would make a strong case for his membership but if the majority went against his
        membership, I would go along with the majority and maintain my friendship with
        him outside.

TABLE 9–2 (*continued*)

——C. I would probably wait and see what the majority finally decided and then go along with them.
——D. I would side with those who were against his admission.
Correlations = .50 and .59

If this person runs for the Presidency of the Student Body at the University,
——A. I would give up a great deal of my study time to campaign for him.
——B. I would give up a little of my time to campaign for him.
——C. I would vote for him.
——D. I would not vote for him.
Correlations = .58 and .51

My sister (brother) takes a strong interest in this person but the rest of my family dislike the person. Under this condition,
——A. I would encourage my sister (brother) to maintain the interest.
——B. I would suggest to my sister (brother) to maintain only a friendly interest in this person.
——C. I probably wouldn't say anything to my sister (brother).
——D. I would warn my sister (brother) of possible adverse consequences.
Correlations = .32 and .64.

---

[a]Data from Tesser, 1969, personal communication.

correlation coefficients represent data concerning responses to two different strangers.

Once again, a series of verbal responses dealing with interpersonal behavior is found to correlate substantially with our standard measure of attraction.

Social Choice

In a Kansas State dissertation, Moss (1969) conducted an experiment which included social choice in a potential dating situation and attraction as measured by the IJS.

The subjects were 40 male undergraduates. The social choice measure is best described by reference to Moss' (1969) instructions to his subjects:

> I am going to show you a series of 8 pictures of girls. I would like you to assume that you were at a party and that these 8 girls were there also. I would like you to look through them, and tell me which one you would approach first with the hope of asking out on a date. Then, place the others in the order that you would approach them. Please be realistic and try to imagine yourself in the situation before deciding which one you would approach. You can take as much time as you like [p. 26].

The slides were reshown later, and the subjects were asked to fill out an IJS concerning each of the eight girls.

The relationship between social choice and the attraction measure may be seen in Table 9–3. The correlation between rank order of choice and attraction was found to be .64.

TABLE 9–3

MEAN ATTRACTION RESPONSES TOWARD
POTENTIAL DATES ARRANGED IN ORDER OF
SOCIAL CHOICE[a]

Rank order of girls as potential dates	Attraction
1	12.30
2	11.30
3	10.98
4	10.45
5	10.00
6	8.48
7	7.98
8	7.32

[a]After Moss, 1969, p. 49.

Dating, Marriage, and Sex

As part of a computer dating experiment in which 44 couples were introduced, spent a brief time together, and afterward evaluated one another, Byrne, Ervin, and Lamberth (1970) asked each subject to rate his or her date with respect to desirability as a date and as a marriage partner and with respect to sexual attractiveness and physical attractiveness.

In Table 9–4 are shown the correlations between attraction responses and each of these four additional rating scales. Again, the data are clear in indicating positive relationships.

In summary, four alternative paper and pencil approaches to the measurement of attraction have been found to correlate significantly with the IJS measure. Although these findings add something to our knowledge of the generality of our response measure, it should also be noted that the correlations are far from 1.00. Thus, not one of the measures described here yields responses sufficiently like our measure of attraction to warrant

TABLE 9–4

CORRELATIONS BETWEEN ATTRACTION RESPONSES AND
RATINGS OF A DATE[a]

Rating Scales	Correlation (male subjects)	Correlation (female subjects)
Desirability as a date	.71	.82
Desirability as a spouse	.66	.73
Sexual attractiveness	.41	.72
Physical attractiveness	.39	.60

[a]Data from Byrne, Ervin, and Lamberth, 1970.

the substitution of one for another. In addition, one could expect these various interrelated measures to yield highly similar but not identical results in a variety of situations. Depending on the particular context and the particular independent variables, one might even obtain uncorrelated or (conceivably) negatively correlated responses in specific situations. An obvious example is the fact that the last two studies involved opposite-sex strangers. If the stranger had been of the same sex, it seems unlikely that attraction would have been significantly related to ratings of desirability as a spouse. The point is simply that a degree of generality of the response measure has been established, but the limitations to that generality must not be ignored.

NONVERBAL MEASURES OF ATTRACTION

The fact that various verbal measures of attraction are intercorrelated is not of great concern to some investigators. In fact, the notion is expressed in a variety of ways that verbal measures, especially those obtained by means of paper and pencil, are inadequate. Verbal behavior is seen as inferior to or not quite as real as nonverbal behavior. An example of this orientation is provided by Aronson (1970):

> Most of the time social psychologists working in this area display a touching and primitive faith in the mightiness of paper-and-pencil measures of attraction. I think that this is a serious example of myopia. Of course, I am as guilty (and as primitive, touching, and myopic) as the next guy on this score. Most of us get stuck on these measures because it's so easy to collect data that way. The problem is that it's also easy for the subject to fill out a rating scale—too easy. Since no commitment and no work is required, there is danger that a subject who is merely required to circle a number reflecting how much he likes another person either may not bother to take it very seriously, or may try to answer in a way that makes him look good to the experimenter [p. 166].

One could argue that the body of research based on the IJS measure would be difficult to explain away on the basis Aronson suggests. For example, subjects would have had to understand relatively complicated theoretical formulations, to take them very seriously, and to try to make themselves "look good" even when the experimenters were confused about the expected outcome (see, for example, the series of studies dealing with topic importance). The Lamberth and Byrne (in press) studies of demand characteristics also argue against Aronson's facile thesis. Nevertheless, the fact remains that the term "attraction" has surplus meaning which suggests its relationship to behavior beyond that of verbal responses to a rating scale. Without evidence that such relationships exist, the meaning of the response measure must necessarily be circumscribed.

What nonverbal behaviors might we expect to be indicative of inter-personal attraction?

Interpersonal Judgment Apparatus

For a series of investigations requiring repeated measures of attrac-tion, it seemed desirable to move away from the paper and pencil IJS. The aim was an apparatus that allowed the subject to indicate attraction by means of a simple physical manipulation. Another goal was to attempt to produce a response dimension which was closely equivalent to the specific numerical values of the IJS. Tongue in cheek, the author considered the construction of a brass instrument on which the IJS items were inscribed along with electronic response buttons next to each statement. A second fantasy was a giant-sized printing of the items on the floor with instructions for the subjects to walk to the statement best indicating his feelings. Our guess was that either the brass-instrument approach or the locomotor ap-proach would impress those who worry about the utility of verbal responses. Instead, we progressed to wooden-instrument psychology. This work was undertaken with William Griffitt and Oliver London.

A 30-in. rectangular wooden box was constructed with a series of 13 round holes cut into the top. The holes on each end and the center hole were labelled with printed statements (see Fig. 9–1) based on the attraction items of the IJS. A subject indicates his response toward a stimulus person by inserting a small round wooden indicator disc into the appropriate slot. Responses are scored on an ordinal scale ranging from 2 to 14.

In a pilot study, 20 subjects who had responded to a 12-item attitude scale were given the usual interpersonal judgment instructions except that there was no mention of intelligence, adjustment, etc. In addition, the use of the Interpersonal Judgment Apparatus (IJA) was explained. The scales

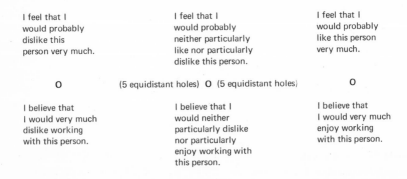

Fig. 9–1. Wording on either extreme and center of Interpersonal Judgment Apparatus.

of the stranger constituted .17, .50, or .83 proportion of similar attitudes.

The attraction responses predicted by the Byrne–Nelson function (with the IJS measure of attraction) would be 7.54, 9.34, and 11.14 for the three conditions. The obtained means were 5.57, 9.00, and 10.75. Though the fit is obviously not as close as would be desired, the general magnitude of the responses correspond reasonably well to those predicted. The three conditions are, of course, significantly different from one another.

These results suggest that the IJA yields responses fairly comparable to the paper and pencil measure. Wooden-instrument psychology proved to be a success.

Proximity

In truth, the critics of paper and pencil measures would not be faked out for long by subterfuges such as the IJA. It is verbal behavior which is actually the crux of their discomfort. Our next step was to consider various behavioral indices of interpersonal attraction.

A promising variable would seem to be what Sommer (1959) and others call "personal space," the physical distance which an individual chooses to place between himself and another person. Propinquity as a determinant of attraction has a relatively long history in psychological and sociological research (e.g., Bossard, 1932; Byrne & Buehler, 1955; Davie & Reeves, 1939; Festinger, Schachter, & Back, 1950; Simon & Lawton, 1967). Attraction as a determinant of propinquity has a somewhat shorter research history. It has been found, for example, that physical distance between two individuals is related to degree of acquaintance or positiveness of the relationship between them (e.g., Duncan, 1969; Levinger & Gunner, 1967; Little, 1965; Mehrabian, 1968). Would the manipulation of attitude similarity have the same effect on voluntary proximity as it has on the IJS responses?

Sitting Side-by-Side. Byrne, Baskett, and Hodges (in press) used 20 male and 20 female undergraduates in what was purported to be a small-group study. Each subject participated with two undergraduate confederates of his or her same sex who posed as students from another class. The three students were asked to indicate to one another their responses to a 24-item attitude scale. It was arranged that the subject would give his or her responses first, followed by one of the confederates who agreed with him on 22 of the issues and then the other confederate who agreed on only 2 of the issues.

Afterward, the three individuals were separated and the subject responded to the IJS. The effect of attitude similarity on attraction was the familiar one, and the means are shown in Table 9–5. The crucial question dealt with the other response measure. The subject was asked to join the

TABLE 9–5
ATTITUDE SIMILARITY AND ATTRACTION
(SIDE-BY-SIDE STUDY)[a]

Subject	Dissimilar confederate	Similar confederate
Males	7.20	11.65
Females	6.55	11.30

[a]After Byrne, Baskett, and Hodges, in press.

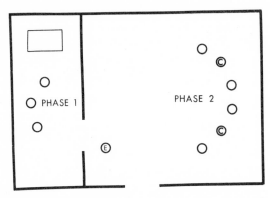

Fig. 9–2. Room arrangement in side-by-side proximity experiment. In phase 1, subject and confederates interacted to discuss attitude topics. In phase 2, after completing the IJS, subject joined the confederates (c) and sat in one of the empty chairs. (After Byrne, Baskett, and Hodges, in press.)

TABLE 9–6
ATTITUDE SIMILARITY AND SEATING CHOICE:
(SIDE-BY-SIDE STUDY)[a]

Subject	Sat beside dissimilar confederate	Sat beside similar confederate
Males	12	8
Females	4	16

[a]After Byrne, Baskett, and Hodges, in press.

two confederates after responding to the IJS; they were seated in an adjoining area as shown in Fig. 9–2. Unlike the IJS findings, seating preferences reveal a decided sex difference. The responses are shown in Table 9–6. Analysis indicated that females showed a significant preference for sitting nearer the agreeing confederate than the disagreeing one, whereas males did not indicate such a preference.

Thus, physical distance as measured in this particular situation was related to the attraction measure only for female subjects. One of the possible explanations for the sex differences was provided by previous research. Sommer (1959) studied the seating arrangements of individuals interacting in small discussion groups. Among the findings were striking sex differences in that "only the females chose to sit alongside the decoy. The males overwhelmingly preferred the chair opposite the decoy. This result parallels the observation that females in our culture will often be seen holding hands or kissing other females, whereas these behaviors are uncommon for males [p. 258]." Therefore, the possibility is raised that the experimental setting was inadvertently designed as one in which females could reasonably express their interpersonal attitudes in behavioral choices but one in which males could not easily do so. To test this proposition, a second proximity study was undertaken.

Sitting Face-to-Face. Once again, subjects were exposed to two confederates who posed as fellow subjects, one of whom expressed views congruent with those of the subject and one of whom expressed divergent views (Byrne *et al.*, in press). Afterward, the subject was asked to sit down with the confederates, the seating choice being confined to sitting opposite the similar stranger or opposite the dissimilar one.

The subjects were 30 males and 30 females. On a supposedly random basis, the subject was chosen to watch a televised interview with the other two students. The responses of the interviewees were arranged to be .17 and .83 similar to those of the subjects on 12 topics. Afterward, the subject evaluated the two strangers on the IJS with results as shown in Table 9–7.

During the interview, the two confederates were seated at a card table facing the camera. After the interview, the subject was asked to enter the video room and sit down at the card table. As may be seen in Fig. 9–3, two chairs were available to the subject, one facing the similar stranger and one facing the dissimilar stranger. The seating preferences are shown in Table 9–8. The hypothesis that males would choose to sit across from the preferred

TABLE 9–7
ATTITUDE SIMILARITY AND ATTRACTION (FACE-TO-FACE STUDY)[a]

Subject	Dissimilar confederate	Similar confederate
Males	7.38	10.69
Females	7.81	10.52

[a]After Byrne, Baskett, and Hodges, in press.

TABLE 9–8
ATTITUDE SIMILARITY AND SEATING CHOICE
(FACE-TO-FACE STUDY)[a]

Subject	Sat across from dissimilar confederate	Sat across from similar confederate
Males	8	21
Females	14	13

[a]After Byrne, Baskett, and Hodges, in press.

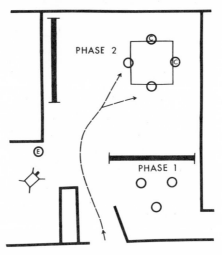

Fig. 9–3. Room arrangement in face-to-face proximity experiment. In phase 1, subject and confederates received instructions and then the subject was taken to a separate room to watch a closed-circuit television broadcast of confederates being interviewed. In phase 2, after completing the IJS, subject joined the confederates (c) and sat in one of the empty chairs. (After Byrne, Baskett, and Hodges, in press.)

stranger was confirmed. In this particular experimental arrangement, it was the females who revealed no systematic preferences.

Before an examination of the meaning of these findings, one additional study of proximity will be described.

Standing Side-by-Side with a Member of the Opposite Sex. A third study of proximity (Byrne, Ervin, & Lamberth, 1970) was included as part of the computer dating experiment mentioned earlier. Following a 30-minute coke date, each of the 44 couples returned to the experimental room for final instructions concerning the IJS, etc. An unobtrusive measure of attraction was obtained while the two subjects were standing together in front of the experimenter's desk. The distance between the two individuals was noted on a simple ordinal scale ranging from 0 (touching one another) to 5 (standing at opposite extremes of the desk).

It was found that IJS attraction correlated between −.36 (females) and −.48 (males) with the physical distance measure. Thus, the greater the liking for the partner, the closer together the two individuals stood.

Cautions about Proximity as an Index of Attraction. As long as the IJS measure and the proximity responses are conceptualized in relative terms, the findings are clear. Differences in attraction as measured by the paper and pencil scale are significantly related to proximity. Can we then say, in Sunday supplement style, that seating choices and standing distances reveal one's likes and dislikes? To an even greater extent than with the verbal measures of attraction, proximity variables cannot be considered as interchangeable indices of that which is measured by the IJS. If one wished to pursue proximity as a primary dependent variable, it should be noted that data of the type just presented constitute only a primitive first step. For example, it appears that the physical arrangement of chairs and probably of the total situation are extremely important determinants of the behavior in question. A considerable amount of systematic research would be required to determine with any degree of confidence precisely what are the relevant and irrelevant aspects of the experimental setting. With those cautions in mind concerning instant adoption of these particular behavioral measures as a substitute for verbal responses, it should also be noted that such findings contribute greatly to the generality of attraction as studied in the paradigm.

Visual Interaction

A somewhat different type of interpersonal behavior, visual interaction, was the focus of two experiments by M. Efran (1969). He cited a number of otherwise divergent investigations which suggest that visual behavior is related to attraction (e.g., Argyle, 1967; J. Efran, 1968; J. Efran & Broughton, 1966; Exline, 1963) and designed two investigations in an attempt to bring this behavioral variable within the present paradigm.

Two Strangers. In the first experiment, 25 female subjects were presented with the supposed attitudinal responses of two bogus strangers. One was similar to the subject on 12 out of 12 items, whereas the other was dissimilar on 12 out of 12 items. The subject filled out an IJS on each stranger and then was asked to interact with two stooges who were supposed to have been the authors of the attitude responses. The subject's visual behavior during the interaction was recorded. The three individuals sat at a circular table, and each told a 2-minute story in response to a TAT card; the subject responded first. After the interaction, the IJS was given again.

TABLE 9–9

MEAN ATTRACTION RESPONSES TOWARD
SIMILAR AND DISSIMILAR STRANGERS BEFORE
AND AFTER INTERACTING[a]

Subjects	Proportion of similar responses	
	.00	1.00
Before interacting	6.33	11.62
After interacting	8.04	10.46

[a]After M. Efran, 1969, p. 67.

Attraction, both before and after the interaction, was found to be determined by attitude similarity. One serendipitous finding, which may be seen in Table 9–9, is that the difference in attraction toward the two strangers decreased following the interaction. The visual behavior of the subject was investigated with respect to amount of time spent looking at each confederate and number of times the subjects looked at each confederate. With neither variable was there a significant difference in visual behavior toward the two strangers.

One Stranger. In the second experiment, each of 34 female subjects received the attitude scale of one stranger who was either similar on 1.00 of 12 attitudes or .00 of 12 attitudes. An IJS was then given, the subject had a brief interaction (again, each told a 2-minute TAT story) with the confederate during which visual behavior was recorded, and then the IJS was readministered.

Once again, attitude similarity was found to have a significant effect on attraction and once again the second administration of the IJS indicated less differential attraction toward similar and dissimilar strangers following interaction. With respect to visual behavior, the looking time was greater when the subject believed the stranger to be attitudinally similar than when she believed the stranger to be dissimilar. The number of gazes did not show a significant effect. An additional analysis revealed a correlation of .37 between attraction as measured by the IJS and total looking time. Thus, the proposed relationship between visual behavior and the paper and pencil measure of attraction was confirmed only under the conditions of Efran's second experiment.

Cautions about Visual Interaction As a Measure of Attraction. As with the other alternative response measures, the findings here suggest that under certain conditions still another behavior is correlated with our attraction measure. It should be even more obvious in the present context that the behavior in question could not be readily substituted for the attraction response (or vice versa) without considerably more knowledge concerning its determinants. M. Efran (1969) suggests:

> Another interpretation of the inconsistent results is that . . . attraction only accounts for a small part of the looking behavior variance. The results are not more consistent because the other determinants of gaze direction were not adequately controlled. One implication of this view is that visual interaction cannot be reliably used as an unobtrusive measure of attraction unless a situation can be devised in which the other determinants of looking can be more fully controlled [p. 99].

Taking Photographs

One of the most ingenious and yet simplest behavioral measures of attraction was devised by Clore and Johnson (1971). The setting was a 1-week summer camp for children sponsored by the Council for Interracial Projects of Champaign, Illinois. The subjects were 48 children from 8 to 12 years of age. Half were black and half white; half were male and half female.

To provide an unobtrusive measure of the development of inter-personal attraction, the experimenters gave half of the children cameras to use during the first part of the week, and the other half of the children had cameras during the second part of the week. Each child had a roll of film to use as he pleased. When the pictures were developed, the experimenters recorded the race of the child and the race of each person appearing in his or her pictures. The question of interest was whether the percentage of opposite race photographs would increase as time in the camp increased.

It was found that in the pictures taken during the first half of the camp, 32.1% were of the opposite race, whereas during the second half, 44.9% were of the opposite race. This change from approximately two-thirds of the photographs of one's own race to an approximately even division was a significant one. The same pattern is shown in the analysis of the pictures taken of the counselors (half black, half white) by the children. The opposite race pictures increased from 42.1% to 50.2% which again shows a significant gain in opposite race photographs.

A similar analysis involved sociometric data. The children were asked to choose partners for a three-legged race on three different occasions. There was a significant increase in the number of opposite-race choices as the experience in the camp increased. The correspondence between these findings and the interracial studies of attraction described in Chapter 6 are, of course, gratifying. Once again, the generality of the at-traction response has been extended. Clore and Johnson (1971) indicate.

> These results are quite encouraging; they show unambiguous evidence that the camp increases the children's attraction toward and willingness to interact with other children

of the opposite race. It is noteworthy that this evidence is concrete, observable behavior as opposed to verbal statements that they like opposite race children. It is also notable that the effects are *mutual*—blacks and whites each show the effects toward one another.

Compliance with the Requests of Liked and Disliked Others

Earlier in this chapter the Tesser and Kian research was described in which subjects gave verbal indications of their willingness to expend effort for another person; those verbal responses were found to be related to IJS responses. Baron (1970b) extended that investigation into the realm of overt behavior.

The subjects were 60 undergraduate females at the University of South Carolina. Each subject and a female confederate responded to 12-item attitude scales and afterward exchanged them. The confederate either was .00 or 1.00 similar to the subject. The subject's responses on the IJS indicated the usual highly significant effect of similarity on attraction (means of 8.37 and 11.70). This manipulation was further strengthened by an exchange of IJS forms in which the subject was either positively or negatively evaluated by the confederate, including written comments that the subject was shallow, immature, and had ridiculous views or that she was mature, sensitive, and had sensible views.

At this point, the experiment was apparently over. The experimenter left the room on a pretext, and the confederate then made one of three requests to the subject. The small request was to ask the subject to return a notebook to a girl who lived in the same dormitory as herself. The moderate request was to ask the subject to return a group of books to the library, a distance of several blocks. The large request was to ask the subject to return the books to the library, then check them out in her own name, and keep them several days until the confederate could pick them up. When the experimenter returned and obtained another IJS rating, the group attraction means were found to be 7.00 and 12.93.

TABLE 9–10

PERCENTAGE OF SUBJECTS COMPLYING WITH
CONFEDERATE'S REQUEST IN EACH CONDITION[a]

Magnitude of confederate's request	Proportion of similar attitudes	
	.00	1.00
Large	50	100
Moderate	30	90
Small	90	100

[a]Data from Baron, 1970b.

Table 9–10 indicates the number of subjects in each group who agreed to perform the requests of the confederate. It may be seen that 29 out of 30 subjects in the high attraction condition complied with the request, whereas only 17 out of 30 in the low attraction condition did so. The difference is a significant one. Since almost all subjects were willing to carry out the small request, it is in the moderate and large request groups where attraction exerted an effect on behavioral compliance.

Commenting on the proximity studies as well as his own work, Baron (1970b) concludes:

> Considered together, the findings of this previous work and those of the present study provide strong support for the view that manipulations of interpersonal attraction conducted in the laboratory are successful in inducing relatively intense levels of positive and negative affect with respect to another person. Thus, they suggest that the results of such research may, with an appropriate degree of caution, be generalized to naturalistic social situations outside the laboratory.

OTHER EVALUATIVE RESPONSES

As will be seen more clearly when the theory of attraction is discussed at greater length in the following section, it is proposed that positive and negative reinforcements elicit differential affect. One of the responses which such affect, in turn, elicits is attraction toward an individual associated with the affect. Thus, positive or negative affect of a given level is associated with a specific individual, and attraction toward that individual is a function of the affect. Attraction is, however, conceptualized as only one representative of a more general class of evaluative responses. Any behavior involving evaluative judgments concerning the individual associated with positive and negative affect should be responsive to the same stimuli that influence attraction. We shall examine a few of these other responses.

Ratings of Various Characteristics

The initial construction of the nonattraction items of the IJS (Byrne, 1961a) was based in part on the rationale outlined above and in part on extrapolation from casual observations and anecdotal evidence. The problem was conceptualized in the following terms. If one is committed to a specific attitudinal position or a series of such positions, how can one explain the fact that another individual holds diametrically opposed positions? Perhaps the rational ideal would be to recognize that there is no definitive empirical test of the relative validity of the opposing positions, that both oneself and the other person are men of good will who have simply reached different conclusions on the basis of differential experiences or differential interpretations of the same experiences, and that no affective and, hence, evaluational reaction need be involved.

In an imperfect world, most individuals do not seem to fit such a pattern, with the possible exception of Mr. Spock during the late 1960s on the television program Star Trek. Instead, much more common reactions include the tendency to question the other person's intelligence ("If he weren't stupid, he would believe as I believe."), or his grasp of the information ("If he knew all that I know, he could not possibly hold his present views."), or his morality ("Assuming that he is sufficiently bright and well informed, I can explain his attitudes only by imputing devious motives to him."), or his adjustment ("Perhaps, after all, he is mentally unbalanced and more to be pitied than attacked."). In an analogous way, the expression of similar attitudes by another person leads to opposite explanations on each dimension. If these observations correspond with typical behavior, it would be hypothesized that such evaluative responses vary as a function of attitude similarity–dissimilarity.

In the first experiment in the present series (Byrne, 1961a), 34 subjects were asked to evaluate a stranger who either expressed complete similarity or complete dissimilarity on 26 attitude items. The first four items of the IJS were built to reflect the four dimensions suggested above: intelligence, knowledge of current events, morality, and adjustment.

The mean evaluation responses are shown in Table 9–11. In each instance, the variable is scored such that 1 is the most negative response and 7 the most positive response. For each evaluation, the difference in response to the similar and dissimilar stranger was significant at beyond the .001 level.

It might be noted that these four scales are retained in the IJS as buffers and to lend credence to our usual instructions to the subjects. In the numerous subsequent studies, these four variables are sometimes found

TABLE 9–11

EVALUATION OF A STRANGER AS A FUNCTION
OF ATTITUDE SIMILARITY–DISSIMILARITY[a]

Variable	Proportion of similar attitudes	
	.00	1.00
Intelligence	3.06	5.65
Knowledge of current events	2.65	4.65
Morality	3.47	5.76
Adjustment	2.71	6.00

[a]After Byrne, 1961a, p. 714.

to yield the same results as the attraction measure and sometimes not. Thus, their responsiveness to attitude similarity–dissimilarity is well documented, though there are evidently additional determinants of such judgments that do not affect attraction. For example, with Stanford undergraduates as subjects who are told that the stranger is another Stanford undergraduate, ratings of intelligence are almost all high and, hence, uninfluenced by attitude similarity–dissimilarity.

In connection with his dissertation research, Baskett factor-analyzed the IJS using a sample of 111 subjects. He found only one factor with an eigenvalue exceeding 1.0. This factor had relatively large loadings for each IJS item. The "evaluation factor" correlated .76 with ratings of intelligence, .50 with ratings of current events, .39 with ratings of morality, .79 with ratings of adjustment, and .88 with the attraction measure.

Desire to Alter the Other Person's Attitudes

Many of the original experimental investigations of attraction dealt with Festinger's (1954) proposal that the occurrence of discrepant opinions within a group will lead to activity aimed at reducing the discrepancy. In general, it was found that subjects in such groups first endeavor to persuade the discrepant individual to alter his beliefs and then tend to reject him when persuasion fails. Byrne (1962) attempted to extend the same proposition to a two-person situation, that of a subject and a simulated stranger.

The experiment was discussed in Chapter 3. Subjects responded to a stranger at one of the eight possible levels of agreement on a seven-item attitude scale. After responding to the IJS, each subject was asked, "What specific changes (if any) would you recommend for this person with respect to self-improvement? How could he (or she) become a better person?" Responses to this question were dichotomized into suggestions involving attitude change versus other suggestions. It was found that the greater the proportion of dissimilar attitudes expressed by the stranger, the greater the tendency of the subject to suggest a change in one or more of that person's attitudes. The hypothesis was confirmed. An interesting side finding is that the tendency was found only for subjects medium or high in affiliation need and not at all for subjects low in affiliation need.

Voting

In most of the experiments on attraction, the stranger has been described as a peer of the subject. If the stranger were a candidate for a political office, there is every reason to expect that the law of attraction would hold— a linear relationship between candidate–subject similarity of attitudes and attraction toward the candidate. And, other evaluative reflections of affect, such as voting, should follow the same pattern.

Byrne, Bond, and Diamond (1969) designed an experiment to bring voting behavior within the more general theory of interpersonal attraction. It was hypothesized that after exposure to the views of two political candidates, subjects vote for the candidate with whom they share the greater proportion of similar attitudes. A second problem considered was the nature of the topics which might influence voting and attraction. It was suggested that candidate–subject similarity on liberal–conservative political issues would have more effect on the voting response than would politically irrelevant issues such as hobbies or reading interests.

The subjects were 134 Stanford students. Several weeks after responding to an attitude scale, the subjects were asked to take part in an investigation of voting behavior. They were read excerpts of material purportedly presented by two candidates in the 1966 congressional election. The statements were labelled as expressions of Candidate A and B, but the statements were prepared to provide either six liberal or six conservative attitudes dealing with topics which appeared on the attitude scale. The statements are presented below:

(Conservative Candidate)

1. The only sensible way to prevent the outbreak of war is to build a sufficiently powerful military force so that no other nation could risk an attack upon us.

2. Had it not been for this nation's continuing superiority in the number and quality of nuclear weapons, I believe that the free world would by this time have been overrun by the aggressors of World War III.

3. Governments representing both political parties have wisely fought against the admission of the Red Chinese into the United Nations; warlike nations must not be allowed to gain entrance at the point of a gun.

4. One of the most frightening prospects I can imagine is any form of socialized medicine in which the government assumes any influence over medical facilities, and the doctor–patient relationship becomes an impersonal interaction with a civil servant.

5. It has always seemed to me that there is an easy cure for nine tenths of the so-called poverty problem and that is a willingness to engage in hard work rather than to lie back and wait for a weekly welfare dole.

6. The most unpleasant aspect of the income tax is its implicit philosophy that financial success is a sin and hence should be penalized by progressively larger tax rates. A sales tax, on the other hand, is tied directly to spending so that all individuals are taxed equally in proportion to their expenditures.

(Liberal Candidate)

1. I think it is almost inevitable that a nation which maintains itself in constant preparation for the possibility of war will, however unwillingly, increase the likelihood of war.

2. One of the tragedies of the cold war period has been the wasted billions spent on the buildup of nuclear armaments because the use of such weapons would mean the end of mankind.

3. It is unthinkable that China, the world's largest nation, is denied admission to the United Nations when that organization represents our best hope of communicating within the family of nations rather than resorting to war.

4. With the progress represented by Medicare, it should be possible to expand its coverage so that every man, woman, and child in this country would be guaranteed medical care throughout his lifetime with all costs paid by tax revenues as with the program in Great Britain.

5. I believe that the time has arrived when it is actually possible to eliminate every aspect of poverty—from inadequate housing to underfed children—simply by diverting our limitless resources from bombs and missiles and space ships into vastly increased welfare programs.

6. The most equitable way to provide the necessary funds for expenses at any level of government is the progressive income tax rather than sales taxes. An income tax levies according to ability to pay while a sales tax places the largest proportional tax burden on those least able to afford it.

Each candidate also made six politically irrelevant statements dealing with topics such as western movies and television programs, tipping, and gardening. After reading the 12 statements of each candidate, the subjects were asked to vote for one of the two candidates.

TABLE 9–12

VOTING FREQUENCIES FOR LIBERAL AND CONSERVATIVE CANDIDATES BY SUBJECTS WITH VARYING PROPORTIONS OF LIBERAL AND CONSERVATIVE ATTITUDES[a]

Subject group (Liberal—Conservative attitudes)	Liberal candidate	Conservative candidate
6–0	14	1
5–1	14	5
4–2	20	6
3–3	12	12
2–4	7	16
1–5	0	14
0–6	0	13
Total votes	67	67

[a]After Byrne, Bond, and Diamond, 1969, p. 256.

The subjects were divided into seven groups on the basis of their own responses to the six liberal–conservative issues. In Table 9–12 may be seen the results of the voting. Clearly, the relative preference for the two candidates is a function of attitudinal similarity. The biserial correlation between the attitudinal grouping of the subjects and candidate choice is .87. If one were to use the similarity hypothesis to predict voting behavior, in the present group there would have been an accurate prediction for 83% of the individuals and an inaccurate prediction for 17%. The mean attraction

TABLE 9–13

MEAN ATTRACTION RESPONSES TOWARD LIBERAL AND
CONSERVATIVE CANDIDATES BY SUBJECTS WITH VARYING
PROPORTIONS OF LIBERAL AND CONSERVATIVE ATTITUDES[a]

Subject group (Liberal–Conservative attitudes)	Liberal candidate	Conservative candidate
6–0	12.07	4.73
5–1	9.60	6.95
4–2	9.37	7.15
3–3	8.71	7.58
2–4	8.61	9.26
1–5	5.00	10.62
0–6	5.85	11.38
Total	8.70	8.03

[a]After Byrne, Bond, and Diamond, 1969, p. 257.

responses, shown in Table 9–13, paralleled the voting response very closely. Attitudes on the politically irrelevant issues influenced neither voting nor attraction.

In addition to extending the generality of the attraction response, these findings suggest the utility of the attraction formulation in the prediction of response to political candidates. It should be noted that the prediction here is not like that of political polls in which individuals are asked for whom they will vote and then are predicted to behave as they said they would. Rather, their voting response is predicted before they are even exposed to the candidates, on the basis of the attitudes they hold in relation to the expressed views of the candidates.

One final aspect of response generality in the experiment is with respect to additional statements about the candidates made by the subjects responding to an open-ended question about the reason for selecting a given candidate. It was observed that the affect connected with opinions about the candidates corresponded well with the attraction and voting responses:

6–0, female: I think [the conservative] programs will lead to destruction, if not to a war of incalculable harm where his sole indication and system of values is conceived as "might makes right"! I'd rather live peacefully than enforce my morality or my culture or ideas on another human being.

3–3, female: Since I had to make a choice on such limited material, I picked [the liberal] because of his views on the war and the income tax. Frankly, neither one was very exciting.

0–6, male: The primary determinants were the principles of [the conservative], a step away from socialism and 1984. I am a staunch and rational conservative and proponent of Ayn Rand's philosophy of objectivism where man is an end, not a means. [The liberal's] principles will lead to political, social, and economic animals. I am for free enterprise, what made this country the greatest the world has ever seen in its history. I could destroy any impractical liberal interpretation where morality is carried to an unreal extreme. If we had a Jesus Christ complex and turned the other cheek, the commies would take over. I could talk forever against insipid, spineless left wingers.

INFERRED ATTRACTION
AND THE APPROVAL-CUE HYPOTHESIS

A somewhat more drastic proposition has been made concerning another response elicited by the attitudes of a stranger. It has been independently proposed by Nelson (1966) and by Aronson and Worchel (1966) that when similar or dissimilar attitudes are expressed by a stranger, the subject assumes that this person would like or dislike him. Further, it is this assumed response on the part of the stranger which elicits the attraction response; attraction was proposed, then, to be a function of inferred attraction rather than of attitude similarity–dissimilarity. Neslon (1966) suggested that:

> . . . the individual may have learned to expect that he is more likely to be approved of ("accepted," "respected," etc.) by someone with attitudes similar to his own than by someone with contradictory attitudes, and that his preference for being with others with attitudes similar to his own may be mediated by expectancies that these others will "approve" of him. Attitude similarity, then, may serve primarily a cue function, relating to increased expectancy of approval, rather than simply as a reinforcement relative to the "need for validation of cognitions."

He reported data from a pilot study indicating that the higher the proportion of similar attitudes expressed by a stranger, the more the subjects expected the stranger to like or approve of them.

In a similar vein, Aronson and Worchel (1966) say:

> It seems reasonable to conjecture that a subject (P) whose attitudes were similar to the (O) would assume that if he *were* to meet O, O would tend to like him . . . It is our prediction that, after a face-to-face interaction, if O likes P, P will like O; the similarity or dissimilarity of O's attitudes to P's attitudes will have a negligible effect [p. 157].

These propositions, which we shall consider together as the approval-cue hypothesis, have generated three testable hypotheses. (*1*) The expression of likes and dislikes is the only variable that influences attraction; attitude similarity in the context of such personal evaluations has a negligible effect (Aronson & Worchel, 1966). A more temperate form of this hypothesis is that evaluations have a greater effect than attitudes and that attitude similarity serves primarily as a cue function (Nelson, 1966). (*2*) Individual differences in the need for approval are predictive of individual differences in the attraction response. (3) Those stimuli that determine the subject's attraction toward the stranger elicit parallel expectancies that the subject will be correspondingly liked by the stranger.

1. As was discussed in Chapter 5, the strong version of the first hypothesis has been repeatedly disconfirmed, and the relative strengths of evaluations versus attitudes has never been in dispute. In both paper and pencil (Byrne & Ervin, 1969; Byrne & Rhamey, 1965) and face-to-face interaction (Aronson & Worchel, 1966; Byrne & Griffitt, 1966b), it is found that subjects are responsive to both attitude similarity and liking with the latter having 3 times the effect of the former. To date, no one has attempted experimentally to differentiate similarity as a cue versus similarity as a reinforcement.

2. In the research described in Chapter 8, support for the second hypothesis was seen to be quite inconsistent. Even if need for approval had been shown to have a powerful and consistent effect on attraction, this would not have constituted evidence that attitude similarity serves as a cue function rather than as a reinforcement function. Approval need could simply be described as an individual differences variable mediating the similarity–attraction effect in that similarity has differential reinforcement value for different individuals.

3. As will be discussed in the following section, only the third hypothesis has received empirical support. It should be noted beforehand, however, that such findings do not indicate a negation of the reinforcement principle. Scotch and soda may quench one's thirst, make one gain weight, and bring about inebriation. The demonstration of any one of these effects does not negate or subordinate the other two. Similarly, agreement may elicit implicit affective responses, attraction responses, and inferences about the other's attraction toward oneself (not to mention other evaluative responses, physical movement toward the other person, visual interaction, etc.). Thus the effect of similarity on inferred attraction may easily be seen as another example of response generality. One of the first demonstrations was provided by McWhirter and Jecker (1967).

Inferring Attraction from Similarity

Subjects were assigned to either a "real" stranger or "mythical" stranger condition and to one of three conditions with respect to proportion of similar attitudes (.28, .57, and .86). In the mythical stranger condition, subjects filled out a seven-item attitude scale, pushed it through a partition to the experimenter who quickly faked another scale at one of the similarity levels and gave it to the subject with information that it was filled out by another subject. In the real stranger condition, the responses were made orally by the subject and a stooge who agreed or disagreed on a prearranged number of items.

After the attitude material was given, subjects received a questionnaire asking them to predict the stranger's behavior. Two of the questions, based on the attraction items of the IJS, asked how much the subject thought the stranger would like him and would want to work with him. The only significant effect was that of proportion of similar attitudes. A highly significant linear trend was also reported.

It seems clear that one of the responses elicited by attitude similarity–dissimilarity is assumed or inferred attraction. The additional proposition that attraction is solely a function of this mediational response has not received empirical support, however. As McWhirter and Jecker (1967) wisely note, "the possibility that both attraction and inferred attraction are determined by attitude similarity remains a viable one [p. 226]."

Inferring Similarity and, Hence, Attraction from Dislike and Vice Versa

The general idea that parallel multiple responses may be evoked by a given stimulus is neither novel nor surprising. When one ignores this possibility, however, theoretical confusions can arise, as we have just seen. Actually, it seems reasonable to suggest that a wide variety of stimuli (all having positive and negative reinforcement properties) elicit affective responses which mediate a wide variety of possible behaviors. In addition, human beings are capable of making complex inferences about stimuli. Thus, when a salesman says, "I like you, you're my kind of people, and I'm going to give you a deal that I wouldn't give to just anyone," one doesn't necessarily feel bathed in positive affect which triggers uncontrolled attraction. Instead, the situation is evaluated and the stimuli are responded to in terms of their meaning. The fact that the same stimuli may have different meaning in different contexts is a seemingly startling concept among some theorists. The influence of contextual meaning is rediscovered periodically as evidence suggesting the sterility and mechanistic simplicity of stimulus–response (S–R) theorists (see, for example, Aronson, 1970). In order to examine further the inferential processes made by subjects and to demonstrate that S–R psychologists have progressed at least a small step beyond the telephone switchboard analogy, Mueller's (1969) dissertation research was undertaken.

A general description of the manipulation is provided by Mueller (1969):

> Suppose a group of subjects were divided into two groups, where the first group was told to express their true attitudes on the Survey of Attitudes, but the second group was told to complete an attitude survey to be the mirror image of their actual

attitudes—a totally false representation. Suppose each is then asked to communicate these attitudes to a stranger (confederate), who in turn is asked to evaluate the subject. For group two (the false group), if the stranger's evaluation is positive, the subject would tend to respond negatively to this stranger, while if these evaluations are negative, the subject would tend to respond positively to this stranger, because in each case, the stranger is responding to a mirror-image of the subject's real attitudes. Now, if the stranger's evaluation is worded to represent only a liking dimension, and the subject in fact responds the opposite of what "self-enhancement" theory would predict for liking, then we must assume that he is no longer simply responding to liking which is directly communicated, but to the only other variable communicated indirectly—similarity. This similarity must be inferred on the assumption that this evaluative statement of liking is based on the attitudes communicated prior to the evaluation [pp. 11–12].

The hypothesis was that attraction would be greater among subjects who gave their true attitudes and received a stranger's positive evaluations or who gave false attitudes and received a stranger's negative evaluations than among subjects in the reverse conditions.

Subjects (80 undergraduates) were asked to express either their true attitudes or the reverse of their attitudes in either written form or in a closed-circuit television broadcast to "another subject." All subjects then received a stranger's televised positive or negative evaluations via television. The feedback was actually a video tape made by a same-sex confederate. The evaluation statements were:

(Positive) Compared to most college students I know, this person seems to be intelligent and well informed. He seems to know what is going on around him. He appears to be an interesting person and basically, he seems to be fairly well adjusted. We'd probably get along real well.

(Negative) Compared to most college students I know, this person doesn't seem to be very intelligent or well informed. He doesn't seem to know what is going on around him. He doesn't appear to be very interesting or basically very well adjusted. We probably wouldn't get along.

Both positive and negative statements were preceded and followed by a short recording of simulated experimenter–confederate interaction to make this appear to be a live presentation.

The subjects then rated the stranger on the IJS.

The results obtained confirmed the hypothesis, as shown in Table 9–14. Their guesses about the stranger's true attitudes followed the same pattern and suggest that evaluative responses led to inferences about attitudes which led to the attraction response. The proportion of similar attitudes guessed to be held by the stranger correlated .62 with attraction toward that stranger. The same overall effects were also found for the four buffer items of the IJS. An additional effect was that positive evaluations elicited more positive (or less negative) responses than did negative evaluations. Once again, subjects are found to be responsive to both attitudes and evaluations even under these complex and atypical conditions.

TABLE 9–14

MEAN ATTRACTION RESPONSE TOWARD STRANGERS
GIVING POSITIVE AND NEGATIVE EVALUATIONS OF
SUBJECTS WHO HAD EXPRESSED EITHER THEIR
TRUE OR FALSE ATTITUDES[a]

Subject	Negative evaluations	Positive evaluations
True attitudes	5.25	11.30
False attitudes	9.45	6.35

[a]Data from Mueller, 1969.

The comparison of video versus paper-and-pencil communication of attitudes indicated no significant effects. The responses toward the stranger were not influenced by the occurrence of the face-to-face (via video) communication to him.

The conclusion could be drawn that subjects respond primarily to similarity rather than to approval–disapproval expressed by the stranger. Within the specific conditions of Mueller's experiment, that conclusion is, of course, an accurate one. In a more general context, it should be clear why inferred similarity was not suddenly assigned a primary theoretical role. As Mueller (1969) suggests, "These results demonstrate the critical importance of specifying theoretical boundary conditions. Within a specified experimental context, liking will exceed similarity in importance in determining attraction; however, under the present design, the reverse was demonstrated [p. 40]."

The Inference Process As Evidence of Cognitive Components in the Similarity–Attraction Relationship

The various experiments in the present section have a common core in suggesting the operation of cognitive components in the similarity–attraction relationship. There is the realization that human subjects do not react as mechanized robots but rather as thinking beings who not only respond to contextual meaning but who are actively engaged in remembering, inferring, expecting, inducing and deducing even in the limiting confines of an experimental situation. Theoretical problems could arise only if anyone were foolish enough to propose that cognitive processes play no part in human behavior or that human behavior is entirely explicable as rational, intellectual activity which involves no affective variables and is independent of reinforcement principles. In the present paradigm, both kinds of variables are recognized as components of the attraction process. Two further examples of the importance of cognition will underline this point. Both experiments indicate that the similarity–attraction relationship is not exclusively limited to affective response to stimuli with reinforcement properties. What is meant is that subjects not only indicate their attraction toward others on the basis of affective determinants but that they also have a reservoir of memories of experiences in such situations and can reproduce them under certain conditions.

Predicting the Attraction Response of Others. Scott (1969) proposed that an intervening motivational construct is unnecessary in the similarity–attraction relationship in that a simple information processing model will account for our various findings. His research involved a situation in which the subject was, in effect, the observer of an attraction experiment and had the task of predicting the attraction responses of another student toward a stranger.

Subjects were assigned to a condition with .00, .33, .66, or 1.00 student–stranger similarity. On a 12-item attitude scale, they read what were purported to be the responses of another student, the responses of a stranger, and then filled out the IJS as they felt the student had done in evaluating the stranger.

The predicted attraction means are shown in Table 9–15. It may be seen that the obtained responses are very close to those usually found in conventional attraction experiments.

Scott perceptively points out that his findings could explain the results of attraction experiments in cognitive as opposed to affective terms but that such findings do not explain how the subject learned an association between attitude similarity and attraction in the first place. He goes on to suggest that the affective model is the most plausible explanation for that original learning. The attraction rating of a stranger is conceptualized as an anticipatory response which prepares the subject for subsequent interaction. Scott (1969)

TABLE 9–15

MEAN ATTRACTION RESPONSES PREDICTED BY SUBJECT
AS ANOTHER STUDENT'S RESPONSE TO STRANGER[a]

Proportion of similar responses between other student and stranger	Mean attraction responses predicted by subject
1.00	11.59
.66	10.60
.33	7.12
.00	5.00

[a]After Scott, 1969.

explains the roles of affective and cognitive components, "The attitude statements function as conditioned reinforcers in the bogus questionnaire procedure and have motivational consequences. The attractiveness of the stranger, however, is a function of the stimulus variables which provide the structure of a social setting and identify its probable consequences."

Inferring Similarity from Attraction. In three separate experiments, the similarity–attraction relationship has been reversed by presenting subjects with attraction responses on the IJS and asking them to create the attitudes of a stranger which would have elicited such a response from them. The first of these experiments was carried out by Baskett and a follow-up study was conducted by Sachs and Byrne. Independently, Moss (1970) investigated the same problem. Because the three experiments yielded quite similar results, only Moss' work will be described here.

Moss created three conditions of liking by filling out the last two items of the IJS to constitute attraction responses of 3, 8, or 13. He asked each subject to assume that he had made those ratings and to complete a 44-item attitude scale as the person being rated had done. That is, what attitudes would the other person have expressed in order to produce those particular IJS responses?

The obtained assumed proportions of similar attitudes for the three groups were .33, .51, and .85. Thus, the reverse relationship between attraction and similarity resembles the usual linear function. The major divergence is that the amount of dissimilarity assumed to elicit extreme dislike is relatively high.

ATTRACTION AS A MEDIATOR OF OTHER INTERPERSONAL RESPONSES

The investigation of the construct validity of the IJS has gradually progressed from a tentative examination of paper and pencil correlates to a more expansive view of attraction as an important index of affect and as a potential predictor of numerous interpersonal responses. Instead of continuing to ask whether the measure of attraction has validity, the question now shifts to inquiries concerning the possible implications of differential attraction.

Anticipatory Responses and Attraction

Extending on the conditioning model to be presented in the following chapter, Griffitt (1969a) proposed that "reinforcing stimuli evoke affective responses which represent, at least in part, reactions which are 'anticipatory' (Doob, 1947), 'hopeful' (Mowrer, 1960), or 'expectative' (Hull, 1952) of future reinforcing situations [p. 153]."

An experiment was designed to test the hypothesis that reinforcing stimuli in the form of agreeing and disagreeing attitudes evoke anticipatory responses relative to anticipated positive and negative interactive consequences associated with the stranger.

The subjects were 27 undergraduates at Kansas State University. The experiment was described as a two-person problem-solving task. Each subject evaluated a same-sex stranger on the basis of attitude responses (.25, .50, or .75 similarity). The stranger was supposed to serve as a partner in the second part of the experiment. In addition to the IJS, subjects were asked to anticipate the nature of the forthcoming interaction on six semantic differential scales, and asked to predict how long they and their partners would take to solve the problem.

The mean attraction responses, anticipated positiveness ratings, and time estimates are shown in Table 9-16. All three variables were significantly influenced by attitude similarity–dissimilarity.

TABLE 9-16

MEAN ATTRACTION, ANTICIPATED POSITIVENESS, AND
TIME ESTIMATE RESPONSES AS A FUNCTION OF
ATTITUDE SIMILARITY[a]

Response variables	Proportion of similar attitudes		
	.25	.50	.75
Attraction	7.22	8.11	10.56
Anticipated positiveness	24.22	25.44	32.33
Time estimates (minutes)	24.22	19.11	16.33

[a]After Griffitt, 1969a, p. 153.

Griffitt proposed that anticipated positiveness of the interaction mediates the similarity–attraction relationship. Whether or not that formulation is precisely accurate, it can be seen that anticipatory affective responses could conceivably influence a wide variety of responses.

Attraction and Interpersonal Bargaining

A popular interpersonal situation for experimenters is the prisoner's dilemma game in which two subjects interact, making cooperative or competitive decisions with differential payoff depending on one's own behavior and the behavior of the other person. Tornatzky and Geiwitz (1968) suggested that the manipulation of liking between the players should affect cooperative behavior and also should exert an influence on the meaning of threat. Previous research (e.g., Krauss, 1966) had shown that interpersonal attraction has a beneficial effect on bargaining. Tornatzky and Geiwitz employed 80 male high-school students as subjects. In the game, subjects received 10 points for mutual cooperation and -10 for mutual competition; if one was competitive and the other cooperative, the former received 15 and the latter -15 points. In addition, an attitude scale of the other player was seen, and it was either .00 or 1.00 similar. The attraction responses were 4.78 and 9.74. In the game, the high mutual attraction pairs chose the cooperative response significantly more often than the low mutual attraction pairs. Differential attraction thus was found to be related to positive interpersonal responses in this situation. In a related study, Fisher and Smith (1969) also found a relationship between attraction as manipulated by attitude similarity and cooperative behavior in the prisoner's dilemma game.

Aggression and Attraction

It has been assumed in our attraction research that the underlying response dimension is one which extends from love to hate. Research on hate, hostility, and aggression has been relatively neglected within the attraction paradigm until very recently. It appears, however, that a blending of attraction and aggression research is not as easy as it might appear.

Aggression toward a Liked or Disliked Stranger in a Competitive Task. Hendrick and Taylor (1971) note that "In everyday life we talk with people toward whom we are attracted, we play with them, we love them, sometimes we get angry at them, and sometimes we kill them (p. 342)." The relation between attraction and these various interpersonal behaviors has gradually begun to be investigated. Their specific interest was in whether belief similarity would affect a behavioral measure of aggression. The underlying hypothesis was that aggression is mediated in some fashion by attraction.

In their experiment, subjects competed with an opponent who was attitudinally similar or dissimilar and who was either aggressive or nonaggressive in his behavior toward the subject. Individuals were told that they were competing with another subject (actually an experimenter-controlled program) in a reaction time experiment. The slower of the two individuals on each trial would receive an electric shock. The intensity of the shock was supposedly controlled by the faster of the two players. The attitude manipulation was a 10-item scale on which the stranger was either .20 or .80 similar. The aggressiveness of the opponent was manipulated by means of the shock intensity received by the subject. The subject's aggression response was defined as the intensity of the setting when he was supposedly shocking his opponent.

It was found that the similarity manipulation influenced the subject's liking of the opponent, but aggression toward the opponent was influenced only by the other person's aggressiveness. The more intense the shock administered by the opponent, the more aggressive was the subject's response. Attraction was also found to be greater toward an opponent low in aggression than toward a highly aggressive one.

Hendrick and Taylor (1971) conclude "It may well be that aggression is not mediated by attraction, but that the two behaviors are independent of each other. We suggest that physical aggression and attraction are different classes of behavior, generally responsive to different sets of independent variables that only partially overlap [p. 347]."

Aggression toward a Liked and Disliked Stranger on the Buss Aggression Machine. Baron (1971) simultaneously investigated several variables hypothesized to influence aggression: magnitude of pain cues given by the victim, level of prior anger arousal, and similarity–dissimilarity of aggressor and victim.

In the similarity condition, the victim was another undergraduate student, normally attired, who agreed with the subject on five out of five topics. In the dissimilar condition, the victim was an apprentice electrician, dressed in a gray work uniform, who disagreed with the subject on all five topics. Male subjects were first angered or were not angered by a confederate (negative evaluation plus high intensity shock or positive evaluation plus low intensity shock) and then provided with an opportunity to aggress against that individual by administering shock on the Buss aggression machine. Each time that the subject administered the shock, he supposedly received information about the amount of pain felt by the other person.

The intensity of the shocks delivered by the subject and the duration of the shocks were each influenced by both the magnitude of the victim's pain cues and by level of prior anger arousal but not by similarity–dissimilarity. The only effect of similarity was in a complex interaction in that one experimental group was quite different from all of the others; the low pain cues, angry, dissimilar group gave longer shocks to the victim than any other group and they increased the duration of these shocks as the experiment progressed.

It once again appears that the determinants of attraction are not identical to the determinants of aggression and that attraction does not play a powerful role in mediating the aggression response.

Imitative Behavior and Attraction

A further extension of the meaning of attraction responses has been provided by the work of Robert Baron at the University of South Carolina and Ronald Smith at the University of Washington. The basic question is whether imitative behavior is influenced by attraction toward the model.

Imitating Aggressive Behavior. In one investigation (Baron & Kepner, 1970), the subjects were angered and then provided with an opportunity to aggress against the one who had angered them. First, however, they were exposed to the behavior of a peer who had also been insulted; this model either showed a low or high level of aggression against the instigator. In addition, attraction toward the model was manipulated by means of attitude similarity (.00 or 1.00) information. The subjects were male undergraduates.

The IJS means of 8.94 and 10.55 were, of course, significantly different. The intensity of shock delivered by the subject to the instigator was strongly influenced by the model's behavior but not by attraction toward the model. For another measure of aggression, duration of shocks administered, both the behavior of the model and attraction yielded minimally significant effects. Low attraction subjects tended to administer shocks of longer duration than did high attraction subjects.

Imitating Betting Behavior. In a related experiment (Baron, 1970a), attraction was found to play a more important role in imitative behavior. It was hypothesized that subjects would show a higher level of imitation and would learn to match a model's behavior more rapidly under conditions of high attraction than under conditions of low attraction. In addition, the model's competence was varied.

The subjects were 48 undergraduates. Attraction was again manipulated by means of .00 or 1.00 similarity on an attitude scale. In addition, personal evaluations were manipulated by showing each subject the purported IJS ratings made by the other person. These ratings were either favorable or unfavorable to the subject. The imitative task concerned betting on electrical "horse races." The feedback about the model's behavior indicated the bets made and the success of the bets. The competent model won on 75% of the races, whereas the low competent model won on 25% of the races. Whenever the subject imitated the model, he was rewarded (by winning the race) 60% of the time.

The attraction means were 8.08 and 11.83. After the experiment, the means were 7.50 and 12.33. In all four conditions, the subjects learned to match the model's behavior over trials. It was found that for subjects with a competent model, high attraction led to more imitative responses than did low attraction. For those with the low competent model, high attraction led to fewer imitative responses than did low attraction. Thus, a high level of attraction toward the model facilitates imitation only when the model is competent in performing the task.

Imitating Behavioral Noninvolvement. Smith, Smythe, and Lien (1971) extended attraction research into the realm of bystander intervention. Under what conditions will a bystander actively intervene to help another individual who is in distress? It has been found that a single individual is more likely to help a stranger in a crisis situation than is a member of a group. The other members of the group seem to inhibit helping behavior. It was proposed that another person's failure to help a stranger in distress will influence the subject's nonintervention behavior to a greater extent if the other person is liked than if he is disliked by the subject.

The subjects were males exposed to an attitudinally similar or dissimilar nonreactive other. Attraction was measured both after exposure to the other person's attitudes and after the "emergency" was over. Shortly after subjects filled out the first IJS, the female experimenter feigned illness, staggered into an adjoining room, lurched into a filing cabinet, and slumped into a chair out of view of the subject. The confederate appeared totally unconcerned during the entire performance. There was also an alone condition in which the subject was exposed to the emergency without the presence of a nonreactive confederate.

It was found that 65% of the subjects in the alone condition intervened, 35% of the subjects with a dissimilar other did so, and only 5% of those with a similar other intervened. Thus, the findings were consistent with previous research in demonstrating the inhibitory effects of a nonreactive other and indicated further that attraction toward that other person is an important factor in determining whether helping behavior is inhibited or not.

An interesting additional finding dealt with changes in attraction toward the dissimilar other by those subjects who followed his lead by not intervening or who reacted in an opposite manner and helped the female experimenter. Of the former group, 78% showed an increase in attraction, whereas only 28% of the latter group showed an increase. It was suggested that engaging in an "undesirable" behavior with another increases attraction toward him.

In conclusion, it may be seen that attraction as measured by the IJS is related to a number of quite different responses and that attraction appears to be of pervasive importance in a varied array of interpersonal interactions.

THEORY-BUILDING

Chapter 10 / **A Reinforcement Model of Attraction**

The broadest and potentially most important avenue of development from a base relationship is the formulation of higher-order generalizations which explain, order, and derive the implications of empirical laws. Theory-building is an attempt to develop general principles which not only encompass the available data but also extend to quite different stimuli and responses in quite different contexts. In the present chapter, the basic principles of a reinforcement model of attraction will be described along with a brief history of the development of this particular approach. In the three chapters to follow, the research which has concentrated on testing hypotheses derived from the model will be presented.

Two major approaches to a theoretical interpretation of attraction phenomena may be roughly categorized as cognitive and reinforcement models. Cognitive theorists (e.g., Festinger, 1950, 1954, 1957; Heider, 1958; Newcomb, 1956, 1959, 1961) have tended to emphasize the homeostatic characteristics of the elements within a closed system. The system encompasses at least two individuals and the "object" of communication (either something or someone). As Berscheid and Walster (1969) suggest, the basic unit of such theories is the cognition, i.e., "any knowledge, opinion, or belief about the environment, about oneself, or about one's behavior that a person might hold." Reinforcement theorists (e.g., Byrne, 1969; Byrne & Clore, 1970; Lott & Lott, 1960; A. W. Staats, 1968, 1969) tend to focus on stimuli and responses as the units comprising interpersonal interaction, on the positive and negative properties of the relevant stimuli, and on the utility of borrowing concepts from learning theory to apply to the attraction situation. These two general themas may be seen as representing two somewhat divergent views of man, and they have been employed repeatedly in contrasting theories of personality, learning, political processes, and numerous other attempts to explain behavioral events. One's relative evaluation of such metatheories probably does not depend on their elegance, their precision, or the number of hypotheses derived and confirmed at a suitable level of statistical significance. Rather, the cognitive or the reinforcement explanation of behavior simply seems more "reasonable" or more "satisfying" to a given individual. The reason for such differential reactions is a suitable topic for future speculation and research. In any event, if the individual happens to be engaged in research, he seeks situations and research designs and data compatible with his viewpoint. If he is sufficiently confused, he may also seek to disprove the opposing viewpoint by means of argument or data and often in a vitriolic way. That opposing attitudes about theory elicit negative interpersonal reactions and negative evaluations should come as no surprise at this point.

With respect to theoretical differences, it may be noted that the established empirical relationships, such as the attitude–attraction function, are interpretable in either cognitive or reinforcement terms. In fact, the two theoretical approaches do not constitute alternative and mutually exclusive explanatory systems. Instead, we have two broadly different interpretational schemas which utilize different languages and which apparently lead to somewhat different types of empirical research. The emphasis here, therefore, will be on the positive characteristics of a reinforcement model and not on the negative characteristics of a cognitive model. There isn't even a compelling necessity to dwell on the intellectual, informational, moral, or adjustment weaknesses of theorists of the cognitive persuasion. The proof of the pudding is not in seeking lumps in rival puddings.

REINFORCEMENT AND ATTRACTION

Development of the Reinforcement Concept within the Paradigm

Interestingly enough, the reinforcement interpretation of attitude similarity was originally introduced to the present author by a leading cognitive theorist, namely, Newcomb (1956). He suggested that attraction between persons is a function of the extent to which reciprocal rewards are present in their interaction; presumably, dislike is a function of reciprocal punishments.

It may be instructive, though somewhat embarrassing, to trace the gradual development of the reinforcement notion within the paradigm by a series of quotes in chronological order. The first step, however, was simply the acceptance of Newcomb's broad suggestion in his American Psychological Association presidential address as intuitively correct. The first experiment in the paradigm was not conceived and carried out until 4 years later, at which time the theoretical statements began to take the following form:

> The accurate prediction of interpersonal attraction and repulsion ... will undoubtedly require that we secure knowledge about several classes of independent variables.
> Probably the most obvious and also best documented variable is that of propinquity.... Once the environmental situation permits or encourages interaction, affiliation need should be helpful in predicting individual differences in interpersonal behavior.... A third class of variables consists of the overt stimulus properties of each individual to which other individuals would be expected to respond on the basis of generalizations from previous interpersonal interactions.
> Once interaction has begun, reciprocal reward and punishment is proposed as the crucial determining factor ... any time that another person offers us validation by indicating that his percepts and concepts are congruent with ours, it constitutes a rewarding interaction and, hence, one element in forming a positive relationship. Any time that another person indicates dissimilarity between our two notions, it constitutes a punishing interaction and thus one element in forming a negative relationship [Byrne, 1961a, p. 713].

> ... the most general explanatory concept in attraction theory is that of reciprocal reward and punishment. The occurrence of any type of interpersonal reward engenders positive affect which is directed toward the rewarding person; punishment in an interpersonal situation engenders negative affect which is directed toward the punishing person. The relative number (and relative intensity) of rewards and punishments associated with a given individual is at least one important determinant of attraction toward him. [Byrne, 1962, p. 164].

> In building a theory of interpersonal attraction, the most inclusive independent variable is almost certainly that of reciprocal reward and punishment. Actually, the other three classes of variables appear to be relevant only as they relate to reward and punishment. [Byrne & Wong, 1962, p. 246]

> Thus, linearity of the relationship is evident across two different experimental conditions but the values of the constants differ. Presumably, the similarity across stimulus conditions is attributable to the common element of positive and negative reinforcements involved. A tentative law of attraction is proposed as $A_x = mPR_x + k$ or attraction toward X is a positive linear function of the proportion of positive reinforcements received from X [Byrne & Nelson, 1965a, p. 662].

The slow progression (painfully slow in retrospect) of our thinking about reinforcement is evident. First, reinforcement constituted one of four classes of stimulus variables determining attraction. Second, reinforcement was described as the most general explanatory concept in attraction theory.

Third, the other three classes of variables were relegated to special instances of varying reward and punishment. Fourth, attraction was formally described as a positive linear function of the proportion of positive reinforcements *received* from *x*.

There was, by the way, a rather deliberate neglect of systematic theoretical development in favor of the search for empirical stability and generality. In part, the choice was the result of the author's early traumatic experiences with (*1*) inconsistent and nonreplicable data in the fields of clinical, personality, and social psychology and with (*2*) metaphorical "theories" in the field of personality which were long on literary quality and short on predictive power. The research was thus guided by a rather vague reinforcement theory and by the desire to establish an empirical law to serve as the foundation for an eventual theoretical superstructure. There was an explicit fear of spinning an elaborate theoretical network to explain a passing chimera composed primarily of error variance. The success of McDonald's (1962) and Golightly's (1965) hypothesis-testing experiments were therapeutic, however. In the spring of 1966 a collaboration with Jerry Clore began which led to a more formal conceptualization of the way in which reinforcement and attraction were linked in antecedent–consequent fashion.

The Byrne–Clore Model

The basic associational theory was developed in a series of three monographs (Byrne & Clore, 1970; Clore, 1966; Clore & Byrne, in press). At a purely tactical level, a reinforcement formulation was seen as having two primary advantages. First, a variety of seemingly different stimulus conditions can be conceptualized in terms of a single unifying construct rather than as an infinite array of unrelated conditions. Basic principles which have maximal generalizability are preferable to situationally specific explanations of events. Second, the concept of reinforcement obviously suggests the possibility of a fruitful relationship between the attraction paradigm and learning theory.

Byrne and Clore (1970) outlined the details of the process which was proposed as the basis for the formation of attraction responses or any other evaluation response. Lott and Lott (1960) presented four assumptions for their reinforcement approach: (*1*) persons represent discriminable stimuli, (*2*) reinforcement results in an overt or covert goal response (R_g or r_g), (*3*) the goal response becomes conditioned to all discriminable stimuli present at the time of reinforcement, and (*4*) if such a goal response is conditioned to a person, then that person in later situations will evoke R_g or $r_g - s_g$.

We had no quarrel with the Lotts' formulation, except that it suggests a stronger commitment to the specifics of Hull–Spence theory than seemed to be required. Our own approach was comparatively cautious in that the language and concepts remained at a more general level (i.e., Thorndike and Pavlov) and, hence, not necessarily committed to the demands of any current theoretical framework. In the present phase of development, there seemed to be no reason to take on borrowed problems from the field of learning. To reverse a metaphor, we wanted to adopt the baby without at the same time contracting for the bath water. Perhaps the best characterization of the present approach is one in which empirical and theoretical work in a quite different research area is viewed as a potentially useful source of general guidelines but not as a detailed and circumscribed blueprint. The only other difference between our and the Lotts' formulation at this point was our greater stress on the affective quality of the mediating response. The schema presented in Fig. 10–1 represents a conditioning model graphically. It was proposed that any stimulus with reinforcement properties functions as an unconditioned stimulus* for an implicit affective response. Such affect is assumed to fall along a subjective continuum that may be characterized as pleasant–unpleasant. Reinforcement properties of stimuli are defined in terms of the empirical law of effect: the capacity to alter response probability. That is, any stimulus is labelled as a reinforcer if it increases or decreases the probability of the occurrence of responses with which it is paired. In Spence's (1951) words, "responses leading to certain types of environmental consequences (called 'rewards') become stronger and are retained, whereas

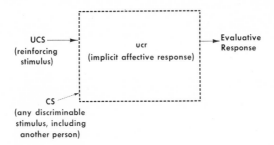

Fig. 10–1. Evaluative responses as a function of reinforcing stimuli associated with a conditioned stimulus. CS, conditioned stimulus; UCS, unconditioned stimulus; UCR, unconditioned response. (After Byrne & Clore, 1970, p. 107.)

*It should be noted that the unconditioned stimulus (UCS) and unconditioned response (UCR) are so identified in relation to the experimental situation. That is, at the beginning of the experiment, certain stimuli are found to elicit certain responses. With human subjects, the UCS is often a conditioned stimulus (CS), the response to which was learned prior to visiting the psychological laboratory. Thus, most of the attraction experiments obviously represent higher-order conditioning.

responses leading to certain other types of after-effects (named non-rewards) become weaker and eventually disappear [p. 708]." Any discriminable stimulus, including a person, which is temporally associated with the unconditioned stimulus can become a conditioned stimulus which evokes the implicit affective response.

The implicit affective response is conceptualized as mediating the relationship between the CS and subsequent evaluative responses. Such an hypothetical response is, of course, a familiar one in behavior theory. Venerable examples include Spence's (1958) hypothetical emotional (pain) response, r_e, Amsel's (1958) hypothetical emotional (anger) response, r_f, and Hull's (1943) fractional antedating goal response, r_g. Evaluation includes verbal responses describing one's assessment of the CS, various types of choice behavior, and approach and avoidance reactions to the CS.

Demonstrating the Conditioning Process

To provide empirical substance for the conditioning model, Byrne and Clore (1970) carried out a simple experimental demonstration of the basic processes involved.

Attitude Statements and Affective Responses. Eight male and eight female undergraduates at the University of Texas were asked to record their "feelings" in response to two different stimulus conditions. With order of presentation counterbalanced, one condition consisted of a tape recording of statements expressing views in agreement with those of the subject concerning 12 miscellaneous issues. The other condition consisted of a recording of 12 statements expressing views dissimilar from those of the subject. Responses were made on six of the evaluative scales* of Osgood's semantic differential (Osgood, Suci, & Tannenbaum, 1957). The scales were comfortable–uncomfortable, bad–good, high–low, sad–happy, pleasant–unpleasant, and negative–positive. Each subject was told that "The purpose of this study is to explore a few of the dimensions of everyday feelings people have. We are asking a number of students to describe their feelings on a series of scales after exposure to several common stimuli."

Individually, a subject listened to a tape recording with either the 12 similar or 12 dissimilar statements, indicated his "immediate feelings at this moment," listened to the second recording, and then responded to the semantic differential again.

---

*Strictly speaking, the implicit affective responses of our model are not observable. When subjects are asked to indicate their feelings, the result is an evaluative response, i.e., an "evaluation" of their internal state. In the two experiments to be described, these responses are treated as if they were direct representations of the affective responses.

Each scale was scored from 1 (negative) to 7 (positive) and a total score obtained. The mean affective response following agreeing statements was 30.56; that following disagreeing statements was 20.88. The two stimulus conditions yielded significantly different responses. It might also be noted that the obtained responses fall, respectively, on the positive and negative sides of the neutral score of 24.

Differential Conditioning with Attitude Statements As Unconditioned Stimuli. A second experiment was undertaken in which 32 undergraduates at the University of Illinois were given a 24-item attitude scale. Several weeks later, each subject participated individually in the conditioning procedure. Subjects sat at a small desk, facing a blank wall. The experimenter sat behind the subject in order to operate a tape recorder and a slide projector.

After the subject was seated, one of two photographs of a same-sex stranger was projected on the wall. Simultaneously, a tape recording of six attitude statements (all similar to or dissimilar from the subject's views) was played. After the sixth statement, the other same-sex picture was projected while six more statements (opposite in attitudinal direction from the first six) were played. The procedure continued with alternating pictures until both sides of all 24 topics had been presented. Thus, for each subject, one picture was consistently paired with statements which agreed with the subject's attitudes, whereas the other picture was paired with disagreements.

Afterward, the semantic differential scales were given to the subject. After reading the instructions, the subject was shown one of the two photographic slides for 15 seconds and instructed to rate his feelings at that moment. The second picture was then projected for 15 seconds, after which the subject's feelings were again recorded. The order of the photographs and of agreements and disagreements was counterbalanced across subjects. The mean response to the CS paired with agreeing statements was 31.84, whereas that to the CS paired with disagreeing statements was 22.22; the difference between the means is significant.

After the experiment, the subjects were asked to indicate if they knew how they had been expected to respond and the purpose of the experiment. Only one individual expressed awareness of the relevant information, and he responded positively to both pictures.

Thus, it was shown that similar and dissimilar attitude statements evoke differential affective responses and that when these stimuli are presented in association with neutral stimuli, the latter will subsequently evoke differential affective responses.

One difficulty with these findings was that the model specifies that simple association between the UCS and CS is sufficient to obtain the conditioning effect. The subjects could, however, have attributed the attitude statements to the depicted stranger. If so, it is not clear whether affective responses elicited by attitudes can be conditioned to a neutral stimulus simply through temporal association. Another experiment was required to resolve this ambiguity.

Differential Conditioning with Attitudes Not Attributable to Conditioned Stimuli. Sachs and Byrne (1970) essentially replicated the second Byrne–Clore experiment with a design in which the attitudes could not be attributed to the CS. The presumed irrelevancy of attitude attribution was tested by (*1*) pairing a human CS of one sex with an attitudinal UCS verbalized by someone of the opposite sex and by (*2*) pairing a nonhuman CS with an attitudinal UCS.

The subjects were 60 University of Texas undergraduates. The procedure followed that of the previous experiment except for the changes in the CS. For half of the subjects, the two CS were pictures of same-sex peers; the UCS was a series of attitude statements taped by an opposite-sex peer. For the other half, the two CS were pictures of 10-sided random figures (Munsinger & Kessen, 1964). Each subject saw one picture consistently paired with agreeing attitudes and one consistently paired with disagreeing attitudes.

In addition to the semantic differential used before, two new scales (slow–fast and hot–cold) were included as nonaffective buffers. Also, those with human CS completed an Interpersonal Judgment Scale (IJS) for each. The subjects who had figures as CS filled out a specially devised Picture Judgment Scale indicating how much they were attracted to the picture and whether they would like to own a copy of it.

On the semantic differential, the results paralleled those of the previous experiment, as shown in Table 10–1, even though attribution of the attitude statements to the CS was not possible. This difference was again significant. On the two buffer scales, there was a marginally significant effect for slow–

TABLE 10–1

MEAN AFFECTIVE RESPONSES TO CONDITIONED
STIMULI PAIRED WITH POSITIVE AND
NEGATIVE ATTITUDINAL UNCONDITIONED
STIMULI[a]

Conditioned stimuli	Unconditioned stimuli	
	Dissimilar attitudes	Similar attitudes
Peer	20.50	30.83
Figure	19.17	31.83

[a]Data from Sachs & Byrne, 1970.

TABLE 10–2
MEAN ATTRACTION RESPONSES TO CONDITIONED
STIMULI PAIRED WITH POSITIVE AND NEGATIVE
ATTITUDINAL UNCONDITIONED STIMULI[a]

Conditioned stimuli	Unconditioned stimuli	
	Dissimilar attitudes	Similar attitudes
Peer	7.30	10.93
Figure	6.07	9.00

[a]Data from Sachs & Byrne, 1970.

fast, and none at all for hot–cold, suggesting that the subjects' responding is not simply an undifferentiated halo affect.

The responses to the judgment scales (evaluative responses) are shown in Table 10–2. Again the differences are significant.

Awareness was again investigated. Subjects were classified as aware, partially aware, or unaware with respect to the reinforcement manipulation of the experiment. It was found that the greatest differential response to positive and negative CS was among the aware subjects, and the least difference was among the unaware subjects. The conditioning effect was present, however, in all three groups.

In summary, these experiments suggest that the association of neutral stimuli with similar and dissimilar attitude statements clearly results in subsequent differential affect evoked by those stimuli and differential evaluation of those stimuli. Such findings are consistent with the reinforcement model.

AN HISTORICAL NOTE ON THE REINFORCEMENT APPROACH TO ATTRACTION AND EVALUATION

It was suggested that no claims are made as to the novelty or uniqueness or even newsworthiness of the basic idea of the Byrne–Clore model. Perhaps that statement can best be verified by noting briefly some of the theoretical predecessors which correspond closely to this formulation.

The Reinforcement Model As Part of Our Western Heritage

It is frequently possible to trace the basis of an idea to at least one Greek philosopher, and the basis of the conditioning model is no exception. In the first century before Christ, Aristotle (translated 1932) sets the stage:

> Further, men love any one who has done good to them or to those for whom they
> are concerned . . .
> Further, men like those who are able and inclined to benefit them in a pecuniary way,
> or to promote their personal safety . . . those who are pleasant to live with, and to spend
> the day with; such as the good-tempered—people who are not given to catching up one's
> mistakes, and are not pertinacious or crossgrained. . . . Further, we like those who praise
> our good qualities, and especially if we are afraid we do not posses them. . . . We like those
> who take us seriously—who admire us, who show us respect, who take pleasure in our
> society. . . . We like those who do not frighten us, and in dealing with whom we do not
> lose our aplomb—for no one likes a person of whom he is afraid [pp. 103–106].

A more general presentation of the idea was made about 2000 years
later in seventeenth century Holland. Spinoza (translated 1951) proposed:

> *Love* is nothing else but *pleasure accompanied by the idea of an external cause*; *Hate* is
> nothing else but *pain accompanied by the idea of an external cause* . . .
> Simply from the fact that we have regarded a thing with the emotion of pleasure or
> pain, though that thing be not the efficient cause of the emotion, we can either love or
> hate it. [pp. 140–141]

Psychological Proponents of a Reinforcement Model

As with many other notions about the nature of man, ideas about the
determinants of attraction have been borrowed from the culture by psychologists as a basis for initiating and conceptualizing scientific investigations.
The following series of selected quotations should provide evidence of the
widespread currency of the reinforcement explanation and a glimpse of the
evolution of a particular idea. The interests of the individuals noted below
have been directed at attitudes, language, prejudice, impression formation,
performance changes in rats, and interpersonal attraction.

Doob (1947) provided the very important opening wedge by attempting
to relate attitudes to behavior theory. His definition of attitude has influenced much of the succeeding work.

> An attitude is an implicit response which is both (a) anticipatory and (b) mediating in
> reference to patterns of overt responses, which is evoked (a) by a variety of stimulus
> patterns (b) as a result of previous learning or of gradients of generalization and discrim-
> ination, which is itself cue- and drive-producing, and which is considered socially
> significant in the individual's society [p. 136].

Among others, Bernice Lott (Eisman, 1955) provided a link between
the conceptualization of attitudes in general and attitudes toward other
human beings.

> It is not too big a step to assume that if children can learn to prefer the color yellow,
> for example, over the colors green and black as a result of the type of training given
> them in this investigation, they can also, as a result of similar training, learn to prefer
> people called Englishmen over those called Poles and Italians, even though they have
> had no differential reward or punishment experience with any of those three national

groups. The essential requirements for this learning are that individuals should learn to attach the same labels to the word "Englishman" as to stimuli with which they have rewarding experience, and to attach the same labels to the words "Pole" or "Italian" as to stimuli with which they have had neutral or punishing experience [p. 325].

Newcomb's use of a reinforcement explanation has been mentioned, but it should be added that he proposed "we acquire favorable or unfavorable attitudes toward persons as we are rewarded or punished by them, and that the principles of contiguity, of reciprocal reward, and of complementarity have to do with the conditions under which rewards are most probable [Newcomb, 1956, p. 577]."

A. W. Staats and his associates (e.g., A. W. Statts & Staats, 1958; C. K. Staats & Staats, 1957) have conducted a series of experiments and have made theoretical contributions which are directly related to the kind of position outlined here. For example:

In [A. W. Staats, 1964] it was suggested that when a stimulus object is paired with word stimuli that elicit evaluative meaning responses (making these words reinforcing stimuli) the object will also come to elicit those evaluative meaning responses, that is, will also come to be a reinforcer. Thus, if words like *beauty, win, gift, sweet, honest, smart, rich, sacred, friend, valuable, happy, pretty, healthy, success, love,* and so on were paired with a person, that person would become a stronger positive reinforcer, and stronger S^D capable of controlling many "positive" verbal and motor behaviors.

It would not even be necessary that the individual himself be paired with the word reinforcers. The same end could be achieved by pairing his name with the word reinforcers. . . . It would also be possible to pair an individual's picture with the reinforcing words and thus produce the conditioning and its effects [A. W. Staats, 1964, pp. 334–335].

. . . it should be possible to manipulate the attitudinal value of a social stimulus (a person) and then test changes in the value of the social stimulus as an ^{UC}S, as a reinforcing stimulus, and as a controlling discriminative stimulus. Thus, the positive attitudinal value of the person could be changed through classical conditioning procedures in which the person is paired with positive attitudinal stimuli. Then the effects of the person would be expected to change. People or other stimuli (messages, for example) paired with this person should acquire more attitudinal value according to classical conditioning principles [A. W. Staats, 1968, pp. 56–57].

The contributions of Albert and Bernice Lott to a reinforcement model of attraction have already been mentioned, but a further example will be given:

There is a clear agreement among many contemporary theorists that attraction will follow if one individual either directly provides another with regard or need satisfaction, is perceived as potentially able to do so, or is otherwise associated with such a state of affairs. Furthermore, the specific antecedent variables which empirical research has shown to be related to interpersonal attraction can, for the most part, be interpreted in support of this general proposition [A. J. Lott & Lott, 1965, p. 287].

The examples given by no means exhaust the possible list of contributors or contributions to this general approach. At a slightly further distance in terms of specific interests one could add individuals such as Anderson (1962, 1965b) and his work with the positive and negative properties of descriptive adjectives and the way in which they affect impression formation, Perkins (1968) and his description of the attractiveness of the stimulus situation in terms of positive and negative reinforcement, and Young (Young & Shuford, 1955) who has dealt extensively with the linear function between performance and the positiveness of the stimulus, using rats as subjects.

CRITICISMS OF THE REINFORCEMENT MODEL

Strangely enough, there are also those who do not feel that reinforcement concepts provide a panacea for attraction research. For anyone interested in theoretical confrontation, however, the stance taken here will be disappointing. No attempt will be made to present all possible criticisms of the reinforcement model, all possible counterarguments, or a critique of all alternative positions. A major reason to avoid such painful exercises is the conviction that theories are neither won nor lost, built nor destroyed, judged successful nor unsuccessful on the basis of debating points. Neither arguments nor crucial experiments are the most important factors influencing the acceptance or rejection of a theoretical position. Kuhn (1962) suggests other factors which lead to the success of a given formulation:

> At the start a new candidate for paradigm may have few supporters, and on occasion the supporters' motives may be suspect. Nevertheless, if they are competent, they will improve it, explore its possibilities, and show what it would be like to belong to the community guided by it. And as that goes on, if the paradigm is one destined to win its fight, the number and strength of the persuasive arguments in its favor will increase. More scientists will then be converted, and the exploration of the new paradigm will go on [p. 158].

Frequently, however, one encounters the belief that by anecdote, argument, assertion, and assumption, it is possible to demonstrate the weakness of a theoretical framework and/or the strength of an alternative formulation. Rather, inadequate theories or their supporters fade away and are replaced by other theories with a new set of proponents. If so, theory confrontation via verbal blitzkrieg constitutes an exercise in futility.

For one thing, there is nothing extraordinary about alternative explanations. Kuhn (1962) indicates "Philosophers of science have repeatedly demonstrated that more than one theoretical construction can always be placed upon a given collection of data. History of science indicates that, particularly in the early developmental stages of a new paradigm, it is not even very difficult to invent such alternates [p. 162]."

Alternative explanations which lead to testable hypotheses that are incompatable with an existing formulation represent a much more difficult achievement than the creation of an alternative explanation. Further, experimental designs that provide unequivocal tests of such hypotheses are quite rare in highly developed sciences and next to impossible in psychology, except in the eye of a naive beholder. It would be exciting to have crucial experiments with a gallery of spectators who exclaim in chorus as the last F ratio is calculated, "Son of a gun! Theory X is 30% better than Theory Y!" To date, the results of such "contests" seem primarily to convince those who perceive their side as the victor.

An additional consideration is that theoretical criticism is likely to represent an abortive attempt to communicate across distant points on a continuum of meaning. When there are divergent basic assumptions about the royal road to science, evaluative communications are seldom productive. For example, if individual A is committed to a view of theory which is closely tied to a specified data base, he will be concerned with such questions as operational consistency and boundary conditions and will consider data obtained using different operations (or otherwise beyond the boundary conditions) as irrelevant to the theory. If individual B is committed to a view of theory which is completely transituational and bound only by the space–time continuum, any datum is equally relevant. Communication between A and B simply cannot lead anywhere except to negative interpersonal evaluations.

Perhaps unfairly, the nature of some of the criticisms of the reinforcement model will be suggested below by quoting a few critical comments, most of which were supplied by anonymous consulting editors. One reaction to any such criticism has best been stated by Charles F. Kettering, the inventor of the first successful electric automobile self-starter. "First they tell you you're wrong, and they can prove it. Then they tell you you're right, but it's not important. Then they tell you it's important, but they've known it for years."

"First They Tell You You're Wrong, and They Can Prove It"

I personally am partial to reinforcement theory. Some of my best friends are.... Yet although the authors [Byrne & Clore] make statements with which I agree, I do not find myself attracted to the model.

If the verbal statement were the reinforcing element, misunderstandings as to meaning or intention could not blur the attraction picture. That the problem of interpretation arises is attested to in everyday life as well as in experimentation on the effect. . . . This point underlines the difficulty associated with the basic assumption of reinforcement research on attraction: if attitudes and their proponents are atomistically separable, ironic effects from misunderstandings could not occur. The speaker's words and his intentions (as discerned by the process of interpretation, involving the verbal statement, nonverbal cues, the environmental contingency, and cognitive reconstructions of his possible intentions culminating in a guess) are the separable elements of interpersonal discourse, not the person and his attitudes.

Another problem, which crucial though it is may only be touched on here, is that of the translation of all value-properties proper to the objects of perception into "reinforcements" without attention to them in their own right. With legitimate behavior specified only in terms of response probabilities, this meagerness of descriptive interest is unavoidable. The assessment of the CS when it possesses properties independent of those associated with it through some UCS can only be specified in terms of additional reinforcing units to be combined with those arising from the UCS. In most experimental settings, this problem is *controlled* by using a stooge, thus providing a constant stimulus object. Quantification has thereby excluded articulate qualification (and perhaps quality as well) from the purview of "legitimate" scientific concern: All it has in fact succeeded in doing has been to impoverish drastically the subject matter to which it may attend.

Apparently, if you are able to come in out of the rain without being told, you provide grist for the model's mill.

"Then They Tell You You're Right, but It's Not Important"

The fact that you can put the observation, "people would rather be patted on the head than kicked in the ass" into S-R talk doesn't render it any more profound.

One begins to wonder where it will all end. Are the various journals of social psychology forever condemned to adorn their issues with ever new instances of the Byrne–Clore function? . . . Surely, before we read more of Byrne's work he should tell us what to do with it.

"Then They Tell You It's Important, but They've Known It for Years"

It is doubtful, however, that most other investigators would share their view that the problem is interesting since it would be highly surprising if their formulation did not hold true.

Hypotheses Derived from the Reinforcement Model

The bare bones of a conditioning model of attraction have been outlined in the simplest manner possible. If this basic idea has utility and power, however, it must lead to the generation of hypotheses which broaden the scope of our inquiry far beyond the similarity–attraction base.

One point to consider is that the most intriguing aspects of the model would seem to be those implications that derive from the attraction literature rather than from classical conditioning or other learning paradigms. Attraction theory and research are not likely to contribute to learning theory nor do they need to be constrained by learning theory. It seems unlikely, as Clore (1966) has indicated, that learning theory will serve as more than a midwife to a theory of attraction. What, then, is the nature of the initial steps in our theory-building enterprise?

Relationship between Reinforcement Magnitude, Affect, and Evaluative Responses

One feature of theory development has already been presented in an earlier context. It deals with the precise way in which stimulus information may by conceptualized as combining to determine attraction.

The modified law of attraction was presented as

$$A_x = m \left[\frac{\Sigma (PR_x \times M)}{\Sigma(PR_x \times M) + \Sigma(NR_x \times M)} \right] + k$$

or attraction toward X is a positive linear function of the sum of the weighted positive reinforcements (Number $\times$ Magnitude) associated with X divided by the total number of weighted positive and negative reinforcements associated with X.

What is suggested here is that all positive and negative stimulus information which is associated with X contributes to the way in which X is evaluated and that all such information is processed according to a relatively straightforward combinational rule. The utility of that concept has been seen with respect to studies of topic importance (Chapter 4), personal evaluations (Chapter 5), physical attractiveness, emotional disturbance, and race (Chapter 6). The general idea that attraction responses may be described by a formula which reduces all stimuli to positive and negative elements of varying weights is deceptively simple. To date, the predictive power of this idea has been shown repeatedly.

The development of the modified law of attraction has been somewhat independent of the conditioning model, but the two may be easily integrated. For example, on the basis of the Byrne–Clore model, it is hypothesized that:

1. The affective response elicited by X is a positive linear function of the sum of the weighted positive reinforcements associated with X divided by the total number of weighted positive and negative reinforcements associated with X.

2. Any evaluative response elicited by X is a positive linear function of the sum of the weighted positive reinforcements associated with X divided by the total number of weighted positive and negative reinforcements associated with X.

3. The greater the reinforcement magnitude of a stimulus, the greater its relative weight as a determinant of affective responses, attraction, and any evaluative response.

4. The greater the relative weight of a stimulus as a determinant of affective responses, attraction, and any evaluative response, the greater its reinforcement magnitude.

These are seen as secondary hypotheses, and very little research has been generated solely to test them. They are dependent upon the following primary hypotheses, and most of the theoretically oriented research has been concentrated on three of them.

Reinforcement, Affect, and Attraction

The three essential elements of the model consist of an independent variable (any stimulus with reinforcement properties), an intervening variable (an implicit affective response), and a dependent variable (any evaluative response such as attraction). Not stated formally in describing the model, but implicit in the formulation is the interrelationship of these elements. The viability of the model depends primarily on whether such interrelationships receive empirical confirmation. The hypotheses fall into three categories.

Stimuli that Have Reinforcing Properties

5a. Any stimulus that has reinforcing properties can determine evaluative responses toward other stimuli through association with them.

5b. Any stimulus that does not have reinforcing properties cannot determine evaluative responses toward other stimuli through association with them.

6a. Any stimulus that has reinforcing properties elicits an affective response.

6b. Any stimulus that does not have reinforcing properties does not elicit an affective response.

Stimuli That Can Determine Evaluative Responses

7a. Any stimulus that can determine evaluative responses elicits an affective response.

7b. Any stimulus that cannot determine evaluative responses does not elicit an affective response.

8a. Any stimulus that determines evaluative responses has reinforcing properties and, hence, can alter the probability of the occurrence of any response with which it is associated.

8b. Any stimulus that cannot determine evaluative responses does not have reinforcing properties and, hence, cannot alter the probability of the occurrence of any response with which it is associated.

Stimuli That Elicit Affective Responses

9a. Any stimulus that elicits an affective response can determine evaluative responses toward other stimuli through association with them.

9b. Any stimulus that does not elicit an affective response cannot determine evaluative responses toward other stimuli through association with them.

10a. Any stimulus that elicits an affective response has reinforcing properties and, hence, can alter the probability of the occurrence of any response with which it is associated.

10b. Any stimulus that does not elicit an affective response does not have reinforcing properties and, hence, cannot alter the probability of the occurrence of any response with which it is associated.

The following three chapters will describe the experiments which have tested these hypotheses.

Chapter 11 / Hypothesis Testing:
I. Stimuli with Reinforcing Properties Can Determine Evaluative Responses

Both within the present research paradigm and in the work of the Lotts', the initial test of the reinforcement formulation involved the effect of nonattitudinal reinforcement on attraction. The basic idea was simply that the association of any positive or negative reinforcement with another person would lead, respectively, to positive or negative attraction responses toward that person.

Actually, there was already a body of research, developed relatively independently of social psychological concerns, which dealt with the effect of differential reinforcement on evaluations of initially neutral stimuli. Primarily, these investigations have been identified with a conditioning model and have been explicitly identified with behavior theory. With children as the most usual class of subjects, manipulation of reinforcement has been found to bring about the predicted attitudinal or preferential responses toward puzzles (Gewirtz, 1959; Rosenzweig, 1933), colors (Eisman, 1955), toys (Filer, 1952; Hunt, 1955), nonsense syllables (Nunnally, Duchnowski, & Parker, 1965; Staats & Staats, 1957), sociopolitical slogans (Razran, 1940), persuasive communications (Janis, Kaye, & Kirschner, 1965), unfamiliar items of information (Carriero, 1967), and proper nouns (Staats & Staats, 1958). Further, when positive reinforcement has been varied in terms of consistency across trials (Staats, Staats, & Heard, 1960) or number of reinforced trials (Nunnally, Stevens, & Hall, 1965), the familiar linear relationship with evaluational responses is reported.

A quite different line of research which also provides supporting evidence for the reinforcement formulation deals with the evaluation of tasks or activities as a function of associated reinforcement. A number of these studies are industrial in orientation and have been conceptualized in terms of variables such as job satisfaction. With tasks initially neutral in eliciting evaluative responses, the differential effects of success and failure on subsequent evaluations have been shown repeatedly (Cartwright, 1942; Gebhard, 1948, 1949; Locke, 1965, 1966, 1967; Nowlis, 1941). Even with an intrinsically dull activity, evaluation becomes more positive as a function of the number of rewards associated with it (Collins, Davis, Myers, & Silk, 1964; Leventhal, 1964). The linearity of the relationship was also supported; Locke (1965), for example, noted, "The findings of the four experiments reported here lend strong support to the generality of a linear relationship between degree of task success and degree of liking for and satisfaction with the task [p. 384]."

The question which remains is whether people learn to like other people in the same way that they learn to like nonsense syllables, puzzles, and repetitive tasks. Of Hypotheses 5 and 6 stated in Chapter 10, only 5a has received intensive study in attraction research to date: *Any stimulus that has reinforcing properies can determine evaluative responses toward other stimuli through association with them.*

In addition, the relationship between such reinforcing stimuli and attraction is given in Hypothesis 2 as: *Any evaluative response elicited by X is a positive linear function of the sum of the weighted positive reinforcements associated with X divided by the total number of weighted positive and negative reinforcements associated with X.*

ATTRACTION TOWARD A PERSON
WHO ADMINISTERS REWARDS AND/OR PUNISHMENTS

Functional Relationship between Proportion of Positive Reinforcements and Attraction

The first experiment within the paradigm to test a reinforcement hypothesis was that of McDonald (1962). His investigation was designed to correspond with that of a previous experiment (Byrne, 1962) in which eight levels of attitude similarity had been found to exert a positive linear effect on attraction.

McDonald considered using traditional reinforcers such as electric shock and monetary reward but decided upon a procedure that utilized an achievement-oriented behavior. Essentially, he devised a task on which subjects would want to do well and then manipulated the feedback as to their success or failure. Since such feedback has been shown to have reinforcement properties in performance tasks, its effect on attraction would provide a crucial first test of the model.

Method. A confederate was used to play the role of a stranger and to provide the reinforcements. When the two students reported for the experimental session, a prearranged drawing was held in which the subject found that he would be the "speaker" and the confederate would be the "listener." The following instructions were then given:

> Creativity and imagination are vague and ambiguous terms. Yet, it is known that these abilities are highly important in determining one's success in his vocation, in school, and in establishing good interpersonal relationships with others. What we are investigating in this experiment are the factors that lead one person to attribute creative ability to another person. In other words, we are trying to discover some of the cues that individual A utilizes in appraising the creativity of individual B.
>
> Here is how we will do this. The person who drew the lot of the "speaker" will demonstrate his capacity for creativity which, in turn, will be evaluated by the person who drew the lot of the "listener." The speaker will demonstrate his creative potential by telling the listener a series of seven brief stories. After hearing each story, the listener will evaluate it and give the story a score. It is important that the person playing the role of the speaker introduce into each of his stories as much imagination, cleverness, and ingenuity as he can. The speaker will be provided with a set of seven pictures to use in making up his stories, and he must tell a story about each picture. The listener's only task is to listen and to appraise each story by giving it a score.
>
> To insure that the listener's judgments of the speaker's stories will be made solely upon the basis of the stories and nothing else, the speaker and listener will not be permitted to see each other during the performance of this task. The speaker will sit in a room and, with the aid of a microphone, tell his stories to the listener, who will be in an adjoining room provided with a loudspeaker.
>
> Here is how the listener will transmit his scores to the speaker. On the table in the speaker's room is a panel containing a horizontal row of lamps numbered 10 through 1. In the listener's room is a panel of corresponding switches numbered 10 through 1. If the listener feels the story is a good one, he should push switch number 10, 9, 8, 7, or 6. Lamp number 10 indicates the maximum positive score. If the listener feels the story is a poor one, he should push switch 5, 4, 3, 2, or 1, with the number 1 indicating the most negative score. Hence, after the completion of each story, the speaker will receive feedback by way of the score lamps as to how the listener evaluated the quality of that story.

Each of the 192 subjects was assigned to one of eight experimental conditions in which a predetermined number of high ratings (lights 7–10) and low ratings (lights 1–4) were given, regardless of the quality of the story told. One group of subjects received seven high ratings and no low ones, the next group received six high ratings and one low one, and so on to the eighth group which received no high ratings and seven low ones. The stimulus pictures were seven TAT cards. Immediately after the story-telling session, the subjects were told:

Your partner, the listener, has been asked to write a personality sketch of you based upon what he thinks he has learned about you as you performed this task. Of course, even though you have been doing all of the talking during the past 15 or 20 minutes, you may have gotten some ideas about the person to whom you have spoken. Remember that you have been engaged in a two-man communication situation, and that even though the listener has not spoken to you, he has been communicating and reacting to you by scoring or evaluating your potential for creativity and originality. There is evidence from other research which shows that an accurate impression of a person can be gained from sources other than his verbal behavior. What we are interested in at this point in the experiment is whether you, the speaker, have learned anything about and formed any impression of the person who has been reacting to you. With this purpose in mind, fill out the accompanying Interpersonal Judgment Scale.

TABLE 11–1

MEAN ATTRACTION RESPONSES TOWARD
STRANGER WHO RATED CREATIVITY OF
STORIES[a]

Proportion of high creativity ratings	Attraction
1.00	11.33
.86	11.08
.71	10.62
.57	10.33
.43	9.88
.29	8.96
.14	9.12
.00	8.38

[a]Data from McDonald, 1962.

Results. The mean attraction responses toward the variously reinforcing strangers are shown in Table 11–1. Analysis indicated that the effects on attraction of varying proportions of high creativity ratings were remarkably like the effects of proportion of similar attitudes. In fact, when this relationship is plotted graphically as in Fig. 11–1, the familiar linear function is immediately evident.

The results confirmed Hypotheses 2 and 5a.

Discussion. McDonald (1962) concluded:

The findings reported above strongly support the hypothesis that interpersonal attraction is a function of reward and punishment. When attitude similarity was utilized as the independent variable (Byrne, 1962), its effect on attraction produced results very similar to those of the present experiment. Thus, it appears that an individual's attraction toward another person may be accurately predicted whether this person is a fictitious stranger with similar and dissimilar attitudes or a peer who is actually present and administering positive and negative evaluations of the individual's creative efforts.

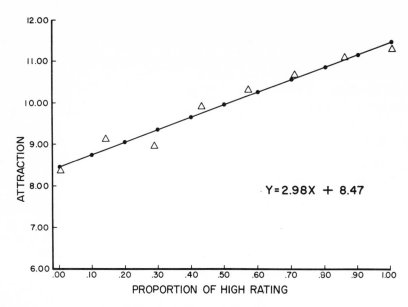

Fig. 11–1. Attraction toward a stranger as a linear function of proportion of high creativity ratings. (After Byrne & Nelson, 1965a, p. 662.)

> The interpretation is clear and straightforward: the combinations of units of reward and punishment represented by high and low scores on the individual's creative stories bear the same functional relationship to interpersonal attraction as do combinations of reward and punishment represented by attitude similarity. Since the attitude similarity variable and the present treatment procedure produce a comparable effect on attraction, it seems reasonable to conceptualize both of these stimulus conditions in terms of a reward–punishment framework [p. 26].

A possible criticism of the McDonald experiment is that the manipulation represented not a new type of reinforcement but simply attitude similarity—the topic being the subject's creativity. McDonald countered this criticism in two convincing ways. First, subjects were asked to give self-ratings of the creativity of their seven stories. It was found that the self-ratings were strongly influenced by the ratings made by the confederates. Therefore, they agreed with the stranger about the creativity of the stories in all eight conditions; attraction was influenced by the positiveness of the ratings and not by agreement. Second, pre-experimental self-ratings of creativity had been obtained. These ratings, presumably, indicated how creative each individual felt himself to be at the beginning of the experiment and, hence, those with high self-ratings should agree with the stranger in the high reward conditions and disagree with him in the low reward conditions; for the low creativity individuals, the reverse should be true. When the subjects were subdivided into high, medium, and low self-rated creativity, these categories were found to be unrelated to the attraction responses; proportion of positive ratings was the only determinant of attraction.

There was, however, another possible criticism of this experiment in that the specific "positive and negative reinforcers" employed by McDonald had not been shown to alter response frequency in a learning experiment. Though there is every reason to believe that they would serve as reinforcing stimuli, additional evidence was required to lay that problem to rest.

Effect of Reinforcements on a Performance Task and on Attraction

In an experimental design to be discussed in greater detail in Chapter 12, Golightly (1965) ran subjects in a discrimination learning task using various reinforcing stimuli including the information "Right" for a correct response and "Wrong" for an incorrect one. Most subjects were able to learn the discrimination easily, so it is clear that the stimuli may be accurately labelled as positive and negative reinforcers.

After the experiment had been completed, each subject was asked to evaluate the experimenter on the Interpersonal Judgment Scale (IJS). The subjects were divided into the 31 who had reached the criterion of learning and the 9 who had failed to do so over the 96 trials. Since the former group had received more positive and fewer negative reinforcements from the experimenter than had the latter group, it was hypothesized that the groups would also differ in attraction toward her. The hypothesis was confirmed, thus adding strength to the McDonald findings.

Combined Effects of Direct Reinforcement and Attitude Similarity on Attraction

Kaplan and Olczak (1970) have provided an additional test of Hypotheses 2 and 5a and have shown that quite different types of reinforcement combine to determine attraction in the manner suggested by the weighted proportion formulation.

Method. The subjects were 135 male undergraduates at Northern Illinois University. The stranger was a female confederate posing as another subject. To eliminate any possible effects of anticipated future interactions, the confederate mentioned that she was transferring to a school on the West Coast in 2 months. Another interesting control was included to hold constant any effect due to the approval cue variable. Before the subject had made his attraction response, the experimenter offhandedly informed him that the girl was quite positive in her evaluation of him.

The experiment was described as one dealing with rewards and learning in which the participants would be attempting to effect learning in their peers and to get to know one another at the same time. First, a 12-item attitude scale was filled out and exchanged; the confederate's scale was simulated to correspond with that of the subject on .00, .50, or 1.00 of the items. Then, the two were brought together, and in a rigged coin toss, the confederate was designated as the experimenter and the subject as the subject.

The task was to cross out the letters M, A, E, I, O, and U in a page of prose, each letter within a 25-second trial. The confederate held a stopwatch and was to reward or punish the subject with tokens after each trial on the basis of his performance. The tokens were redeemable for cigarettes or money at the conclusion of the experiment. Within each similarity condition, the subjects were given two tokens on each trial (1.00 reward), two tokens on half the trials (.50 reward), or no tokens (.00 reward). Afterward, the two participants were separated, and the IJS was administered.

TABLE 11–2
MEAN ATTRACTION RESPONSES AS A FUNCTION
OF DIRECT REINFORCEMENT
AND ATTITUDE SIMILARITY[a]

Proportion of positive reinforcements in learning task	Proportion of similar attitudes		
	.00	.50	1.00
1.00	10.60	11.60	11.67
.50	10.07	10.13	11.73
.00	9.60	9.87	10.60

[a]After Kaplan & Olczak, 1970, p. 187.

Results. The mean attraction responses are shown in Table 11–2. As hypothesized, both attitude similarity and direct reinforcement significantly affected attraction, and there was no interaction. Again, the reinforcement model is supported.

Another interesting feature of the Kaplan and Olczak experiment is the possibility of examining the way in which three different types of stimulus information may be combined in influencing attraction. Each subject received 12 units of attitude information, 6 units of direct reinforcement, and the information that the female confederate was quite positive in her evaluation of him. The latter was said while the subject was filling out the IJS, so we shall assume that its effect is the same as that found in four experiments described in Chapters 5 and 6 (Aronson & Worchel, 1966; Byrne & Ervin, 1969; Byrne & Griffitt, 1966b; Byrne & Rhamey, 1965): a value of +3 for each IJS item or a total of +18 received by all subjects. Further, we can use the established values of $+1$ for each similar attitude and -1 for each dissimilar attitude. The only unknown is the reinforcement manipulation, but it seems reasonable to assume that each reinforced trial is $+1$ and each non-reinforced trial -1. The weighted reinforcement values were computed for each experimental condition, and the resulting proportion entered in the Byrne–Nelson formula. Table 11–3 presents the predicted attraction responses and those actually obtained by Kaplan and Olczak. The correspondence is obvious. The authors pointed out the similarity between this approach and Anderson's (1967) linear-averageing model of impression formation.

TABLE 11–3

PREDICTED AND OBTAINED ATTRACTION RESPONSES
BASED ON POSITIVE EVALUATION, DIRECT REINFORCEMENT,
AND ATTITUDE SIMILARITY

Weighted proportion of positive reinforcements	Predicted attraction response	Obtained attraction response
1.00	12.06	11.67
.92	11.62	11.73
.83	11.14	11.10
.75	10.70	10.13
.67	10.26	10.24
.58	9.78	10.07
.50	9.34	9.60

Beyond documenting the effects of direct reinforcement and the way in which diverse stimulus information may be combined, this experiment also provides scant support for the approval cue or implied liking hypotheses as the basic explanation for all attraction effects. The stranger approved of or liked all of the subjects. In addition, the authors suggest that balance theory would have difficulty in explaining their results:

> A comment, based on indirect evidence, may be made concerning a balance theory approach to attraction. It should be noted that attraction means for the 100% similarity, 0% reward and 0% similarity, 100% reward conditions were identical. This finding can be accounted for by balance theory only by considering reinforcement as a statement of agreement, one with much greater potency than agreement on the 12 attitudinal statements. This interpretation requires the assumption that S uniformly thought his performance was above average, a questionable assumption in such an ambiguous task.

A Further Examination of Direct Reinforcement. Olczak (1969) extended the work of the previous investigation by utilizing direct reinforcement plus attitudes about a third person. The latter variable involves a situation of balance or imbalance, replicating a situation used by Aronson and Cope (1968). It was expected that, in determining attraction, direct reinforcement would combine linearly with the kind of reinforcement provided by shared attitudes about another person.

The experimental design was one in which the subject was treated harshly or pleasantly by an experimenter, eliciting a negative or positive interpersonal attitude. Then the subject overheard the experimenter's supervisor treating the experimenter harshly or pleasantly, thus behaving congruently with the subject's feelings (harsh–harsh or pleasant–pleasant) or incongruently (harsh–pleasant or pleasant–harsh). The supervisor dispensed one of three levels of direct reinforcement to the subject (cigarettes or money representing .00, .50, or 1.00 reinforcement based on story creativity in McDonald's TAT task). The subject's attraction toward the supervisor was measured by means of the IJS.

An overall reinforcement effect was found with attraction increasing as the amount of direct reinforcement increased. The balanced triads yielded more positive responses than the imbalanced ones, but only in the condition of 0% reinforcement. Thus, "my enemy's enemy is my friend" only when no other reinforcement is provided. Reinforcement acted to obscure or completely override the balance effects. Olczak (1969) concluded that "reinforcement was effective in increasing attraction, and predictions stemming from balance theory were not supported [p. 34]."

ATTRACTION TOWARD A PERSON WHO IS SIMPLY ASSOCIATED WITH REWARDS AND/OR PUNISHMENTS

Originally, within the paradigm, the reinforcement proposal was that attraction toward X is determined by the relative amount of positive and negative reinforcements received from X. In the attitude experiments, for example, similar and dissimilar attitudes were expressed by the stranger to the subject. In the formal statement of the model, however, the implications of classical conditioning led to the necessary conclusion that simple association between the neutral stimulus and the reinforcing stimuli was a sufficient condition for the attraction effect. The attitude studies are not designed to test this hypothesis, though the findings are obviously compatible with it. The three experiments just reported also provide data compatible with the theory but fail to put the associational model to a stringent test. An adequate test requires a conditioned stimulus (CS) and an unconditioned stimulus (UCS) to be temporally paired, with the UCS not attributable to the CS. Several investigations have employed such a design.

Success within a Group and Attraction toward Group Members

Lott and Lott (1960) conducted the first experiment to test the hypothesized effect of associated reinforcement. Specifically, they predicted that if a person is rewarded in the presence of others, he will develop positive attitudes toward them.

Method. The subjects were 48 elementary school children. They were divided into 16 three-member groups homogeneous as to sex. Each group was composed of children who had not chosen one another on two sociometric tests administered by their teachers.

The situation in which rewards and nonrewards were manipulated was a board game called "Rocket Ship." The object of the three-person game was to land a cardboard rocket ship on planets. There were different paths to each goal with four choice points or "danger zones." The children in each group took turns in being first to cross a danger zone, so the experimenters could arrange to have some succeed and some fail in reaching the planets safely. When a planet was safely reached, the child received a small plastic auto model as a prize.

Each group tried to reach six planets. Half of the subjects were allowed to land safely on four planets, whereas the other half were prevented from reaching any of the planets. The former returned to their classroom with four model cars and the latter with none. The number of subjects rewarded in each group was systematically varied: zero, one, two, or all three.

At the end of the school day, after all of the games had been played, the classroom teacher administered another sociometric test:

> Suppose your family suddenly got the chance to spend your next vacation on a nearby star out in space . . . you can invite two children to go on this trip . . . and spend the holiday with you on the star. Which two children in this class would you choose to take with you?

Results. The sociometric choices are shown in Table 11–4. The relative number of play-group members chosen by the rewarded subjects was significantly greater than the number chosen by the nonrewarded subjects.

Discussion. It should be noted that the results are somewhat weak, but they are clearly in the predicted direction. One difficulty lies in the dependent variable consisting of relative choice responses rather than an absolute rating such as the IJS. Thus, the 37 rewarded subjects who chose friends outside of the play group may well have liked those associated with positive reinforcement, but they just liked some other individuals better. The fact that 11 of these rewarded subjects dropped at least one friend (as measured by the pre-experimental sociometric tests) and named someone associated with reward suggests the potential power of the reinforcement effect.

TABLE 11-4
CHOICES MADE BY SUBJECTS
ON SOCIOMETRIC TEST[a]

	Choices	
Subjects	Member of play group	Nonmember of play group
Rewarded	11	37
Not rewarded	3	45

[a]After Lott & Lott, 1960, p. 299.

Success—Failure and Performance Similarity

Senn (1971) investigated the combined effects of task success and performance similarity on attraction. The subjects were 60 undergraduate males at Franklin and Marshall College. On a reaction time task, pairs of subjects were either both successful, both unsuccessful, or one was successful and the other unsuccessful. During the task, subjects were aware of both their own and the other person's performance. Attraction ratings were obtained afterward.

It was found that attraction was greater in the success—success condition than in the failure—failure condition. Presumably, both similarity of performance and task success contributed to attraction in the former group, whereas only performance similarity was operative in the latter group. The mixed group was as negative as the totally unsuccessful group, and the attraction of the successful and unsuccessful members of the pair did not differ. Since both subjects were exposed to a dissimilar other, differential success should have led to differential attraction.

Combined Effects of Direct and Associated Reinforcement

Griffitt (1968b) tested both Hypotheses 2 and 5a with a convincing demonstration of the way in which direct and associated reinforcement may be combined in determining attraction. He hypothesized that attraction is a positive function of both proportion of similar attitudes expressed by a stranger (direct reinforcement) and amount of reinforcement from another source while the stranger is present (associated reinforcement).

Method. The subjects were 40 undergraduates at the University of Hawaii. Students in the introductory course at Hawaii may add points to their final course total by participating in research projects. One point is given for each participation up to a maximum of 5.

In this experiment, subjects participated in the usual attitude–attraction task with the stranger either .25 or .75 similar. For the manipulation of associated reinforcement, half of the subjects in each condition were told that they would receive 4 bonus points of experimental credit for participating in the experiment in addition to the usual credit of 1 point. Thus, the stranger was directly responsible for the attitudinal similarity and had absolutely no responsibility for the awarding of bonus points.

TABLE 11–5

MEAN ATTRACTION RESPONSES TOWARD
STRANGERS AS A FUNCTION OF ATTITUDE
SIMILARITY AND BONUS CREDIT POINTS[a]

Bonus point credit	Proportion of similar attitudes	
	.25	.75
+4	8.60	10.90
+0	6.70	9.60

[a] After Griffitt, 1968b, p. 147.

Results. The mean attraction responses are shown in Table 11–5. Both types of reinforcement were found to have a significant effect on attraction, and there was no interaction.

In addition, by assigning a weight of +2 to each bonus point (and the usual +1 for similar attitudes and −1 for dissimilar attitudes), Griffitt was able to obtain a linear function between the combined types of reinforcement and attraction.

As Griffitt (1968b) concluded, "It is apparent that attraction responses are influenced by reinforcement associated in time with a stranger in much the same way as by reinforcement directly attributable to him [p. 147]."

Associated Reinforcement and Evaluation of Human and Non-human Conditioned Stimuli

The success of the previous experiment led Griffitt and Guay (1969) to conduct a more elaborate test of the reinforcement model. They point out that the model states that the CS need only be present and discriminable at the time positive or negative reinforcement occurs in order to acquire positive or negative qualities for the subject. They categorized the various types of CS as a human responsible for the reinforcement (HR), human not responsible (HNR), nonhuman responsible (NHR), and nonhuman not responsible (NHNR). Evaluation of each type should be determined in the same way.

With a human CS, supporting evidence consists of the kind of experiments reported in the present chapter. With respect to nonhuman CS, they pointed to the effect of reinforcement on evaluation of nonsense syllables, proper nouns, puzzles, etc.

> With respect to NHR stimuli the data are anecdotal but quite convincing. Consider an individual's evaluation of a dog which has just bitten him, his response to a door which has smashed his finger, or one's evaluation of his automobile which has just broken down on the freeway. Experience, as well as the reinforcement model, would predict negative evaluations of such NHR stimuli. In contrast, positive responses would be predicted to the computer which has just efficiently completed the analysis of one's research data or to a racehorse which wins one a large sum of money. Such evaluative responses are consistent with the reinforcement model even though systematic data are not available. It should be noted that cognitive theories make no predictions concerning evaluations of HR, HNR, NHR, or NHNR stimuli in settings such as those described above. In the absence of communication between S and a second individual concerning the object to be evaluated, no predictions are possible within the boundaries of the cognitive framework [Griffitt & Guay, 1969, p. 3].

In their first experiment, subjects received positive or negative reinforcements from one individual (direct reinforcement, HR) in the presence of a second individual (associated reinforcement, HNR). On the basis of the model, it was hypothesized that attraction toward both individuals would be a positive function of the proportion of positive reinforcements received by the subject.

HR and HNR Conditioned Stimuli. McDonald's (1962) procedure was altered so that evaluation could be of a stranger who made the ratings of the subject's creativity or of a stranger who was present during the reinforcement but not responsible for it. The subjects were 48 students at the University of Hawaii.

The subject was seated at one of two facing booths and asked to fill out an attitude scale. During this period, a confederate (unseen by the subject) entered, introduced himself and a third (mythical) subject to the experimenter, and apologized for being late. One was asked to sit at the second booth and the other at a nearby table.

The experimenter then described the creativity experiment and explained that only the two subjects in the booths would participate. On the seven stories, half of the subjects received all positive ratings, and half received all negative ratings. Afterward, subjects were asked to evaluate one of the other "subjects" on the IJS. First, in order to provide a rationale for the judgments, an attitude scale (each of which was simulated as .50 similarity) was given to each subject.

TABLE 11–6

MEAN ATTRACTION RESPONSES TOWARD
HUMAN RESPONSIBLE (HR) AND
HUMAN NOT RESPONSIBLE (HNR) FOR
REINFORCEMENT AS A FUNCTION OF
PROPORTION OF POSITIVE REINFORCEMENT[a]

Stimulus	Proportion of positive reinforcement		
	.32	.68	Total
HR	9.00	11.42	10.21
HNR	9.25	11.33	10.29
Total	9.12	11.38	—

[a]After Griffitt & Guay, 1969, p. 4.

The mean attraction responses are shown in Table 11–6. The only significant effect was that of proportion of positive reinforcements. As hypothesized, whether a stranger is the direct source of reinforcement or merely present when reinforcement is received, attraction is a positive function of the proportion of positive reinforcements associated with that stranger.

Griffitt and Guay went on to examine the effects of reinforcement on the evaluation of nonhuman, nonresponsible stimuli.

HR and NHNR Conditioned Stimuli. The subjects were 36 University of Hawaii undergraduates, and the general procedure was identical to that of the previous experiment. Only four TAT pictures were used, and they were matched in a pilot study with respect to evaluative ratings on the semantic differential scale. Instead of a confederate, the experimenter served as the human, nonresponsible stimulus.

Subjects received either .25, .50 or .75 positive ratings for their stories. All possible orders of positive and negative ratings on the four stories were employed. Afterward, the subject was asked to rate the confederate on the IJS and then to rate the experimenter, the apparatus, each TAT picture, and the experiment in general on semantic differential scales.

The evaluations of the various conditioned stimuli are shown in Table 11–7, and the differences are significant for each of the first four stimuli. In addition, these various evaluative responses are (with one exception) positively intercorrelated.

It might be thought that such results could be interpreted as some sort of general set or halo effect which carries across the various rating scales. The ratings of the four TAT pictures disconfirm that notion. That is, the total

TABLE 11-7
MEAN EVALUATIVE RESPONSES TOWARD
HUMAN RESPONSIBLE (HR),
HUMAN NOT RESPONSIBLE (HNR), AND
NONHUMAN NOT RESPONSIBLE FOR REINFORCEMENT
(NHNR) AS A FUNCTION OF PROPORTION OF
POSITIVE REINFORCEMENT[a]

Stimulus	Proportion of positive reinforcement		
	.25	.50	.75
Confederate (HR)	8.92	9.33	10.67
Experimenter (HNR)	35.67	36.67	39.00
Apparatus (NHNR)	31.58	32.67	33.58
Experiment (NHNR)	32.17	40.17	41.25
Positively reinforced picture (NHNR)	27.83	27.25	26.78
Negatively reinforced picture (NHNR)	19.61	23.17	24.08

[a]After Griffitt & Guay, 1969, p. 6.

proportion of positive reinforcements did not affect the picture ratings, but there was a highly significant effect of positive versus negative ratings on each picture. That finding is even more important when analyzed further. The apparatus, for example, was associated with all four ratings and, hence, evaluation of it was determined by the proportion of those four ratings which was positive. A given TAT picture for a given subject, however, was present and associated with only one rating and, hence, it was associated with either .00 or 1.00 reinforcement. The findings constitute powerful evidence not only for the reinforcement model but for the sensitivity and selectivity of subjects in responding to different stimuli.

Griffitt and Guay (1969) also discuss other implications of such findings:

> In light of the findings of the present studies, it is interesting to speculate concerning the "rationality" of one's evaluational and attitudinal processes. For example, in the present studies Ss evaluated the *same* experimenter, apparatus, experiment, TAT pictures, and unseen persons more positively when associated with positive stimulus conditions than when associated with negative stimulus conditions. Such differential evaluation is clearly not solely based on a "logical" and "rational" process of examination of the positive and negative attributes of the stimuli in question but to a large extent on the less rational basis of conditioned affect. It is not surprising then, that, other things being equal, or perhaps even unequal, the salesman who creates the most positive conditions for his customers will make the most sales. "Rational cognition" is not a necessary element of the reinforcement model of evaluational responses [pp. 7-8].

Limits of Associated Reinforcement. In the Griffitt and Guay situation, the affect elicited by the ratings serves to influence the subject's evaluations of a wide variety of stimulus objects associated with that affect. Hughes (1969) questioned the extent to which this "irrational evaluation" would occur if the stimulus objects themselves were not only present in the situation but also provided direct reinforcement. Would the resulting evaluations be a blend of the two sources of reinforcement or would subjects sharply differentiate one reinforcing stimulus from another?

Hughes' experiment again employed the McDonald procedure but with two judges to rate the subject's creativity—one consistently positive and the other consistently negative. A further manipulation was that the two judges were either both present during the reinforcement sequences or each was only present while giving his own creativity judgments. Hughes hypothesized that the simultaneous presence of two individuals providing contrasting reinforcements would, through association, alter the evaluation of each, compared to the situation in which the reinforcing individuals were physically segregated.

The subjects were 32 undergraduates at the University of Texas. As in the second Griffitt and Guay experiment, four TAT stories were told and evaluated. For half of the subjects, Confederate A waited outside the room while Confederate B heard and judged the stories; then Confederate B left during Confederate A's judging procedure. For the remaining subjects, Confederates A and B remained in the room continuously. In each instance, one confederate rated two stories positively and the other rated two stories negatively. The order of positive and negative ratings was counterbalanced. Afterward, subjects completed the IJS and the Griffitt and Guay rating scales.

The mean attraction responses are shown in Table 11–8. The only

TABLE 11–8
MEAN ATTRACTION RESPONSES TOWARD
POSITIVELY AND NEGATIVELY REINFORCING STRANGERS[a]

No. of strangers	Negatively reinforcing stranger	Positively reinforcing stranger
One stranger present during reinforcement	9.19	11.06
Both strangers present during reinforcement	8.94	11.00
Total	9.06	11.03

[a] Data from Hughes, 1969, p. 12.

significant effect on attraction was that of positive and negative reinforcement. The reinforcement provided by one stranger had no effect on the evaluation of a second reinforcing stranger regardless of whether or not both were physically present during the two reinforcement sequences.

Hughes suggested that the failure of Reinforcer A to affect evaluations of Reinforcer B (and vice versa) may be the result of a failure of the IJS to measure small differences. He also suggested that it is possible that the susceptibility of a stimulus to conditioned affect is altered by the extent to which that stimulus is perceived as a responsible reinforcer. That is, the evaluation of a previously neutral stimulus is totally determined by the reinforcers with which it is associated. The evaluation of a reinforcing stimulus is totally determined by the reinforcement for which it is reponsible. Should this formulation be supported, an alteration or further specification of Hypothesis 5a is obviously required. Hughes (1969) suggests the following reformulation:

> Affect will be conditioned to multiple stimulus objects (responsible and nonresponsible) to the extent that the subject does not isolate the source of his affect. To the degree that the subject is unable to confidently identify the source of his affect, all stimuli present and discriminable at the time of reinforcement will be treated as responsible sources and will hence be susceptible to conditioned affect [p. 17].

Further Evidence of Stimulus Discrimination. In support of Hughes' point, it has been found that the ability of subjects to identify and discriminate differentially reinforcing stimuli is excellent. In a laboratory project directed by Robert Godbout and David Ziff, subjects were given a 12-item attitude scale on which the responses of two strangers were recorded in two different colored check marks. One of the strangers was .17 similar to the subject, and the other was .83 similar. Thus, in reading through the scale, each subject received two bits of information concerning each item. The task at the end was to indicate attraction toward the two different strangers.

The obtained attraction responses of 6.71 and 9.07 suggest that even in this potentially confusing situation, individuals are able to make quite precise discriminations when each of two stimuli is clearly associated with different proportions of reinforcement.

Attitudes as Unconditioned Stimuli. Since attitude statements are conceptualized as reinforcers, their effect on evaluative responses should not be limited to the stranger associated with them. Hence, any other discriminable stimulus in the situation should also play the role of CS.

Baskett (1971) exposed 111 subjects to one of three levels of similarity (.20, .50, or. 80) on a 24-item attitude scale. In addition to measuring attraction toward the stranger, Baskett also administered an 11-item

7-point agree–disagree scale (Holmes, 1967) to measure the subject's reaction to the experiment. It was hypothesized that as the proportion of similar attitudes increased, the evaluation of the experiment would be increasingly positive.

Factor analysis isolated two primary factors comprising seven items in the scale, and they were labelled by Baskett as Effort and Evaluation of Psychological Experiments. The items are as follows:

(Effort)

1. In psychological experiments I try to cooperate as much as possible.

2. I have a strong desire to perform at my very best in psychological experiments.

3. I try to the best of my ability to do what is asked of me in experiments.

4. As a subject in psychological research I try to figure out what an experiment is all about.

(Evaluation)

1. I see considerable meaning in the experiment in which I have participated.

2. If I were performing psychological experiments I would try to emulate the methods I have seen others use.

3. So far, I have been very impressed by what I have seen concerning psychological experiments.

Scores on each factor were positively related to the similarity of the stranger to whom the subjects were exposed. The more similar the stranger, the more likely the subject was to say that he wanted to cooperate, wanted to perform at his best, could see meaning in the experiment, was impressed by the experiment, etc.

Descriptive Adjectives as Unconditioned Stimuli. It has been found repeatedly in research on human learning that descriptive adjectives have reinforcement properties (e.g., Finley & Staats, 1967; Stalling, 1970). In addition, such stimuli have been used extensively in studies of impression formation (e.g., Anderson, 1965a,b, 1966, 1968b; Asch, 1946). It is not an astounding conceptual leap to suggest, then, that such stimuli should be able to function as UCS in determining atttraction.

Griffitt, Byrne, and Bond (1971) hypothesized that attraction toward a stimulus person is a positive linear function of the proportion of positive adjectives associated with that person. An additional manipulation was a variation in the context in which the adjectives were presented.

The subjects in the first sample were 63 students at Stanford University, whereas the second sample was composed of 90 students at the University of Texas.

Three proportions of positive adjectives were created by using words prescaled as to favorableness by Anderson (1968a). In the .20 condition each subject was presented with a list of 20 adjectives of which 4 were positive and 16 negative. The .80 condition was the reverse of this. In the .50 condition the lists consisted of 10 positive and 10 negative adjectives. A separate list was prepared for each subject in each condition with the serial position of positive and negative adjectives randomly determined within each.

In each sample and within each proportion condition, one-third of the subjects was assigned to each of three instructional conditions designed to vary the relevance of the adjective descriptions to the subject. In the low relevance condition, each subject was told that the adjective description he was to read had been randomly generated by a computer as a description of a hypothetical person. In the medium relevance condition, subjects were told that the adjectives applied to an anonymous real person who had been described by a fellow student following a brief interaction. High relevance condition subjects were told that the adjective description was of themselves.

The low and medium relevance subjects rated the stimulus person on the IJS, whereas the high relevance subjects rated the person who had written the description.

The Stanford and Texas samples did not differ, so their data were

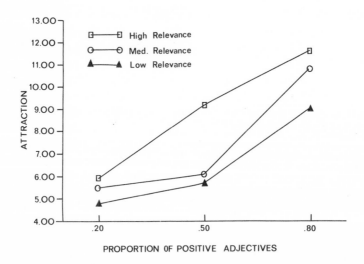

Fig. 11–2. Attraction as a function of proportion of positive adjectives and personal relevance of adjective descriptions. (After Griffitt, Byrne, & Bond, 1971, p. 116.)

combined. The effect of proportion of positive adjectives and of personal relevance are depicted in Fig. 11–2. Each of these variables and the interaction significantly affected attraction. An additional finding in the high relevance condition was that the more positive the adjective description the more accurate the descriptions were judged to be.

Thus, attraction was found to be a positive linear function of the proportion of positive descriptive adjectives associated with a target person. Further, the function was also found to be influenced by the context in which the adjectives and target person were presented. Consistent with the reinforcement model, individuals respond to positive and negative descriptive adjectives much as they do to other, quite different positively and negatively reinforcing stimuli. Cognitively, however, quite different meanings are ascribed to acts which are behaviorally similar. For example, in the .20 condition subjects in one group indicated dislike for a person described by mostly negative adjectives, whereas subjects in another group indicated dislike for a person who had described them with those same adjectives (and incorrectly so, they felt). These divergent situations become functionally similar if one conceptualizes them as involving positive and negative stimuli associated with previously neutral stimuli. The specific characteristics of the neutral stimulus (hypothetical person, stranger from one's peer group, or stranger who emitted the stimulus words) are irrelevant to the association process.

Comparative Effects of Attitudes and Descriptive Adjectives. Rosenblood's (1970) research was explicitly designed to determine the relationship between the variables used in attraction research and in research on impression formation. The subjects were 79 Ohio State undergraduates who received seven randomly marked attitude items for four stimulus persons. Each stranger was rated on Anderson's (1968a) 8-point favorable–unfavorable scale and on the IJS. The correlation between the two dependent variables was found to be .68.

In a second experiment, using 66 Ohio State students, Rosenblood exposed the subjects to attitudes of varying similarity and to adjectives of varying favorableness. The dependent variables were attraction and favorability ratings. The findings were clear (Rosenblood, 1970):

> The data conclusively demonstrate that both the independent variable, adjective evaluative scale value used in impression formation, and the independent variable, similarity–dissimilarity used in similarity–attraction research, both have the same monotonic relation to the dependent variables used in both paradigms. While this does not exclude the hypothesis that these are different processes, it does demonstrate that results on the relevant dependent variables are the same [p. 29].

Anticipated Reinforcement and Attraction

Griffitt (1968a) pointed out that the implicit affective responses elicited by reinforcing stimuli represent reactions which are in part "expectative" (Hull, 1952) or "hopeful" (Mowrer, 1960) of future reinforcement. Thus, any variables that influence anticipations of future reinforcement should have an effect on attraction.

Money versus Pain. Griffitt (1968a) hypothesized that subjects are more attracted to a stranger from whom they anticipate positive reinforcement than to one from whom they anticipate negative reinforcement.

The subjects were 40 undergraduates at the University of Hawaii. They were given the attitude scale of a stranger (.25 or .75 similar) with whom they supposedly were to interact in a second experiment. Each subject was told that the other student would be assigned the role of experimenter in a discrimination learning task in which he would be the subject. Half of the subjects were told that the student experimenter would positively reinforce each correct response with 5 cents and ignore incorrect responses. The remaining subjects were told that the student experimenter would negatively reinforce each incorrect response with a painful shock and ignore correct responses. It might be noted that the reinforcement is in the future and that its characteristics are not the responsibility of the student experimenter.

The mean attraction responses are shown in Table 11–9. Both the similarity variable and the manipulation of anticipated reinforcement had a highly significant effect on attraction. It will be remembered from Chapter 9 that in another investigation, Griffitt (1969a) found that manipulation of reinforcement (attitude similarity) leads to differential anticipations of future reinforcement. The two experiments together provide a consistent picture of the relationship between anticipatory responses and attraction.

TABLE 11–9

MEAN ATTRACTION RESPONSES AS A
FUNCTION OF ATTITUDE SIMILARITY
AND ANTICIPATED REINFORCEMENT[a]

Anticipated reinforcement	Proportion of similar attitudes		
	.25	.75	Total
Positive	9.40	11.60	10.50
Negative	7.70	10.30	9.00
Total	8.55	10.95	—

[a]After Griffitt, 1968a, p. 355.

Observed Benevolence and Hostility. When one person observes the behavior of another and then evaluates him, the possible determinants of that evaluation are quite varied. The behavior itself may have acquired reinforcement value and, hence, the tendency to elicit an affective response in the observer. The behavior may have been observed previously in other individuals and the evaluation beif of them generalized to the person being observed. An anticipatory response may be involved if the observer assumes that a stranger who behaves in, for example, a rewarding manner to others is likely in the future to behave in a rewarding manner to himself. The anticipatory hypothesis was adopted by Hewitt and Chung (1969).

They had 42 female subjects listen to a tape recording in which the experimenter asked two female confederates (A and B) a series of questions. Person B was asked about her interests, goals, and problems, and A was asked to give her impression of B. Then, the procedure was reversed. The impressions which were given were either generally positive or generally negative. After listening to this tape, the subjects were asked to evaluate B.

It was found that attraction toward B was more positive when B's evaluation of A was positive than when it was negative. This was true regardless of A's evaluation of B. An additional finding was that when B evaluated A negatively, dislike of B was greater when A had evaluated B positively.

These findings are consistent with the notion of anticipatory rewards and punishments, and they serve to extend further the predictive power of the model. "Merely observing one person act in an unfriendly manner toward someone else is apparently sufficient to create a dislike, and merely observing the context in which these actions occur is apparently sufficient to alter the magnitude of the dislike [Hewitt & Chung, 1969, p. 82]."

LEARNING PRINCIPLES AND THE ATTRACTION RESPONSE

If, as the preceding experiments strongly suggest, reinforcing stimuli determine evaluative responses such as attraction, these responses would seem to be acquired through a simple learning process. That conceptualization leads to the proposition that various learning principles should be applicable to the acquisition of attraction. Lott, Aponte, Lott, and McGinley (1969) indicate, "By placing the concept of attraction within the larger framework of general behavior principles it has been possible to derive testable hypotheses regarding the conditions necessary for the development of liking and its effect on subsequent behavior of the liker [p. 101]." Three examples of such hypotheses will be presented in the present chapter involving delay of reward, incentive value, and drive.

Immediate versus Delayed Reward and Attraction

Lott *et al.* (1969) based their attraction predictions on Hull's (1952) proposal that "the greater the delay in reinforcement, the weaker will be the generalized r_G, the weaker the S_G, and consequently the weaker the secondary reinforcement [p. 128]." A number of animal experiments have provided support for the proposed effects of delay of reward on performance as have experiments with children dealing with instrumental responses and discrimination learning.

Method. First-grade children ($N = 48$) participated individually in the experiment. There were two separate but identical cubicles at each of which sat an adult male assistant. When a subject was seated with one assistant, he could not see the other.

With one of the assistants, immediate reward always followed task completion, whereas there was a 10-second delay between completion and reward with the other assistant. The subjects filled the holes in a board with marbles and were rewarded with a dried bean after each board was filled. They were told that as soon as they had filled up a tube with the beans, they would receive a toy which they had previously selected. Subjects alternated between assistants across trials.

Afterward, the assistants left the room, and the experimenter showed the subject a photo of each assistant. He asked, "Which helper did you like the best?" Each was also rated on a 15-point scale and on a semantic differential scale.

A control group went through the same procedure except that each assistant used both immediate and delayed reward.

Results. On the liking scale, there was a significant preference for the assistant providing immediate reward over the one providing delayed reward; there was no difference in the control group. Parallel results were obtained on the semantic differential and on the question about which helper was liked best.

Thus, attraction seems to be greater toward a stimulus person associated with immediate reward than toward one associated with delayed reward.

Incentive, Drive, and Attraction

Lott, Bright, Weinstein, and Lott (1970) investigated attraction as a function of reinforcement in situations of varying incentive value (or goal quality) and varying drive level. They proposed that previously neutral stimulus persons who are associated with positive reinforcement will evoke greater attraction in individuals who received the positive reinforcement under appropriate high drive than under appropriate low drive. Further, attraction should be greater toward a stimulus person associated with a more desirable drive-relevant reward than toward one associated with a less desirable reward.

Differentially Preferred Food, Hunger, and Attraction. The subjects were 60 first-grade children. The stimulus persons were photographs of male and female college seniors previously scaled as eliciting neutral liking responses from other first graders. Drive was manipulated by running half of the subjects before and half after lunch. Incentive was manipulated by obtaining each subject's preferences among five snack foods (pretzel stick, peanut, cheese cracker, corn chip, oysterette). The most and least preferred snacks were assumed to differ in incentive value.

Again, there was a marble task. When the board was filled, the subject received a box with one of the photographs on it and one of the snacks inside. In 28 trials, half of the time the reward box was covered with a photo of Adult A and half of the time with Adult B.

Afterward, each subject was shown first one photograph and then the other and asked to respond to each on the 15-point liking scale.

It was found that attraction was influenced by variation in incentive value but not by drive level. Control groups who received only high incentive or only low incentive rewards did not show differential preference. It was suggested that the experience of contrasting incentives may be necessary for stimuli associated with them to become differentially attractive. The failure of the drive manipulation was attributed to individual differences in hunger and satiety and to the possible arousal of an appetitional drive by the sight of the snacks.

Need for Academic Recognition and Attraction. In a second experiment, Lott *et al.* (1970) employed a different drive, need for academic recognition, and a different subject population, college students.

The subjects were 31 undergraduates. Differences in drive were measured by Liverant's (1958) Goal Preference Inventory. Academic recognition is defined as the need to be considered competent or good in academic situations, to have academic behaviors approved and admired by others, and to gain academic status. High and low drive subjects were selected for the experiment.

The experimenter administered two paper and pencil timed tests identified as measures of intelligence. Half of the subjects were assigned to a reward condition and half to a nonreward condition. The former received easier items and norms indicating they had done very well (percentile of 85 or above). The nonreward subjects received harder items and norms indicating they had not done well.

The experimenter who administered the tests was rated on a semantic differential, the liking scale from the IJS, and a 30-point liking scale.

The entire procedure was repeated in a second session except that the reward and nonreward groups switched places, and a different experimenter administered.the tests.

The high drive subjects were found to be more interested in the task than were the low drive subjects. As hypothesized, subjects high in need for academic recognition manifested significantly more positive attraction toward the stimulus person who was present when this need was satisfied than toward a person present when this need was not satisfied. As expected, low need subjects were not differentially attracted to the two stimulus persons.

Lott *et al.* (1970) suggest:

> It seems reasonable to conclude, on the basis of the obtained data, that there is a positive relation between variation in drive level of a rewarded individual and his acquisition of a positive attitude toward person stimuli associated with that reward. What is called rewarding, in other words, appears to be only functionally so if it satisfies a drive, which is what a drive-reduction approach to reinforcement would suggest [p. 74].

CONCLUSIONS

These investigations support the hypothesis that stimuli with reinforcing properties can, through association with neutral stimulus objects, determine evaluative responses toward those objects. The reinforcement may be administered by the stimulus or simply be associated with it, may involve anticipation of future reinforcement rather than actual reinforcement, and its effects depend on such familiar learning principles as immediate versus delayed reward, incentive value of the reinforcement, and drive level of the subject. These effects hold across a wide variety of reinforcing stimuli and quite different motivational states. These effects seem to conform to the linear function first derived in attitude studies, and the combined effects of different types of reinforcement are predictable on the basis of the combinational rules developed in the attitude–evaluation studies. Thus, Hypotheses 2 and 5a have received considerable empirical support and conceptual elaboration.

Chapter 12 / Hypothesis Testing: II. Stimuli That Can Determine Evaluative Responses Elicit Affective Responses and Have Reinforcing Properties

In many respects the reasoning underlying the experiments to be reported in the present chapter is complementary to that described in the previous chapter. That is, various stimuli have been found to influence attraction. If the reinforcement model is a useful explanation of that relationship, it not only follows that any stimuli that are known to have reinforcement properties would be expected to influence attraction but also that any stimuli that are known to influence attraction would be expected to have reinforcement properties.

A few studies have been conducted which are relevant to Hypothesis 7a (Chapter 10): *Any stimulus that can determine evaluative responses elicits an affective response.* A detailed discussion of the affective response will be deferred until the following chapter, but some of the relevant data will be presented here.

Most of the research to be discussed is based on Hypothesis 8a: *Any stimulus that can determine evaluative responses has reinforcing properties and, hence, can alter the probability of the occurrence of any response with which it is associated.*

AFFECTIVE RESPONSES ELICITED BY STIMULI
THAT DETERMINE ATTRACTION

The notion that the stimuli determining attraction also elicit affect has not been a primary focus of extensive research. One such finding has already been described in Chapter 10. In the experiment by Byrne and Clore (1970), it was found that similar attitude statements tended to elicit semantic differential responses indicative of positive affect (comfortable, good, high, happy, pleasant, positive), whereas dissimilar attitude statements tended to elicit responses indicative of negative affect (uncomfortable, bad, low, sad, unpleasant, negative). If one is willing to accept these self-ratings of feelings, these findings are supportive of Hypothesis 7a. If the semantic differential scales are seen as minor variants of the kinds of questions asked on the IJS, such findings would not generate intense excitement. Two other kinds of evidence are available, however.

Attitude Similarity–Dissimilarity and Effectance Arousal

In research to be described in Chapter 13, Byrne and Clore (1967) characterized the specific quality of the affective state aroused by attitudinal disagreement as "effectance." Arousal was described as unpleasurable with a negative emotional tone. The specific characteristics postulated were tenseness or uneasiness, confusion, sense of unreality, dreamlike feeling, and desire for social comparison. A self-rating scale was built to measure these responses. It was hypothesized that exposure to the similar and dissimilar attitudes of a stranger arouses the effectance motive and that dissimilar attitudes are more arousing than similar ones.

The subjects were 46 undergraduates at the University of Texas. They took part in a typical similarity–attraction experiment and, in addition to the Interpersonal Judgment Scale (IJS), were asked to fill out the effectance arousal scale. For comparison purposes, 95 additional subjects were shown either a neutral control movie or a movie specifically designed to arouse the effectance motive.

In Table 12–1 are shown the mean effectance arousal scores of subjects in response to the neutral movie, the attitudes of a stranger, and the effectance arousal movie. As expected, the attitude material was more arousing than the neutral movie and less arousing than the effectance movie.

The subjects in the attraction experiment were subdivided into those receiving relatively similar strangers (.58 to 1.00 similarity) and those receiving relatively dissimilar strangers (.25 to .50 similarity). The mean effectance arousal score of the former group was found to be 8.83, whereas that of the

TABLE 12–1

MEAN EFFECTANCE AROUSAL SCORES IN
RESPONSE TO CONTROL MOVIE, ATTITUDES OF
A STRANGER, AND EFFECTANCE AROUSAL
MOVIE[a]

Neutral control movie	Attitudes	Effectance arousal movie
7.82	9.52	12.73

[a]After Byrne and Clore, 1967, p. 12.

latter was 10.22. Not only does attitudinal material arouse the effectance motive, but arousal is differentially influenced by similar and dissimilar attitude statements.

Attitude Similarity–Dissimilarity and Physiological Arousal

Self-ratings of feelings are consistent with Hypothesis 7a, but it would be more convincing to have independent evidence that attitudes elicit affect. Clore and Gormly (1969) have provided such evidence using a physiological indicator of arousal.

The subjects were 49 undergraduates at the University of Illinois. At the laboratory, each subject met a same-sex confederate who was supposed to be another subject. The two individuals completed a 12-item attitude survey and then were placed in an interactive situation. The session consisted of each subject stating his responses to the attitude scale with the confederate agreeing on .25 or .75 of the items. Continuous recordings of autonomic activity were made during the interaction and a measure of skin conductance was obtained.

As usual, a similar stranger was liked better than a dissimilar one. The skin conductance measure* indicated differences between the agree–disagree groups. As may be seen in Fig. 12–1, these differences were clearly established by the time seven attitudes had been stated. Disagreement appears to produce arousal as measured physiologically.

Attitude Similarity—Dissimilarity, Enjoyment, and the Perception of Time

Meadow (1971) approached the problem of the affective consequences of attitude similarity both directly and indirectly. With 30 Purdue undergraduates as subjects, the design involved the presentation of the attitudes

---

*Highest point of conductance during a 5-second interval, corrected for individual differences in range.

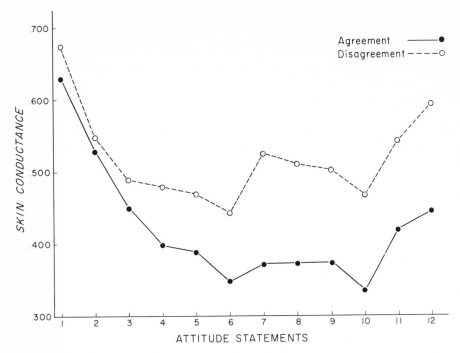

Fig. 12–1. The effect of attitudinal agreement and disagreement on skin conductance level. (After Clore & Gormly, 1969.)

of a stranger who was either .17 or .83 similar. While engaging in this task, the subjects were asked to estimate when 5 minutes had elapsed by pressing a buzzer (which stopped a timing device). In addition, subjects responded to the stranger on the IJS and completed an enjoyment scale. The latter measure asked them to indicate the extent to which the experimental period

TABLE 12–2
EFFECTS OF ATTITUDES ON ATTRACTION,
ENJOYMENT, AND TIME ESTIMATION[a]

	Proportion of similar attitudes	
Response measures	.17	.83
Attraction	5.33	10.93
Enjoyment (5-point scale)	2.6	3.8
Estimation of 5-minute period	5' 58"	4' 37"

[a]Data from Meadow, 1971.

was enjoyable on a scale ranging from 1 (extremely displeasurable) to 5 (extremely enjoyable).

As may be seen in Table 12–2, proportion of similar attitudes had the familiar effect on attraction and the hypothesized effects on the direct measure of affect (enjoyment ratings) and on the indirect measure of affective state (time estimation). In associational terms, attraction was found to correlate .62 with enjoyment ratings and –.49 with time estimations. As Meadow and others have noted, time sure flies by when you're having a good time; also similar attitudes appear to provide a much better time than dissimilar attitudes.

ATTITUDE STATEMENTS AS POSITIVE AND NEGATIVE REINFORCERS

Similar and Dissimilar Attitudes and Response Probability

To provide an initial test of Hypothesis 8a, it was necessary to devise a learning task in which similar and dissimilar attitude statements could be substituted for traditional reinforcers. In the first experiment in this series, Golightly and Byrne (1964) hypothesized that the probability of the occurrence of a response increases if that response is followed by the presentation of a statement consonant with an attitude held by the responder and decreases if that response is followed by the presentation of a statement dissonant with an attitude held by the responder.

The subjects were 60 undergraduates at the University of Texas who had responded to a 45-item attitude scale. The learning task consisted of a simple discrimination problem. The subjects sat in front of a large wooden apparatus which contained a window for the presentation of the stimulus cards. Each of 96 cards contained a circle and a square. One was black and one white, one large and one small. There were eight possible combinations of shape, size, color, and position, and they appeared in random order in each block of eight trials.

The subjects were run individually, and they were told that the experiment dealt with learning. When a stimulus card appeared in the window, the subject was supposed to choose one of the two figures and say it aloud ("circle" or "square"). Immediately afterward, a card was presented through a slit in the apparatus. The subject read the information printed on the card and then discarded it. The subjects were randomly assigned to one of three experimental conditions. The discrimination to be learned was small–large. Small was correct for half of the subjects, and large correct for the other half. In the traditional reward–punishment group, the choice of the correct stimulus was followed by a card saying "Right"; choice of the incorrect stimulus was followed by "Wrong." The attitude similarity–

dissimilarity group received cards containing statements agreeing or disagreeing with their own position, depending on whether they gave correct
or incorrect responses. For example, the statement would read "There is
definitely a God" or "There is no God" depending on the subject's belief
in God and whether he had just given a correct or incorrect response. In the
control group, the subjects received cards containing neutral statements
of fact relevant to the attitude topics, regardless of whether correct or incorrect responses were given. An example is "Most modern religions are
monotheistic." Trials were continued until the subject reached a criterion
of eight consecutive correct responses or until 96 trials were completed.

The relationship between trials and number of correct responses is
depicted in Fig. 12–2. As hypothesized, the attitude similarity–dissimilarity
group performed better than the control group. The presentation of statements with attitudes similar to and dissimilar from those of the subject acted
to change response probability.

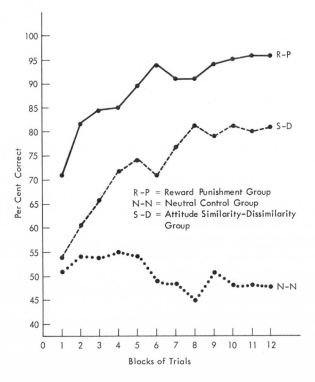

Fig. 12–2. Acquisition curves showing performance changes as a function of traditional
and attitudinal reinforcers. (After Golightly & Byrne, 1964, p. 798.)

An additional finding was that the traditional reward–punishment group performed better than either the control group or the similarity–dissimilarity group. The possibility was raised that such reinforcement was more powerful than attitudinal reinforcement. A different possibility will be discussed shortly.

It was pointed out that the particular research design employed in this experiment made it impossible to determine if similar and dissimilar attitudes must both be used to bring about learning or if either one of these stimuli alone would serve as a reinforcer or even if only one of them had reinforcement properties. Additional research was necessary to identify which of these alternative analyses was correct.

Similar or Dissimilar Attitudes and Response Frequency

Similar or Dissimilar Attitudes versus Neutral Statements. Byrne, Young, and Griffitt (1966) carried out a replication of the Golightly–Byrne experiment and added two conditions in an attempt to test separately the reinforcement properties of similarity and dissimilarity.

The 75 subjects were randomly assigned to one of five experimental conditions. Three of the conditions were precisely like those of the preceding investigation. The two new conditions were a similar–neutral group in which correct responses were followed by an agreeing attitude statement and incorrect responses by a neutral statement and also a neutral-dissimilar group in which neutral statements followed correct responses and disagreeing statements followed incorrect responses.

Another addition to the experimental design was a series of 64 extinction trials following the 96 acquisition trials. Beginning with the 97th trial for all subjects, all responses were followed by the presentation of a blank card.

The acquisition and extinction curves for the five groups are shown in Fig. 12–3. For the three replication groups, the findings are just as in the previous study; both the reward–punishment and similar–dissimilar conditions resulted in the predicted changes in performance, and again the reward–punishment group was superior to the attitude group. In the new groups, there was a surprise. The neutral–dissimilar group clearly learned the discrimination, but the similar–neutral group did not differ from the control group. For the three groups that learned the discrimination, there was an extinction effect.

A straightforward summary of the results for the four attitude groups is that learning takes place only when incorrect responses are followed by a dissimilar attitude statement. Thus, a reasonable conclusion is that the effects of attitude similarity–dissimilarity in either learning or attraction studies are simply a function of the dissimilar attitude statements and that

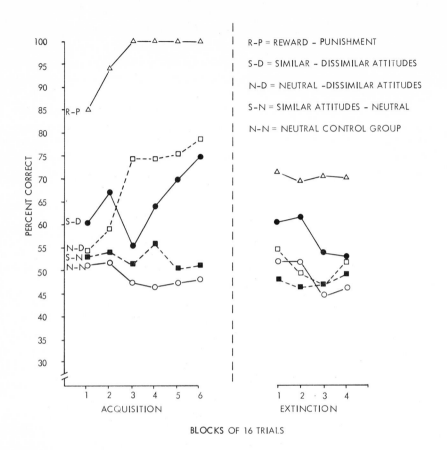

Fig. 12–3. Acquisition and extinction curves showing percentage of correct responses as a function of traditional and attitudinal reinforcers in five experimental conditions. (After Byrne, Young, & Griffitt, 1966, p. 268.)

similar attitudes are irrelevant. A second possibility was advanced, however. Perhaps the results in the similar–neutral group were artifactual as a function of unsuspected attributes of the neutral statements. Such statements are actually statements of fact, and they could be conceptualized as constituting instances of consensual validation about noncontroversial issues. If so, subjects in the similar–neutral group were receiving some degree of positive reinforcement for both correct and incorrect responses and, hence, were unable to learn the discrimination. Byrne *et al.*, (1966) designed a test of the second possibility by using a blank card as the non-reinforcing stimulus in place of the neutral statement card.

Similar, Neutral, or Dissimilar Attitudes versus Blank Cards. The same general procedures were followed as in the two previous experiments. A new sample of 45 subjects was drawn. Each individual was assigned to one of three experimental conditions. In the similar-blank group, the choice of the correct stimulus was followed by an agreeing statement, and an incorrect choice was followed by a blank card. In the neutral-blank group, correct responses were followed by a neutral statement and incorrect responses by a blank card. There was also a blank–dissimilar group in which correct responses were followed by a blank card and incorrect responses by a disagreeing statement.

The acquisition curves for the three groups are shown in Fig. 12–4. All three groups learned the discrimination, and they did not differ from one

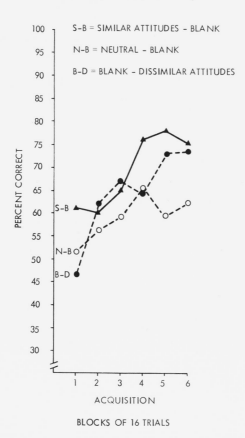

Fig. 12–4. Acquisition curves showing percentage of correct responses as a function of similar, dissimilar, and neutral attitudinal statements. (After Byrne, Young, & Griffitt, 1966, p. 270.)

another. There was also a weak tendency for the attitude groups to perform at a higher level than the neutral statement group.

These results clarified the findings of the previous investigation. Similar and dissimilar attitude statements each have reinforcement properties. Neutral statements of fact also can serve as positive reinforcers. Thus, when similar statements were contrasted with neutral statements, the subjects received two different positive reinforcers and, hence, would not be expected to show performance changes.

Attitude Statements As Discriminating Stimuli. A possible alternative explanation of the attitudinal reinforcement phenomenon is that the attitude statements serve as discriminating stimuli. What we have labelled as reinforcers may only be cues to inform the subject that "large" and "small" are the relevant stimulus dimensions. If discriminating stimuli only informed the subject of the experimenter's definition of the relevant dimensions, performance on the task would remain unaffected. Clore (reported in Byrne *et al.,* 1966) ran 15 subjects on the discrimination apparatus with discriminable but nonreinforcing stimuli presented after each response. Correct responses were followed by a card containing a nonsense syllable beginning with the letter "b," and incorrect responses were followed by a nonsense syllable beginning with "d." After each set of 24 trials, subjects were asked to verbalize their thoughts about the experiment.

By the end of the 96 acquisition trials, the majority of the subjects indicated awareness that b and d syllables were associated with the large and small stimulus figures. Performance remained at the level of chance, nevertheless, for both aware and unaware subjects. Neither type of nonsense syllable was reinforcing, so subjects did not prefer one over the other. Discrimination alone does not lead to performance changes. Once the discrimination is made, performance is affected only if differential reinforcement is provided. It is possible that similar versus dissimilar attitudes on right versus wrong or money versus electric shock are interpreted cognitively by subjects to mean "correct" and "incorrect," so they perform accordingly. If so, the designation "reinforcement" is still an accurate one in that response probability is altered in the predicted direction by such material.

The data in this series of experiments suggest that subjects are motivated to receive attitude statements supporting their views **and also** declarative factual statements. In addition, they are motivated **to avoid** attitude statements contradicting their views.

Individual Differences in Responsiveness to the Reinforcement
Properties of Attitude Statements

Fear of Negative Evaluation. Smith and Jeffery (1970) assumed that attitude statements acquire reinforcing properties because of past discriminative training involving situations of social approval and disapproval. A personality variable, social-evaluative anxiety, was proposed as a characteristic which should mediate the effects of attitudinal reinforcement. Those high in social-evaluative anxiety are motivated primarily to avoid social disapproval. Therefore, the reinforcement properties of attitude statements should be greater for them than for individuals low in social-evaluative anxiety.

The subjects were 38 female undergraduates at the University of Washington who were drawn from the upper and lower extremes of scores on the Fear of Negative Evaluation Scale (Watson & Friend, 1969). This is a 30-item scale dealing with apprehension about the evaluations of others, worry over negative evaluations, and avoidance of evaluative situations. Examples of items are

I become tense and jittery if I know someone is sizing me up.

When I am talking to someone, I worry about what they might be thinking of me.

The procedure was a modified version of the discrimination learning task, with 80 acquisition trials. Awareness of reinforcement contingency was assessed after the completion of the 80 trials.

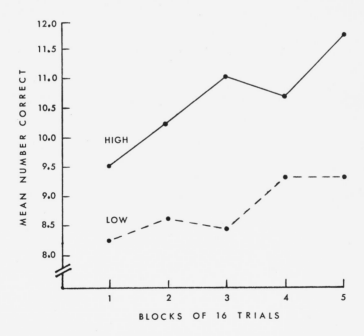

Fig. 12–5. Discrimination learning curves for the high and low social anxiety groups. (After Smith & Jeffery, 1970, p. 278.)

The acquisition curves for the high and low anxiety groups are shown in Fig. 12–5. Not only did the high social-evaluative anxiety subjects show superior performance, but the low anxiety subjects actually showed no learning effects over trials. Awareness was indicated by only five of the subjects and, hence, was not found to be a necessary concomitant of learning in this situation.

Social Avoidance and Distress. As was reported in Chapter 8, several investigators have found that the second measure of social-evaluative anxiety devised by Watson and Friend (1969), social avoidance and distress (SAD), influences the attitude–attraction relationship. Individual differences on this scale would, therefore, be expected to have an analogous influence in a learning situation involving attitudinal reinforcers.

R. E. Smith (1970) selected 15 high and 15 low scorers on the SAD scale to take part in the Golightly–Byrne discrimination learning task.

The results correspond closely with those of the previous study. Subjects low on the SAD scale showed no significant improvement in performance over trials, whereas the high SAD individuals showed the expected learning effects.

It could be concluded that the reinforcement properties of agreeing and disagreeing attitude statements are dependent upon the presence of social–evaluative anxiety.

Attitude Statements versus Traditional Reinforcers

In the two experiments in which attitude statements and a traditional reinforcer (right–wrong) were used, the latter was in each instance more effective. This finding was not particularly surprising, and it was suggested that attitude statements involved reinforcement of smaller magnitude than familiar stimuli such as the words "right" and "wrong." Then, Willard Reitz and his colleagues wisely challenged this assumption.

Homogeneity and Centrality of Attitudinal Reinforcers. Reitz, Douey, and Mason (1968) suggested that one reason for the differential effects of the two kinds of reinforcers was the homogeneity of the traditional reinforcers in contrast to the heterogeneity of the diverse attitudinal statements. Further, if the attitudes were focused on a single topic which was of great importance or relevance to the subjects, the magnitude of the attitudinal statements would be further enhanced. The experimenters selected religion as the topic domain, and chose 40 students in a Catholic high school as subjects. All of the subjects had received high religiosity scores on two measures and were identified as intrinsically or extrinsically motivated. The attitude statements all dealt with religion (e.g., On the whole, religious beliefs are necessary to better and happier living; it makes no difference to me whether religious beliefs are true or false). In addition to the intrinsically and extrinsically motivated groups who received attitudinal reinforcement, there was a traditional right–wrong group, and a control group who received neutral religious statements regardless of the correctness of each response. A modified version of the Golightly–Byrne task was used.

The results are shown in Fig. 12–6. The two groups receiving attitude statements did not differ from the traditional reward–punishment group; all three showed the expected performance changes. No learning was shown by the control group.

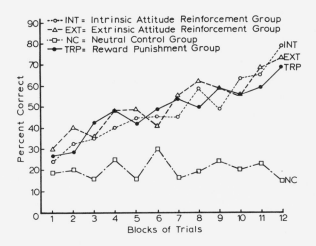

Fig. 12–6. Acquisition curves for the four groups showing percentage of correct responses as a function of traditional and high valence attitudinal reinforcers. (After Reitz, Douey, & Mason, 1968, p. 122.)

Homogeneity and Noncentrality of Attitudinal Reinforcers. Reitz *et al.* (1968) next asked whether their results would remain the same if their subjects had been at the opposite pole of religiosity. They raised the possibility that anti religion is less likely to be a central, integrative value than is pro religion, so the reinforcing effects of antireligious attitudes may be relatively low.

From a pool of 150 students at the University of Western Ontario, 60 with extreme scores on a religion attitude scale were selected as subjects. Each was assigned to either an attitudinal, a traditional reinforcement or a control group. The Golightly–Byrne procedure was again used.

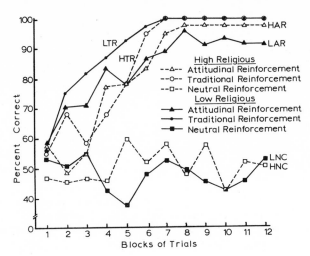

Fig. 12–7. Acquisition curves for the six groups showing percentage of correct responses as a function of traditional reinforcers and religious attitudes for individuals high and low in religiosity. LTR, low religiosity, traditional reinforcement; HTR, high religiosity, traditional reinforcement; HAR, high religiosity, attitudinal reinforcement; LAR, low religiosity, attitudinal reinforcement; LNC, low religiosity, neutral control; HNC, high religiosity, neutral control. (After Reitz, Douey, & Mason, 1968, p. 123.)

In Fig. 12–7 are shown the results. Again, both attitudinal and traditional reinforcers produced learning. Also, the various reinforcements were equally effective for both low and high religiosity groups. So, attitudinal reinforcement was again as effective in producing learning as was a traditional reinforcer, and this held true for both antireligious and religious individuals.

It was concluded that "This attitudinal reinforcement effect appears to be as potent as that produced by traditional reinforcement under conditions of attitude homogeneity and centrality [Reitz *et al.*, 1968, p. 124]."

Homogeneity or Centrality? A question unanswered by the previous two experiments is whether attitudinal reinforcement is equal to traditional reinforcement only when both homogeneity and centrality are present. Byrne, Griffitt, and Clore (1968) manipulated only the homogeneity–heterogeneity of attitudinal reinforcement across a series of topics to determine whether this was the crucial variable in Reitz' experiments.

Again, the Golightly–Byrne procedure was used. The subjects were 45 Texas undergraduates. The three groups used were a traditional reward–punishment (right–wrong) group, a heterogeneous or complex attitude group in which agreements and disagreements were drawn from the full array of 45 topics, and a homogeneous or simple attitude group in which

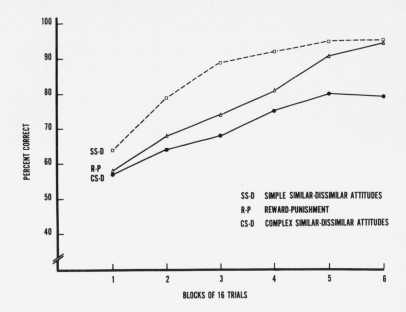

Fig. 12–8. Acquisition curves for the three experimental groups showing percentage of correct responses as a function of traditional reinforcers and simple versus complex attitudinal reinforcers. (After Byrne, Griffitt, & Clore, 1968, p. 963.)

only one topic of similarity–dissimilarity was used for each subject (although a different topic was used for each of the 15 subjects in this condition). The acquisition curves are shown in Fig. 12–8. Both the traditional reward–punishment group and the homogeneous attitude group were superior to the heterogeneous attitude group.

It was concluded that (a) the original findings of the superiority of traditional reinforcers was artifactual in that stimulus homogeneity was not controlled and (b) that the Reitz results were a function of the homogeneity rather than the centrality of the attitude domain.

Learning Instructions versus Preference Instructions. As part of his dissertation research, Clore (1966) used the discrimination learning apparatus with two different instructional conditions. Subjects receiving learning instructions were told that some of the feedback statements indicated that their previous response had been correct and some of the statements indicated that their previous response had been incorrect. In the preference instruction group, subjects were told that there were no right or wrong responses in the experiment and that they were to choose the figure that results in the kind of statement they would like to obtain.

It was found that both groups learned the discrimination and that performance was better under learning instructions than under preference instructions.

Clore concluded that learning in the preference group, in the absence of motivation to be correct, constituted strong support for the reinforcement model.

Verbal Conditioning. It must be remarked that everything touched by similar and dissimilar attitudes does not automatically turn to research gold. Edwards (1970) employed attitude statements in a verbal conditioning task with 84 students at McGill University. Subjects were shown 100 cards on which were printed a past-tense verb and, below this, the pronouns I, we, you, he, she, and they in random order. The task was to make up a sentence choosing a pronoun and using the verb. On the reinforced trials, the experimenter said "good" for "I" and "we" sentences or he presented a card with a similar attitude statement for "I" or "we" sentences and a card with a dissimilar attitude statement for the other four kinds of sentences. There were no significant effects on frequency of "I" or "we" sentences, even for the the subjects in the group receiving "good" as a reinforcer.

OTHER DETERMINANTS OF ATTRACTION
AS POSITIVE AND NEGATIVE REINFORCERS

Self-Statements As Reinforcers

In Chapter 7, several experiments were described which dealt with the effect of similarity of statements about self on attraction. It was consistently found that similarity to self functioned in precisely the same manner as attitude similarity. It follows, then, that self-statements should function as reinforcers in a learning task. Reitz, Robinson, and Dudley (1969) pointed out that such a finding would serve as a step in linking self-theory with behavior theory.

Individuals with High Self-Esteem. Reitz et al. (1969) selected the 30 highest scoring individuals on Dymond's (1954) self-attitude items out of a group of 180 introductory psychology students. Response to the 74 items is on a 9-point scale with high scores indicating positive self-attitudes. Each subject was assigned to one of three experimental conditions in the Golightly–Byrne learning task. In the high reinforcement condition, subjects were positively reinforced with self-statements they had endorsed with an 8 or 9 and negatively reinforced with statements they had endorsed with a 1 or 2. In the moderate reinforcement condition, items given a 6 or 7 were positive reinforcements, whereas items given a 3 or 4 were negative

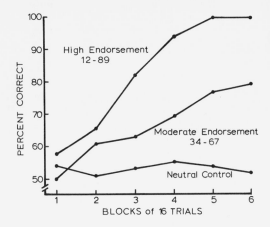

Fig. 12–9. Acquisition curves for the three groups showing percentage of correct responses as a function of self-statements with high and moderate endorsement. (After Reitz, Robinson, & Dudley, 1969.)

reinforcements. The control group received objective, factual, and non-evaluative self-statements regardless of the correctness of their responses.

The results are shown in Fig. 12–9. It may be seen that the positive self-statements served as reinforcing stimuli. Both the strongly endorsed and moderately endorsed statements altered response probability, and the former produced greater performance changes than the latter.

Individuals with Low Self-Esteem. Reitz *et al.* (1969) point out that problems are involved in postulating reinforcing effects of similar self-statements for subjects low in self-esteem. On the basis of studies of self-concept and attraction, it is clear that similarity (even on negative characteristics for low self-esteem individuals) leads to attraction. It would be predicted, then, that similarity should be reinforcing in a learning task. On the other hand, studies of the effects of personal evaluations on attraction suggest that almost all subjects prefer to be evaluated positively and like those who so evaluate them. On this basis it would be predicted that dissimilar self-statements would be reinforcing for low self-esteem individuals.

From the same subject pool as was used in the previous experiment, the lowest scoring 40 individuals were selected. Each was assigned to one of four reinforcing conditions for the discrimination learning task. Positive and negative self-statements were used as the reinforcers. Either a positive reinforcement followed correct responses, and a neutral self-statement followed incorrect responses or a negative reinforcement followed incorrect responses and a neutral self-statement followed correct responses.

It was found that learning took place only when positive self-attitudes were used as positive reinforcers. Because of the extreme variability of the groups, the authors suggested that some other variable such as social desirability was unintentionally manipulated. They found that the reinforcing effectiveness of their materials was highly related to social desirability ratings. It was also noted that (in contrast to previous studies) many of the subjects showed signs of emotional distress. In addition, many of the subjects learned in the incorrect direction.

One possibility which might be raised to explain the variability of the responses, the learning reversals, the emotional responses, and the differences between these findings and those of the self-attraction studies is that subjects interpreted the reinforcing stimuli in diverse ways. That is, a negative self-statement expressed by someone else is a positive stimulus for an individual who describes himself negatively in that way. The same negative statement directed toward the individual who describes himself negatively is a negative stimulus. In the learning situation, the meaning of these statements could be ambiguous and, hence, could lead to quite different reactions in different subjects. Additional research would be required to test the validity of this suggestion.

Interest Items As Reinforcers

Reitz and McDougall (1969) used items from the Strong Vocational Interest Blank (SVIB) as reinforcing stimuli in the discrimination learning task. As reported in Chapter 2, this test has been successfully used in attraction research. Subjects were 48 male undergraduates at the University of Western Ontario. They responded to the first 280 items of the SVIB on a 9-point scale ranging from liking to disliking of the item's content. On the basis of previously obtained ratings, items were selected for the learning task which were either high or low in social desirability. Some subjects received items which they had endorsed moderately (3, 4, 6, or 7), whereas others received items to which they had given extreme endorsements (1, 2, 8, or 9).

It was found that these interest items functioned as reinforcers and produced performance changes. Although social desirability had no effect, items that the subject had marked with extreme endorsement were effective reinforcers, whereas those items marked with moderate endorsement were not.

ATTITUDE STATEMENTS AS REINFORCERS: ADDITIONAL IMPLICATIONS

Opinion Change

Corrozi and Rosnow (1968) were interested in the effects of positive and negative reinforcement on opinion change. When a positive or negative reinforcer is presented immediately before or after a two-sided persuasive communication, subjects' opinions tend to change in the direction of the argument which is temporally closer to the positive or further from the negative stimulus. On the basis of the kind of attitudinal reinforcement experiments just described, they proposed that similar and dissimilar attitudes should be able to serve as reinforcers in the opinion change situation.

The subjects were 152 high-school juniors and seniors. The two-sided communication was about Pablo Picasso, and the order of positive and negative arguments was counterbalanced. On the basis of other data, the dissimilar attitude was the advocation of a longer school week, whereas the similar attitude was the position that the school week was already sufficiently long. Measures of opinions about Picasso were obtained 2 weeks before the experiment and shortly after the communications.

Opinion change following the persuasive message was found to be strongly influenced by the position of the irrelevant attitude material. The first argument tended to be more effective if it was preceded by a similar attitude or if the second argument was followed by a dissimilar attitude. The second argument tended to be more effective if it was followed by a similar attitude or if the first argument was preceded by a dissimilar attitude.

Thus, in a situation quite different from the discrimination learning task, attitude statements are once again found to function as reinforcers. It should be noted that Simons, Berkowitz, and Moyer (1970) have argued against the generality of this finding.

Learning of Similar and Dissimilar Attitudes

Stefaniak (1967) proposed that if attitude statements constitute positive and negative reinforcers, material dealing with the former would be learned more readily than material dealing with the latter. He pointed out that in previous research on this topic (e.g., Alper & Korchin, 1952; Edwards, 1941: Jones & Kohler, 1958; Levine & Murphy, 1943) only one general topic was used and pro and con paragraphs were the material to be learned. Because the subject was allowed to study the material in his own way, it is possible that differential time was spent on the similar and dissimilar paragraphs and that this difference accounted for the obtained effects. Stefaniak designed two experiments in which learning time was controlled and in which a variety of attitudes was employed.

Attitude Statements and Recognition. From a pool of 60 Texas undergraduates who had taken the 56-item survey of attitudes, 29 subjects who had expressed 12 or more extreme attitudes were selected. For each subject, six topics were randomly selected for agreement and six for disagreement. Each subject was asked to learn six statements congruent with his attitudes, six opposed to his attitudes, and six neutral statements. Each statement was typed on cards, presented once for a 2-second period, followed by a 2-second interstimulus interval. Immediately after the presentation of the 18 statements, subjects were required to recognize each statement from among three other statements on cards. Each recognition card contained one statement congruent with the subject's attitude, one opposed, one neutral, and one statement reading "None of the above." There were 24 recognition cards, of which six contained no statements presented during the learning period.

The mean number of statements of each type correctly recognized is shown in Table 12–3. As hypothesized, the highest recognition score was for the similar attitude statements and the lowest recognition score was for the dissimilar attitude statements.

TABLE 12–3
MEAN NUMBER OF STATEMENTS
CORRECTLY RECOGNIZED[a]

Type of statement	Mean recognition score
Similar attitudes	4.83
Neutral	4.21
Dissimilar attitudes	3.90

[a] After Stefaniak, 1967, p. 9.

Attitude Statements in Paired Associate Learning. In Stefaniak's (1967) second experiment, a 40-item attitude survey was administered to a large group of undergraduates. From this group, 20 subjects were selected on the basis of having six or more attitudes on which they responded at one extreme or the other. For each subject three topics were chosen for agreement and three for disagreement. The number of syllables in the similar and dissimilar statements for a given topic was matched. Nine nonsense syllables were paired with three similar, three dissimilar, and three neutral statements. The same nonsense syllables were used for all subjects, but they were randomly paired with the statement for a particular subject.

All statements and nonsense syllables were typed on index cards. The cards were exposed in windows cut into a wooden shield. The nonsense syllables appeared on the subject's left and the statements on his right. Three randomly assigned lists of the nine pairings were administered to each subject. The nonsense syllable was presented for 7 seconds, following which the syllable and statement were presented for 4 seconds. After one practice trial through the list, the subject was supposed to state verbatim the statement upon seeing the nonsense syllable. Subjects continued until they had gone through two consecutive presentations of the list without an error or until a total of twelve presentations was completed.

The mean number of errors for the three types of statements is shown in Table 12–4. In this paired associate learning task, more errors were made on the pairs involving dissimilar statements than on the pairs involving similar statements.

Thus, the two experiments indicated that similar attitude statements produce better recognition and more rapid learning than do dissimilar attitude statements.

TABLE 12–4
MEAN NUMBER OF ERRORS IN LEARNING
NONSENSE SYLLABLES PAIRED WITH
DIFFERENT TYPES OF STATEMENTS[a]

Type of statement	Mean errors
Similar attitudes	8.90
Neutral	8.45
Dissimilar attitudes	11.05

[a]After Stefaniak, 1967, p. 11.

Effects of Differential Magnitude of Reward

Given the preceding body of evidence indicating that similar and dissimilar attitude statements function as positive and negative reinforcers, it follows that attitudinal material would be expected to parallel various other effects of traditional reinforcers. For example, variations in reward magnitude are known to have specific effects on performance. If the stimuli which influence attraction are conceptualized as reinforcers and if differential effects on attraction are conceptualized to occur as a function of differential reinforcement magnitude, it should be possible to demonstrate magnitude effects for such stimuli in a learning task.

Reinforcement Magnitude. Clore (1966) conducted the first of the magnitude experiments. He pointed out that magnitude of reinforcement in classical conditioning refers to the intensity of the unconditioned stimulus. Conditioned responses are thought to be influenced directly by the intensity of the stimulus and by the increase in drive level elicited by the stimulus. In earlier attraction research, the effects of topic importance and evaluations on attraction had been conceptualized as resulting from differential reinforcement magnitude. Clore decided to test this magnitude formulation by using such stimuli in the discrimination learning task.

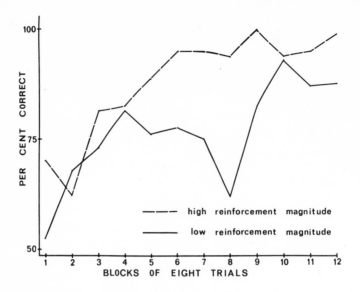

Fig. 12–10. Acquisition curves for groups receiving high and low reinforcement magnitude. (Data from Clore, 1966.)

In his research,* Clore (1966) selected attitude statements and personal evaluations as representing two levels of effect on attraction and, hence, theoretically, two levels of reinforcement magnitude. The Golightly–Byrne procedure was used except that one group received attitude statements as reinforcers, whereas another received evaluative statements (e.g., I believe that this person is above average in intelligence), supposedly written about them by another subject. The subjects were Texas undergraduates.

The results are shown in Fig. 12–10. Once again, stimuli that influence attraction are shown to influence learning and, more importantly, stimuli that differentially affect attraction also differentially affect performance. As hypothesized, performance level is higher when evaluations are used as the feedback than when attitude statements constitute the feedback.

It is possible that the high magnitude group performs better because it is easier to translate the evaluations into "right–wrong" than it is to translate the attitude material. If so, learning should occur more rapidly with the evaluations than with the attitudes, but Clore found that the two groups did not differ with respect to the trial on which they became aware

---

*For the present exposition, some portions of Clore's experiments are not reported.

of the reinforcement contingencies. Also, with awareness held constant, the high magnitude group still performed at a higher level than the low magnitude group. The alternative explanation, that these stimuli differ in affective quality and, hence, in reinforcement magnitude, is quite consistent with the data.

Reinforcement Magnitude on a Performance Task. Lamberth and Gay (1969) broadened the study of magnitude effects to a performance task. They hypothesized that a group receiving a large magnitude of reward would have faster speeds on a performance measure than would a group receiving a small magnitude of reward.

The subjects were 27 female undergraduates at Texas. The apparatus developed for this research consists of a panel with an aluminum lever in the center that can be depressed 15 ins. At the upper right of the panel is a "ready" light, with a slit underneath through which reinforcements can be delivered. When the light goes on, Clock I is activated. When the subject begins pressing the lever, Clock I is terminated and Clock II is activated. When the lever is fully depressed, Clock II is terminated. In this and subsequent research, the time recorded on Clock II has proved to be the more reliable performance measure. Subjects, run individually, were told that the experiment involved learning. When the light came on, they pressed the lever and afterward received either personal evaluations or factual statements. The evaluations were purportedly based on statements written about them by other students who had read their attitude scales. Each subject was given 40 trials, with one group receiving all large reward magnitude (positive personal evaluations) and another group receiving all small reward magnitude (neutral statements of fact).

On Clock II, the large magnitude group performed significantly faster than the small magnitude group, as hypothesized.

Magnitude and Magnitude Shift. Lamberth and Craig (1970) extended the research on magnitude effects. They proposed that the use of reinforcement concepts in attraction research requires that various learning phenomena be demonstrable with attitudinal stimuli. In addition to reinforcement magnitude leading to simple performance differences, there is an another magnitude effect of interest to learning theorists—magnitude shift. When animals are shifted from large to small magnitude of reward, performance declines; a shift in the opposite direction facilitates performance (Amsel, 1967; Capaldi, 1967; Crespi, 1946; Spear & Spitzner, 1966). Lamberth and Craig believed that the same effects would occur with human subjects responding to the kind of stimuli that influence attraction.

The subjects were 36 Texas undergraduates who were run on the discrimination learning task. Positive personal evaluations were used as the large magnitude, and factual neutral statements as the small magnitude. All incorrect responses were followed by a blank card. The subjects were assigned to one of four experimental conditions, and the acquisition trials were divided into two phases of 48 trials each. One group received the large magnitude of reward in both phases and one received the small magnitude of reward in both phases. In a third group, the large magnitude was given in the first phase and the small magnitude in the second phase. The fourth group received the small magnitude in the first phase and was then shifted to the large magnitude in the second phase. Only subjects who had learned the discrimination in Phase 1 were used for Phase 2.

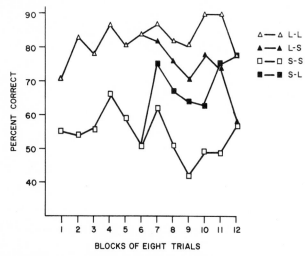

Fig. 12–11. Performance curves as a function of differential magnitude of reward. L–L, large magnitude reward in both phases; L–S, large magnitude reward in first phase and small magnitude reward in second phase; S–S, small magnitude reward in both phases; S–L, small magnitude reward in first phase and large magnitude reward in second phase. (After Lamberth & Craig, 1970, p. 283.)

The results are presented in Fig. 12–11. In Phase 1, there was a significant performance difference between the high and low magnitude groups. In Phase 2, following the shift, the performance of each group was altered as predicted. A change in the magnitude of the reinforcing stimuli resulted in a change in performance level.

Lamberth and Craig (1970) point out "The fact that they respond to changes in reward magnitude in virtually the exact way that animals respond to changes in the amount of food in a similar situation greatly strengthens the conceptualization of these stimuli as reinforcers [p. 284]."

Sequential Variables and Attitudinal Stimuli. Perhaps the most ambitious employment of attraction variables in a learning situation has been Lamberth's (1970) use of attitudinal stimuli in research relevant to Capaldi's (1967) sequential theory of instrumental learning. One goal was to take attraction research beyond the concern with first impressions toward the study of lasting relationships such as long-term friendships. Lamberth selected sequential theory as a promising approach. Capaldi (1967) gives as a background to his theoretical schema the basic notion that "performance on some trial Tn is regulated extensively by the stimuli contributed from earlier or preceding trials in the series [p. 67]."

Lamberth (1970) first examined the effect of *N*-length, the number of consecutive nonrewarded trials followed by a rewarded trial, on extinction. With percentage of reinforcement controlled, sequential theory predicts that a long *N*-length group is more resistant to extinction than a short *N*-length group. The subjects were 102 undergraduates at Purdue University, and the lever-pressing apparatus was used. The reinforcements consisted of homogeneous similar attitudes; the subjects received nothing on the nonreinforced trials. The short *N*-length group (Group 12) received two conditionings of an *N*-length of one and four conditionings of an *N*-length of two; the long *N*-length group (Group 37) had one conditioning of an *N*-length of three and one of seven. The reinforcement schedules for the 20 trials were as follows:

Group 12:   *R N N R N N R R R N R R N R N N R N N R*
Group 37:   *R R R R N N N R R R N N N N N N N R R R*

It may be seen that each group received reinforcement on 50% of the trials; they differed only in the sequence in which those reinforcements were given. Both groups then were given 20 extinction trials. As is shown in Fig. 12–12, the long *N*-length group was more resistant to extinction than the short *N*-length group, as hypothesized. A second measure of extinction was a verbal inquiry at the end of the 20 extinction trials as to whether the subject expected to receive more cards or when he had quit expecting to receive more. On this measure, there was a highly significant difference between the 12 and 37 groups in the predicted direction.

In Lamberth's (1970) second experiment, it was hypothesized that a group receiving all of its nonrewarded trials prior to its rewarded trials would show greater resistance to extinction than a continuously rewarded group. One group (*RR*) was reinforced on 10 trials, and the other (*NR*) received 5 nonrewarded trials followed by 5 rewarded trials on the lever-pressing apparatus. Again, both groups received 20 extinction trials. As Fig. 12–13 indicates, there was a considerable difference between the groups, with the *NR* group showing greater resistance to extinction than the *RR* group, as hypothesized.

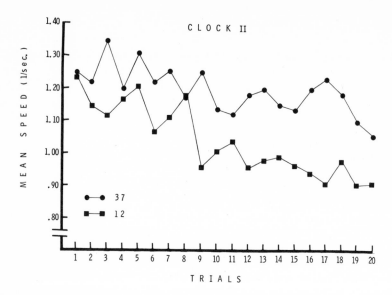

Fig. 12–12. Mean extinction speeds for groups receiving long (37) and short (12) *N*-lengths in acquisition. (After Lamberth, 1970, p. 23.)

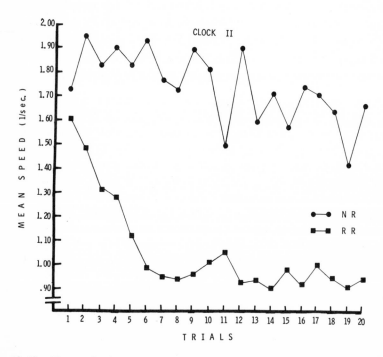

Fig. 12–13. Mean extinction speeds for groups receiving continuous reinforcement (RR) and reinforcement preceded by nonreinforcement (NR). (After Lamberth, 1970, p. 25.)

Lamberth concluded that the results of these two experiments lend support to the feasibility of pursuing a sequential analysis in research on interpersonal attraction.

OTHER PERSONS
AS REINFORCING STIMULI

There is still another aspect of the reinforcement model to be considered. Stimuli that influence attraction elicit implicit affective responses and have reinforcing properties. When they are temporally associated with neutral stimuli (such as other persons), attraction toward the neutral stimuli is affected. That is, the other person now elicits implicit affective responses which mediate evaluative responses. An additional implication is that these previously neutral stimuli now have reinforcing properties. Thus, people who are liked and disliked should serve, respectively, as positive and negative reinforcers.

Photographs As Reinforcers: Discrimination Learning

Lott and Lott (1969) indicated that a liked person is conceptualized as one who evokes implicit anticipatory goal responses, whereas disliked persons evoke implicit anticipatory punishment or frustration. They employed the Golightly–Byrne discrimination learning task to test the reinforcing effectiveness of photographs of liked, neutral, and disliked peers on performance. The subjects were 100 ninth-grade students. Each had been asked to rate all of their same-sex classmates on 30-point liking scales. On the basis of these ratings, peers could be chosen who were strongly liked, strongly disliked, or toward whom the subject felt neutral. Experimental conditions included a group who received the word "right" for a correct response, a photograph of a liked peer for a correct response, a photograph of a neutral peer for a correct response, and a photograph of a disliked peer for an incorrect response. A blank card followed the other response in each condition.

It was found that the right–blank group performed best followed by the like–blank group. The neutral–blank and blank–dislike groups also increased their percentage of correct responses. Awareness was found to affect performance only in the right–blank condition in which the aware subjects performed better than those who were unaware.

The authors concluded that liked persons can function as effective positive reinforcers, whereas disliked persons can function as negative reinforcers.

Names As Reinforcers: Paired Associates Learning

Following the same line of reasoning as in the previous experiment, Lott, Lott, and Walsh (1970) conducted two studies in which subjects learned to associate names with nonsense syllable trigrams.

In the first experiment, Kentucky students indicated their feelings toward various public figures and later had to learn name–trigram pairs. Significantly more errors were made in learning the pairs with neutral names than the pairs containing the names of either liked or disliked persons, and the liked person pairs yielded the least number of errors. Presumably, the greater the affect associated with a name, the easier to learn associates to it.

In a second study, undergraduates at the University of California, Riverside, listed the names of two acquaintances whom they liked, two they disliked, and two about whom they felt neutral. These names were later used in the learning task in which they were paired with nonsense syllable trigrams. In this experiment, once again the fewest errors were made with the liked person pairs and the most errors made with the neutral person pairs.

The authors (Lott, Lott, & Walsh, 1970) conclude; "These data lend credence to the theoretically derived assumptions regarding differences in salience among liked, disliked, and neutral persons, as well as differences in their drive-arousing properties. The approach cue value of a liked person, as compared with a disliked or neutrally regarded person, was supported [p. 280]."

CONCLUSIONS

The experiments presented in the present chapter have consistently shown that stimuli which can determine evaluative responses elicit affective responses and have reinforcing properties. The affective responses have been measured with self-rating scales, with a physiological index, and indirectly through time perception. In a series of learning studies, attitudes and other stimuli known to determine attraction have been found to function very effectively as reinforcers. With such stimuli conceptualized in reinforcement terms, it is found that differential effects on attraction are paralleled in the learning situation as reinforcement magnitude effects. In addition, learning phenomena associated with magnitude shifts and with sequential effects can be reproduced, using stimuli from attraction research. Not only do attitudes and other attraction-determining stimuli have reinforcing properties, but the objects of attraction responses also are found to be effective reinforcers. Thus, Hypotheses 7a and 8a seem to be well supported by empirical evidence.

Chapter 13 / Hypothesis Testing: III. Stimuli That Elicit Affective Responses Have Reinforcing Properties and Can Determine Evaluative Responses

In the classical conditioning model of attraction, the implicit affective response may be treated in a strictly formal sense as an intervening variable which is ultimately reducible to the stimuli that elicit it and the responses that it mediates. Implicit affective responses could serve simply as logical abstractions. There is something to be gained, however, by pursuing this intervening variable by seeking other stimuli which might be expected to elicit affect and other responses which might be expected to be influenced by affect. An emphasis on the importance of affect as a mediator of attraction has been of unique interest in the present paradigm.

In addition, at a somewhat speculative level, there has been the attempt to explain the effect of attitudes. That is, attitude statements may unequivocally be said to determine attraction and to possess reinforcement properties. Why? What is it about statements such as "The Vietnam war is immoral" or "The Vietnam war is a tribute to America's love of freedom" which can bring about extreme emotional responses, determine friendships or enmities, and alter the probability of responses with which they are associated? The ability to answer that question satisfactorily is obviously not essential to the conditioning model nor even a necessary part of it. Attitudes may simply be treated as stimuli which have certain properties and, hence, have certain effects. On the other hand, the reason for the attitudinal effect is intriguing and the pursuit of an explanation might serve to expand the theory in a new direction. That particular pursuit has been a sometimes rewarding and sometimes frustrating endeavor within the attraction paradigm.

   Much of the research to be described in this chapter is either a test of Hypothesis 9a (Chapter 10) or is directly relevant to it: *Any stimulus that elicits an affective response can determine evaluative responses toward other stimuli through association with them.* In addition, a vital connecting link between the affective studies and the learning studies is provided by experimental evidence relevant to Hypotheses 10a and 10b: *Any stimulus that elicits an affective response has reinforcing properties and, hence, can alter the probability of the occurrence of any response with which it is associated* and *Any stimulus that does not elicit an affective response does not have reinforcing properties and, hence, cannot alter the probability of the occurrence of any response with which it is associated.*

AFFECTIVE RESPONSES AND CONDITIONING

   Stalling (1970) correctly pointed out that the effect of similarity on attraction and on performance in a learning task is dependent on the ability of the similar stimuli to elicit affective responses (pleasant versus unpleasant). Thus, if similarity and affect could be separated, it would be hypothesized that the reinforcement effects are attributable to the latter variable rather than to the former. In a design based in part on the work of A. W. Staats (1968), Stalling carried out a test of this hypothesis.

   The subjects were 16 students at the University of Hawaii. On a pretest, subjects responded to 121 of Anderson's (1968b) adjectives on two scales: pleasant–unpleasant and like me–unlike me. For each subject, four 12-adjective lists were constructed. With respect to the ratings of each individual, the lists consisted of words pleasant and like me, unpleasant but like me, pleasant but unlike me, and unpleasant and unlike me.

   In the conditioning experiment, four trigrams (yof, laj, wuh, and xeh) served as conditioned stimuli. Each was projected for 5 seconds, during which time one of the adjectives (unconditioned stimuli) was spoken by the experimenter and repeated by the subject. All 12 adjectives of a given list were consistently paired with a particular trigram for each subject. Each adjective was used once, so a subject received 48 trigram–adjective pairings. Afterward, subjects rated the pleasantness-unpleasantness of the four trigrams. Only subjects who were unaware of the relationship between the kind of adjectives and a particular trigram were retained in the data analysis.

   In Table 13-1 are the mean evaluative ratings of the trigrams associated

TABLE 13-1
MEAN EVALUATIVE RATINGS OF CONDITIONED
STIMULI TRIGRAMS ASSOCIATED WITH
FOUR TYPES OF ADJECTIVES[a]

Similarity dimension	Affective dimension		
	Unpleasant	Pleasant	Total
Like me	3.94	4.44	4.19
Unlike me	3.00	5.12	4.06
Total	3.47	4.78	—

[a]Data from Stalling, 1970.

with the four kinds of adjectives. The adjective characteristic which affected learning was that of pleasant–unpleasant, whereas the similarity variable was not found to exert a significant influence.

As hypothesized, the crucial element for the conditioning effect was that of affective quality rather than similarity per se. Stalling also presented evidence suggesting an explanation for the usual similarity effect. In the original rating of the 121 adjectives by 89 subjects, the correlation between the similarity and affective ratings was found to be .88.

Generalizing Stalling's results to attitudinal stimuli, we can point to evidence in the foregoing chapters that attitude statements elicit affect, influence attraction, and have reinforcement properties. If affect is the central characteristic, we are faced with the unresolved question of why attitudes elicit affect.

THE EFFECTANCE MOTIVE

One theoretical means of seemingly bypassing the problem of explaining attitudinal effects has been discussed previously with respect to the approval cue hypothesis. That is, attitude similarity or dissimilarity simply serves as a cue (based on past experience) that the other person will like or dislike the subject. Although that assertion is undoubtedly correct, it begs the question as to why in past experience similarity should have been associated with liking and dissimilarity with disliking. There is not much gained in explanatory power by transporting the attitude–attraction effect from the experimental room to the scene of the subject's early childhood experiences. An adequate explanation must deal with what it is about the attitudes themselves which elicits affect.

Theoretical Background

With a general framework borrowed from Festinger (1950, 1954) and Newcomb (1953, 1956, 1959, 1961), it may be suggested that the expression of similar attitudes by a stranger serves as a positive reinforcement because consensual validation for an individual's attitudes and opinions and beliefs is a major source of reward for the drive to be logical, consistent, and accurate in interpreting the stimulus world. In an analogous way, the expression of dissimilar attitudes by a stranger provides consensual invalidation, is therefore frustrating, and acts as a negative reinforcement.

The reasoning behind this proposition was spelled out in some detail by Byrne and Clore (1967). It was proposed that the motive which is presumably activated by attitudinal material is not unique to that particular stimulus. Rather, the motivational properties of attitude statements represent a special instance of a more general phenomenon. It was suggested that the type of secondary motive described in the attraction studies has appeared under various labels and in various contexts. Examples are the need for cognition or the need to experience an integrated and meaningful world (Cohen, Stotland, & Wolfe, 1955), the need to be able to know and predict the environment (Kelly, 1955; Pervin, 1963), the desire for certainty which involves understanding the environment and making it predictable (Brim & Hoff, 1957), and the drive to evaluate one's own opinions and abilities (Festinger, 1954). In order to provide a common term to designate all of these various motives, it was decided to borrow the term *effectance motive* from White (1959) in that the various concepts each involve a process related to effective interaction with the environment. White said:

> . . . it is maintained that competence cannot be fully acquired simply through behavior instigated by [primary] drives. It receives substantial contributions from activities which, though playful and exploratory in character, at the same time show direction, selectivity, and persistence in interacting with the environment. Such activities in the ultimate service of competence must therefore be conceived to be motivated in their own right. It is proposed to designate this motivation by the term effectance, and to characterize the experience produced as a *feeling of efficacy* [p. 329].

One point made by Byrne and Clore (1967) has been ignored by several critics of the concept; our use of effectance and that of White differ in one major respect. White stressed the "positive" aspects of the motive to explain why organisms avoid the monotonous and repetitive and familiar in order to seek stimulation via exploration, play, intellectual curiosity, and manipulation of the environment. Byrne and Clore proposed, however, that the same motivational construct that accounts for a preference for stimulation also accounts for a negative response to stimuli which lie further along the continuum of unfamiliarity, unpredictability, and unexpectedness.

A speculative description of the development of such a motive system has been provided by Dollard and Miller (1950) in discussing the learned drive to be logical and to make a correct report of the environment.

> While learning to talk the child receives training in matching words, sentences, and descriptive paragraphs with important features of the environment. He is trained not to call the sky "green" or the grass "blue." He is corrected for mistakes, and eventually learns to have anxiety about responding differently from other people. He is also taught to distinguish between the make-believe and the real—in other words, between the situations in which sentences that do not run parallel to sequences in the environment will be tolerated and those in which they will not. He is taught to discriminate between his own private dreams, images, and phantasies, and the perceptions that can be verified by cross-checking with other senses and that agree with the reports of other people . . .
>
> We believe that his training serves to provide motivation against hallucinations and delusions. The strength of this motivation is shown by the anxiety that a normal person will show if through some unexpected illusion he seems to be seeing things others do not see [p. 119].

At the anecdotal level, it can be observed that small children appear to experience pleasure in simply learning the correct verbal label to apply to any new object or event, in repeating endlessly a previously experienced sequential activity such as a game or a familiar story, or in grasping the meaning of that which was previously puzzling. With respect to such activity, Woodworth (1958) suggested:

> Its long-range value as the means of making the child acquainted with the world he has to deal with later, and so equipping him through play for the serious business of life, can scarcely lie within the little child's horizon. His goals are more limited and direct: to see this or that object more closely, to find what is behind an obstacle, to hear the noises an object makes when it strikes the floor, to be told the name of a thing or person [p. 78].

If, however, the stimulus events are sufficiently unfamiliar, unpredictable, or inexplicable, they arouse anxiety and fear. The desire to deal effectively with the environment can thus lead either to pleasurable exploration or to fearful withdrawal.

Adulthood does not alter these relationships. Rather, the well-adjusted adult simply has a wider sphere of knowledge and familiarity than does the child, so that the physical world offers fewer day to day surprises which either challenge or frighten him (Hebb & Thompson, 1968). White (1959) indicated "The building of houses, roads, and bridges, the making of tools and instruments, the domestication of plants and animals, all qualify as planful changes made in the environment so that it comes more or less under control and serves our purposes rather than intruding upon them [p. 324]."

Nevertheless, when adults are confronted with unfamiliar, unpredictable, or inexplicable events, it appears that the consequent distress equals in intensity that of childhood.

Thus, well-adjusted adults in a relatively stable, civilized society should be protected against unpleasant levels of effectance arousal by effective social training in childhood, years of experience in which to build up conceptual capacity, and a stable environment with built-in predictability. There may be occasional minor jolts (momentary forgetting of the location of one's car after a football game, minor loss of orientation just after moving to a new house, seeing a familiar face but not remembering where or when the person was known) and at times major disruptions (economic depression, automobile accident, earthquake, riot, war) which prevent in varying degrees the satisfaction of the effectance motive. The reality to which we have adapted becomes altered, things seem unreal, and new adjustments must be made. For most of us most of the time, physical reality does not actually pose major problems related to effectance. Under what conditions, then, is effectance aroused? There remains what Festinger (1950) called "social reality," in which there is a much greater degree of unpredictability, lack of necessary knowledge, and the occurrence of seemingly illogical events. Dollard and Miller (1950) noted, "The training in matching words to important features of the environment applies to the social as well as the physical environment. The child is trained to give an accurate account of social events and to make his statements about the probable social consequences of acts match the cultural pattern [p. 119]."

Included here are all of the major aspects of our world about which we hold attitudes, opinions, beliefs, and values. Is there a God? What are the consequences of assuming an aggressive military posture toward Communist China? Is it immature to enjoy situation comedies on television? Has the radical movement gone too far or not far enough? How should one raise his children? Should marijuana be legalized? To what extent should sexual intercourse between consenting adolescents be proscribed? It is obvious that the list can be extended almost endlessly and that the resolution of such questions in terms of discovering the correct answer, mastering the problem, dealing effectively with the issue, or testing the empirical consequents of one's assumptions is not possible. Thus, the raising of such issues should arouse the effectance motive. Further, almost the only relevant evidence which could bring about effectance reduction lies in consensual validation. This occurs when others agree with or share our outlook and, hence, provide satisfaction of the effectance motive. Consensual invalidation occurs when others disagree with us and, hence, frustrate the satisfaction of the effectance motive.

The attitudes of others are important to us because human beings depend on one another as sources of information about countless aspects of the environment. People are rewarding to one another as "suppliers of new information and as confirmers or correctors of old [Newcomb, 1959,

p. 386]." Heider (1958) stated, "The power of similarity of beliefs or attitudes derives from the identity of the environment to which they refer, and from the fact that it is satisfying to find support for one's own view [p. 196]." Similarly, Festinger (1950) proposed, "if there are other people around him who believe the same thing, then his opinion is, to him, valid. If there are not others who believe the same thing, then his opinion is, in the same sense, not valid [p. 272]."

In terms of providing a descriptive and speculative rationale for the effects of attitude similarity–dissimilarity on attraction, the notion of effectance may or may not provide instant *Verstehen*. The research problem, however, is to seek a means to arouse this hypothesized motive independently of the attitude situation, to devise a reliable behavioral index of arousal, and to determine experimentally the way in which effectance arousal influences the attitude–attraction relationship.

Verifiability of Attitudinal Position

The first experimental attack on the effectance concept was by Byrne, Nelson, and Reeves (1966). The starting point was Festinger's (1950) distinction between social reality and physical reality. With respect to issues concerning physical reality (e.g., "Is it raining?," "Is the book on the third shelf?"), it is possible to verify a given hypothesis relatively directly and relatively easily with empirical observations. In such situations, differences of opinion should have little influence on the effectance motive, consensual validation or invalidation should have little reward or punishment value, and attraction toward those who express similar or dissimilar opinions about such issues should be relatively undifferentiated. When, however, the issues involve social reality (e.g., "Can meaningful reform take place within the established political system?", "Should racial integration in the schools be attained through bussing?"), the observable consequences of one's viewpoint are difficult or impossible to test (Newcomb, 1953). Here, differences of opinion should have considerable influence on the effectance motive, motive satisfaction or nonsatisfaction should depend entirely on consensual validation or invalidation, and attraction should be strongly affected by the expression of similar or dissimilar views.

Going beyond a simple dichotomy of physical reality versus social reality, Byrne *et al.* (1966) proposed that the degree to which effectance motivation is aroused by a given issue varies as an inverse function of the ease with which empirical verification may be attained. Festinger (1954) had suggested, "When an objective, non-social basis for the evaluation of one's ability or opinion is readily available persons will not evaluate their opinions or abilities by comparison with others [p. 120]." If that proposition is correct, the effects of similarity–dissimilarity of opinions on attraction would also be an inverse function of ease of empirical verification. An experiment was designed in which the attitudinal topics were varied in terms of the possibility of verifying one's opinion empirically. It was hypothesized that as verifiability increases, the effect of attitude similarity–dissimilarity on attraction decreases.

Three 12-item attitude and opinion scales were constructed to provide the three degrees of verifiability. On the unverifiable (UV) scale the correctness of one's position was not open to empirical verification. Examples are "I strongly believe that Red China should not be admitted to the U.N." and "I strongly believe that Red China should be admitted to the U.N." On the verifiable in future (VF) scale, one's opinion about each issue could be empirically verified at some future date. Examples are "Red China will be overwhelmingly denied admission to the U.N. next year." and "Red China will be overwhelmingly approved for admission to the U.N. next year." On the verifiable at present (VP) scale, one's opinions could be verified at any time by referring to a library source, encyclopedia, newspaper file, etc. Examples are "Nationalist China has strongly opposed the admission of Red China to the U.N." and "Nationalist China has strongly favored the admission of Red China to the U.N." Specific topic areas remained the same across the three conditions, and each was arranged on a 6-point scale as in the ordinary attitude–attraction studies.

One of the three types of scales was administered to each of 168 undergraduates at the University of Texas. Subjects were assigned to one of four levels of attitude similarity in a standard attitude–attraction experimental design.

The mean attraction responses are shown in Table 13–2. As expected,

TABLE 13–2

MEAN ATTRACTION RESPONSES TOWARD
STRANGERS WITH VARYING PROPORTIONS OF
SIMILAR ATTITUDES ON TOPICS DIFFERING IN VERIFIABILITY[a]

Proportion of similar attitudes	Verifiability of attitudes			
	Unverifiable	Verifiable in future	Verifiable at present	Total
1.00	12.14	10.00	10.92	11.02
.67	9.92	9.14	9.57	9.54
.50	8.85	8.85	8.28	8.66
.33	6.64	8.57	7.28	7.50
Total	9.39	9.14	9.01	—

[a]After Byrne, Nelson, and Reeves, 1966, p. 102.

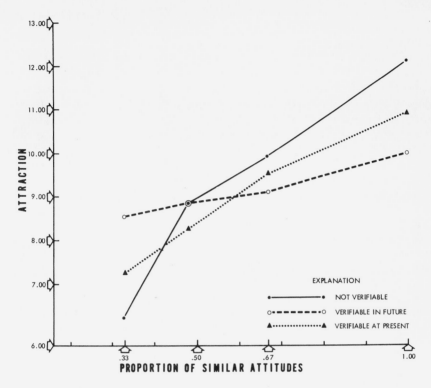

Fig. 13–1. Attraction toward a stranger as a linear function of proportion of similar attitudes on topics differing in verifiability. (After Byrne, Nelson, & Reeves, 1966, p. 103.)

there was a significant effect for proportion of similar attitudes and a significant interaction between similarity and verifiability. The interaction is best seen in Fig. 13–1. The three groups yielded linear trends which were significantly different from one another. The only unexpected finding was a reversal in the positions of the VF and VP groups. The least effect of similarity on attraction was with respect to attitudinal topics verifiable in the future.

Thus, the hypothesis regarding the effect of verifiability on response to similarity–dissimilarity was partially supported. One explanation for the reversed groups is that for these undergraduate students, the possibility of verifying the correctness of opinions on certain topics through information obtained in reference books, newspaper files, encyclopedias, etc., is not evident or is seen as an extremely difficult task. Thus, given the relative difficulty in actually obtaining the appropriate factual information, verification through consensual validation becomes quite important, though not as much so as in the instance where there actually is no way to determine correctness or incorrectness. In retrospect, it could be seen that it was the future events for which verification was easiest to attain. That is, what happens with respect to Red China and the U.N. will be generally known without the necessity of any special effort to obtain the information. The obvious ease of verification concerning such issues renders the agreement or disagreement on the part of strangers almost irrelevant.

Arousing and Measuring the Effectance Motive

If the notion of an effectance motive were to become a basic concept in attraction research, it appeared vital to devise operations which reliably arouse this motive and others which serve as a reliable index of its arousal. Byrne and Clore (1967) suggested that any situation that provides evidence of one's predictive accuracy, ability to understand, correctness, logicality, reality orientation, or behavioral appropriateness would satisfy the effectance motive. Any situation providing the opposite kind of evidence would arouse and fail to satisfy the effectance motive. Arousal conditions would include stimuli which are unfamiliar or strange, ambiguous, variable, uncertain, unexpected, unpredictable, or which represented a discrepancy from an expected outcome.

A response measure for this motive was sought in the form of a verbal self-report. The problem was to define the content which would be crucial as an index of arousal. Arousal should be unpleasurable and, hence, should evoke a negative emotional response. On the basis of previous research, five more specific characteristics were suggested: tenseness or uneasiness, confusion, sense of unreality, a dreamlike feeling, and desire for social comparison.

The first research step was to devise a standard, controlled stimulus with ambiguous, nonpredictable, unexpected qualities. An 8-mm sound color movie was made. The rationale was simply to produce a series of scenes having no meaningful interrelationship and in which the sequence of events within a scene followed no logical schema. Three investigators worked independently, and the resultant edited version consists of 10 minutes and 23 seconds of continuing meaninglessness. Scenes include ceramic figures of cannibals cooking a missionary, an aerial view of a toy battleship, Mr. Ed the talking horse, a flushing toilet, a chess game played with cosmetic bottles, black children playing, a girl swimming, a dizzying ride through treetops, and a variety of animals. The sound track is predominantly that of "Voodoo Suite" played by Perez Prado with occasional interpolations of other sounds. This unusual production will be referred to as *Nonpredictable Movie I*.

The arousal scale consists of five 5-point self-rating scales dealing with the response characteristics listed above (see Appendix I). Items are scored from 1 to 5, and the total arousal score can range from 5 to 25.

For purposes of comparison, two other movies were also used. A neutral predictable movie was a documentary entitled *Life in Morocco*. It was also decided to secure a predictable film which was drive-arousing. The selection was a medical film entitled *Extracapsular Cataract Operation with Peripheral Iridectomy* which depicts the painfully detailed procedures of a cataract operation in living color.

The subjects were 120 undergraduates. They were shown one of the three movies and then asked to fill out the rating scale. The mean effectance scores are shown in Table 13-3. The nonpredictable movie yielded the highest effectance arousal score, as hypothesized.

TABLE 13-3

MEAN EFFECTANCE AROUSAL SCORES IN RESPONSE TO
NONPREDICTABLE AND PREDICTABLE MOVIES[a]

Neutral predictable movie	Arousing predictable movie	Nonpredictable movie I
7.20	9.60	12.48

[a]After Byrne and Clore, 1967, p. 6.

The internal consistency of the effectance arousal score was investigated and each of the items was found to correlate significantly with the total score of the other four items combined. The corrected split-half reliability was found to be .69.

*Influence of Effectance Arousal on Response to Attitude
Similarity–Dissimilarity*

If the effectance arousal score represents nothing more than unpleasant affect, it would be expected to show a simple negative relationship with attraction. If, however, effectance represents a motivational state crucial to the attitude–attraction relationship, arousal would be expected to increase the slope of the linear function. In the Byrne *et al.* (1966) experiment, the unverifiable topics were presumably the most arousing and it was found that similarity–dissimilarity on these topics yielded the steepest slope and the lowest *Y* intercept.

In an attempt to test the hypothesis that increased arousal leads to increased slope, three experiments were conducted. In each, there was a manipulation of the effectance motive followed immediately afterward by an attraction task in which subjects were exposed to either a relatively similar or relatively dissimilar stranger (Byrne & Clore, 1967). Because none of the three experiments confirmed the hypothesis, their methodology and results will be summarized very briefly.

In the first experiment, subjects saw either *Nonpredictable Movie I* or *Life in Morocco* and immediately afterward took part in a standard attitude–attraction experiment. In the second experiment, subjects saw either *Nonpredictable Movie I* or *Nonpredictable Movie II* (different in content from the first movie but identical in unpredictability and confusingness); immediately afterward they were asked a series of attitudinal questions about the film and then exposed to the responses of a stranger on these film-relevant attitudes. The third experiment involved a quite different arousal task in that a bogus intelligence test was administered, subjects predicted how well they would do, and the task was arranged so that their predictions were either confirmed or disconfirmed. An attitude–attraction experiment then was conducted.

TABLE 13–4

ATTRACTION RESPONSES TOWARD SIMILAR AND DISSIMILAR STRANGERS BY SUBJECTS AT HIGH AND LOW LEVELS OF EFFECTANCE AROUSAL[a]

Effectance arousal	Proportion of similar attitudes	
	Low	High
Experiment I		
High	7.67	9.88
Low	6.00	11.33
Experiment II		
High	8.76	9.06
Low	7.46	9.92
Experiment III		
High	7.71	9.57
Low	6.43	10.71

[a]Data from Byrne and Clore, 1967.

The results of all three experiments are presented in Table 13–4. Two findings are consistent across the experiments. First, the effect of proportion of similar attitudes on attraction is replicated in each instance. Second, instead of the hypothesized increased slope in the attitude–attraction function as a result of effectance arousal, there is a significant interaction in the opposite direction. That is, those subjects who were high in effectance arousal were less negative toward a dissimilar stranger and less positive toward a similar stranger than the subjects who were low in effectance arousal.

On purely logical grounds, a convincing case could be made at this point for giving the experimental manipulations a label quite different from that of effectance arousal—anxiety arousal, ambiguity, failure, ego threat, etc. Given the failure of the original hypotheses about the consequents of effectance arousal, it would be perfectly appropriate to explore some of these other possibilities. One difficulty should be noted concerning such an attempt, however. The fact that the arousal conditions interact with the similarity–dissimilarity conditions means that any explanation must account for some of the aroused subjects responding *more positively* and some responding *more negatively* to strangers, compared to the responses of the nonaroused subjects. This would suggest that something more is involved than unpleasant affect. It seemed that a reexamination of effectance motivation might prove more fruitful than a search for a completely different explanation.

Why should arousal lead to a dampening effect on the similarity–attraction relationship? One possibility is that these experimental manipulations raise drive level to such a point that it is disruptive. It had been suggested that a highly aroused state of effectance motive should characterize very young children and psychotics. The scale includes self-ratings of confusion, unreality, and a dreamlike state. Thus, a high level of arousal may simply disorient the subject and leave him less sure of his attitudes, less discriminating of the attitudes of others, and perhaps less inclined to express strongly positive or strongly negative evaluations of others. Among the many research possibilities suggested by this formulation is the comparison of schizophrenics and normals in their response to attitude similarity–dissimilarity. Schizophrenics should be characterized by an arousal state higher than that of normals. If the experimental arousal is analogous to the schizophrenic state, such patients should respond like the high arousal group: a dampened similarity–attraction relationship. It may be remembered that the Byrne, Griffitt, Hudgins, and Reeves (1969) experiment described in Chapter 8 found precisely this difference between schizophrenics and normals.

Is the idea of an increased similarity–attraction effect as the result of effectance arousal completely incorrect or had we overlooked something in our analyses? A new approach was sought.

Effect of Low, Moderate, and High Effectance Arousal on Attraction

In Chapter 12 it was reported that subjects in a typical attitude–attraction experiment were found to yield effectance arousal scores midway between that of a neutral control movie and the nonpredictable movie. It was also reported that arousal was greater following exposure to dissimilar attitudes than to similar attitudes. As a consequence of these findings, Byrne and Clore (1967) decided to measure effectance arousal in the attitude situation and examine differential effects on attraction for relatively aroused and nonaroused subjects. The general levels of arousal in this situation are, of course, much lower than in the experiments with the nonpredictable movies and the intelligence test manipulation.

Subjects in a standard attitude–attraction experiment were asked to fill out the effectance arousal scale to indicate their feelings while reading the stranger's attitudes. They were then divided into those who were least aroused (scores of 5 to 9) and those who were most aroused (scores of 10 to 14). The mean attraction responses of these groups are shown in Table 13–5. It may be seen that the direction of the interaction between arousal and similarity is that which was originally hypothesized. As arousal increases, there is a more negative response to a dissimilar stranger and a more positive response to a similar stranger.

TABLE 13–5

MEAN ATTRACTION RESPONSES OF
MODERATELY AROUSED AND NONAROUSED
SUBJECTS TOWARD SIMILAR AND DISSIMILAR
STRANGERS[a]

	Proportion of similar attitudes	
Effectance arousal	Low	High
Moderate	6.00	10.96
Low	7.50	10.31

[a]After Byrne and Clore, 1967, p. 13.

This finding led us to seek further an explanation for the failure of the experimental movies to influence responses to similar and dissimilar attitudes in the expected way. The effectance scores of the subjects in the two nonpredictable movie studies were reanalyzed. The "low arousal" subjects yielded a mean arousal score of 10.71, whereas the mean of the high arousal subjects was 16.06. Obviously, the meaning of "low" and "high" arousal is quite different in the movie and the attitude studies.

Subjects from the two movie experiments were combined to form four groups (moderate and high arousal conditions exposed to similar and dissimilar strangers). Low arousal consisted of subjects who had seen *Life in Morocco*. The relationship between attitude similarity and attraction as a function of low, moderate, or high effectance arousal may be seen in Fig.

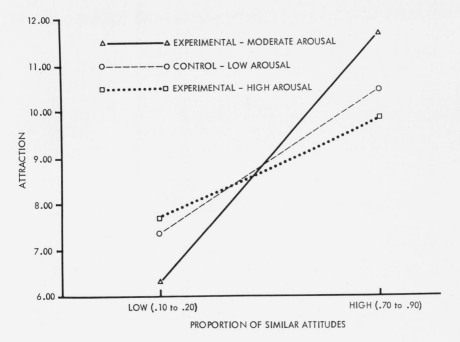

Fig. 13–2. Attraction toward a stranger as an interactive function of proportion of similar attitudes and level of effectance arousal. (After Byrne & Clore, 1967, p. 14.)

13–2. Compared to a low arousal control condition, moderate effectance arousal leads to an increased negative response toward a dissimilar stranger and an increased positive response toward a similar one. When effectance arousal reaches a still higher level, however, the effect is opposite to that of moderate arousal and the proportion of similar attitudes has less effect on attraction than in either of the other two conditions.

Additional Studies of Effectance Arousal and Attraction

Though a number of investigations and several false starts were required, the status of the concept of effectance seemed relatively firm at the time the Byrne and Clore (1967) monograph was written. We had progressed from a theoretical interpretation of the attitude–attraction findings in terms of effectance as an intervening variable to a set of operations designed to arouse that motive, a set of operations designed to measure motive arousal, and seemingly stable findings concerning the opposite effects of moderate and high arousal on the similarity–attraction function. Further, attitudinal material was found to arouse effectance, and arousal was found to increase as dissimilarity increased. The findings at that point provided us with an orderly world and a meaningful addition to the theory of attraction. Effectance seemed likely to play a major role in subsequent attraction research. Unfortunately for this happy state of affairs, additional research was conducted.

Consensual Validation and Differential Arousal. Wiener's (1969) dissertation research involved consensual validation on a perceptual task and included the measurement of effectance arousal. Because of problems with a number of the manipulations, only the relevant portions of the research design will be described.

He proposed that challenge to the subject's competence at a perceptual task should constitute an effectance-arousing situation much as the attitudinal confrontation does. In the perceptual experiment, it was hypothesized that attraction would be greater toward a consensually validating stranger than toward an invalidating stranger. On the basis of the Byrne–Clore findings, differential effectance arousal was also expected to influence this relationship.

The subjects were 64 male undergraduates at the University of Texas. The perceptual task consisted of twenty color slides depicting aerial views of three- and four-lane highways containing 26 to 67 vehicles. The study was described as one dealing with the feasibility of using helicopters to spot traffic congestion and to coordinate routing of traffic. Guesses as to number of vehicles on each slide were made in response to a multiple-choice answer sheet. Afterward, the subjects gave their response to each item aloud; the confederate then responded to each. In the consensual validation condition, the confederate gave identical responses on 15 items, was one alternative away on 2 items, and two alternatives away on 3 items. In the consensual invalidation condition, the confederate gave 5 identical responses, 2 that were one alternative away, and 13 that were two alternatives away. Subjects responded to the confederate on the IJS and also filled out the effectance arousal scale.

The mean attraction response toward the validating stranger (10.18) was not significantly higher than the mean response toward the invalidating one (9.41). One of the reasons for this finding became clear when the subjects were divided into those showing relatively high (10–16) and low (5–9) effectance arousal. The mean attraction responses toward validating and invalidating strangers are shown in Table 13–6. Thus, as in the Byrne–Clore research, moderate levels of effectance arousal lead to a positive relationship between consensual validation and attraction. In the absence of that level of arousal, there is no significant relationship between validation and attraction. Considering the differences between this experimental situation

TABLE 13-6
MEAN ATTRACTION RESPONSES TOWARD
CONSENSUALLY VALIDATING AND INVALIDATING STRANGERS
BY SUBJECTS LOW AND MODERATE IN
EFFECTANCE AROUSAL[a]

	Stranger's responses	
Effectance arousal	Consensually invalidating	Consensually validating
Moderate	9.27	10.73
Low	9.47	9.90

[a]Data from Wiener, 1969.

and the ones used previously, Wiener's findings constitute very strong support for the effectance conceptualization.

In an experiment described in some detail later in this chapter, Stapert and Clore (1969) had five experimental groups designed to differ in effectance arousal. The effectance arousal scale revealed no significant differences across conditions. It was found, however, that attraction toward an agreeing stranger was significantly related to effectance scores ($r = .28$). Thus, Stapert and Clore found a positive relationship between effectance and attraction toward an agreeing stranger, again supporting the previous findings.

Attitude Similarity and Differential Arousal. In Baskett's (1968) study of the effect of cognitive complexity on the similarity–attraction function, 111 subjects were given the effectance arousal scale immediately after responding to the Interpersonal Judgment Scale (IJS). Table 13–7 presents the mean attraction responses of the subjects indicating moderate and low effectance arousal at three levels of attitude similarity. It was found

TABLE 13-7
MEAN ATTRACTION RESPONSES OF SUBJECTS INDICATING
MODERATE AND LOW EFFECTANCE AROUSAL IN RESPONSE
TO A STRANGER AT ONE OF THREE LEVELS
OF ATTITUDE SIMILARITY[a]

	Proportion of similar attitudes		
Effectance arousal	Low	Medium	High
Moderate	6.21	6.56	9.05
Low	6.66	8.33	10.84

[a]Data from Baskett, 1968.

that effectance yields only a main effect, not an interaction; effectance arousal was negatively related to attraction. This is a perfectly reasonable finding and one that fits in well with other studies of affect arousal to be reported subsequently. The difficulty, of course, is that the results here are unlike those of Byrne and Clore, of Wiener, and of Stapert and Clore.

Attitude Similarity, Patterning, and Effectance Arousal. In a dissertation project at Iowa State University, Sherman (1969) was interested in the intensity of attraction responses as a function of attitude similarity, effectance level, and patterning. The subjects were 240 Iowa undergraduates. The 12 most important attitude topics from the 56-item survey of attitudes were selected; similarity levels of .17, .50, and .83 were created. Patterning was defined as the relative strengths of response choices across the attitude items. A highly patterned set was characterized by responses that were all the same scale distance from the neutral point (in this instance, 2 scale points from neutral). Thus, intensity of response was the same across topics. A low patterned set was characterized by inconsistency of intensity across topics (randomly determined). A modified IJS was the measure of attraction. Sherman constructed a nonpredictable video tape following the rationale of the Byrne–Clore movies. The effectance arousal scale was used as the measure of drive. The control film was *The Columbia River.* The mean arousal score in response to the unpredictable tape was 12.49 and to the control film 7.19; these means are quite comparable to the ones obtained in our earlier research. In the experiment, subjects were exposed to either the unpredictable tape or the control film and then were given the attitude survey of a stranger which was at one of two levels of patterning and at one of three levels of similarity.

Of greatest concern among Sherman's findings are those dealing with effectance arousal. When the "high drive" group was divided into moderate and high subgroups, a partial replication of the Byrne–Clore results was obtained. That is, the high arousal group was less responsive to attitude similarity than was the moderate arousal group. There were, however, no significant differences between the low and moderate groups in response to attitude similarity.

Sherman proposed an interesting hypothesis to account for the difference in findings: the Byrne–Clore unpredictable movies were interpersonal in context, whereas his tape was largely concerned with things. He suggested that a different type of effectance arousal may be involved in the two varieties of unpredictable stimuli.

Other Determinants of Attraction and Effectance Arousal. In two experiments discussed previously, the effectance arousal scale was administered in an attempt to extend the generality of the motivational studies. The experiments dealt with similarity on the repression–sensitization scale (Byrne & Griffitt, 1969) and positiveness of descriptive adjectives (Griffitt, Byrne, & Bond, 1971). In both experiments, effectance level was not influenced by the experimental conditions and was not related to the attraction response. Such findings may be seen as sharply limiting the generality of the effectance concept or as convincing support for the specificity of effectance as a mediator of the attitude–attraction relationship.

Need for Vindication

Reanalyzing the Effectance Motive. In analyzing the theoretical description of the effectance motive, Palmer (1969) has proposed that two distinct and to some extent mutually exclusive motivational constructs are implied. He labels these constructs as the *need for vindication* and the *need for evaluation*. If attitude dissimilarity is threatening and arouses the effectance motive, is it because we need to acquire a valid opinion on an issue regardless of our current position (evaluation) or because we need to defend the validity of whatever opinion we currently hold (vindication)? The Byrne–Clore description of effectance fails to make such a distinction, and Palmer suggests that the two constructs lead to different implications or predictions. For example, if evaluation were the goal, individuals would find any additional information on an issue rewarding, would be eager to compare and discuss their opinions with others, and would be attempting to seek the 'truth.' If vindication were the goal, individuals would find additional information rewarding only if it were consistent with their current beliefs, would avoid social interaction with those who held dissimilar beliefs, and any discussions would involve an attempt to win the argument.

This distinction might constitute an individual differences variable, but it also leads to the possibility of modifying the conceptualization of the effect of attitudes on attraction. Palmer argues that the need for vindication provides a more satisfactory explanation of the attitude–attraction findings than does the need for evaluation. He also notes that the need for evaluation is a closer approximation of the effectance motive as originally described by White (1959). Further, the unpredictable movies as arousal stimuli and the effectance arousal scale as an index of motive level are much more closely related to the evaluation construct than to the vindication construct. Palmer proposes that effectance be dropped from the attraction paradigm and replaced by the need for vindication.

Competence versus Incompetence. In the first experiment based on this theoretical analysis, Palmer (1969) hypothesized that the competence of the stranger should affect the attitude–attraction relationship in one of two ways, depending on whether the motivational variable were evaluation or vindication. If evaluation were the goal, either agreeing or disagreeing views from a competent stranger should be rewarding, whereas those from an incompetent stranger should be irrelevant. If vindication were the goal, agreement from a competent stranger would be more rewarding than agreement from an incompetent stranger, whereas disagreement from a competent stranger would be more punishing than disagreement from an incompetent stranger. Thus, vindication leads to a predicted interaction between similarity and competence, whereas evaluation leads to a predicted main effect for each.*

In manipulating competence, Palmer (1969) defined such a stranger as one having the ability to form valid opinions on important social, moral, and political issues. Specifically, the competent stranger was one who had a dominant profile on Leary's Interpersonal Checklist, scores of 675 to 750 on the verbal and quantitative subsections of the Scholastic Aptitude Test, and an A− average in his freshman year with the highest grades in courses such as American Government and Philosophy of Ethics. The incompetent stranger was submissive, had verbal and quantitative scores of 350 to 425, and had a C− average with the lowest grades in the courses such as government and ethics. In addition to the competence information, subjects also were given the stranger's attitudes on 12 important topics which represented either .17 or .83 similarity. The subjects were 180 male and female undergraduates at the University of Texas.

In a pilot study not involving attitudes, the competence manipulation was found to be effective in that the competent stranger was judged to be better adjusted, more intelligent, and more knowledgeable about current events than the incompetent stranger. Attraction also yielded a significant difference with the competent stranger being preferred.

In the experiment itself, the vindication hypothesis was partially vindicated in that attitude similarity interacted with competence in determining attraction. The mean attraction responses are shown in Table 13–8. It might be noted that the interaction is the result of the differential effect of the competent and incompetent strangers in the high similarity condition. Compared with a control condition in which competence information was omitted, the greatest similarity–attraction effect was in response to a competent stranger ($p < .001$) and the least effect was in response to an incompetent stranger (not significant). An intermediate effect was found in the control condition ($p < .01$).

---

*Palmer made this prediction only with respect to important attitudinal topics. He suggested and, subsequently, found that competence was irrelevant with respect to trivial topics.

TABLE 13–8

MEAN ATTRACTION RESPONSES TOWARD
COMPETENT AND INCOMPETENT STRANGERS
AT TWO LEVELS OF ATTITUDE SIMILARITY[a]

	Proportion of similar attitudes	
Stranger	.17	.83
Competent	6.27	9.93
Incompetent	6.07	7.13

[a] Data from Palmer, 1969.

In Chapter 6, the way in which Palmer conceptualized the competence information as involving both positive and negative reinforcement was discussed. He was also able to establish appropriate weights so that the results in the competent, incompetent, and control conditions on both important and trivial topics for similar and dissimilar strangers could be included in one linear equation: $Y = 6.42X + 5.11$. This function can also be described by a multiple correlation of .51.

AFFECT AND ATTRACTION

Leaving aside the specific question of the motivational consequences of attitudinal stimuli, a more general and potentially more important aspect of the model is contained in Hypothesis 9a. That is, any affect that is associated with any stimulus influences the evaluation of that stimulus. This proposition has been empirically tested in a variety of ways.

Effectance Arousal and Attraction

The first experiment directly relevant to the general affective hypothesis once again dealt with the effectance motive but from a different viewpoint than has been discussed so far. In research by Schwartz (1966), effectance was conceptualized as one type of negative affect. Anyone responsible for arousing that affect, regardless of the way in which it was accomplished, should be disliked.

The subjects were 109 high-school juniors and seniors in Austin, Texas. The affect-arousing stimulus was *Unpredictable Movie I* from the Byrne–Clore experiments. The neutral stimulus was a movie made by Schwartz, *Highland Lakes Area of Central Texas*, which was an 8-mm sound color movie of lake scenes and countryside with narration and music. After seeing one of the two films,* subjects responded to the effectance arousal scale and filled out an IJS with respect to the individual who had made the film. The films and their makers were described as follows:

> I would like to introduce this film with a few remarks. This is part of a national research project. Because of the large number of high school juniors and seniors and because of the importance of your learning and attitudes now and in the future, much of the research concerns students like yourselves. A large part of the project involves the development of varied approaches to learning and communication. Several students working in different parts of the country in special classes were requested to develop films specially designed for instructional purposes in the areas of communication and learning. Each of us working independently produced a film, one of which you will view in a few moments. Students like yourselves are seeing the other films. We are interested in what kind of learning takes place while a person watches the film. Since we are interested in the learning process, it is *most important* that you do not talk to each other or share your reactions either during the movie or after it is over until we are completely finished today. There will be some questions asked after the film.

It was found that effectance arousal was significantly higher in response to the experimental movie (13.69) than to the control movie (9.76). The attraction responses were significantly more negative toward the maker of the effectance arousal movie (7.69) than toward the maker of the control movie (9.04). Because of wide variations in arousal in each condition, the most meaningful analysis seems to be that which examines the attraction responses of high and low aroused subjects, regardless of experimental condition. The mean attraction responses are presented in Table 13–9. Attraction was shown to be strongly influenced by effectance arousal for

TABLE 13–9

MEAN ATTRACTION RESPONSES OF MALE AND FEMALE
SUBJECTS HIGH AND LOW IN EFFECTANCE AROUSAL
TOWARD THE INDIVIDUAL RESPONSIBLE
FOR THE AROUSAL[a]

Subjects	Effectance arousal	
	Low (13−)	High (14+)
Male	7.50	6.00
Female	9.75	7.50

[a]Data from Schwartz, 1966.

* Schwartz actually showed both films to each subject (in counterbalanced order), but order effects tended to obscure a number of the findings. For this reason, the present discussion deals only with the first movie seen by each subject.

both sexes, and, in addition, males responded more negatively than females at each level of arousal.

It might be noted that this experiment was conducted prior to the change in our theoretical emphasis to a simple associational model. Thus, Schwartz hypothesized and found that attraction toward an individual responsible for the arousal of negative affect is relatively negative. Whether the mere association of an individual with an affective state is sufficient to influence attraction toward him remained to be tested.

Ambient Effective Temperature and Attraction

In an experiment of considerable potential importance for both theory and application, Griffitt (1970) provided the first stringent test of Hypothesis 9a; he suggests that "If one is made to feel 'bad' (uncomfortable, unhappy, unpleasant, etc.), the evaluation of persons in such a context would be expected to be more unfavorable than in a situation in which one feels 'good' (comfortable, happy, pleasant, etc.) [pp. 240–241]." The specific situational variable he chose to manipulate was temperature:

> The very ubiquity of its potential influence on social-affective behavior would seem to render the effective temperature of the environment a variable of particular interest to social psychologists. At the anecdotal level, many interpersonal affective situations which are seemingly influenced by temperature conditions become apparent. Responses to wives, colleagues, and students are often noted as being more negative when one is "hot and grouchy" than when one is comfortably located in an air-conditioned setting. The "long hot summers" of ghetto riots are often partially attributed to the effects of high temperature on emotional and affective responses. Given the magnitude and practical implications of the problem, there is surprisingly little evidence (at the human level) concerning the effects of temperature conditions on social-affective behavior [p. 241].

His experiment involved the manipulation of a combination of temperature and humidity (effective temperature) in addition to a standard attitude–attraction task. It was expected that attraction would be a joint function of attitude similarity and effective temperature.

The subjects were 40 male and female undergraduates at Kansas State University. Attitude similarity was manipulated in the standard way on a 44-item scale with strangers simulated at either .25 or .75 similarity. Each subject reported to the Kansas State University Environmental Research Institute for the experiment. Subjects were run in small same-sex groups. The subjects in the unpleasant affect condition were run with the temperature at 100°F and the relative humidity at 60%. This results in an effective temperature of 90.6°. The normal affect condition consisted of temperature at 74°F and 30% relative humidity which results in an effective temperature of 67.5°. Previous research had shown the former to be perceived as uncomfortable and the latter as comfortable. During a 45-minute period, the subjects responded to several paper and pencil tasks including six semantic differential scales and ratings as to how they felt. Following all of this, the attitude–attraction task was introduced. Afterward, the subjects again rated their feelings, warmth, and responded to various semantic differential scales.

The effects of the temperature–humidity manipulation on affect were as expected. The high effective temperature condition was rated as more unpleasant and as warmer than the control condition. Further, the temperature and pleasantness ratings were negatively correlated at both the first ($r = -.40$) and the second ($r = -.65$) assessment periods.

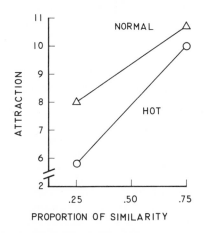

Fig. 13–3. Mean attraction responses as a function of effective temperature (normal = 67.5°, hot = 90.6°) and proportion of similar attitudes. (After Griffitt, 1970, p. 243.)

The mean attraction responses under the two environmental conditions are depicted in Fig. 13–3. The attraction responses were more negative in the "hot" condition than in the "normal" condition in addition to the usual similarity effect.

Attraction was thus found to be a function of two independent determinants: effective temperature and attitude similarity. The multiple correlation between the two independent variables and attraction was found to be .68. In addition, those subjects who reported the greatest increase in negative affect and the greatest increase in perceived temperature from beginning to end of the session responded most negatively to the stranger. Griffitt (1970) concluded:

> The findings of the present investigation support the hypothesis drawn from an affective model of evaluative behavior and everyday observation that interpersonal

evaluative responses are more negative under conditions of personal discomfort than under conditions of relative comfort. It is suggested that the effective temperature manipulations affected subjective experience of affective feelings which in turn influenced the positiveness of overt evaluative (attraction) responses to the anonymous stranger [p. 243].

It was noted in Chapter 9 that two studies of aggressive responses were based on the notion that the variables determining attraction would have an analogous effect on aggression. Neither experiment supported that proposition. With respect to the temperature effect of Griffitt, Baron (in press) hypothesized that under appropriate instigation conditions, aggression as defined by responses on the Buss aggression machine would be greater under uncomfortably hot than under comfortably cool temperatures. His findings were the reverse of this, once again suggesting that there is not a simple relationship between attraction and aggression.

Induced Mood and Attraction

In an extension of the research of Griffitt on the effects of both positive and negative affect, Gouaux (1969) drew upon research in the area of moods. He suggested that work on mood and affect arousal indicates that the quality of a person's general affective state determines much of his behavior. If the quality of a person's affective life contributes to the quality of his interpersonal relations, mood should have an effect on attraction. On the basis of the reinforcement model, that same prediction would be made.

Elation, Depression, and Attraction. Gouaux (1969) used a method developed by Velten (1967, 1968) to induce affective differences.* Subjects, run individually, were assigned to an elation or depression condition. Each was presented with cards containing 60 self-referent statements which were to be read aloud. The statements involve a progression of affect as shown by the following examples:

Elation
1. Today is neither better nor worse than any other day.
10. I'm glad I'm in college—it's the key to success nowadays.
20. I feel enthusiastic and confident now.
30. I feel so vivacious and efficient today—sitting on top of the world.
40. I feel that many of my friendships will stick with me in the future.
50. Things will be better and better today.
60. God, I feel great!

*A neutral group was also run but is omitted from the present description.

Depression

1. Today is neither better nor worse than any other day.

10. I've had important decisions to make in the past, and I've sometimes made the wrong ones.

20. Just to stand up would take a big effort.

30. I feel worn out. My health may not be as good as it's supposed to be.

40. I feel tired and depressed; I don't feel like working on the things I must get done.

50. My thoughts are so slow and downcast I don't want to think or talk.

60. I want to go to sleep and never wake up.

The subjects were female Texas undergraduates. Immediately after reading the 60 statements, each subject was given a stranger's 20-item attitude scale which was simulated at .00 similarity for all subjects. After evaluating the stranger on the IJS, the subject completed a Multiple Affect Adjective Checklist (MAACL) (Zuckerman, Lubin, & Robins, 1965) to indicate their feelings.

The mood manipulation was apparently successful in that depression scores on the MAACL were significantly higher in the depression condition than in the elation condition. Attraction was, as hypothesized, affected by mood in that the mean response in the elation condition (8.74) was significantly higher than in the depression condition (6.43). Correlational analysis indicated a significant negative relationship ($r = -.29$) between attraction and depression scores on the MAACL. The semantic differential ratings of the experimenter were also higher in the elation than in the depression condition.

Thus, both positive and negative affect seem to have the expected influence on attraction responses.

Combined Effects of Mood and Attitude Similarity on Attraction. Gouaux (1970a) carried his research on induced affective states a step further by manipulating mood states prior to the exposure of subjects to various levels of attitude similarity.

The subjects were undergraduate females at Purdue University. The mood manipulation in this experiment was accomplished by means of movies which had been used successfully in previous research (Averill, 1969). The elation film was a comedy, *Good Old Corn*, from Warner Brothers. The depression film was *John F. Kennedy, 1917–1963* from 20th Century Fox. Following the film, subjects responded to a stranger's attitudes at .15, .50, or .85 similarity. Again, the MAACL was administered as an index of mood.

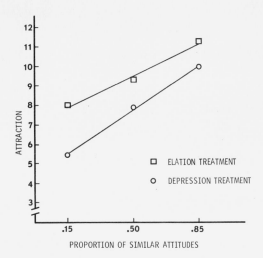

Fig. 13–4. Attraction toward a stranger as a linear function of proportion of similar attitudes and affect treatment conditions. (After Gouaux, 1970a.)

The mood manipulation was found to be effective. The attraction results are shown in Fig. 13–4. Both the stranger's attitudes and the induced mood had the expected effects on attraction.

Gouaux (1970a) concluded that, "These findings support the assumption that positive affect is associated with more positive interpersonal perceptions and evaluations and that negative affect is associated with more negative interpersonal perceptions and evaluations."

Prevailing Mood and Attraction

If mood manipulations affect attraction responses, it follows that individual differences in mood at a given point in time should be related to differences in attraction responses at that time. Gouaux, Lamberth, and Friedrich (to be published) conducted an experiment in which several state variables were assessed and contrasted with equivalent trait measures of the same variables. Our focus here will be on their measurement of mood. The subjects were 111 students at Purdue University. They were given a general form of the MAACL during a pretesting session (trait measure) and a "today" form of the same instrument at the time of the attraction experiment (state measure). The experiment involved responses to a stranger who was .17 or .83 similar to the subject on a 24-item attitude scale.

In Table 13–10 are shown the mean attraction responses as a function of depression–elation scores on both the state and trait measures. In each

TABLE 13–10
MEAN ATTRACTION RESPONSES TOWARD
SIMILAR AND DISSIMILAR STRANGERS
FOR SUBJECTS HIGH, MEDIUM, AND LOW
ON STATE AND TRAIT MEASURES
OF DEPRESSION[a]

Measures of depression	Proportion of similar attitudes	
	.17	.83
Depression trait		
High	6.05	9.68
Medium	6.85	10.53
Low	7.83	11.27
Depression state		
High	5.44	9.00
Medium	6.69	10.68
Low	9.00	11.25

[a]Data from Gouaux, Lamberth, and Friedrich, to be published.

instance, attitude similarity and depression were found to influence attraction. In associational terms, the trait measure of depression was found to correlate $-.29$ with attraction, whereas the state measure correlated $-.57$. Each of these relationships is significant, and the state measure is a significantly better predictor than the trait measure. A multiple correlation between attraction and the variables of attitude similarity and state depression was found to be .85.

Gouaux *et al.* (to be published) concluded that state measures of affect are better predictors of attraction than are trait measures and that "The findings of this study provide additional support for Byrne's affective theory of interpersonal attraction. Namely, the affective state of the subjects which is associated with a stranger significantly influences the evaluation of that stranger."

Affect As a Cue to Social Approach and Avoidance Motivation

An Alternative View of the Affect Experiments. Gouaux (1970b) has provided an alternative conceptualization to account for the influence of affective states on attraction. As opposed to a simple additive model of affect, Gouaux proposes that elation arouses social approach motivation, whereas depression arouses social avoidance motivation. He cites a number of investigations in which positive affect is found to be related to social approach behavior and negative affect related to avoidance behavior (Exline & Winters, 1965; Wehmer & Izard, 1962; Wessman & Ricks, 1966). The induction of affective states arouses the appropriate social motivation which, in turn, energizes, regulates, and directs social approach or avoidance behavior. Attraction varies as a function of affect not because various reinforcing stimuli contribute to the net implicit affective response but because affect arouses a specific motive of which differential attraction is one consequence.

Obviously, either formulation is an adequate way of describing the affect–attraction findings. Gouaux (1970b) has, however, attempted to derive differential predictions for the two formulations. The background for his research consists of animal experiments (e.g., Hull, 1933, Kendler, 1946) and research with children (e.g., Gewirtz & Baer, 1958a, b) in which for a given drive state, certain types of reinforcers are appropriate and relevant to the drive reduction and are found to have a greater effect on performance than inappropriate or irrelevant reinforcers. Specifically, he hypothesized that after affect arousal, a social reinforcer will have different effects on the performance of elated, neutral, and depressed individuals, whereas a nonsocial reinforcer will not differentially influence individuals differing in affect state.

Affect and Social versus Nonsocial Reinforcers in an Instrumental Learning Task. Gouaux (1970b) used the lever-pulling apparatus developed by Lamberth and described in Chapter 12. The subjects were 123 female undergraduates at Purdue University. Subjects were randomly assigned to the elation, neutral, or depression condition. Affect arousal was accomplished by the use of the mood-induction cards described previously. The neutral group read 60 factual statements which were not self-referent. Semantic differential scales were administered before and after the mood manipulation and again after the learning task. On each acquisition trial, the social reinforcements consisted of statements of positive personal evaluations supposedly written by other students who had seen the subject's attitude responses. The nonsocial reinforcement was 5 cents given on each acquisition trial. All subjects received 16 acquisition trials and 20 extinction trials. After the learning task, subjects once again filled out the semantic differential scales.

The six groups did not differ in their initial mood, but they did differ significantly in the expected direction at both of the postmanipulation measuring periods. The performance results are best seen in Fig. 13–5 and 13–6. The predicted reinforcement by affective state interaction for the acquisition trials was not significant. Instead, the depression group performed less rapidly than the elation and neutral groups in response to both types of reinforcement. In extinction, however, the predicted reinforcement

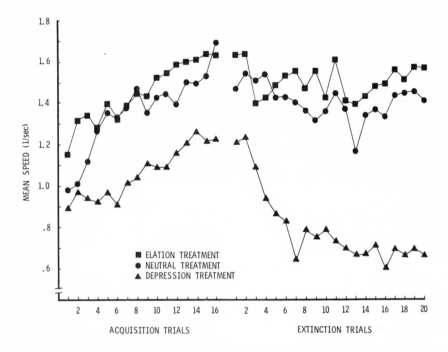

Fig. 13–5. Mean acquisition and extinction speeds for Clock II for elation, neutral, and depression groups receiving social reinforcers. (After Gouaux, 1970b, p. 44.)

by affective state interaction was confirmed. As may be seen in the figures, all three affect groups show the same extinction patterns following nonsocial reinforcement, whereas the depression group extinguishes much faster than the other two groups after social reinforcement.

The results for affective state in acquisition parallel the influence of affect on attraction. Both performance on an instrumental task and attraction toward a stranger are higher when the subject is elated than when he is depressed. The extinction findings are quite different, though, and are supportive of Gouaux's hypothesis. If the neutral group is ignored, the findings become more clear. With social reinforcement, the elated group is extremely resistant to extinction, whereas the depressed group extinguishes very rapidly. With nonsocial reinforcement, the two affect groups extinguish at an intermediate level and at the same rate. Because of the differences in acquisition and extinction, the proposal that affect is a cue to social approach and avoidance motivation may be said to have been equivocally supported.

If Gouaux's formulation had been unequivocally supported, what conclusions might be drawn? Gouaux (1970b) suggests that support for

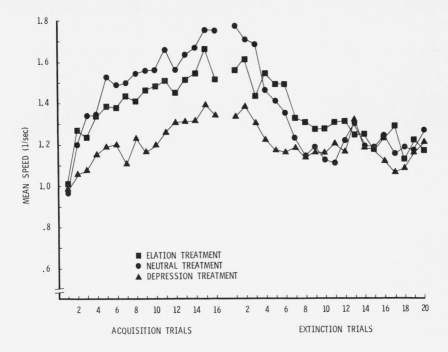

Fig. 13–6. Mean acquisition and extinction speeds for clock II for elation, neutral, and depression groups receiving nonsocial reinforcers. (After Gouaux, 1970b, p. 45.)

this theoretical proposal would be incompatible with the reinforcement approach presented earlier:

> Griffitt's reinforcement interpretation of affect-inducing stimulus conditions associated in time with direct reinforcement from a stranger clearly is opposed to the motivational interpretation suggested in this paper. Rather than accepting Griffitt's interpretation, it is suggested that the results of his two studies can more properly be understood in motivational language. Namely, both the manipulations of bonus points (Griffitt, 1968b) and effective temperature (Griffitt, 1970) induced affective states in the subjects and thereby aroused a social motive. Whereas the four bonus points in the first study induced a positive affective state and aroused approach social motivation, the "hot" condition in the second study induced a negative affective state and aroused avoidance social motivation [p. 14].

The either–or conclusion is not a necessary one. If the manipulation of affect influences attraction in the manner specified by the conditioning model, it may be that affect also has other effects such as the arousal of social approach–avoidance motivation, an enhancing or deleterious effect on performance, and bringing about differential responsiveness to various reinforcers. These findings are not incompatible with one another or with the reinforcement model. That affect has multiple properties adds to the complexity and completeness of the theoretical picture, but the picture remains basically the same. Acceptance of the social approach–avoidance findings does not require a rejection or even a modification of previous formulations, but rather an additon.

CONTEXTUAL MANIPULATIONS OF AFFECT

One direction in which attraction research has progressed is the study of situations in which there are multiple strangers. The general question is whether information about more than one stranger is maintained in discrete and independent categories or whether the various sets of information have some effect on one another. The question is not whether a subject can discriminate between or among multiple strangers but whether there are any contextual effects attributable to the multiple-stranger situation. The problem is directly relevant to the question of affect because those working in this area have tended to interpret such effects as based on affective variations.

Disagreement-Produced Arousal

Stapert and Clore (1969) point out that in the conditioning model, it is specified that disagreement arouses unpleasant affect or an unpleasant drive state. They further note that it has frequently been shown that drive arousal increases the effectiveness of reinforcers. If disagreement is drive arousing and if agreement is positively reinforcing, it follows that similar attitudes should have a greater effect on attraction following disagreement than following agreement.

In a previous experiment (Worchel & Schuster, 1966), using an attraction measure related to our standard one, each of five subjects was asked to pick one of two solutions to a problem. Then, he was given the bogus responses of the other four subjects. In one condition, the bogus responses were all in agreement with the subject (AAAA) and in another the first three were in disagreement followed by one in agreement (DDDA). It was found that attraction toward the fourth stranger was significantly more positive in the second condition than in the first. The result was interpreted as supporting a reinforcement model.

Stapert and Clore (1969) also noted that two attitudinal studies within the paradigm had reported no sequence effects. One (Byrne & London, 1966) was discussed in Chapter 4. In addition, an unpublished study, conducted in Hawaii by Byrne and Griffitt involved a similar (.86) and a dissimilar (.14) stranger presented in various combinations. As may be seen

TABLE 13–11
MEAN ATTRACTION RESPONSES WITH
AGREEMENTS (A) AND DISAGREEMENTS (D)
ON DIFFERENT ISSUES[a]

Condition	Stranger 1	Stranger 2
AA	10.80	11.00
DA	7.20	11.40
AD	11.00	7.40
DD	7.30	6.50

[a]Byrne and Griffitt data reported in Stapert and Clore, 1969, p. 66.

in Table 13–11, subjects responded to the proportion of similar attitudes irrespective of contextual effects. Stapert and Clore suggested that the failure of the two experiments in finding an effect involved agreements and disagreements on *different issues* and that disagreement-produced arousal would influence response to similarity only on the same issues (as in the Worchel–Schuster experiment). They employed the same kinds of attitudes as used in the two studies that did not find effects but in a design in which agreements and disagreements would be on the *same issues*. They also varied the number of disagreers preceding an agreeing stranger in order to determine the functional aspects of the relationship. They hypothesized that attraction toward an agreer would be an increasing function of the number of disagreers preceding him and that attraction toward a disagreer would be a decreasing function of the number of disagreers preceding him.

The subjects were 110 undergraduates at the University of Illinois. Each subject received two to four 15-item attitude scales purportedly filled out by strangers. Each stranger was simulated at either .20 or .80 similarity and each was evaluated on the IJS before the subject went on to the next stranger.

The various conditions and the mean attraction responses are shown in Table 13–12. The ratings of a series of agreeing strangers is relatively stable with no significant effects attributable to serial position. In support of the first hypothesis, attraction toward an agreeing stranger increases as the number of preceding disagreers increases.

With respect to the second hypothesis, however, the findings were the reverse of the prediction: attraction toward disagreers increased after prior disagreement. A fifth group was run with three disagreers, a re-assessment of the subject's attitudes, and then an agreeing stranger. On the attitude scale, it was found that subjects shifted their opinion to the opposite side of the issue on 3.2 of the 15 items following exposure to the

TABLE 13–12

MEAN ATTRACTION RESPONSES TOWARD STRANGERS AGREEING (A)
AND DISAGREEING (D) ON THE SAME TOPICS IN VARIOUS SEQUENCES[a]

Condition	Stranger 1	Stranger 2	Stranger 3	Stranger 4
AAAA	9.04	8.50	8.63	8.33
DA	6.04	11.22	—	—
DDA	5.88	7.00	11.63	—
DDDA	6.20	8.00	9.00	12.10

[a]After Stapert and Clore, 1969, p. 67.

three disagreers. It seems quite possible that this attitude change was responsible for some of the increase in attraction toward successive disagreeing
strangers. The possibility was also raised that dislike is not a function of
association with constant states of unpleasant affect but with the arousal of
unpleasant affect. Thus, the first disagreer would be more disliked than
subsequent ones because he is the one most closely associated with arousal.

Stapert and Clore concluded that their results supported the notion
that arousal produced by disagreement is topic-specific and that agreement
must validate the subject's view on the topic of previous disagreement in
order to reduce the arousal. They also compare the conditioning model
with balance theory as to the adequacy of explanation of such data (Stapert
& Clore, 1969):

> Like the conditioning model, balance theory posits a disagreement-produced state
> of arousal to which either dislike of the disagreer or attitude change are probable
> responses. However, for balance theory these responses both serve a homeostatic
> function; they reduce the arousal by keeping the relations in balance. This aspect
> of the theory makes a balance interpretation of the present data rather awkward.
> Specifically, if disagreement-produced arousal is reduced by attitude change or dis-
> like, then we are left without arousal to explain the increased attraction toward
> subsequent agreers. Of course the conditioning model also assumes that attitude change
> reduces arousal, since such change does away with the reason for arousal, but according
> to a conditioning analogy, the formation of dislike for the disagreer is a by-product of
> his *association* with unpleasant arousal rather than a means of reducing it. In the present
> study both rejection of the initial disagreer *and* intensification of attraction to a later
> agreer occurred. These findings appear more consistent with an association than a
> homeostasis model [p. 68].

Contrast Effects

Griffitt (1971) approached the same general problem from a somewhat different direction. He noted that in studies of judgment a consistent
finding is that the judged brightness, loudness, pitch, size, numerosity,
etc., of various target stimuli is a function of the objective attributes of the

target and of the stimulus context. When stimuli are rated or judged in contexts of higher or lower values, either assimilation or contrast effects are reported, depending on several aspects of the conditions. Assimilation and contrast refer to judgmental shifts toward or away from the context stimuli. In the experiments of Worchel and Schuster and of Stapert and Clore, contrast effects were found. Griffitt (1971) designed a series of experiments in order to examine some of the determinants of such context effects.

Agreement and Disagreement on Different Topics. The subjects were 40 undergraduates at Kansas State University. Subjects who had been pretested on 44 items were asked to listen to the tape-recorded attitudinal responses of two strangers. With two recorders, the experimenter played the tapes alternating between the first stranger's responses on each of 22 items and the second stranger's responses on each of another set of 22 items. One voice was male and the other female. After hearing all 44 attitudinal responses, the subjects evaluated each stranger on the IJS. Each stranger was either .18 or .91 similar and the context was either consistent (AA or DD) or inconsistent (AD or DA).

The results are shown in Fig. 13–7. There was the usual significant effect of agreement on attraction and the hypothesized interaction between agreement and context. That is, attraction was greater toward an agreer

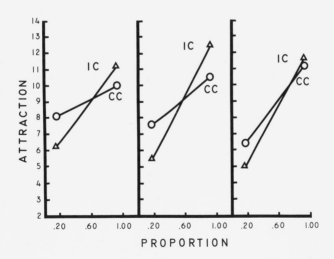

Fig. 13–7. Mean attraction responses as a function of proportion of "simultaneously" presented similar attitudes and context consistency (left panel), proportion of sequentially presented similar attitudes and context consistency (center panel), and proportion of simultaneously presented positive adjectives and context consistency (right panel). IC, inconsistent context; CC, consistent context. (After Griffitt, 1971, p. 28.)

paired with a disagreer than when paired with another agreer. Also, attraction was less toward a disagreer paired with an agreer than when paired with another disagreer. Thus, a contrast effect was found.

Agreement and Disagreement on the Same Topics. Griffitt's (1971) second experiment in this series was designed to determine whether these same contrast effects would be found if the two strangers were responding to the same attitude items.

The subjects were again 40 Kansas State undergraduates. In this experiment the strangers were represented by mimeographed attitude scales. Each was at either .18 or .91 similarity, and the subject evaluated each after having read both attitude scales. As in the previous experiment, there was either agreement or disagreement in a consistent or inconsistent context.

The results were shown in Fig. 13–7, and it is obvious that they closely parallel those of the previous experiment. Once again, a contrast effect was evident.

Descriptive Adjectives and Context Effects. Griffitt's (1971) third experiment again employed 40 subjects. Each was asked to examine adjective descriptions of two individuals provided by a psychologist who had purportedly interviewed each. There were two stacks of cards labelled Person A and Person B. Subjects picked up the first card in the Person A stack, read aloud the adjective typed on it, then picked up the first card of Person B, etc. There were 11 adjectives for each stranger. After reading through both stacks, subjects rated both strangers on the IJS. The adjectives were arranged as either .18 or .91 positive. Analogous to the other two experiments, each stranger was either positive or negative in a consistent or inconsistent context.

The results, also shown in Fig. 13–7, were precisely the same as in the two attitude experiments. Contrast effects were again found.

Griffitt's Affect Formulation. Griffitt (1971) proposed a modification of the Stapert and Clore sequential hypotheses:

> Stimulus persons who agree with S, positively evaluate S, or are positively described (P), are hypothesized to evoke positive affective arousal (PAA) in S while those who disagree with S, negatively evaluate S, or are negatively described (N), evoke negative affective arousal (NAA). Thus, the sequencing of separate P and N stimulus persons is seen as the critical determinant of whether or not a contrast effect is obtained. Stapert and Clore (1969) hypothesize that the magnitudes of evoked PAA and NAA sequentially decrease across a series of P stimulus persons and N stimulus persons, respectively. Thus, response to an initial P stimulus person is more positive than to subsequent Ps due to the greater amount of PAA associated with the former. Similarly, response to an initial N person is more negative than to subsequent Ns due to decreasing NAA. In addition,

responses to Ps preceded by Ns are more positive than to Ps preceded by Ps since in the former condition a greater amount of PAA is associated with the P person. Finally, responses to Ns preceded by Ps would be expected to be more negative than responses to Ns preceded by Ns since in the former condition NAA associated with N is greater due to the precedence of Ps which have reduced negative affect to a minimal level. This "sequential" hypothesis adequately accounts for the findings of studies involving sequential variations of P and N . . .

In the present investigations, however, contrast effects were obtained in the absence of sequential variations of P and N orders. In Experiments I and III, P and N presentation was essentially simultaneous, while in Experiment II no order effects were obtained. In order to account for the present findings, a modification of the sequential hypothesis appears necessary. In the PN conditions the P person does not precede the N person but is presented essentially at the same time and vice versa with respect to the NP conditions. P is simply presented in a context of N and N is presented in a context of P. In the PN and NP conditions the sequencing of single positive (p) stimuli (PAA) associated with P alternating with single negative (n) stimuli (NAA) associated with $NP_{(p)}(PAA) - N_{(n)}(NAA) - P_{(p)} - N_{(n)}$, etc. results in a situation in which a large magnitude of PAA is consistently produced by P and a large magnitude of NAA is consistently produced by N. Thus, as opposed to the PP and NN conditions in which the magnitudes of PAA or NAA associated with each stimulus person are sequentially decreasing, each stimulus person in the PN or NP conditions is repeatedly associated with either a large magnitude of PAA or NAA and consequently attraction responses are more extreme in the PN and NP situations [pp. 31–32].

CONCLUSIONS

The investigations discussed in the present chapter are consistent with the proposal that affective responses play a crucial role in the attraction phenomenon. The possibility of any stimulus influencing attraction or influencing performance in a learning task is dependent on its affect-eliciting properties. Within the attraction paradigm, affect has been investigated with respect to differential stimulus properties and differential self-ratings of subjects, and there have been attempts to induce affect by means of varying the characteristics of the stimulus, the context in which the stimulus occurs, and through the creation of independent arousal conditions. As an explanation for the effects of attitudinal material, the concept of effectance motive is somewhat appealing and has the virtue of bringing together the cognitive and reinforcement approaches to attraction. The research engendered by this idea has been of only limited success, however, and tends to be characterized by unexpected and in part inconsistent findings. At best, the operations employed to manipulate and to measure effectance are in need or refinement. As a criticism and suggested redefinition of the effectance concept, Palmer's work on the need for vindication provides a promising guideline for future research. Beyond the concern with the affective properties of attitude statements, the research on affect arousal as a determinant of attraction is basic to the general theoretical model, and the data have consistently supported the hypotheses. The manipulation of affect by means as diverse as effective temperature and contextual arrangements would seem to be the royal road to predicting and controlling evaluative responses. Hypothesis 9a has received solid empirical support.

APPLICATIONS

Chapter 14 / **Toward Applications Based on the Attraction Paradigm**

One of the more difficult tasks in evaluating any research program at a given point in time is in determining its broad implications for further research, for theory-building, and for application. At various points in time, the present paradigm has been criticized for being at a dead end with no-where further to go (this observation was first made in 1961 after the initial experiment was published) and for being empirical and atheoretical (this criticism was justified in the early 1960s for the reasons outlined in Chapter 10). The preceding 13 chapters should serve to answer both of these points. One may not care for either the research or the theory, but they do exist. Actually, the implications of the attraction paradigm for research in person-ality and social psychology are perhaps of greater importance than any specific concern with attraction. For those interested in messages and/or morals, interwoven throughout the description of the attraction experi-ments there was a general message or moral concerning a way to approach research. The possibility of applications will be considered in some detail in the present chapter. As was noted in Chapter 1, one effect of seeking gen-erality from the base relationship is to move closer to the everyday world and closer to possible applications to the concerns of that world. The research to be discussed in the present chapter could easily have been included in the earlier chapters and vice versa. It is premature to expect the attraction paradigm to produce a technology, but a number of investigations serve to outline several possibilities concerning the nature of a future technology.

MAXIMIZING INTERPERSONAL HARMONY

Perhaps the most obvious application of attraction research is in seeking to increase attraction and to decrease rejection in various two-person situations: friendship, courtship, and marriage. If we have gained predictive knowledge about many of the variables that determine attraction and if we value positive interpersonal relationships, the next step would seem to be that of determining how we can move from laboratory research to the control of interpersonal relationships.

Moving from the Prediction of Interpersonal Attraction to the Control of Interpersonal Attraction

For most of us, a term such as "control" is sufficiently frightening to evoke unpleasant associations of the sort dramatized in *Brave New World, 1984*, and *This Perfect Day*. Farber (1964) has discussed this problem:

> It was stated earlier that, if the determinants of behavior were known, and if enough of them were susceptible to manipulation, then it would be possible to control behavior. It was also noted that this proposition arouses the most intense annoyance and anxiety in many people, including psychologists, who for good reasons, abhor the idea of a totalitarian technocracy (Bergmann, 1956). In its superficial aspects, one can rather readily understand why the concepts of "control" and "despotism" are sometimes equated. If behavior can indeed be controlled by manipulating its determinants, then individuals with the requisite knowledge could and very possibly would exercise this control. On the one hand, we must recognize that different societies and different individuals have different goals. What is desirable or reinforcing for one may be frustrating and punishing for another. We are only too liable to the delusion that our own goals are the only reasonable ones. Thus, when I try to change a person's behavior or attitudes, I am appealing to his better judgment; when you try to do so, you are using propaganda; and when "they" do so, they are brainwashing. To complicate matters further, this multiplicity of motives and goals extends to the intrapersonal sphere. The behavior that is instrumental to the satisfaction of one motive may frustrate the satisfaction of another.
>
> On the other hand, our respect for the rights of others to their particular goals and the instrumental acts whereby they are achieved should not lead us to the romantic delusion that these are spontaneous products of unfettered choice. No one escapes control by the physical environment short of death; and no one escapes control by his social environment short of complete isolation. Almost the entire period of childhood is given over to the acquisition of new behaviors, goals, and motives, under the guidance of parents, family, and teachers. Be it wise or unwise, deliberate, impulsive, or unconscious, such guidance inevitably has its effects. It is difficult, in fact, to think of any kind of social interaction that has absolutely no effect on behavior. That the effects are unintentional or unwanted does not negate them [pp. 12–14].

In the present context, we may note that people become friends, go on dates, and get married regardless of whether behavioral scientists interfere or not. The only justifiable reason to seek application is to make the process more beneficial to those concerned. For example, a research goal of reducing the divorce rate and increasing the proportion of happy marriages does not appear to be a fascist plot any more than is the irradication of polio. Perhaps the only difference is that all of us are accustomed to successful applications in fields other than behavioral science.

If one can accept the notion that specific applied goals are both feasible and moral, the battle has only begun. It is a familiar but never totally resolved problem with any experimental data to specify the extent to which they may be generalized to the nonlaboratory situation. At least three viewpoints about the problem may be discerned. First, and perhaps most familiar, is instant generalization from the specific and often limited conditions of an experiment to any and all settings even remotely related. This tendency is most evident at cocktail parties after the third martini and on television talk shows featuring those who popularize psychology. Second, and almost as familiar, is the notion that the laboratory is a necessary evil. It is seen as an adequate substitute for the real world only to the extent that it reproduces that world. For example, Aronson and Carlsmith (1968) ask, "Why, then, do we bother with these pallid and contrived imitations of human interaction when there exist rather sophisticated techniques for studying the real thing? [p. 4]" They enumerate the advantages of experiments over field studies but emphasize that good experiments must be realistic in order to involve the subject and have an "impact" on him. Concern with experimental realism often is expressed in the context of positing qualitative differences between the laboratory and the outside world; it is assumed that in moving from simplicity to complexity, new and different principles emerge. Third, and least familiar in personality and social psychology, is a view which is quite common in other fields. Laboratory research is seen not as a necessary evil but as an essential procedure which enables us to attain isolation and control of variables and thus makes possible the formulation of basic principles in a setting of reduced complexity. If experiments realistically reproduce the nonlaboratory complexities, they provide little advantage over the field study. Continuity is assumed between the laboratory and the outside world and complexity is seen as quantitative and not qualitative. To move from a simple situation to a complex one requires detailed knowledge about the relevant variables and their interaction. Successful application and the attainment of a valid technology depend upon such an approach.

Considering the effect of attitude similarity on attraction, why is it not reasonable to propose an immediate and direct parallel between laboratory and nonlaboratory responses? One reason is simple and quite obvious, but it seems often to be overlooked. Laboratory research is based on the isolation of variables so that one or a limited number of independent variables may be manipulated while, if possible, all other stimulus variables are controlled. In the outside world, multiple uncontrolled stimuli are always present. Thus, if all an experimental subject knows about a stranger is that he holds opinions similar to his own on six out of six political issues, the stranger will be liked (Byrne, Bond, & Diamond, 1969). We cannot, however, assume that any two interacting individuals who agree on these six issues will become fast friends because (*1*) they may never get around to discussing those six topics at all, and (*2*) even if these topics are discussed, six positive reinforcements may simply become an insignificant portion of a host of other positive and negative reinforcing elements in the interaction. A second barrier to immediate applicability of a laboratory finding lies in the nature of the response. It is good research strategy to limit the dependent variable [as with the Interpersonal Judgment Scale (IJS) measure of attraction], but nonlaboratory responses tend to be as varied and uncontrolled as the stimuli. The third barrier lies in the nature of the relationship investigated. For a number of quite practical reasons, the laboratory study of attraction is limited in its time span and hence might legitimately be labelled the study of first impressions. Whether the determinants of first impressions are precisely the same as the determinants of a prolonged friendship, of love, or of marital happiness is an empirical question and one requiring a great deal of research before it will be possible to offer definitive answers.

Despite the barriers to extralaboratory application of experimental findings, we shall examine some research steps which may take us toward the engineering enterprise.

Correlational Studies of Husbands and Wives

In Chapter 2, it was pointed out that some of the earliest attraction research dealt with husband–wife similarity on numerous characteristics. Beginning with the work of Galton (1870, republished 1952) and of Schuster and Elderton (1906), it has consistently been found that spouses are more similar than would be expected on a chance basis. Applied implications were drawn by Terman and Buttenwieser (1935a,b) who found suggestive evidence that differential similarity is related to differential marital success. Relatively recent research on the relationship between marital success and personality or attitudinal similarity has tended to confirm the Terman and Buttenwieser findings (e.g., Cattell & Nesselroade, 1967; Pickford, Signori, & Rempel, 1966a,b, 1967; Signori, Rempel, & Pickford, 1968). Pickford, Signori, and Rempel (1966b) concluded "it can be stated that there is fairly consistent evidence indicating that marital happiness or adjustment is related to similarity of personality traits in husband and wife and that dissimilarity is related to marital unhappiness or maladjustment [p. 192]." If reliable correlates of marital success were established, it would seem reasonable to attempt to determine whether premarital similarity is predictive of successful marriages. If so, the implications for marital counseling are obvious. Research dealing with these possibilities has been conducted only sporadically.

Similarity and Assumed Similarity of Attitudes. Byrne and Blaylock (1963) suggested that the number and intensity of reciprocal rewards exchanged by spouses would be greater than the number and intensity of reciprocal punishments. Otherwise, the relationship would not be maintained. It was also noted that attempts to predict the reward pattern for any single type of interaction (e.g., sexual behavior, economic attitudes) are likely to be incorrect, because maintenance of the relationship would depend on the total array of rewards and punishments rather than any limited class of them. With respect to attitude similarity, happily married individuals would be expected to offer one another frequent rewards via consensual validation about a variety of topics, but not about all topics. Political attitudes, for example, might or might not be an important area of discussion for a particular couple. With college students or college-educated individuals, it seems likely that those who marry will be found to be similar in their general political orientation.

Another aspect of the Byrne and Blaylock (1963) investigation was based on balance theory. Presumably, attitude similarity is one of the variables that increases the probability of two individuals deciding to marry. In real life, however, it is almost impossible to find a suitable mate who is 1.00 similar. What happens, then, when a reasonably happy husband and wife find that they disagree about some topics? According to balance theory, one of the simplest resolutions of such a problem is misperception. That is, if a husband and wife like one another and if they disagree about topic X, the potential problem disappears if each decides that the other really holds similar rather than dissimilar views. This misperception is much easier than achieving balance by altering feelings about one's spouse or by persuading one's spouse to adopt a different position or by changing one's own attitudes about X. It was hypothesized, then, that assumed similarity of political attitudes is greater than actual similarity of political attitudes among married couples.

The attitudes were measured by means of Rokeach's (1960) left opinionation and right opinionation scales. In addition, more general attitudes were assessed by his dogmatism scale. The subjects were 36 married couples. The husbands were either students at the University of Texas or in various professions ranging from research engineer to real estate developer. The wives included students, housewives, secretaries, and teachers. Each subject filled out the questionnaire and then was asked to respond to the

TABLE 14-1

ACTUAL SIMILARITY AND ASSUMED SIMILARITY OF POLITICAL ATTITUDES
BETWEEN HUSBANDS AND WIVES[a]

Scale	Similarity actually found for couples	Assumed by husband	Assumed by wife
Left opinionation	.30	.74	.79
Right opinionation	.44	.69	.89
Dogmatism	.31	.70	.85

[a] After Byrne and Blaylock, 1963, p. 638.

scales again as the spouse would have done. For each subject on each of the three scales, two scores were obtained: self-score and assumed spouse score.

It may be seen in Table 14–1 that the husband–wife correlations indicated significant similarity on all three scales. Much higher relationships are obtained, however, with respect to assumed similarity. Both the husbands and the wives assumed that there was much greater similarity than was actually the case. It was also thought possible that the length of time a couple had been married might affect these relationships. Length of marriage ranged from 4 months to 37 years. It was found that regardless of length of marriage, the same relationships held true: moderate correlations between self-scores of husbands and wives and significantly higher correlations between self-scores and assumed spouse scores.

For individuals with strong political concerns, consensual validation versus consensual invalidation concerning political beliefs and attitudes could conceivably contribute a great deal to the total proportion of positive reinforcements provided by a relationship. Despite other possible rewards in an interaction, it is difficult to imagine a member of the John Birch Society marrying a member of the Students for a Democratic Society (SDS). Similarity of political beliefs is rewarding, and there is a strong tendency to distort modest actual similarities in the direction of much greater congruence than is objectively present. Thus, rewards are increased by means of misperceptions. One suggestion made was that assumed similarity probably contributes to and is an index of the positiveness of the relationship.

Similarity and Marital Satisfaction. Levinger and Breedlove (1966) replicated the general Byrne–Blaylock design in a nonstudent sample and tested the hypothesis that assumed similarity varies directly with marital satisfaction.

The subjects were 60 married couples; 24 of these were clients at a family service agency and 36 were parents of elementary school children.

During an interview session, conducted separately with the husband and wife, each was assessed with respect to attitudes toward family life on a number of measures. The spouse's assumed attitudes were determined concerning the relative importance of 9 different marriage goals and of 11 marital communication topics. Marital satisfaction was measured by an index composed of each individual's factor score derived from 15 indices. Husbands and wives correlated .45 on this index.

TABLE 14–2
ACTUAL VERSUS ASSUMED AGREEMENT ABOUT MARITAL GOALS[a]

Topics	Agreement actually found for couples	Assumed by husband	Assumed by wife
Communication goals	.39	.62	.68
General goals	.44	.60	.46

[a]After Levinger and Breedlove, 1966, p. 369.

In Table 14–2 the results are shown, comparing actual and assumed agreement, and the findings are very much like those of the Byrne–Blaylock study. In Table 14–3 are shown the correlations between marital satisfaction and assumed agreement. The results clearly support the hypothesis of a positive relationship between degree of assumed similarity and satisfaction, and this was especially true for the husbands.

TABLE 14–3
CORRELATIONS BETWEEN MARITAL SATISFACTION
AND ASSUMED AGREEMENT[a]

Topics	Husbands	Wives
Communication goals	.39	.19
General goals	.45	.29

[a]After Levinger and Breedlove, 1966, p. 369.

It was noted that:

... marital satisfaction is significantly associated with the degree to which a partner overestimates—or underestimates—in stating his assumed agreement with his spouse. A number of spouses, whose marital satisfaction was low, reported even less agreement with their partner than was actually the case. One can infer that, in accordance with Newcomb's model, these distortions are rewarding to these individuals [Levinger & Breedlove, 1966, p. 370].

Levinger and Breedlove had also proposed that actual agreement and attraction should be related only to the extent that such agreement promotes the achievement of the group's goals. Thus, the more the agreement is instrumental for furthering the goals of the marital relationship, the higher should be the correlation with marital satisfaction. Their test of this was a comparison of agreement about the importance of specific communication topics with agreement about the importance of general goals for the marriage. The expected difference was not found. After the fact, it might be argued as to which if either of these areas of agreement is more instrumental in furthering marriage goals. The general idea of instrumentality sounds plausible, however, and seems to be well worth pursuing.

Sexual Needs and Attraction. At a more mundane level than communication topics or general goals is the array of attitudes, values, and responses concerned with sex. Because sexual behavior is one of the major sources of both positive reinforcement and frustration in or out of marriage, it seems likely that agreement about sexuality would be a vital element in determining marital success. Both common sense and the data supplied by marital counselors and divorce courts support this proposition. In addition, whether for cultural or biological reasons, spouses often are quite different in sexual proclivities (e.g., Wallin & Clark, 1958). Systematic research dealing with similarity of sexual attitudes and values has only recently gotten underway.

In Chapter 6, it was noted that response to the same- and opposite-sex strangers tends to be the same in the attitude similarity experiments. In the study of physical attractiveness (Byrne, London, & Reeves, 1968), it was proposed that response to the same and opposite-sex strangers would differ, but that turned out to be incorrect. A further attempt to explore differential responses to the two sexes was made by Byrne, Lamberth, and Mitchell (to be published, b). For heterosexual individuals, sexual needs are instrumental to attaining certain goals in relationships with members of the opposite sex but not with members of the same sex (Banta & Hetherington, 1963; Murstein, 1961). Therefore, on sexually relevant issues, similarity of same and opposite-sex strangers should be differentially relevant; on nonsexual issues, the sex of the other person should be irrelevant.

A preliminary experiment was conducted at Stanford University with 70 male and female undergraduates. Because of a shortage of subjects, only a portion of the appropriate conditions could be run. Subjects responded to a 15-item version of the Edwards Personal Preference Schedule (EPPS) and were later exposed to the responses of a stranger on the same scale. The stranger was either of the same or opposite sex and either similar on .40 or .60 of the items. Nine of the items involved the need for heterosexuality and included choices such as "I like to read books and plays in which sex plays a major part," "I like to kiss attractive persons of the opposite sex," and "I like to become sexually excited." The other six items were randomly chosen from other EPPS scales. The simulation of the stranger was such that .40 similarity consisted of similarity on the nonsexual items and dissimilarity on all of the choices involving sex; .60 similarity consisted of similarity on the sexual items and dissimilarity on the others. The results are shown in Table 14–4. The proposed interaction was found in that differential similarity on the sexual items had the greatest effect on responses to an opposite-sex stranger.

TABLE 14–4

MEAN ATTRACTION RESPONSES TOWARD
SAME- AND OPPOSITE-SEX STRANGERS
WHO WERE SIMILAR OR DISSIMILAR ON
SEXUAL ITEMS

	Proportion of similar responses	
Sex of stranger	.40 (Dissimilar on sexual items)	.60 (Similar on sexual items)
Same sex	8.01	9.50
Opposite sex	7.46	10.89

On the basis of these findings, Byrne, Lamberth, and Mitchell (to be published, b) conducted a more elaborate experiment using 302 University of Texas undergraduates. The subjects were given the full EPPS (A. L. Edwards, 1959) and scored for need for heterosexuality and need for achievement. Half of the subjects were divided into high and low subgroups on one of the needs and half were divided on the other need. In the experiment itself, each subject received a 28-item EPPS scale containing all heterosexual or all achievement items. The stranger was either of the same or opposite sex and agreed with the subject on .25 or .75 of the items. Items of agreement were randomly selected except that a .75 similar stranger was similar to the subject with respect to need level while a .25 stranger was dissimilar from the subject in need level.

Because males and females did not differ in their responses and because high and low need level made little difference, the results are shown in Table 14–5 for the two levels of similarity with same- and opposite-sex strangers for the two kinds of material. Again, there was support for the general idea. That is, for both kinds of stimulus material, there is a significant similarity effect but only on the sexual material does the sex of

TABLE 14-5
MEAN ATTRACTION RESPONSES
TOWARD SAME- OR OPPOSITE-SEX STRANGERS
AT TWO LEVELS OF SIMILARITY ON
SEXUAL OR ACHIEVEMENT ITEMS[a]

	Proportion of similar responses	
Sex of stranger	.25	.75
Need for heterosexuality		
Same sex	8.24	9.28
Opposite sex	9.50	10.56
Need for achievement		
Same sex	8.34	9.97
Opposite sex	9.03	10.90

[a]After Byrne, Lamberth, and Mitchell, to be published, b.

the stranger significantly influence attraction. A stranger of the opposite sex is liked better than a stranger of the same sex only when the stimulus material deals with sexual activity.

Similarity of Sexual Responses of Husbands and Wives. Returning to the study of similarity in marriage, Byrne, Lamberth, and Mitchell (to be published, a) conducted an experiment at Purdue University with 42 married couples in which the subjects were exposed to a variety of erotic stimuli and independently assessed as to their general feelings about the experience, the degree to which the stimuli were sexually arousing, whether or not each stimulus was pornographic, and their opinions about various legal restrictions which might be placed on such stimuli. A week after the experiment, each responded to a follow-up questionnaire dealing with the relative frequency during that week of various kinds of sexual activity. The stimuli consisted of 19 sexual themes presented pictorially on slides, verbally in printed form, or simply described with instructions to think about the theme. In the results to be discussed, the three modes of presentation do not yield differential results. It might be noted that this investigation differs from previous studies of marital partners in that the subjects were exposed to a series of specific experimental stimuli and also that the responses deal entirely with reactions and judgments about sex.

In Table 14-6 are shown several of the husband–wife correlations plus the average correlations of 41 random pairs of males and females in the sample. Two factors are striking about these findings. First, those who

TABLE 14–6
HUSBAND–WIFE CORRELATIONS
ON VARIOUS RESPONSES TO EROTIC STIMULI
COMPARED WITH AVERAGE CORRELATIONS FOR
41 MALE–FEMALE PAIRS

Responses	Spouses r	Random pairs r
Preexperimental feelings		
Sexually aroused	.50	−.01
Bored	.44	−.01
Excited	.32	−.01
Postexperimental feelings		
Nauseated	.63	−.02
Sexual arousal to specific erotic stimuli		
Total arousal	.60	−.02
Dorsal–ventral intercourse	.57	−.01
Homosexual fellatio	.54	−.01
Partially clad heterosexual petting	.41	−.01
Nude female	.40	−.01
Cunnilingus	.40	−.01
Nude heterosexual petting	.39	−.01
Male masturbating	.38	−.01
Ventral–ventral intercourse	.31	−.01
Male torturing female	.31	−.01
Group oral sex	.30	−.01
Nude male	.26	−.01
Judgments about pornography		
Total No. of themes judged pornographic	.43	−.01
Legal restrictiveness		
Total restrictiveness	.31	−.01
Forbid production and sale	.42	−.01
Forbid sale to teenagers	.36	−.01
Follow-up: relative frequency of sexual behavior		
Thinking about sexual matters	.41	−.01
Talking about sexual matters	.34	−.01
Reading books about sex	.29	−.01
Dreaming about sexual activity	.31	−.01
Engaging in sexual activity	.38	−.01
Sexual behavior different from usual pattern	.42	−.01
Hostility toward the experiment	.49	−.01

TABLE 14–7

HUSBAND–WIFE SIMILARITY IN SEXUAL
AROUSAL IN RESPONSE TO THE THEME
OF DORSAL–VENTRAL INTERCOURSE

Type of response	No. of couples
Similar in finding theme relatively unarousing sexually	23
Similar in finding theme relatively arousing sexually	10
Dissimilar with husband finding theme more arousing than wife did	4
Dissimilar with wife finding theme more arousing than husband did	5

marry show greater than chance similarity in their positive and negative reactions to erotic stimuli, their evaluative judgments about these stimuli, and even in the effects of these stimuli on subsequent behavior. It might be noted that the coefficients reported in Table 14–6 are much higher than those normally found in studies of husband–wife similarity. Second, even with this impressive degree of marital similarity, there is a considerable degree of dissimilarity in individual couples. For example, the extent to which the theme of dorsal–ventral intercourse is sexually arousing or unarousing is much more similar between those who marry one another than is true for random pairs of individuals ($r = .57$ versus $-.01$). In theoretical terms, this is a high degree of similarity. In practical terms, however, that finding means that only 32% of the variance in the responses of one member of the pair is accounted for by the responses of the other member. Another way to consider the same point is through examining the actual responses of the 42 couples. As may be seen in Table 14–7, 33 of the couples are similar and possibly reciprocally reinforcing with respect to sexual response to dorsal–ventral intercourse either because they both find it arousing or both find it unarousing. For the other 9 couples, however, there is dissimilarity and the potentiality of reciprocal punishment. It remains to be determined, however, whether individuals in the former group are happier in their marriage and less likely to contemplate divorce than are the members of the latter group. All of our research to date would lead to the prediction that total proportion of such similarities would be a decisive determinant of the emotional climate of the marriage.

Applied Implications. The line of investigation just described represents a beginning in the attempt to apply principles derived from the attraction experiments to the problem of maximizing marital happiness. A point might be made concerning the type of additional evidence needed prior to application. First, it would seem wise to have evidence from varied samples confirming and documenting and detailing the relationship between similarity and marital satisfaction. Second, extensive evidence is needed that premarital characteristics are predictive of subsequent marital happiness. It could be, for example, that satisfied couples are those who learn to conform to one another in marriage rather than having been similar prior to marriage. Third, a considerable amount of systematic research is needed to show the differential effects of various kinds of agreement and disagreement. Presumably, appropriate weighting coefficients could be established either normatively or for each individual. Fourth, it would be necessary to learn the effects of such demographic variables as educational level, social class, and ethnic background which could be found to alter the weighting coefficients or even reverse certain relationships. Fifth, if the suggested research were well executed and if it led to consistent and convincing results, one could comfortably suggest wide-scale application. At that point, it would seem reasonable to propose that individuals considering marriage might wish to consider an assessment procedure covering numerous attitudinal and behavioral areas and a determination of similarity profiles. With sufficient data, it should be possible to assess degree of similarity, assign appropriate weights, and derive a prediction concerning probable marital happiness and even probability of divorce.

It should go without saying, but in a democratic society one would hope that the decision to avail oneself of the proposed premarital assessment and the decision to respond to or ignore the predictions would remain a matter for the individuals involved and not for a superordinate governmental body.

Experimental Studies of Dating

Research on marital satisfaction is almost certainly limited to the correlational approach in field studies. It is not feasible to determine pairings according to a prearranged design such that one group of couples is expected to have a happy marriage, whereas a second group is expected to be miserable. This kind of manipulation is, however, possible and defensible in the dating situation.

One point should be made prior to a description of such experiments. It may well be that the prediction of satisfactory dating relationships is only partially related to or even unrelated to the prediction of satisfactory marital relationships. The potential problem is not that different laws are operative but that different variables are present. One can imagine, for example, an entire series of interactions in marriage which would not be expected to occur during the dating process. Thus, it could be that husband–wife similarity with respect to a comfortable setting of the thermostat, whether to spend money on a new dishwasher or a new stereo, neatness in disposing of dirty socks, interest in morning sex, disciplinary decisions about children, whether to squeeze the toothpaste tube on the bottom or in the middle, etc., etc., could summate to determine the outcome of a marriage. The same variables would quite probably remain useless as predictors of the outcome of a dating relationship and would probably never be identified in such experiments. Analogously, a variety of considerations in dating (e.g., dancing ability, acceptability to one's high school friends, interest in petting in drive-in movies) might be found to be predictive of attraction in that situation but irrelevant to marriage. The general principles (e.g., attraction as a function of reinforcement) remain the same, but the identification of specific relevant reinforcers is a vital practical matter which cannot be ignored.

Simulated Dating Relationship. Shaughnessy and Levinger (1969) have described a methodology for the study of the development of any pair relationship. Their approach was a computer-assisted technique for investigating social encounters. The situation was one in which the subject was led to believe that he was interacting with another person by means of a teletype used to ask questions, receive answers, and to receive questions and to answer them. The other person did not exist; the behavior of the stranger was controlled and the entire process was monitored.

The subjects were 34 male undergraduates at the University of Massachusetts. Each filled out a 40-item questionnaire. The items were in the form of two-value preferences ranging from ("Do you prefer summer or winter?" to "Would you prefer to find out that your parents are getting a divorce or that your parents are having extramarital relations?" The "other subject" was described as an undergraduate female. The subject was instructed to ask her a question about one of the items, and he then received an answer to it. Then, he was asked a question about another item and gave his response. Through the sequence, each member of the pair asked questions concerning 20 of the 40 items. Half of the subjects received answers from "the girl" which were all similar (1.00) to their own whereas the other half received dissimilar responses (.20). At the end of the session, subjects were asked to rate the girl with respect to how much he would like her as a potential date.

The hypothesis that subjects would prefer a similar over a dissimilar other as a potential dating choice was strongly confirmed. There was also a tendency for similarity to evoke more questions on intimate items than was the case for dissimilarity.

Actual Dating Relationship. Though field studies of dating have been conducted (e.g., Walster, Aronson, Abrahams, & Rottman, 1966), manipulations in which specific matchings are experimentally assigned have been lacking. In Chapters 6 and 9, two findings from such an experiment were described (Byrne, Ervin, & Lamberth, 1970). The aim was to create a limited dating situation as a direct link between laboratory studies of attraction and "real life" dating. Independent variables identified in laboratory research (attitude and personality similarity, physical attractiveness) were varied in a real life situation, an attempt was made to minimize the occurrence of other stimulus events, and the IJS attraction measure was employed as a point of reference.

In order to provide a relatively broad base on which to match couples for the dating process, a 50-item questionnaire was constructed. Each of five variables identified in previous research was represented by 10 items: authoritarianism, repression–sensitization, attitudes, EPPS items, and self-concept. The questionnaire was administered to 420 introductory psychology students at the University of Texas. By means of a computer program, the responses of each male were compared with those of each female. For any given couple, the number of possible matching responses could range from 0 to 50; the actual range was from 12 to 37. From these distributions of matches, male–female pairs were selected to represent either the greatest or the least number of matching responses. There was a further restriction that the male be as tall as or taller than the female. The selected subjects consisted of 24 high similar pairs (.66 to .74) and 20 low similar (.24 to .40) pairs.

The experiment was run with one of the selected couples at a time. In the experimental room they were introduced to each other and told that the study involved computer dating and that they had been matched with respect to either high or low similarity. They were asked to spend the following 30 minutes together on a coke date in the Student Union, with 50¢ spending money. They were told to return to the experimental room afterward and that they would be asked questions about one another.

As in the laboratory investigations, attraction was significantly influenced by proportion of similar responses on the questionnaire. With respect to the prediction of attraction, it seemed likely that a combination of the similarity and attractiveness variables would provide the optimal information. In Table 14–8 are shown the mean attraction responses toward attractive and unattractive dates at two levels of response similarity. For both sexes, each of the two independent variables was found to affect attraction. The most positive response was toward similar attractive dates, and the least positive response was toward dissimilar unattractive dates. Similarity was also found to have a significant effect on ratings of the date's intelligence, desirability as a date, and desirability as a marriage partner.

TABLE 14–8

MEAN ATTRACTION RESPONSES
OF MALES AND FEMALES WITH SIMILAR
OR DISSIMILAR DATES WHO WERE
RELATIVELY ATTRACTIVE OR UNATTRACTIVE[a]

Physical attractiveness of date	Proportion of similar responses	
	Low	High
Male subjects		
Attractive	10.55	12.00
Unattractive	9.89	10.43
Female subjects		
Attractive	11.25	12.71
Unattractive	9.50	11.00

[a]After Byrne, Ervin and Lamberth, 1970, p. 162.

In a follow-up investigation at the end of the semester, several questions were asked about the date. When those who had a similar attractive date were compared with those who had a dissimilar unattractive date, it was found that the more positive the stimulus conditions at the time of the date, the more likely was the subject to remember correctly the date's name, to have talked to the other individual during the period since the experiment, and to indicate a desire to date the other person in the future.

The results were seen as evidence indicating the continuity between the laboratory study of attraction and its manifestation under field conditions. Physical attractiveness and similarity of attitudes and personality characteristics were found to influence real life attraction in a highly predictable manner. Other studies of computer dating at Illinois (Curran, 1970) and Purdue (Tesser & Brodie, 1971) have confirmed these general findings.

It might be noted that the subjects' written comments at the end of the Byrne, Ervin, and Lamberth experiment suggested that their responses involved more than simply checkmarks on a piece of paper. Besides enjoying and being interested in the experiment, the following comments are typical of their remarks written at the conclusion of the date:

I think computer dating is a great thing and I can see how it would have picked her and myself but there seems to be a lack of visual correspondence which should somehow be corrected. I mean interests and personality, yes. Her looks, no.

Does she date much? Is she already taken?

We both felt it was a funny kind of experiment, but we had fun doing it. I felt both of our reactions to one another were friendly.

I very much enjoyed this experiment and I feel that I am inclined to be somewhat less suspicious of computer dating as a method of matching people of similar personalities.

Our religious views clashed. He is an agnostic while I'm Lutheran. My chief reaction was based on this fact.

At first I didn't like him because he seemed too quiet and withdrawn, then he began talking and it turned out he had a really pleasant personality. He reminded me also of a person I once disliked—until he began talking.

He is a hard person to talk to and I couldn't talk to him about subjective things, only objective. The friends I go around with up here now are not at all like him and I guess it is partly my fault for not being able to talk to him since I haven't spoken to people of his type in quite a while.

DETERMINATION OF OTHER EVALUATIVE RESPONSES

Friendships and successful marriages are of unquestioned importance in determining the quality of our lives, but it seems quite likely that the attraction paradigm will expand beyond a concern with who likes whom and how much. The general model deals with evaluative responses. That which affects attraction should also influence other evaluative responses. The general meaning of that statement becomes increasingly clear (and to some extent increasingly frightening) as we examine the research which has been guided by that premise.

Judgments about the Performance and Aptitude of Others

Much of Chapter 9 dealt with the way in which various evaluations are determined. One not very surprising example is the Byrne *et al.* (1969) experiment on voting behavior. It seems that people vote for the candidates they like; votes are cast for those who express views with which we agree. That possibility seems to be a perfectly acceptable aspect of the democratic process, except for the unhappily frequent instances in which the candidate lacks credibility. To use Jones' (1964) terminology, one can never be certain whether a given candidate believes what he is saying and intends to behave accordingly or whether he is merely practicing ingratiation. There is another familiar problem associated with the attitude expressions of candidates. In addition to the issues of the day on which honest and reasoned disagreement is possible, the attitudes which determine voting also might be expected to include the expression of interracial hate, antiintellectualism, and lurid fears of domestic and foreign conspiracies to any audience receptive to such views. Attitude similarity can represent the lowest common denominator of a people's conscience.

Going a step beyond the effect of attitudes on voting, consider an extension of the more general propositions of the paradigm. Candidates associated with the greatest proportion of positive reinforcements should win, and those reinforcements include variables such as physical attractiveness, race, the kind of public relations image which can be manufactured, and association (even noncausal) with affectively pleasant or unpleasant events. For example, it is probably good for a candidate to be standing by when astronauts return successfully from a mission and bad to be standing by when news of increased unemployment is announced. It is proposed then, that voting behavior may be predicted on the same basis on which attraction responses are predicted and that voting behavior may be manipulated by anyone conversant with the relevant general principles. Since successful politicians and political managers are already quite familiar with this idea, let us examine some parallel extensions of the paradigm into areas that are less obvious.

Evaluating the Performance of Others. Smith, Meadow, and Sisk (1970) extended the similarity–attraction effect by examining the determinants of the evaluative perception of an observed stranger's performance.

The subjects were 44 undergraduate males at Purdue University. They were exposed to a 12-item attitude scale of a stranger who was simulated as either .17 or .83 similar. Each subject then was told that he would observe the stranger participating in another experiment and would be asked several questions about him afterward. The stranger (a confederate) was observed through a one-way vision mirror while taking part in a learning experiment involving electric shock. The confederate was engaged in a paired associates learning task in which incorrect responses were followed by a brief electric shock administered through electrodes on his right hand. All subjects saw the confederate receive seven paired associate items via tape recording over four trials; performance was identical in each instance such that it conformed to a typical learning curve across four trials. With incorrect responses, a loud switch was activated on an illuminated panel, and the confederate jerked his hand as if shocked. The confederate was unaware as to whether his observer was in a similar or dissimilar condition. The subject evaluated the stranger's performance on a 7-point rating scale.

In addition to the usual effects of attitude similarity on attraction, it was found that the proportion of similar attitudes attributed to the stranger significantly affected the ratings of the stranger's performance on the learning task. The similar stranger received a mean rating of 4.68, whereas the dissimilar stranger received a mean rating of 3.95.

Thus, all subjects saw the same stranger performing in the same way, but prior information about his attitudes led to differential judgments about the quality of that performance. Is it possible that such judgmental effects occur in other situations?

Evaluating Candidates for a Teaching Position. In a dissertation project at Syracuse University, Merritt (1970) examined the effects of attitude similarity on evaluations in a very realistic situation, that of a principal examining the credentials of teacher candidates who differed as to their qualifications. He suggested that the selection of teaching personnel is one of the primary functions of educational administrators and that the consequences of placing an unsuitable teacher in a teaching situation may be psychologically tragic and permanent for particular children. The basic research question was the extent to which the reaction of principals to potential teachers are based on educational qualifications versus attitudinal similarity. Merritt hypothesized that principals would respond to both characteristics and that with increasing administrative experience, principals would respond less to attitude variables and more to educational variables.

The subjects were 140 elementary school principals in New York State in urban, suburban, and rural school districts. The attitude material consisted of responses to a 20-item education scale. Items included "Teachers, like university professors, should have academic freedom—freedom to teach what they think is right and best," "Teachers should encourage pupils to study and criticize our own and other economic systems and practices," and "One of the big difficulties with modern schools is that discipline is often sacrificed to the interests of children." Information about the teacher candidates was simulated such that a principal received either the folder of a similar (1.00) or a dissimilar (.00) prospective teacher. The qualifications of the candidates varied with respect to certification, educational level, degrees earned, practice teaching experience, actual teaching experience, related educational experience, references, course work taken, and grades earned. Each of these characteristics was manipulated to yield a low versus high quality candidate. Candidates were evaluated on the IJS. The subjects were divided into subgroups on the basis of years of experience as an elementary school principal.

In a nonattitudinal pilot study with a different set of 100 principals, the candidate with high qualifications was preferred to one with low qualifications. In the experiment itself, it was found that the principal's response to the candidates was greatly affected by attitude similarity and to a much less extent by the qualifications of the candidate. The mean attraction responses are shown in Table 14–9.

TABLE 14–9

MEAN ATTRACTION RESPONSES
TOWARD SIMILAR AND DISSIMILAR TEACHER
CANDIDATES WITH DIFFERENTIAL
QUALIFICATIONS[a]

	Proportion of similar attitudes	
Qualifications	.00	1.00
High	6.90	11.51
Low	6.37	10.28

[a]After Merritt, 1970.

The principals were divided into low and high experience subgroups
at the median (8 years of experience). In addition to the similarity effect,
an interaction between similarity and experience was found. It may be seen
in Table 14–10 that the similarity effect is greater among the less experienced
principals. Nevertheless, over 8 years of experience has only a mild effect
on the phenomenon in that even the most experienced principals respond
strongly to the similarity of the candidate.

TABLE 14–10

MEAN ATTRACTION RESPONSES TOWARD
SIMILAR AND DISSIMILAR TEACHER CANDIDATES
BY PRINCIPALS WITH DIFFERENTIAL EXPERIENCE[a]

	Proportion of similar attitudes	
Experience	.00	1.00
High	7.05	10.57
Low	6.00	11.24

[a]After Merritt, 1970.

Personnel Selection. Griffitt and Jackson (1970) examined the effects
of attitude similarity on decisions concerning the hiring of students as
undergraduate research assistants in the psychology department at Kansas
State University. On the basis of the reinforcement model, it was hypothesized
that decisions to hire or reject an applicant are based on the extent to which
items of information concerning the applicant elicit positive or negative
affect. Griffitt and Jackson emphasized that the nature of such information
may often be irrelevant to job performance. In their experiment, two

factors were manipulated, one relevant to task success (intellectual ability) and one irrelevant (proportion of similar attitudes), and it was proposed that selection recommendations would be a positive function of each of the two factors.

The subjects were 78 Kansas State undergraduates who had been pretested on a 24-item attitude scale. In the experiment, they were asked to make judgments and recommendations concerning another same-sex student who had applied for a position as a research assistant. The information on a Summary Data Sheet included his grade point average during two semesters at the university and his scores on a fictitious scholastic ability test. Three levels of ability were created: low, medium, and high. The nonability information consisted of an attitude scale simulated at .25 or .75 similarity. Decisions about hiring were made on a 7-point scale ranging from strong recommendation to hire to strong recommendation not to hire. After that, subjects were told to assume that the applicant would be hired and to suggest the appropriate salary per hour ranging from $1.50 to $2.50 in 10¢ steps. The IJS and a semantic differential were also given.

The mean recommendations with respect to hiring the applicant are given in Table 14–11. Analysis revealed that hiring was significantly affected by both the attitude and the ability variables. Attraction was found to correlate significantly with hiring recommendations ($r = .53$) and with salary recommendations ($r = .41$).

TABLE 14–11
MEAN HIRING RECOMMENDATIONS AS A
FUNCTION OF ATTITUDE SIMILARITY AND
ABILITY LEVEL[a]

Ability level	Proportion of similar attitudes	
	.25	.75
High	4.38	5.38
Medium	2.31	5.31
Low	3.00	3.69

[a]After Griffitt and Jackson, 1970, p. 961.

Attitude similarity was also found to influence (in addition to attraction) ratings of the applicant with respect to reliable–unreliable, bad–good, high–low, attractive–unattractive, pleasant–unpleasant, negative–positive, warm–cold, worthy–unworthy, cooperative–uncooperative, and flexible–inflexible.

The authors (Griffitt & Jackson, 1970) suggested that attitude similarity:

> ... is an unlikely candidate for a valid predictor of an applicant's job performance and may well represent a reasonably potent variable in influencing an evaluator's decision concerning an applicant. It is not suggested that attitudinal information is exchanged during interviews or through application forms; however, it is not unlikely that an evaluator might be indirectly exposed to an applicant's opinions through knowledge of the latter's association with such groups as Young Democrats, Young Republicans, or other organizations whose political and social orientations are well known [pp. 961–962].

Approving a Loan. Another situation in which interpersonal evaluations might be expected to influence decision-making is that in which an individual makes application for a loan. Golightly, Huffman, and Byrne (to be published) provided 53 business students with a loan application form. Identical background information was given to all subjects concerning the applicant's age, income, assets, etc. In addition, the subjects were provided with attitudinal information about the applicant, using the standard stranger technique, and subject–stranger similarity ranged from .12 to .88. The major dependent variable, besides attraction, was the amount of money which would be approved as a loan to the applicant.

It was found that proportion of similar attitudes had a highly significant effect on attraction and on the magnitude of the loan which would be approved. The correlation between the two dependent variables was found to be .38.

As a follow-up to this investigation, Golightly proposed a brothel experiment to determine whether prostitute–client similarity had any effect on the price charged. As yet, this project has not gotten underway.

These four investigations of the relationship between attraction and evaluative judgments will be discussed further following an examination of a somewhat different kind of interpersonal evaluation.

Decisions of Jurors

One of the comforting cornerstones of a democratic society is the right to a trial by a jury of one's peers. Objective evidence is presented and weighed carefully by the jurors, and they arrive at a decision. Thus, the determination of guilt and innocence and often the setting of appropriate penalties for guilt are reached in a fair and impartial manner. Of course, ambiguities in the evidence, inaccurate perception or recall by witnesses, and the behavior of a biased judge can serve to detract from the ideal. What if other variables are operative? Is it possible that, with all other things equal, decisions of guilt and decisions of appropriate punishment simply represent evaluative responses? If so, it would be expected that the kinds of variables identified in the attraction paradigm act to determine these responses. That would seem to be a horrendous possibility. Mitchell (1970) notes. "To the extent that extra-legal and irrelevant variables are found to affect judicial decisions, the objectivity and impartiality of the legal system will obviously suffer [p. 5]." What evidence is there that such variables are operative in the courtroom situation?

Sentencing a Murderer. Mahaffey (1969) approached the problem by conceptualizing dissimilar attitudes in terms of punishment or frustration. Drawing on various kinds of evidence and theorizing, he suggests that in our culture, individuals are taught to respond to frustration with aggressive responses, but only when an "appropriate target" is available. It was hypothesized that positive affect associated with the target would result in a relatively lower magnitude of aggressive response than would negative affect. In his experiment, the culturally appropriate target of aggression was a convicted murderer and the aggressive response was the legal punishment deemed appropriate for that individual.

The subjects were eight pairs of middle-class married couples in Austin, Texas. One member of each pair was assigned to the high similar and one to the low similar condition. After being pretested on a 24-item attitude survey, the subjects were asked to take part in a research project. First, they were asked to read the attitude scale of another person (either high or low in similarity). Then, they were given a sheet which read:

> You have just read a set of attitudes belonging to a convicted murderer. Please check the punishment which you think that this particular individual should receive. Then fill out the Interpersonal Judgment Scale attached to this page, and give the completed forms back to me. *Please do not talk or ask any questions* until both you and the others filling out these forms have completed and returned them. Thank you for your cooperation.
>
> —a. A sentence of committment to a mental institution until judged sane.
> —b. A sentence of life in prison.
> —c. A sentence of death.
> —d. A suspended sentence of 1–10 years.
> —e. A sentence of 3–10 years in prison.

The responses of both groups on a preliminary measure of suitable punishment for the crime of murder were consistently and severely punitive. It was found that the magnitude of punishment selected for the specific murderer whose attitudes were known was significantly lower in the similar condition ($M = 1.63$) than in the dissimilar condition ($M = 4.75$).

Mahaffey concluded that there seemed to be a definite relationship between high interpersonal attraction and the mitigation of socially permissible punishment. He also raised the question of whether attraction might be related to severity of punishment in such varied situations as child discipline and the punishment of a defeated enemy.

Guilt and Sentencing of Defendant in a Case of Negligent Homicide. In a more elaborate investigation of the jury process, Griffitt and Jackson (to be published) utilized 122 undergraduates at Kansas State University who had been pretested on an attitude scale. Each subject was exposed to one of two versions of a video-tape description of the details of a trial involving negligent homicide. The evidence was the same in each version with the exception of the attitudinal information about the defendant. On one of the tapes, it was indicated that he believed in God, favored the American way of life, felt that men were superior to women in coping with stress and in handling the family finances, enjoyed sports and dancing, and was in favor of racial integration in schools. On the other tape, the opposite views were ascribed to the defendant. With these seven topics in a standard stranger design, agreement between subject and defendant varied from .00 to 1.00. Subjects were asked to rate the defendant's guilt on a 7-point scale, to assign a sentence ranging from 1 to 25 years in prison, and to recommend the time period before he would be eligible for parole.

TABLE 14–12

MEANS OF EVALUATIVE AND DECISION RESPONSE
VARIABLES AS A FUNCTION OF PROPORTION OF SIMILAR
ATTITUDES BETWEEN DEFENDANT AND JUROR[a]

Response variable	Mean proportion of similar attitudes	
	.12	.91
Guilt	2.25	2.66
Sentence length (years)	6.00	4.13
Length of imprisonment prior to parole eligibility (years)	3.02	2.13
Attraction	6.38	10.00
Intelligence	4.53	5.06
Knowledge of current events	4.00	5.06
Morality	3.55	4.90
Adjustment	3.24	4.83
Bad–good	3.22	4.66
High–low	3.31	4.39
Attractive–unattractive	3.57	4.55
Pleasant–unpleasant	3.36	5.00
Positive–negative	3.33	4.48
Warm–cold	3.17	4.84
Worthy–unworthy	3.50	4.84

[a]After Griffitt and Jackson, to be published.

The findings are summarized in Table 14–12. All of the mean differences shown in the table are significant except for that dealing with years of imprisonment prior to parole eligibility. Even that variable was found to be significantly related to attitude similarity in a correlational analysis. On the various rating scales, the meaning of divergent scale points may be ambiguous, but with respect to sentence length, the meaning is clear: 2 additional years of prison for the defendant who is attitudinally dissimilar from the juror.

Griffitt and Jackson thus created a situation very much resembling that faced by a juror and found that the decisions made were a function of proportion of similar attitudes attributed to the defendant. It should be noted that the evidence relevant to guilt and innocence was identical for all subjects and that the same specific attitudes which led some jurors to decide on innocence or a brief prison sentence were those attitudes which led other jurors to decide on guilt and a long prison sentence. Griffitt and Jackson (to be published) noted:

> Within the philosophy of the American judicial system, the social and political orientations and behaviors of individuals accused of criminal acts are factors which are to be ignored in considerations of guilt and punishment. The findings of the present experiment and those discussed previously serve to question the objectivity and impartiality of the jury process. Jurors are people and people are known to respond in an evaluative fashion to many characteristics of other individuals which are philosophically irrelevant to criminal evidence.

Stealing an Examination: Similarity and Authoritarianism. With Mitchell and Byrne (1971) the judicial studies were applied to a third type of wrongdoing, i.e., the stealing of a final examination by a college student. In addition, it was proposed that authoritarianism would prove to be a relevant variable in this situation even though it had been found not to have any effect on the standard similarity–attraction relationship (see Chapter 8). In the context of an immoral act, it was hypothesized that individuals high in authoritarianism would respond with moralistic aggression toward anyone who has violated societal values. Thus, the most negative judgments should be those of an authoritarian juror confronted by an attitudinally dissimilar defendant.

The subjects were 139 undergraduates at Purdue University who had been pretested on an attitude scale. In the experiment, each subject was given a legal brief describing a case which had supposedly been presented to a student court at another university. There was an official-looking document with information such as the trial number, university code number, the trial date, etc. The description of the offense was the same for all subjects as was the description of the defendant's background. A portion of the description, however, contained five bits of attitudinal information which were prepared for each specific subject such that the defendant was either .00 or 1.00 similar. After reading the summary of the hearing, subjects were asked to make the following decisions about the defendant:

      1. Judgment of guilt:

__1__ I feel that the defendant is definitely guilty.

__2__ I feel that the defendant is guilty.

__3__ I feel that probably the defendant is guilty.

__4__ I feel that I cannot make a judgment concerning the defendant's guilt or innocence.

__5__ I feel that probably the defendant is not guilty.

__6__ I feel that the defendant is not guilty.

__7__ I feel that the defendant is definitely not guilty.

      2. Disposition of the hearing:

__1__ Dismissal of the case

__2__ Warning

__3__ Reprimand

__4__ Social probation

__5__ One week suspension

__6__ One month suspension

__7__ Semester suspension

__8__ Year suspension

__9__ Permanent expulsion

      Because of the nature of the evidence presented, most of the subjects believed that the defendant was guilty. There was a significant interaction, as shown in Table 14–13, between similarity and authoritarianism in the extent to which subjects were convinced of the defendant's guilt. Those

TABLE 14–13

MEAN GUILT JUDGMENTS TOWARD
AN ATTITUDINALLY SIMILAR
OR DISSIMILAR DEFENDANT
BY SUBJECTS LOW OR HIGH
IN AUTHORITARIANISM[a]

Authoritarianism	Proportion of similar attitudes	
	.00	1.00
High	1.92	2.45
Low	2.19	1.72

[a]After Mitchell and Byrne, 1971.

TABLE 14–14
MEAN JUDGMENTS OF SEVERITY OF PUNISHMENT
TOWARD AN ATTITUDINALLY SIMILAR
OR DISSIMILAR DEFENDANT BY SUBJECTS
LOW OR HIGH IN AUTHORITARIANISM[a]

Authoritarianism	Proportion of similar attitudes	
	.00	1.00
High	5.13	3.58
Low	3.84	3.69

[a]After Mitchell and Byrne, 1971.

most sure of his guilt were high authoritarians responding to a dissimilar defendant and low authoritarians responding to a defendant with similar attitudes. The findings with respect to severity of punishment are shown in Table 14–14. Here, there was a similarity effect, an authoritarianism effect, and a significant interaction. The attitude similarity effect was greatest for high authoritarian subjects in that they recommended the most severe punishment toward a dissimilar defendant and the least severe punishment toward a similar defendant. Subjects were also asked to indicate their attraction toward the defendant and their perception of his morality. Attitude similarity had a significant influence on both responses, and authoritarianism was found to be related to attraction responses. In this specific situation at least, high authoritarians were more negative toward the stranger than were low authoritarians.

Can the Similarity Effect Be Controlled?

In considering research on friendship, dating, and marriage, the implications for further research and for application seemed relatively straightforward. It is easy to reach a consensus that positive interpersonal relationships are to be preferred over negative ones and that happy marriages are preferable to unhappy ones. Further, the available research findings are clearly suggestive of the direction which additional research might take in order to reach such goals. With the research just described on personnel selection and judicial decisions, the applications are not as readily apparent or as unambiguous.

Personnel Selection. In the personnel selection situation, as in the case of voting, a possible application for job applicants is in ascertaining the appropriate attitudes and verbalizing those views which will elicit a positive response. One would guess that job applicants have utilized such ploys at least as frequently as political candidates.

A second possibility is to assume that in work situations, as in marriage, attitudinally compatible employees should be sought openly and deliberately in order to increase the positiveness of interpersonal interactions within the institution. Merritt (1970) suggests:

> ... that at the practical level we might be concerned with establishing reliability among interviewers as to what is deemed generally favorable or unfavorable organizational attitudes. This also suggests that recruiting teams, with high inter-rater reliability on important "company" attitudes or beliefs, may be a more efficient method of getting the teachers who are more compatible with the attitudinal set of the school districts [p. 87].

Such an approach would make a virtue out of what is probably an unconscious process and it leads to a number of research possibilities. What are the consequents of forming attitudinally homogeneous work units in various work situations (Moos & Speisman, 1962)? Are the individuals happier working under these conditions than in a situation based entirely on ability with random attitudinal structure? Is productivity influenced by a high level of attraction within a factory or office or academic setting? It has been found, for example, that attitudinally similar pairs of students perform a simple physical task more effectively than attitudinally dissimilar pairs (Meadow, 1971). In short, if it makes sense to maximize attraction in marriage, does the same reasoning hold true for fellow employees?

A third consideration was raised by Griffitt and Jackson (1970) and Merritt (1970). If one assumes that the goal is to obtain the best qualified teachers or undergraduate research assistants or employees in any other occupation, decisions based on irrelevant attitudes can be considered as irrational and as interfering with the appropriate decisions. The question, then, is how to prevent such irrationality. Griffitt and Jackson quote Guion's (1967) notion that research in the selection process has led to some optimism "based on the untested assumption that knowledge about the irrational bases for interviewer decisions will show the way to overcome such tendencies [p. 200]." In a similar vein, Merritt (1970) proposes that "Those concerned with training interviewers might wish to include experiences which concentrate on developing an awareness of the attraction process [p. 87]." Obviously, a great deal of work is needed to determine whether or not awareness of the similarity–attraction function or special training in differentiating affective and cognitive judgments would lead to more objective selection decisions.

Judicial Decisions. The problem with juror evaluative responses seems more difficult to alleviate than that of personnel selection. There are twelve individuals plus a judge, each of whom is presumably responding in part, at least, to attitude variables.

One obvious implication of the present findings is that the attorneys for the defense and for the prosecution might strive to select jurors who are, respectively, similar to or dissimilar from the defendant. Such attempts may not further the cause of justice, but they are realistic aspects of the adversary system. It should be noted, concern with attraction variables are already part of the lore of the jury selection process as Clarence Darrow pointed out in 1938. The outcome is likely a balance with respect to attitudes, with the similarity of some jurors balanced by the dissimilarity of others.

Another possibility to consider is an attempt to prevent these variables from contaminating jury trials by screening out high authoritarians or by eliminating attitudinal material from testimony. The former possibility seems to be a questionable procedure in that neither our science nor our society seem ready for psychological testing to select jurors. The elimination of attitude variables is probably impossible in that attitudes are suggested by many aspects of one's life and even by one's clothing, style of speech, or hair length. If we consider the plight of a black defendant facing a jury of prejudiced whites or a long-haired, bearded, young radical collegian facing a jury of middle-aged, lower middle-class workers and housewives, attitudinal variables might even constitute the predominant factor in the decision process.

The third alternative is that suggested for personnel selection, that of attempting to eliminate the attitude effect through awareness or special training. If it were found to be possible to eliminate this source of irrationality from judicial decisions, then this could be one of the more important applications to grow out of the attraction paradigm.

INCREASING TOLERANCE FOR DISSIMILARITY

Implicit in most of the situations examined so far is the apparent inevitability of the similarity–attraction relationship. Certainly, the bulk of this book consisted of descriptions of research which documented the power and the ubiquity of attitude effects. One critic even placed this research in the role of the king's messenger; the Byrne–Nelson function was somehow attributed a degree of responsibility for intolerance of dissimilarity. Most of us recognize, of course, that a low level empirical law is not necessarily immutable. What if it were possible to change this relationship? What if there were a way to reduce the threat posed by dissimilarity? Hodges (1970) notes:

> The enormous variability among human cultures, groups, and individuals seems to be obvious and relatively inevitable. Furthermore, as the Earth's unoccupied "buffer" space decreases and as human populations become more and more inter-

dependent, contacts between very dissimilar people become increasingly unavoidable. Under these circumstances, tolerance of dissimilarity among people would seem to be an essential prerequisite for peace and harmony [p. 1].

Wheel a Mile in My Chair

In the Smith *et al.* (1970) experiment described earlier, subjects who had observed the stranger receive electric shock in the learning experiment were asked to indicate how painful the shock was to the stranger. Those in the high similarity condition tended to rate the shock supposedly received by the stranger as more painful than did those in the low similarity condition. Thus, another person with whom one agrees and who is liked must feel more pain than someone with whom one disagrees and who is disliked. It is possible, then, that the greater the difference between A and B, the less compassion A can feel for B. Anecdotally, it could be suggested that slavery, atomic bombing, gas chambers, the dropping of napalm, and the massacre of civilians is facilitated by one's perception that the victims are different from oneself, and, hence, what happens to them is not quite the same as if it had happened to real people. In any event, one approach to the problem of negative reactions to dissimilarity would be an attempt to get individuals to perceive the world from the other's point of view.

One class of overt stimulus characteristics which identifies an individual as dissimilar from the majority group and which elicits negative responses is that of physical handicaps (e.g., Farina, Sherman, & Allen, 1968; Matthews & Weslie, 1966; Nunnally, 1961). Individuals tend to feel guilty about responding negatively to someone with a handicap, but the negative reaction occurs nevertheless. Clore and Jeffery (1971) employed a role-playing technique as a way to alter the negative response to physical dissimilarity.

The subjects, undergraduates at the University of Illinois, were instructed to propel themselves in a wheelchair across the campus to the student union, have a cup of coffee, and return to the experimenter. The task was a difficult one involving an uphill sidewalk, two elevator rides, several ramps and doors, and a complicated procedure for obtaining coffee. Each subject was told to imagine that it was his first day back on campus after an automobile accident. Subjects responded quite strongly to the experience as suggested by comments of the following variety:

> The looks that I received were very interesting and were consistently the same. People look out of the corner of their eyes and then a downward glance past my legs. They seemed a bit embarrassed.

> I am surprised what effect this had on me. I was alone the entire time, I saw no one that I knew, so perhaps this made me take it all very seriously. All I know is that my eyes filled up with tears coming back up alone in that elevator.

Two other experimental conditions were also created. One group of subjects served as passive controls. They followed behind the role-playing subjects, observing and participating in the experience vicariously. Still a third group had no knowledge of the wheelchair experiment and simply spent an equivalent amount of time walking on the campus. Immediately after the experience, subjects were asked to indicate their attitudes toward spending funds on increasing facilities for disabled students. Such attitudes were assessed again 4 months later in a telephone survey. In addition, the subjects made confidential evaluations of the experimenter (who was in a wheelchair) for her supervising professor.

The role-playing subjects, both active and passive, indicated more positive attitudes about funds for disabled students both immediately after the experiment and 4 months later. Attraction toward the experimenter paralleled these attitude change results as shown in Table 14–15. The closer the subject's experience to that of the individual being rated, the greater the attraction toward that person.

TABLE 14–15

MEAN ATTRACTION TOWARD A HANDICAPPED
EXPERIMENTER AS A FUNCTION OF EXPERIENCE
IN PLAYING ROLE OF HANDICAPPED PERSON[a]

Control group	Vicarious role-playing	Active role-playing
10.20	11.40	12.40

[a]Data from Clore and Jeffery, 1971.

Innumerable research possibilities and applications are suggested by the Clore and Jeffery findings. If tolerance for various kinds of dissimilarity can be fostered through role-playing experiences, it would obviously be advantageous to develop techniques and procedures to facilitate the development of tolerance. A second approach, should this line of research prove to be fruitful, would be to determine the extent to which children might be taught generalized tolerance through role-playing, either vicariously or directly. Children are notoriously intolerant of dissimilarity and openly express their rejection in various unpleasant ways. At the same time, children would be expected to be more amenable to tolerance training than their older counterparts. There is evidence that massive educational campaigns, often employing vicarious role-playing, have been effective in diminishing interracial prejudice. Analogous attempts to teach tolerance for dissimilar attitudes, beliefs, and values, would, if successful, result in a dramatic change for the better in interpersonal behavior.

Reducing the Threat of Dissimilar Attitudes

Most of the research approaches to increased tolerance, both successful and unsuccessful, have concentrated on the response and the responder. For example, much of the research on individual differences cited in Chapter 8 was aimed at identifying those who do not respond negatively to the dissimilar attitudes of others. Had the research on authoritarianism or dogmatism, for example, been successful, our next plan was to identify the child-rearing practices or childhood experiences which were responsible for attitudinal tolerance. In a related way, research such as that of Clore and Jeffery involves a manipulation of an individual's experience in the expectation that he will behave differently afterward. If it can be assumed that we have learned to respond intolerantly, it follows that we can learn a different response under appropriate conditions. There is every reason to continue this line of attack on the problem.

A complementary approach was undertaken by Hodges and Byrne (in press) in which attention is concentrated on the stimulus. It has been proposed that dissimilar attitudes lead to dislike because they elicit negative affect and that they elicit negative affect because dissimilarity is threatening. Palmer's vindication proposal implies that the threat involves our fear of being incorrect and, hence, made to appear to be a fool. It might be speculated that much of this reaction rests on repeated childhood experiences in which mistakes in language, in reasoning, or in understanding are met with ridicule. Such mistakes are the source of amusement, sometimes benign and sometimes quite viscious, from parents, siblings, peers, and educators. A common defense against that kind of ridicule and derogation appears to be the tendency to accept majority opinion, to identify with the aggressors in rejecting deviants, and to state that which we believe in strident terms. There is a strong and seemingly increasing tendency to shout one's own position in unrelentingly dogmatic terms while villifying those who hold opposing views. In the late 1960s and early 1970s, it has become a common practice to wrap one's own political views, for example, in fiery rhetoric. It is ironic that the peace sign and the American flag have become opposing attitudinal symbols with hate-arousing properties. Whether the verbal attacks are directed against fascist pigs or filthy anarchists, the meaning is the same. My side is correct and your side is the last refuge for scoundrels and fools. The Hodges and Byrne (in press) research dealt with the premise that if the attitudinal stimulus could be defused of its dogmatic certainty and its implied ridicule and rejection of those who disagree, the threat and, hence, the negative affect would be lessened, and as a result interpersonal rejection of those who disagree would be lessened. Two experiments were conducted in which the attitude stimulus was altered as a possible way of decreasing the negative effect of dissimilarity on attraction. Specifically, the wording of a stranger's attitude statements was manipulated in a way designed to reduce the implied threat. It was hypothesized that attraction would be higher toward an open-minded dissimilar stranger than toward a dogmatic dissimilar stranger.

Response to Paper and Pencil Dogmatism and Open-mindedness. The subjects were 42 male undergraduates at the University of Texas. Attitude statements were presented in the form of handwritten answers on a 16-item open-ended questionnaire. Dogmatic and open-minded attitude statements were composed by deducing implications for verbal behavior from dictionary definitions and from Rokeach's (1960) description of open and closed minds. Examples are:

Belief in God

Open-minded: Personally I do believe there is a God, but I believe this is purely a matter of belief, rather than of knowledge.

Dogmatic: There's no doubt in my mind about it. There is a God.

Open-minded: Actually I cannot say that I do believe in God unless I define the term in an unconventional way.

Dogmatic: No, I don't believe there is a God. There's no proof. A person would have to be naive to believe there is a God.

The subject's task was to evaluate the stranger on the basis of information gained from reading his attitude statements. Each subject received a questionnaire containing all dogmatic or all open-minded statements. The statements were either .25 or .75 similar to the attitudes of the subject. The mean attraction responses are shown in Table 14–16. Attraction was significantly influenced by both similarity and the stranger's dogmatism. Further analysis revealed that the dogmatism effect was significant only in response to the dissimilar stranger, as hypothesized.

In order to extend this finding to a more realistic situation, a second experiment was undertaken.

TABLE 14–16

MEAN ATTRACTION RESPONSES TOWARD
OPEN-MINDED OR DOGMATIC STRANGER ON
BASIS OF EXPOSURE TO SIMILAR OR
DISSIMILAR WRITTEN STATEMENTS[a]

	Proportion of similar attitudes	
Stranger's statements	.25	.75
Open-minded	9.09	11.20
Dogmatic	6.64	9.71

[a]After Hodges and Byrne, in press.

Face-to-Face Confrontation with Dogmatism or Open-mindedness. The major differences between these two experiments were that the second involved an oral presentation of attitudes, two strangers who disagreed with one another, and a live visual presentation on closed-circuit television.

The subjects were 60 male and female undergraduates at the University of Texas. Each subject met two same-sex undergraduate confederates who posed as fellow subjects. Through a rigged drawing, subjects were assigned the role of watching the other two "subjects" being interviewed via television concerning 12 topics. One of the strangers expressed views which were .17 similar to those of the subject, and the other expressed views .83 similar to those of the subject. For any given subject, both strangers were dogmatic or both were open-minded. After the interview, the subject was asked to evaluate each of the confederates.

TABLE 14–17
MEAN ATTRACTION RESPONSES TOWARD
OPEN-MINDED OR DOGMATIC STRANGER ON
BASIS OF EXPOSURE TO SIMILAR AND
DISSIMILAR ORAL STATEMENTS[a]

	Proportion of similar attitudes	
Stranger's Statements	.17	.83
Open-minded	8.16	10.23
Dogmatic	6.85	10.88

[a]After Hodges and Byrne, in press.

The mean attraction responses are shown in Table 14–17. In this experiment, there was a significant similarity effect and a significant interaction between similarity and dogmatism. Actually, as in the first experiment, the dogmatism effect is significant only in the dissimilar condition and not in the similar condition. Once again, under quite altered experimental circumstances, open-mindedness is found to reduce the negative response toward a dissimilar stranger.

Discussion. Both experiments provide support for the hypothesis that open-minded disagreement is more tolerable than dogmatic disagreement. It was suggested that the stimulus variable being manipulated was tolerance for opposing views or implied respect for those who disagree. The findings are at least consistent with the theoretical statement that intolerance toward persons with dissimilar attitudes is a defensive reaction against threat to one's own feeling of competence.

Once again, examination of the possible applications of such findings leads to some challenging possibilities. Is it possible to teach ourselves, to teach others, and/or to teach children to express their views in an open-minded way? Can people learn to think and speak so as to express the idea:

There are arguments for *X* and arguments for *Y*. There is no way to determine conclusively whether *X* or *Y* is correct. Intelligent individuals of good will may come to support *X* or to support *Y*. I am strongly in favor of *X* for what I believe to be excellent reasons, but I may be wrong and I respect your right to support *Y*.

Offhand, it appears much easier for people to learn to think dogmatically and to reject the opponents with insulting epithets, rotten eggs, rocks, and bullets.

Efforts to change the way in which attitudes are expressed will obviously be difficult. It might be noted in passing that part of the difficulty lies in the cultural support for dogmatic views. As with the classic Sherif and Sherif (1953) findings in which the arbitrary grouping of boys at a camp into the "Bull Dogs" and "Red Devils" led quickly to intergroup hate, there is a great deal of societal support from schools, advertisers, and political leaders to take the position that my side is right and their side is wrong. Whether "my side" is the brand of Scotch I drink, the political party I support, the music I prefer, the school I attended, the professional football team with which I identify, my sexual identity, the country in which I happened to be born, or my child's elementary school home room, chauvinism is widely encouraged. It might be difficult to sell soap with the argument that all soaps are basically the same, but our brand comes in a pretty blue box and our company badly wants to make a profit. It might, nevertheless, be a less threatening stimulus world if soaps, Scotches, political ideologies, musical tastes, schools, football teams, the sexes, nationality, and home rooms were described in that manner. The difference would be in the direction of greater honesty, less threat, and less negative interpersonal relationships. As hokey as it all may sound, such changes may turn out to be essential not only to the quality of our lives on a crowded planet but to our continued existence on that planet.

OTHER EXTENSIONS OF THE PARADIGM

Education

A. J. Lott (1969) has argued persuasively that there is both theoretical and empirical evidence indicating that learning is enhanced by positive interpersonal relationships. Historically, our educational endeavors have either ignored the role of interpersonal attraction in the learning process or have wittingly or unwittingly fostered a negative situation. From the type of schoolroom experiences described by Dickens to last week's Ph.D. oral examination, negative affect and consequent dislike have been a part of our educational heritage. It could be argued that if the same learning could take place under pleasant as under unpleasant interpersonal conditions, pleasantness is to be preferred to unpleasantness. There is evidence, however, that learning is actually enhanced by positive relationships. Two examples of the kind of research which leads to such conclusions will be presented.

Learning and Attraction toward the "Teacher". Sapolsky (1960) investigated the effects of interpersonal relationships on learning in a laboratory context. He hypothesized that a liked experimenter would have a greater effect on performance than a disliked experimenter in a verbal conditioning task.

The subjects were female undergraduates at Adelphi College. In two investigations the experimenter was another undergraduate female or a female graduate student posing as an undergraduate. Half of the subjects were given information designed to induce them to like the experimenter and half were given negative information. Attraction was manipulated with respect to simulated or actual similarity on the FIRO-B. In a verbal conditioning task, the experimenter used "mmm-hmm" to reinforce sentences which the subject began with the words "I" or "we."

In each experiment, there were dramatic differences in acquisition between the high and low attraction groups with the positive group showing the greatest changes in performance. Sapolsky (1960) concluded:

> When there was either High-Attraction or Compatibility between S and E, the reinforcing value of "mmm-hmm" was enhanced, presumably by the additional reinforcing qualities that E represented, and a typical learning curve was obtained during acquisition. When the Attraction between S and E was low (or S and E were Incompatible), no significant increase in the use of the reinforced pronouns occurred during the acquisition period of either experiment. The personal quality of E can here be viewed as having taken on the aspects of an aversive stimulus which resulted in a decrement in the observed strength of the conditioned response [p. 245].

Learning and Attraction toward Peers. Lott and Lott (1966) proposed that the greater the degree of intermember liking within a group, the better will be individual learning within that group. They cited some previous evidence (e.g., Shaw & Shaw, 1962) which support the general proposition.

Their subjects were fourth- and fifth-grade children. On the basis of a previously administered sociometric test, subjects were placed in small same-sex groups ($N = 3$ or 4) which were high or low in intermember attraction. Groups were also homogeneous with respect to IQ. Several tasks involving the learning of Spanish equivalents of English words were given.

It was found that for high IQ subjects the high attraction groups did consistently better than the low attraction groups. The low IQ subjects did consistently less well on the task, and their performance was not affected by attraction.

These two investigations suggest the possibility of a line of research to determine the effects of attraction on learning and performance in various educational settings. The potential importance of the application of such findings is apparent.

Psychotherapy

The interest of psychotherapists in the attraction process has two somewhat distinct origins. First, many therapists have a learning orientation, and any variables that are relevant to learning are potentially relevant to psychotherapy. In the present context, not only has the conditioning model proved to be a useful description of the attraction phenomenon, but studies such as that of Sapolsky and the Lotts serve as a direct link between attraction and therapylike learning. Second, at a much broader level, most clinical theorists stress the importance of the therapist–patient relationship to the quality and outcome of the therapeutic interaction. That relationship would seem to be in some ways analogous to that investigated in attraction research (e.g., Mendelsohn & Rankin, 1969; Sapolsky, 1965).

The Syracuse Experiments. In a research program too extensive and too detailed to be covered here, Goldstein (in press) has brought together the social psychological concern with attraction and clinical concerns with psychotherapy. His general rationale has been stated as:

All of the investigations we will have to report derive from social-psychological research. Consistent with our desire to more adequately define "relationship," the specific research literature to which we have turned consists of investigations of interpersonal attraction. Interpersonal attraction is a variable with a long and fruitful research history. As such, many of its antecedents, concomitants and consequences are relatively known—at least in the social-psychological laboratory. If there is indeed a unity to psychological change processes, be they called psychotherapy or something else, procedures which augment interpersonal attraction in the social-psychological laboratory may well be relevant to increasing such attraction as it operates between patient and therapist in clinical settings. Thus, it is a series of extrapolatory studies upon which we are embarking here—from the social-psychological laboratory to settings more relevant to clinical concerns.

In a series of systematic investigations, Goldstein and his colleagues have employed attraction-enhancement procedures in an attempt to improve the therapist–patient relationship in psychotherapy. Their procedures were found to be successful with what are labelled YAVIS (young, attractive, verbal, intelligent, and successful) subjects—both college students and YAVIS patients. They were notably unsuccessful with non-YAVIS patients. Goldstein (in press) writes "We may thus generally conclude that our research program provides a major initial step toward a technology of psychotherapeutic attraction-enhancement. Yet, this is a most crucial stipulation, as is true of so many aspects of contemporary psychotherapy, we have here a contribution to primarily a YAVIS-relevant technology."

A Word of Caution. In three independent experiments with quite different aims, the attraction manipulations have proven ineffective when the subjects were of low intellectual or educational level (Byrne, Griffitt, Hudgins, & Reeves, 1969; Goldstein, in press; Lott & Lott, 1966). In each instance, a different explanation was offered. Whether the problem lies in some artifact of the experimental situations (verbal tasks with subjects who have reading difficulty) or in the possibility that different laws are required to explain the behavior of low ability individuals, it is necessary to consider intellectual and educational deficiency as a possible limiting condition for the attraction paradigm as it presently is conceived.

Population Density

There is another broad consideration, as yet barely tapped, in the implications of the affective portion of the reinforcement model. Broadly speaking, any evaluative response should be in part a function of the individual's affective state. Extrapolating a bit from the research which has been conducted, jury decisions should be influenced by room temperature, personnel decisions should be influenced by the quality of the interviewer's sex life, and a riot policeman's willingness to pull a trigger should be influenced by the dogmatism of the verbalizations hurled at him.

Griffitt and Veitch (1971) have pursued such implications experimentally. They point out that systematic knowledge of the role of environmental conditions in influencing social behavior will become crucial when variables such as pollution and population density reach critical degrees of stressfulness.

In addition to Griffitt's (1970) temperature experiment described in Chapter 13, there are a number of intriguing leads as to the generality of the affective proposition. In studying the effects of high temperatures on physiological, intellectual, and physical functioning, Rohles (1967) observed "continual arguing, needling, agitating, jibing, fist-fighting, threatening, and even an attempted knifing [p. 59]." When the U.S. Riot Commission (1968) analyzed the occurrence of ghetto riots, it was reported that "In most instances, the temperature during the day on which the violence first erupted was quite high [p. 123]."

Griffitt and Veitch (1971) extended the search for environmental determinants of affect to the situation of overcrowding or population density. The U.S. Riot Commission (1968) noted the "crowded ghetto living conditions, worsened by summer heat [p. 325]." Numerous animal experiments (e.g., Calhoun, 1962; Christian, 1963; Greenberg, 1969; Thiessen, 1966) report that crowded conditions precipitate numerous behavior disruptions. Griffitt and Veitch hypothesized that attraction and subjective evaluations of affect would be more negative under conditions of high population density than under low density.

In the attitude manipulation, subjects responded to an anonymous same-sex stranger who was either .25 or .75 similar on a 24-item scale. The subjects were 121 undergraduates at Kansas State University. In addition to population density, the effective temperature experiment was replicated; the room was either at a normal effective temperature (73.4°) or at a hot effective temperature (93.5°). In addition to the two levels of attitude similarity and two temperature conditions, there were two levels of population density in that subjects were run in small (3–5) or large (12–16) groups in a chamber 7 ft by 9 ft. There was an average of 12.73 ft² per person in the low density condition and 4.06 ft² per person in the high density condition. Subjects were seated in rows to minimize eye contact and were run in same-sex groups. Subjects were initially assessed on six semantic differential scales, self-ratings of hot-cold, and a mood adjective checklist. Then the attitude–attraction task was carried out. Afterward, the ratings of feelings, etc., were repeated as well as ratings of the room and the experiment.

It was found that self-ratings of affect were more negative under high density conditions than under low density conditions as well as more negative under hot than under normal temperature. Self-ratings of temperature were

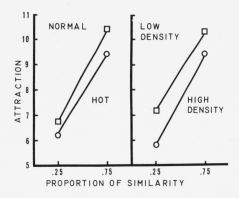

Fig. 14–1. Mean attraction responses as a function of effective temperature and proportion of similar attitudes (left panel) and population density and proportion of similar attitudes (right panel). (After Griffitt and Veitch, 1971, p. 95.)

also influenced by the two environmental manipulations; the actual effective temperature was the same under high and low density, but the subjects rated themselves as warmer in the high density than in the low density condition. The effects of each environmental condition and the effects of attitude similarity are depicted in Fig. 14–1. It was also reported that ratings of personal affective experience, attraction, and the evaluative ratings of the room and experiment were all positively interrelated.

Thus, the previous temperature effect was replicated and the effect on evaluative responses of a new variable, crowding, was demonstrated for the first time with human subjects. It might be speculated that a variety of environmental stressors including effective temperature, population density, noise pollution, dirty air, contaminated water, traffic snarls, power failures, unpleasant national and international news reports, malfunctioning appliances, and inaccurate computer billings will each be found to contribute to negative affect and, hence, to negative evaluative responses directed toward both social and nonsocial stimuli. The way in which these instigators interact and combine in determining negative responses will undoubtedly be the focus of considerable research in the near future.

In describing the response to dissimilarity in an atmosphere of increased polarization, it was suggested that we pursue ways to alter this response and to alter the way in which attitudinal stimuli are expressed. There is a third possibility to consider. It seems possible that much of the public overreaction to the dissimilarity of others, whether from the revolutionary left or the hard hat right, is a function of summated negative affect. The individual or group with whom one disagrees is an identifiable and specific target to hate and to attack in contrast to the diffuse and nonspecific agent responsible for one's malfunctioning telephone or for the particles in the air causing one's upper respiratory irritation. It follows that if there were a melioration of the numerous sources of negative affect, the specific affect aroused by dissimilarity would evoke less negative responses. The research of Griffitt and his colleagues offers a promising conceptual and empirical beginning for solving some of our more crucial societal problems.

Some Concluding Remarks

The primary emphasis of this book has been on the way in which research is conducted and on the way in which both theoretical and applied research may be seen to grow out of a base relationship.

In addition to the beginning steps toward a technology described in the present chapter, another effect of the paradigm might be noted in passing. Many of us who have been integrally caught up in attraction research find it impossible not to restructure our concepts of the world in ways congruent with the model. Part of the change is an affective conception of man in which individuals are responsive (consciously or not) primarily to their feelings rather than to intellectual or cognitive factors. And, if evaluative responses really are a simple mathematical function of associated reinforcement, one's judgments about and liking for the members of one's family or Communism or Richard Nixon or Cincinnatti or French poodles or the Methodist Church are necessarily perceived in a different manner than previously. These altered perceptions may or may not represent an improvement over other ways of perceiving the world but they do represent a change and a kind of unanticipated by-product of attraction theory.

In any event, the attraction paradigm represents a continuing research program which may constitute a useful model for other research, and, if it has anything to offer, should continue to grow and to change. The present volume may be seen as a progress report covering approximately a decade of research. I personally am eager to learn where the paradigm leads in the next decade.

Appendix A / **Fifty-Six Item Attitude Scale**

Survey of Attitudes

Name:_____Psychol:____Sect:____Date:_____
Age:_____Sex:_____Class: Fr._____Soph._____Jr._____Sr._____
Hometown:_____

    1. Fraternities and Sororities (check one)
— I am very much against fraternities and sororities as they usually function.
— I am against fraternities and sororities as they usually function.
— To a slight degree, I am against fraternities and sororities as they usually function.
— To a slight degree, I am in favor of fraternities and sororities as they usually function.
— I am in favor of fraternities and sororities as they usually function.
— I am very much in favor of fraternities and sororities as they usually function.

    2. Western Movies and Television Programs (check one)
— I enjoy western movies and television programs very much.
— I enjoy western movies and television programs.
— I enjoy western movies and television programs to a slight degree.
— I dislike western movies and television programs to a slight degree.
— I dislike western movies and television programs.
— I dislike western movies and television programs very much.

    3. Undergraduates Getting Married (check one)
— In general, I am very much in favor of undergraduates getting married.
— In general, I am in favor of undergraduates getting married.
— In general, I am mildly in favor of undergraduates getting married.
— In general, I am mildly against undergraduates getting married.
— In general, I am against undergraduates getting married.
— In general, I am very much against undergraduates getting married.

4. Situation Comedies (check one)
— I dislike situation comedies very much.
— I dislike situation comedies.
— I dislike situation comedies to a slight degree.
— I enjoy situation comedies to a slight degree.
— I enjoy situation comedies.
— I enjoy situation comedies very much.

5. Belief in God (check one)
— I strongly believe that there is a God.
— I believe that there is a God.
— I feel that perhaps there is a God.
— I feel that perhaps there is no God.
— I believe that there is no God.
— I strongly believe that there is no God.

6. Professors and Student Needs (check one)
— I feel that university professors are completely indifferent to student needs.
— I feel that university professors are indifferent to student needs.
— I feel that university professors are slightly indifferent to student needs.
— I feel that university professors are slightly concerned about student needs.
— I feel that university professors are concerned about student needs.
— I feel that university professors are very much concerned about student needs.

7. Draft (check one)
— I am very much in favor of the draft.
— I am in favor of the draft.
— I am mildly in favor of the draft.
— I am mildly opposed to the draft.
— I am opposed to the draft.
— I am very much opposed to the draft.

8. Necking and Petting (check one)
— In general, I am very much against necking and petting among couples in college.
— In general, I am against necking and petting among couples in college.
— In general, I am mildly against necking and petting among couples in college.
— In general, I am mildly in favor of necking and petting among couples in college.
— In general, I am in favor of necking and petting among couples in college.
— In general, I am very much in favor of necking and petting among couples in college.

9. Smoking (check one)
— In general, I am very much in favor of smoking.
— In general, I am in favor of smoking.
— In general, I am mildly in favor of smoking.
— In general, I am mildly against smoking.
— In general, I am against smoking.
— In general, I am very much against smoking.

10. Integration in Public Schools (check one)
— Racial integration in public schools is a mistake, and I am very much against it.

— Racial integration in public schools is a mistake, and I am against it.
— Racial integration in public schools is a mistake, and I am mildly against it.
— Racial integration in public schools is a good plan, and I am mildly in favor of it.
— Racial integration in public schools is a good plan, and I am in favor of it.
— Racial integration in public schools is a good plan, and I am very much in favor of it.

11. Comedians Who Use Satire (check one)
— I very much enjoy comedians who use satire.
— I enjoy comedians who use satire.
— I mildly enjoy comedians who use satire.
— I mildly dislike comedians who use satire.
— I dislike comedians who use satire.
— I very much dislike comedians who use satire.

12. Acting on Impulse vs. Careful Consideration of Alternatives (check one)
— I feel that it is better if people always act on impulse.
— I feel that it is better if people usually act on impulse.
— I feel that it is better if people often act on impulse.
— I feel that it is better if people often engage in a careful consideration of alternatives.
— I feel that it is better if people usually engage in a careful consideration of alternatives.
— I feel that it is better if people always engage in a careful consideration of alternatives.

13. Social Aspects of College Life (check one)
— In general, I am very much against an emphasis on the social aspects of college life.
— In general, I am against an emphasis on the social aspects of college life.
— In general, I am mildly against an emphasis on the social aspects of college life.
— In general, I am mildly in favor of an emphasis on the social aspects of college life.
— In general, I am in favor of an emphasis on the social aspects of college life.
— In general, I am very much in favor of an emphasis on the social aspects of college life.

14. Birth Control (check one)
— I am very much in favor of most birth control techniques.
— I am in favor of most birth control techniques.
— I am mildly in favor of most birth control techniques.
— I am mildly opposed to most birth control techniques.
— I am opposed to most birth control techniques.
— I am very much opposed to most birth control techniques.

15. Classical Music (check one)
— I dislike classical music very much.
— I dislike classical music.
— I dislike classical music to a slight degree.
— I enjoy classical music to a slight degree.
— I enjoy classical music.
— I enjoy classical music very much.

16. Drinking (check one)
— In general, I am very much in favor of college students drinking alcoholic beverages.
— In general, I am in favor of college students drinking alcoholic beverages.

—In general, I am mildly in favor of college students drinking alcoholic beverages.
—In general, I am mildly opposed to college students drinking alcoholic beverages.
—In general, I am opposed to college students drinking alcoholic beverages.
—In general, I am very much opposed to college students drinking alcoholic beverages.

17. American Way of Life (check one)
—I strongly believe that the American way of life is not the best.
—I believe that the American way of life is not the best.
—I feel that perhaps the American way of life is not the best.
—I feel that perhaps the American way of life is the best.
—I believe that the American way of life is the best.
—I strongly believe that the American way of life is the best.

18. Sports (check one)
—I enjoy sports very much.
—I enjoy sports.
—I enjoy sports to a slight degree.
—I dislike sports to a slight degree.
—I dislike sports.
—I dislike sports very much.

19. Premarital Sex Relations (check one)
—In general, I am very much opposed to premarital sex relations.
—In general, I am opposed to premarital sex relations.
—In general, I am mildly opposed to premarital sex relations.
—In general, I am mildly in favor of premarital sex relations.
—In general, I am in favor of premarital sex relations.
—In general, I am very much in favor of premarital sex relations.

20. Science Fiction (check one)
—I enjoy science fiction very much.
—I enjoy science fiction.
—I enjoy science fiction to a slight degree.
—I dislike science fiction to a slight degree.
—I dislike science fiction.
—I dislike science fiction very much.

21. Money (check one)
—I strongly believe that money is not one of the most important goals in life.
—I believe that money is not one of the most important goals in life.
—I feel that perhaps money is not one of the most important goals in life.
—I feel that perhaps money is one of the most important goals in life.
—I believe that money is one of the most important goals in life.
—I strongly believe that money is one of the most important goals in life.

22. Grades (check one)
—I am very much in favor of the university grading system as it now exists.
—I am in favor of the university grading system as it now exists.
—I am mildly in favor of the university grading system as it now exists.
—I am mildly opposed to the university grading system as it now exists.

—I am opposed to the university grading system as it now exists.
—I am very much opposed to the university grading system as it now exists.

23. Political Parties (check one)
—I am a strong supporter of the Democratic party.
—I prefer the Democratic party.
—I have a slight preference for the Democratic party.
—I have a slight preference for the Republican party.
—I prefer the Republican party.
—I am a strong supporter of the Republican party.

24. Group Opinion (check one)
—I feel that people should always ignore group opinion if they disagree with it.
—I feel that people should usually ignore group opinion if they disagree with it.
—I feel that people should often ignore group opinion if they disagree with it.
—I feel that people should often go along with group opinion even if they disagree with it.
—I feel that people should usually go along with group opinion even if they disagree with it.
—I feel that people should always go along with group opinion even if they disagree with it.

25. One True Religion (check one)
—I strongly believe that my church represents the one true religion.
—I believe that my church represents the one true religion.
—I feel that probably my church represents the one true religion.
—I feel that probably no church represents the one true religion.
—I believe that no church represents the one true religion.
—I strongly believe that no church represents the one true religion.

26. Musical Comedies (check one)
—I dislike musical comedies very much.
—I dislike musical comedies.
—I dislike musical comedies to a slight degree.
—I enjoy musical comedies to a slight degree.
—I enjoy musical comedies.
—I enjoy musical comedies very much.

27. Preparedness for War (check one)
—I strongly believe that preparedness for war will not tend to precipitate war.
—I believe that preparedness for war will not tend to precipitate war.
—I feel that perhaps preparedness for war will not tend to precipitate war.
—I feel that perhaps preparedness for war will tend to precipitate war.
—I believe that preparedness for war will tend to precipitate war.
—I strongly believe that preparedness for war will tend to precipitate war.

28. Welfare Legislation (check one)
—I am very much opposed to increased welfare legislation.
—I am opposed to increased welfare legislation.
—I am mildly opposed to increased welfare legislation.
—I am mildly in favor of increased welfare legislation.
—I am in favor of increased welfare legislation.
—I am very much in favor of increased welfare legislation.

29. Creative Work (check one)
— I enjoy doing creative work very much.
— I enjoy doing creative work.
— I enjoy doing creative work to a slight degree.
— I dislike doing creative work to a slight degree.
— I dislike doing creative work.
— I dislike doing creative work very much.

30. Dating (check one)
— I strongly believe that girls should be allowed to date before they are in high school.
— I believe that girls should be allowed to date before they are in high school.
— I feel that perhaps girls should be allowed to date before they are in high school.
— I feel that perhaps girls should not be allowed to date until they are in high school.
— I believe that girls should not be allowed to date until they are in high school.
— I strongly believe that girls should not be allowed to date until they are in high school.

31. Red China and the U.N. (check one)
— I strongly believe that Red China should not be admitted to the U.N.
— I believe that Red China should not be admitted to the U.N.
— I feel that perhaps Red China should not be admitted to the U.N.
— I feel that perhaps Red China should be admitted to the U.N.
— I believe that Red China should be admitted to the U.N.
— I strongly believe that Red China should be admitted to the U.N.

32. Novels (check one)
— I dislike reading novels very much.
— I dislike reading novels.
— I dislike reading novels to a slight degree.
— I enjoy reading novels to a slight degree.
— I enjoy reading novels.
— I enjoy reading novels very much.

33. Socialized Medicine (check one)
— I am very much opposed to socialized medicine as it operates in Great Britain.
— I am opposed to socialized medicine as it operates in Great Britain.
— I am mildly opposed to socialized medicine as it operates in Great Britain.
— I am mildly in favor of socialized medicine as it operates in Great Britain.
— I am in favor of socialized medicine as it operates in Great Britain.
— I am very much in favor of socialized medicine as it operates in Great Britain.

34. War (check one)
— I strongly feel that war is sometimes necessary to solve world problems.
— I feel that war is sometimes necessary to solve world problems.
— I feel that perhaps war is sometimes necessary to solve world problems.
— I feel that perhaps war is never necessary to solve world problems.
— I feel that war is never necessary to solve world problems.
— I strongly feel that war is never necessary to solve world problems.

35. State Income Tax (check one)
— I am very much opposed to a state income tax.

—I am opposed to a state income tax.
—I am mildly opposed to a state income tax.
—I am mildly in favor of a state income tax.
—I am in favor of a state income tax.
—I am very much in favor of a state income tax.

36. Tipping (check one)
—I am very much opposed to the custom of tipping.
—I am opposed to the custom of tipping.
—I am mildly opposed to the custom of tipping.
—I am mildly in favor of the custom of tipping.
—I am in favor of the custom of tipping.
—I am very much in favor of the custom of tipping.

37. Pets (check one)
—I enjoy keeping pets very much.
—I enjoy keeping pets.
—I enjoy keeping pets to a slight degree.
—I dislike keeping pets to a slight degree.
—I dislike keeping pets.
—I dislike keeping pets very much.

38. Foreign Movies (check one)
—I enjoy foreign movies very much.
—I enjoy foreign movies.
—I enjoy foreign movies to a slight degree.
—I dislike foreign movies to a slight degree.
—I dislike foreign movies.
—I dislike foreign movies very much.

39. Strict Discipline (check one)
—I am very much against strict disciplining of children.
—I am against strict disciplining of children.
—I am mildly against strict disciplining of children.
—I am mildly in favor of strict disciplining of children.
—I am in favor of strict disciplining of children.
—I am very much in favor of strict disciplining of children.

40. Financial Help from Parents (check one)
—I strongly believe that parents should provide financial help to young married couples.
—I believe that parents should provide financial help to young married couples.
—I feel that perhaps parents should provide financial help to young married couples.
—I feel that perhaps parents should not provide financial help to young married couples.
—I believe that parents should not provide financial help to young married couples.
—I strongly believe that parents should not provide financial help to young married couples.

41. Freshmen Having Cars on Campus (check one)
—I am very much in favor of freshmen being allowed to have cars on campus.
—I am in favor of freshmen being allowed to have cars on campus.

— I am in favor of freshmen being allowed to have cars on campus to a slight degree.
— I am against freshmen being allowed to have cars on campus to a slight degree.
— I am against freshmen being allowed to have cars on campus.
— I am very much against freshmen being allowed to have cars on campus.

42. Foreign Language (check one)
— I am very much in favor of requiring students to learn a foreign language.
— I am in favor of requiring students to learn a foreign language.
— I am mildly in favor of requiring students to learn a foreign language.
— I am mildly opposed to requiring students to learn a foreign language.
— I am opposed to requiring students to learn a foreign language.
— I am very much opposed to requiring students to learn a foreign language.

43. College Education (check one)
— I strongly believe it is very important for a person to have a college education in order to be successful.
— I believe it is very important for a person to have a college education in order to be successful.
— I believe that perhaps it is very important for a person to have a college education in order to be successful.
— I believe that perhaps it is not very important for a person to have a college education in order to be successful.
— I believe that it is not very important for a person to have a college education in order to be successful.
— I strongly believe that it is not very important for a person to have a college education in order to be successful.

44. Fresh Air and Exercise (check one)
— I strongly believe that fresh air and daily exercise are not important.
— I believe that fresh air and daily exercise are not important.
— I feel that probably fresh air and daily exercise are not important.
— I feel that probably fresh air and daily exercise are important.
— I believe that fresh air and daily exercise are important.
— I strongly believe that fresh air and daily exercise are important.

45. Discipline of Children (check one)
— I strongly believe that the father should discipline the children in the family.
— I believe that the father should discipline the children in the family.
— I feel that perhaps the father should discipline the children in the family.
— I feel that perhaps the mother should discipline the children in the family.
— I believe that the mother should discipline the children in the family.
— I strongly believe that the mother should discipline the children in the family.

46. Nuclear Arms Race (check one)
— I am very much opposed to the federal government's buildup of nuclear arms.
— I am opposed to the federal government's buildup of nuclear arms.
— I am mildly opposed to the federal government's buildup of nuclear arms.
— I am mildly in favor of the federal government's buildup of nuclear arms.
— I am in favor of the federal government's buildup of nuclear arms.
— I am very much in favor of the federal government's buildup of nuclear arms.

47. Community Bomb Shelters (check one)
— I strongly believe that the federal government should provide community bomb shelters.
— I believe that the federal government should provide community bomb shelters.
— I feel that perhaps the federal government should provide community bomb shelters.
— I feel that perhaps individuals should provide their own bomb shelters.
— I believe that individuals should provide their own bomb shelters.
— I strongly believe that individuals should provide their own bomb shelters.

48. Divorce (check one)
— I am very much opposed to divorce.
— I am opposed to divorce.
— I am mildly opposed to divorce.
— I am mildly in favor of divorce.
— I am in favor of divorce.
— I am very much in favor of divorce.

49. Gardening (check one)
— I enjoy gardening very much.
— I enjoy gardening.
— I enjoy gardening to a slight degree.
— I dislike gardening to a slight degree.
— I dislike gardening.
— I dislike gardening very much.

50. Dancing (check one)
— I enjoy dancing very much.
— I enjoy dancing.
— I enjoy dancing to a slight degree.
— I dislike dancing to a slight degree.
— I dislike dancing.
— I dislike dancing very much.

51. A Catholic President (check one)
— I am very much in favor of a Catholic being elected president.
— I am in favor of a Catholic being elected president.
— I am mildly in favor of a Catholic being elected president.
— I am mildly against a Catholic being elected president.
— I am against a Catholic being elected president.
— I am very much against a Catholic being elected president.

52. Women in Today's Society (check one)
— I strongly believe that women are not taking too aggressive a role in society today.
— I believe that women are not taking too aggressive a role in society today.
— I feel that perhaps women are not taking too aggressive a role in society today.
— I feel that perhaps women are taking too aggressive a role in society today.
— I believe that women are taking too aggressive a role in society today.
— I strongly believe that women are taking too aggressive a role in society today.

53. Family Finances (check one)
— I strongly believe that the man in the family should handle the finances.

—I believe that the man in the family should handle the finances.
—I feel that perhaps the man in the family should handle the finances.
—I feel that perhaps the woman in the family should handle the finances.
—I believe that the woman in the family should handle the finances.
—I strongly believe that the woman in the family should handle the finances.

54. Exhibitions of Modern Art (check one)
—I dislike looking at exhibitions of modern art very much.
—I dislike looking at exhibitions of modern art.
—I dislike looking at exhibitions of modern art to a slight degree.
—I enjoy looking at exhibitions of modern art to a slight degree.
—I enjoy looking at exhibitions of modern art.
—I enjoy looking at exhibitions of modern art very much.

55. Careers for Women (check one)
—I am very much in favor of women pursuing careers.
—I am in favor of women pursuing careers.
—I am mildly in favor of women pursuing careers.
—I am mildly opposed to women pursuing careers.
—I am opposed to women pursuing careers.
—I am very much opposed to women pursuing careers.

56. Men's Adjustment to Stress (check one)
—I strongly believe that men adjust to stress better than women.
—I believe that men adjust to stress better than women.
—I feel that perhaps men adjust to stress better than women.
—I feel that perhaps men do not adjust to stress better than women.
—I believe that men do not adjust to stress better than women.
—I strongly believe that men do not adjust to stress better than women.

Appendix B / Interpersonal Judgment Scale

Your name: _____

1. Intelligence (check one)
— I believe that this person is very much above average in intelligence.
— I believe that this person is above average in intelligence.
— I believe that this person is slightly above average in intelligence.
— I believe that this person is average in intelligence.
— I believe that this person is slightly below average in intelligence.
— I believe that this person is below average in intelligence.
— I believe that this person is very much below average in intelligence.

2. Knowledge of Current Events (check one)
— I believe that this person is very much below average in his (her) knowledge of current events.
— I believe that this person is below average in his (her) knowledge of current events.
— I believe that this person is slightly below average in his (her) knowledge of current events.
— I believe that this person is average in his (her) knowledge of current events.
— I believe that this person is slightly above average in his (her) knowledge of current events.
— I believe that this person is above average in his (her) knowledge of current events.
— I believe that this person is very much above average in his (her) knowledge of current events.

3. Morality (check one)
— This person impresses me as being extremely moral.
— This person impresses me as being moral.
— This person impresses me as being moral to a slight degree.

426

— This person impresses me as being neither particularly moral nor particularly immoral.
— This person impresses me as being immoral to a slight degree.
— This person impresses me as being immoral.
— This person impresses me as being extremely immoral.

4. Adjustment (check one)
— I believe that this person is extremely maladjusted.
— I believe that this person is maladjusted.
— I believe that this person is maladjusted to a slight degree.
— I believe that this person is neither particularly maladjusted nor particularly well adjusted.
— I believe that this person is well adjusted to a slight degree.
— I believe that this person is well adjusted.
— I believe that this person is extremely well adjusted.

5. Personal Feelings (check one)
— I feel that I would probably like this person very much.
— I feel that I would probably like this person.
— I feel that I would probably like this person to a slight degree.
— I feel that I would probably neither particularly like nor particularly dislike this person.
— I feel that I would probably dislike this person to a slight degree.
— I feel that I would probably dislike this person.
— I feel that I would probably dislike this person very much.

6. Working Together in an Experiment (check one)
— I believe that I would very much dislike working with this person in an experiment.
— I believe that I would dislike working with this person in an experiment.
— I believe that I would dislike working with this person in an experiment to a slight degree.
— I believe that I would neither particularly dislike nor particularly enjoy working with this person in an experiment.
— I believe that I would enjoy working with this person in an experiment to a slight degree.
— I believe that I would enjoy working with this person in an experiment.
— I believe that I would very much enjoy working with this person in an experiment.

Appendix C / **Attitudinal Sentences**

1. Integration in Public Schools
   A. Public schools should not be integrated.
   B. Public schools should be integrated.
   C. School integration has been in the news a great deal in recent years.

2. Birth Control
   A. Birth control is a good practice.
   B. Birth control is a bad practice.
   C. Birth control is an issue of great importance throughout the world.

3. Money
   A. Money should not be a major factor in choosing a career.
   B. Money should be a major factor in choosing a career.
   C. The United States has a relatively high per capita income.

4. Grades
   A. The current college grading system is a fair one.
   B. The current college grading system is an unfair one.
   C. College students are often concerned about grades.

5. Political Parties
   A. The Democratic party is best.
   B. The Republican party is best.
   C. Political conventions are usually held in large cities.

6. One True Religion
   A. There is only one true religion.
   B. There is no such thing as "one true religion."
   C. Religious beliefs have often affected the course of history.

7. Preparedness for War
   A. Preparedness for war helps prevent war.
   B. Preparedness for war may start a war.
   C. War games form a part of military training.

8. Necking and Petting
   A. It is a very bad idea for college students to engage in necking and petting.
   B. It is a very good idea for college students to engage in necking and petting.
   C. Necking and petting have been known by a number of different names over the years.

9. Welfare Legislation
   A. Public welfare programs should be reduced.
   B. Public welfare programs should be increased.
   C. Most states have some sort of public welfare program.

10. War
    A. Some disputes can only be resolved by war.
    B. All world disputes can be resolved without war.
    C. Weapons of war have grown more complex and more powerful in recent years.

11. Strict Discipline
    A. Children should not be strictly disciplined.
    B. Children should be strictly disciplined.
    C. Some parents use strict discipline and some do not.

12. Careers for Women
    A. Women should be able to have a career if they wish.
    B. Women should be discouraged from having a career.
    C. A great many women are employed in this country.

Appendix D / Computer Dating
Interpersonal Judgment Scale Items

7. Dating (check one)
— I believe that I would probably like to date this person very much.
— I believe that I would probably like to date this person.
— I believe that I would probably like to date this person to a slight degree.
— I believe that I would neither particularly like nor particularly dislike dating this person.
— I believe that I would probably dislike dating this person to a slight degree.
— I believe that I would probably dislike dating this person.
— I believe that I would probably dislike dating this person very much.

8. Marriage (check one)
— I believe that I would very much dislike this person as a spouse.
— I believe that I would dislike this person as a spouse.
— I believe that I would dislike this person as a spouse to a slight degree.
— I believe that I would neither particularly dislike nor particularly enjoy this person as a spouse.
— I believe that I would enjoy this person as a spouse to a slight degree.
— I believe that I would enjoy this person as a spouse.
— I believe that I would very much enjoy this person as a spouse.

9. Sexual attraction (check one)
— This person impresses me as being extremely attractive sexually.
— This person impresses me as being sexually attractive.
— This person impresses me as being sexually attractive to a slight degree.
— This person impresses me as being neither particularly sexually attractive nor unattractive.
— This person impresses me as being sexually unattractive to a slight degree.

— This person impresses me as being sexually unattractive.
— This person impresses me as being extremely unattractive sexually.

10. Physical Attractiveness (check one)
— This person is extremely attractive physically.
— This person is physically attractive.
— This person is somewhat attractive physically.
— This person is neither particularly attractive nor unattractive physically.
— This person is somewhat unattractive physically.
— This person is physically unattractive.
— This person is extremely unattractive physically.

Appendix E / **Homogeneous Behavior Questionnaire**

Behavior in Groups

Name _____ Psychology ___ Section ___ Date _____ Age ___ Sex: F___ M___
Class: Fr. ___ Soph. ___ Jr. ___ Sr. ___

Below are listed six questions related to *your* behavior in a decision-making group. Read the two alternatives for each question, then check one of the statements following the two alternatives.

1. In general, what function, or activities, do you *prefer* to perform in a decision-making group:

A. I prefer to help others participate, give moral support to members who are "on the spot," and test to see if people agree on a possible solution.

B. I prefer to supply information, evaluations, and ground rules for reaching the decision, seeing that everyone stays on the task.

— Item A is very characteristic of me.
— Item A is characteristic of me.
— Item A is somewhat characteristic of me.
— Item B is somewhat characteristic of me.
— Item B is characteristic of me.
— Item B is very characteristic of me.

2. In a decision-making group, where a number of different judgments are possible on an issue of vital importance to you, with whose judgments do you feel most confident?

A. Although I have ideas of my own, I characteristically feel most confident with the judgments which meet with the least initial disagreement among members.

B. I characteristically feel most confident with my own judgments regardless of whether they are in agreement with those of the other group members.

— Item A is very characteristic of me.

432

—Item A is characteristic of me.
—Item A is somewhat characteristic of me.
—Item B is somewhat characteristic of me.
—Item B is characteristic of me.
—Item B is very characteristic of me.

3. In general, when *you* see a conflict arising in the group, what action do you normally take?

A. I try to forestall conflict before it erupts openly by breaking the tension with humor, suggestions for a coffee break, or the like.

B. I continue to push for completion of the task because conflict is inevitable and it's the decision which must be put first.

—Item A is very characteristic of me.
—Item A is characteristic of me.
—Item A is somewhat characteristic of me.
—Item B is somewhat characteristic of me.
—Item B is characteristic of me.
—Item B is very characteristic of me.

4. How would you prefer that final decisions be reached if *you* were the leader of a decision-making group?

A. Since I would be responsible for the outcome, I would prefer to have the final say as to the solutions incorporated in all group decisions.

B. I would prefer that *all* members be equal parties to the decision, and that the final decision should reflect those ideas with which each of us can most agree.

—Item A is very characteristic of me.
—Item A is characteristic of me.
—Item A is somewhat characteristic of me.
—Item B is somewhat characteristic of me.
—Item B is characteristic of me.
—Item B is very characteristic of me.

5. What kind of leader, in terms of the functions he performs, do *you* prefer in a decision-making group?

A. I prefer the leader who gets the most out of group members in terms of relevant information and effort and who accomplishes the task in the most efficient manner with minimal loss of time.

B. I prefer the leader who keeps things running smoothly, gives support to members when needed and provides the opportunity for everyone to participate in the discussions.

—Item A is very characteristic of me.
—Item A is characteristic of me.
—Item A is somewhat characteristic of me.
—Item B is somewhat characteristic of me.
—Item B is characteristic of me.
—Item B is very characteristic of me.

6. How do you normally react when someone challenges your ideas?

A. I frequently feel uncertain and, often find myself agreeing with the other person's point of view.

B. I feel compelled to prove my point and continue to defend my position even becoming angry and excited at times.

— Item A is very characteristic of me.

— Item A is characteristic of me.

— Item A is somewhat characteristic of me.

— Item B is somewhat characteristic of me.

— Item B is characteristic of me.

— Item B is very characteristic of me.

7. When you experience strong negative feelings toward other members of the group which interferes with your ability to work with them effectively, how do you normally relate to these persons during the course of decision making?

A. I believe in getting feelings out in the open and I let people know what I think about them and what it is they are doing to irritate me.

B. I try to overcome my feelings of hostility without letting the other persons know I am upset and strive to better understand their actions.

— Item A is very characteristic of me.

— Item A is characteristic of me.

— Item A is somewhat characteristic of me.

— Item B is somewhat characteristic of me.

— Item B is characteristic of me.

— Item B is very characteristic of me.

Appendix F / **Heterogeneous Behavior Questionnaire**

Social Behaviors

Name _____ Psychology ____ Section ____ Date _____ Age ____ Sex: F___ M___
Class: Fr. ____ Soph. ____ Jr. ____ Sr. ____

Below are listed seven statements related to your behavior in a variety of situations. Read the two alternatives for each statement, then check the most appropriate item following the alternatives.

1. When I enter a theater, I usually:
A. Proceed down the right aisle first.
B. Proceed down the left aisle first.
— Item A is very characteristic of me.
— Item A is characteristic of me.
— Item A is somewhat characteristic of me.
— Item B is somewhat characteristic of me.
— Item B is characteristic of me.
— Item B is very characteristic of me.

2. When I am seated at a restaurant with a member of the opposite sex, we usually:
A. Sit on the same side of the table.
B. Sit on opposite sides of the table.
— Item A is very characteristic of me.
— Item A is characteristic of me.
— Item A is somewhat characteristic of me.
— Item B is somewhat characteristic of me.
— Item B is characteristic of me.
— Item B is very characteristic of me.

435

3. In classes where seats are not assigned, I usually:
   A. Select a seat and retain it for the entire semester.
   B. Change seats from one class meeting to the next.
— Item A is very characteristic of me.
— Item A is characteristic of me.
— Item A is somewhat characteristic of me.
— Item B is somewhat characteristic of me.
— Item B is characteristic of me.
— Item B is very characteristic of me.

4. When walking across the campus, I find:
   A. Most people walk faster than I do.
   B. Most people walk slower than I do.
— Item A is very characteristic of me.
— Item A is characteristic of me.
— Item A is somewhat characteristic of me.
— Item B is somewhat characteristic of me.
— Item B is characteristic of me.
— Item B is very characteristic of me.

5. In traveling to and from class, I usually:
   A. Come and go by different routes.
   B. Come and go by the same route.
— Item A is very characteristic of me.
— Item A is characteristic of me.
— Item A is somewhat characteristic of me.
— Item B is somewhat characteristic of me.
— Item B is characteristic of me.
— Item B is very characteristic of me.

6. After I have written a letter:
   A. I always mail it immediately.
   B. Frequently, a day or so passes before I mail it.
— Item A is very characteristic of me.
— Item A is characteristic of me.
— Item A is somewhat characteristic of me.
— Item B is somewhat characteristic of me.
— Item B is characteristic of me.
— Item B is very characteristic of me.

7. My social activities:
   A. Are usually planned well in advance.
   B. Are often determined on the spur of the moment.
— Item A is very characteristic of me.
— Item A is characteristic of me.
— Item A is somewhat characteristic of me.
— Item B is somewhat characteristic of me.
— Item B is characteristic of me.
— Item B is very characteristic of me.

Appendix G / **Homogeneous Attitude Questionnaire**

Survey of Attitudes

Name _____ Psychology ____ Section ____ Date _____ Age ____ Sex: F____ M____
Class: Fr. ____ Soph. ____ Jr. ____ Sr. ____

  1. In general, I find working cooperatively with others
— a highly satisfying experience.
— a satisfying experience.
— a somewhat satisfying experience.
— a somewhat unsatisfying experience.
— an unsatisfying experience.
— a highly unsatisfying experience.

  2. As for effectiveness, most groups are
— usually effective.
— frequently effective.
— slightly more effective than ineffective.
— slightly more ineffective than effective.
— frequently ineffective.
— usually ineffective.

  3. When I meet someone who has held several elective offices, I am usually
— very favorably impressed.
— favorably impressed.
— somewhat favorably impressed.
— somewhat unfavorably impressed.
— unfavorably impressed.
— very unfavorably impressed.

4. Group leaders are
— always the most able group members.
— usually the most able group members.
— frequently the most able group members.
— occasionally the most able group members.
— seldom the most able group members.
— rarely the most able group members.

5. As for organized activities, personally, I am
— strongly for organized activities.
— for organized activities.
— mildly for organized activities.
— mildly against organized activities.
— against organized activities.
— strongly against organized activities.

6. When I am working in a group, the people I work with are
— the most important single variable.
— an important variable.
— a somewhat important variable.
— a somewhat unimportant variable.
— an unimportant variable.
— the least important variable.

7. In comparison to individual decisions, the decisions made by groups are
— always superior.
— usually superior.
— frequently superior.
— occasionally superior.
— seldom superior.
— rarely superior.

Appendix H / **Children's Interpersonal Judgment Scale**

Rating Scale

Your name: _____

1. Intelligence (check one)
— I believe that this person is very much above average in intelligence.
— I believe that this person is above average in intelligence.
— I believe that this person is a little above average in intelligence.
— I believe that this person is average in intelligence.
— I believe that this person is a little below average in intelligence.
— I believe that this person is below average in intelligence.
— I believe that this person is very much below average in intelligence.

2. Good or Bad (check one)
— This person impresses me as being very good.
— This person impresses me as being good.
— This person impresses me as being a little bit good.
— This person impresses me as being neither good nor bad.
— This person impresses me as being a little bit bad.
— This person impresses me as being bad.
— This person impresses me as being very bad.

3. Personal Feelings (check one)
— I feel that I would probably like this person very much.
— I feel that I would probably like this person.
— I feel that I would probably like this person a little bit.
— I feel that I would probably neither like nor dislike this person.
— I feel that I would probably dislike this person a little bit.
— I feel that I would probably dislike this person.
— I feel that I would probably dislike this person very much.

4. Working Together (check one)

— I believe that I would very much dislike working with this person.

— I believe that I would dislike working with this person.

— I believe that I would sort of dislike working with this person.

— I believe that I would neither dislike nor enjoy working with this person.

— I believe that I would sort of enjoy working with this person.

— I believe that I would enjoy working with this person.

— I believe that I would very much enjoy working with this person.

Appendix I / **Effectance Arousal Scale**

Reaction Scale

Name _____

How did you feel while you were watching the movie? (reading the stranger's attitudes?)

1. Entertained (check one)
— Not at all entertained
— Slightly entertained
— Moderately entertained
— Entertained
— Quite entertained

2. Disgusted (check one)
— Not at all disgusted
— Slightly disgusted
— Moderately disgusted
— Disgusted
— Extremely disgusted

3. Unreality (check one)
— Strong feelings of unreality
— Feelings of unreality
— Moderate feelings of unreality
— Slight feelings of unreality
— No feelings of unreality at all

4. Anxious (check one)
— Not at all anxious
— Slightly anxious
— Moderately anxious
— Anxious
— Extremely anxious

5. Dreaming (check one)
— Very similar to feelings I have when I'm dreaming
— Similar to feelings I have when I'm dreaming
— Moderately similar to feelings I have when I'm dreaming
— Slightly similar to feelings I have when I'm dreaming
— Not at all similar to feelings I have when I'm dreaming

6. Bored (check one)
— Extremely bored
— Bored
— Moderately bored
— Slightly bored
— Not at all bored

7. Uneasy (check one)
— Not at all uneasy
— Slightly uneasy
— Moderately uneasy
— Uneasy
— Quite uneasy

8. Confused (check one)
— Not at all confused
— Slightly confused
— Moderately confused
— Confused
— Quite confused

9. Others' thoughts (check one)
— Strong desire to know what others thought
— Desire to know what others thought
— Moderate desire to know what others thought
— Slight desire to know what others thought
— No desire to know what others thought at all

References

Adorno, T. W., Frenkel-Brunswik, E., Levinson D. J., & Sanford, R. N. *The authoritarian personality.* New York: Harper, 1950.

Allport, G. W. Traits revisited. *American Psychologist,* 1966, **21**, 1–10.

Alper, T. G., & Korchin, S. J. Memory for socially relevant material. *Journal of Abnormal and Social Psychology,* 1952, **47**, 25–37.

Altrocchi, J. Dominance as a factor in interpersonal choice and perception. *Journal of Abnormal and Social Psychology,* 1959, **59**, 303–308.

Amsel, A. The role of frustrative nonreward in noncontinuous reward situations. *Psychological Bulletin,* 1958, **55**, 102–119.

Amsel, A. Partial reinforcement effects on vigor and persistence. In K. W. Spence and J. T. Spence (Eds.), *The psychology of learning and motivation: Advances in research and theory.* Vol. 1. New York: Academic Press, 1967. Pp. 1–65.

Anderson, N. H. Application of an additive model to impression formation. *Science,* 1962, **138**, 817–818.

Anderson, N. H. Test of a model for number-averaging behavior. *Psychonomic Science,* 1964, **1**, 191–192.

Anderson, N. H. Averaging versus adding as a stimulus-combination rule in impression formation. *Journal of Experimental Psychology,* 1965, **70**, 394–400.   (a)

Anderson, N. H. Primacy effects in personality impression formation using a generalized order effect paradigm. *Journal of Personality and Social Psychology,* 1965, **2**, 1–9.   (b)

Anderson, N. H. Component ratings in impression formation. *Psychonomic Science,* 1966, **6**, 279–280.

Anderson, N. H. Averaging model analysis of set-size effect in impression formation. *Journal of Experimental Psychology,* 1967, **75**, 158–165.

Anderson, N. H. Likeableness ratings of 555 personality-trait words. *Journal of Personality and Social Psychology,* 1968, **9**, 272–279.   (a)

Anderson, N. H. A simple model for information integration. In R. P. Abelson, E. Aronson, W. J. McGuire, T. M. Newcomb, M. J. Rosenberg, and P. H. Tannenbaum (Eds.),

Theories of cognitive consistency: a sourcebook. Chicago: Rand-McNally, 1968. Pp. 731–743. (b)

Anderson, N. H., & Barrios, A. A. Primacy effects in personality impression formation. *Journal of Abnormal and Social Psychology*, 1961, **63**, 346–350.

Anderson, N. H., & Hubert, S. Effects of concomitant verbal recall on order effects in personality impression formation. *Journal of Verbal Learning and Verbal Behavior*, 1963, **2**, 379–391.

Anderson, N. H., & Norman, A. Order effects in impression formation in four classes of stimuli. *Journal of Abnormal and Social Psychology*, 1964, **69**, 467–471.

Argyle, M. *The psychology of interpersonal behavior.* Middlesex, England: Penguin, 1967.

Aristotle. *The rhetoric.* New York: Appleton-Century-Crofts, 1932.

Aronson, E. Some antecedents of interpersonal attraction. In W. J. Arnold and D. Levine (Eds.), *Nebraska symposium on motivation, 1969.* Vol. 17. Lincoln, Nebraska: Univ. of Nebraska Press, 1970. Pp. 143–173.

Aronson, E., & Carlsmith, J. M. Experimentation in social psychology. In G. Lindzey and E. Aronson (Eds.), *The handbook of social psychology.* (2nd ed.), Vol. 2. Reading, Mass.: Addison-Wesley, 1968. Pp. 1–79.

Aronson, E., & Cope, V. My enemy's enemy is my friend. *Journal of Personality and Social Psychology*, 1968, **8**, 8–12.

Aronson, E., & Linder, D. Gain and loss of esteem as determinants of interpersonal attractiveness. *Journal of Experimental Social Psychology*, 1965, **1**, 156–171.

Aronson, E., & Worchel, P. Similarity versus liking as determinants of interpersonal attractiveness. *Psychonomic Science*, 1966, **5**, 157–158.

Asch, S. E. Forming impressions of personality. *Journal of Abnormal and Social Psychology*, 1946, **41**, 258–290.

Asch, S. E. The doctrine of suggestion, prestige, and imitation in social psychology. *Psychological Review*, 1948, **55**, 250–276.

Atkinson, J. W. *Motives in fantasy, action, and society.* Princeton, N.J.; Van Nostrand, 1958.

Atkinson, J. W., Heyns, R. W., & Veroff, J. The effect of experimental arousal of the affiliation motive on thematic apperception. *Journal of Abnormal and Social Psychology*, 1954, **49**, 405–410.

Averill, J. R. Autonomic response patterns during sadness and mirth. *Psychophysiology*, 1969, **5**, 399–414.

Banta, T. J., & Hetherington, M. Relations between needs of friends and fiances. *Journal of Abnormal and Social Psychology*, 1963, **66**, 401–404.

Baron, R. A. Attraction toward the model and model's competence as determinants of adult imitative behavior. *Journal of Personality and Social Psychology*, 1970, **14**, 345–351. (a)

Baron, R. A. Behavioral effects of interpersonal attraction: compliance with the requests of liked and disliked others. Submitted for publication, 1970. (b)

Baron, R. A. Aggression as a function of magnitude of victim's pain cues, level of prior anger arousal, and aggressor-victim similarity. *Journal of Personality and Social Psychology*, 1971, **18**, 48–54.

Baron, R. A. Aggression as a function of ambient temperature and prior anger arousal. *Journal of Personality and Social Psychology*, in press.

Baron, R. A., & Kepner, C. R. Model's behavior and attraction toward the model as determinants of adult aggressive behavior. *Journal of Personality and Social Psychology*, 1970, **14**, 335–344.

Baskett, G. D. Dogmatism and response to attitude similarity–dissimilarity. Unpublished master's thesis, University of Texas, 1966.

Baskett, G. D. Interpersonal attraction as a function of attitude similarity–dissimilarity and cognitive complexity. Unpublished doctoral dissertation, University of Texas, 1968.

Baskett, G. D. Evaluation of experiments as a function of attitude similarity–dissimilarity. Unpublished manuscript, Georgia Institute of Technology, 1971.

Batchelor, T. R., & Tesser, A. Attitude base as a moderator of the attitude similarity–attraction relationship. *Journal of Personality and Social Psychology*, in press.

Becker, G. The complementary-needs hypothesis, authoritarianism, dominance, and other Edwards Personal Preference Schedule scores. *Journal of Personality*, 1964, **32**, 45–56.

Bergmann, G. The contribution of John B. Watson. *Psychological Review*, 1956, **63**, 265–276.

Berkowitz, L. Repeated frustrations and expectations in hostility arousal. *Journal of Abnormal and Social Psychology*, 1960, **60**, 422–429. (a)

Berkowitz, L. Some factors affecting the reduction of overt hostility. *Journal of Abnormal and Social Psychology*, 1960, **60**, 14–21. (b)

Berkowitz, L., & Howard, R. C. Reactions to opinion deviates as affected by affiliation need (*n*) and group member interdependence. *Sociometry*, 1959, **22**, 81–91.

Bermann, E., & Miller, D. R. The matching of mates. In R. Jessor and S. Feshbach (Eds.), *Cognition, personality, and clinical psychology*. San Francisco: Jossey-Bass, 1967. Pp. 90–111.

Berscheid, E., & Walster, E. H. *Interpersonal attraction*. Reading, Mass.: Addison-Wesley, 1969.

Berscheid, E., & Walster, G. W. Liking reciprocity as a function of perceived basis of proffered liking. Unpublished manuscript, University of Minnesota, 1970.

Bjerstedt, A. A field-force model as a basis for predictions of social behavior. *Human Relations*, 1958, **11**, 331–340.

Blank, E. P., & Arenson, S. J. Effects of previous order and proportion of similar attitude statements on attraction during a subsequent series of dissimilar statements. *Psychonomic Science*, 1971, **22**, 245–246.

Bloom, R. F. The measurement of interpersonal attraction as a function of need for approval and attitude dissimilarity. Unpublished master's thesis, University of Texas, 1968.

Bond, M. H., Byrne, D., & Diamond, M. J. Effect of occupational prestige and attitude similarity on attraction as a function of assumed similarity of attitudes. *Psychological Reports*, 1968, **23**, 1167–1172.

Bonney, M. E. Relationships between social success, family size, socioeconomic home background, and intelligence among school children in grades III to V. *Sociometry*, 1944, 7, 26–39.

Bonney, M. E. A sociometric study of the relationship of some factors to mutual friendships on the elementary, secondary, and college levels. *Sociometry*, 1946, **9**, 21–47.

Bordin, E. S. Curiosity, compassion, and doubt: the dilemma of the psychologist. *American Psychologist*, 1966, **21**, 116–121.

Bossard, J. H. S. Residential propinquity as a factor in marriage selection. *American Journal of Sociology*, 1932, **38**, 219–224.

Boswell, J. *The life of Samuel Johnson L.L.D.* 1791. Vol. 2 (Republished: New York, Heritage, 1963.)

Bowerman, C. E., & Day, B. R. A test of the theory of complementary needs as applied to couples during courtship. *American Sociological Review*, 1956, **21**, 602–605.

Brehm, J. W., & Behar, L. B. Sexual arousal, defensiveness, and sex preferences in affiliation. *Journal of Experimental Research in Personality*, 1966, **1**, 195–200.

Brewer, R. E. & Brewer, M. B. Attraction and accuracy of perception in dyads. *Journal of Personality and Social Psychology*, 1968, **8**, 188–193.

Brim, O. G., Jr., & Hoff, D. B. Individual and situational differences in desire for certainty. *Journal of Abnormal and Social Psychology*, 1957, **54**, 225–229.

Brock, T. C. Communicator–recipient similarity and decision change. *Journal of Personality and Social Psychology*, 1965, **1**, 650–654.

Brown, T., & Eng, K. The effects of race, physical attractiveness, and value similarity on interpersonal attraction. Unpublished manuscript, University of British Columbia, 1970.

Byrne, D. Interpersonal attraction and attitude similarity. *Journal of Abnormal and Social Psychology*, 1961, **62**, 713–715. (a)

Byrne, D. Interpersonal attraction as a function of affiliation need and attitude similarity. *Human Relations*, 1961, **3**, 283–289. (b)

Byrne, D. Response to attitude similarity–dissimilarity as a function of affiliation need. *Journal of Personality*, 1962, **30**, 164–177.

Byrne, D. Assessing personality variables and their alteration. In P. Worchel and D. Byrne (Eds.), *Personality change*. New York: Wiley, 1964. Pp. 38–68. (a)

Byrne, D. Repression–sensitization as a dimension of personality. In B. A. Maher (Ed.), *Progress in experimental personality research*. Vol. 1. New York: Academic Press, 1964. Pp. 169–220. (b)

Byrne, D. Authoritarianism and response to attitude similarity–dissimilarity. *Journal of Social Psychology*, 1965, **66**, 251–256.

Byrne, D. *An introduction to personality: a research approach*. Englewood Cliffs, N.J.: Prentice-Hall, 1966.

Byrne, D. Attitudes and attraction. In L. Berkowitz (Ed.), *Advances in experimental social psychology*. Vol. 4. New York: Academic Press, 1969. Pp. 35–89.

Byrne, D. Can Wright be wrong? Let me count the ways. *Representative Research in Social Psychology*, in press.

Byrne, D., & Andres, D. Prejudice and interpersonal expectancies. *Journal of Negro Education*, 1964, **33**, 441–445.

Byrne, D., Barry, J., & Nelson, D. Relation of the revised Repression-Sensitization Scale to measures of self-description. *Psychological Reports*, 1963, **13**, 323–334.

Byrne, D., Baskett, G. D., & Hodges, L. Behavioral indicators of interpersonal attraction. *Journal of Applied Social Psychology*, in press.

Byrne, D., & Blaylock, B. Similarity and assumed similarity of attitudes between husbands and wives. *Journal of Abnormal and Social Psychology*, 1963, **67**, 636–640.

Byrne, D., Bond, M. H., & Diamond, M. J. Response to political candidates as a function of attitude similarity–dissimilarity. *Human Relations*, 1969, **22**, 251–262.

Byrne, D., & Buehler, J. A. A note on the influence of propinquity upon acquaintanceships. *Journal of Abnormal and Social Psychology*, 1955, **51**, 147–148.

Byrne, D., & Clore, G. L. Predicting interpersonal attraction toward strangers presented in three different stimulus modes. *Psychonomic Science*, 1966, **4**, 239–240.

Byrne, D., & Clore, G. L. Effectance arousal and attraction. *Journal of Personality and Social Psychology*, 1967, **6**, (4, Whole No. 638).

Byrne, D., & Clore, G. L. A reinforcement model of evaluative responses. *Personality: An International Journal*, 1970, **1**, 103–128.

Byrne, D., Clore, G. L., & Griffitt, W. Response discrepancy versus attitude similarity–dissimilarity as determinants of attraction. *Psychonomic Science*, 1967, **7**, 397–398.

Byrne, D., Clore, G. L., & Worchel, P. The effect of economic similarity–dissimilarity on interpersonal attraction. *Journal of Personality and Social Psychology*, 1966, **4**, 220–224.

Byrne, D., & Ervin, C. R. Attraction toward a Negro stranger as a function of prejudice, attitude similarity, and the stranger's evaluation of the subject. *Human Relations*, 1969, **22**, 397–404.

Byrne, D., Ervin, C. R., & Lamberth, J. Continuity between the experimental study of attraction and "real life" computer dating. *Journal of Personality and Social Psychology*, 1970, **16**, 157–165.

Byrne, D., Gouaux, C., Griffitt, W., Lamberth, J., Murakawa, N., Prasad, M. B., Prasad, A., & Ramirez, M., III. The ubiquitous relationship: attitude similarity and attraction. *Human Relations*, in press.

Byrne, D., & Griffitt, W. A developmental investigation of the law of attraction. *Journal of Personality and Social Psychology*, 1966, **4**, 699–702. (a)

Byrne, D., & Griffitt, W. Similarity versus liking: a clarification. *Psychonomic Science*, 1966, **6**, 295–296. (b)

Byrne, D., & Griffitt, W. Similarity and awareness of similarity of personality characteristics. *Journal of Experimental Research in Personality*, 1969, **3**, 179–186.

Byrne, D., Griffitt, W., & Clore, G. L. Attitudinal reinforcement effects as a function of stimulus homogeneity–heterogeneity. *Journal of Verbal Learning and Verbal Behavior*, 1968, **7**, 962–964.

Byrne, D., Griffitt, W., & Golightly, C. Prestige as a factor in determining the effect of attitude similarity–dissimilarity on attraction. *Journal of Personality*, 1966, **34**, 434–444.

Byrne, D., Griffitt, W., Hudgins, W., & Reeves, K. Attitude similarity–dissimilarity and attraction: generality beyond the college sophomore. *Journal of Social Psychology*, 1969. **79**, 155–161.

Byrne, D., Griffitt, W., & Stefaniak, D. Attraction and similarity of personality characteristics. *Journal of Personality and Social Psychology*, 1967, **5**, 82–90.

Byrne, D., & Lamberth, J. Reinforcement theories and cognitive theories as complementary approaches to the study of attraction. In B. I. Murstein (Ed.), *Theories of love and attraction*. New York: Springer, in press.

Byrne, D., Lamberth, J., & Mitchell, H. E. Husband–wife similarity in response to erotic stimuli. To be published. (a)

Byrne, D., Lamberth, J., & Mitchell, H. E. The instrumentality of sexual needs in male–female relationships. To be published. (b)

Byrne, D., Lamberth, J., Palmer, J., & London, O. Sequential effects as a function of explicit and implicit interpolated attraction responses. *Journal of Personality and Social Psychology*, 1969, **13**, 70–78.

Byrne, D., & London, O. Primacy–recency and the sequential presentation of attitudinal stimuli. *Psychonomic Science*, 1966, **6**, 193–194.

Byrne, D., London, O., & Griffitt, W. The effect of topic importance and attitude similarity–dissimilarity on attraction in an intrastranger design. *Psychonomic Science*, 1968, **11**, 303–304.

Byrne, D., London, O., & Reeves, K. The effects of physical attractiveness, sex, and attitude similarity on interpersonal attraction. *Journal of Personality*, 1968, **36**, 259–271.

Byrne, D., McDonald, R. D., & Mikawa, J. Approach and avoidance affiliation motives. *Journal of Personality*, 1963, **31**, 21–37.

Byrne, D., & McGraw, C. Interpersonal attraction toward Negroes. *Human Relations*, 1964, **17**, 201–213.

Byrne, D., & Nelson, D. Attraction as a function of attitude similarity–dissimilarity: the effect of topic importance. *Psychonomic Science*, 1964, **1**, 93–94.

Byrne, D., & Nelson, D. Attraction as a linear function of proportion of positive reinforcements. *Journal of Personality and Social Psychology*, 1965, **1**, 659–663. (a)

Byrne, D., & Nelson, D. The effect of topic importance and attitude similarity–dissimilarity on attraction in a multistranger design. *Psychonomic Science*, 1965, **3**, 449–450. (b)

Byrne, D., Nelson, D., & Reeves, K. Effects of consensual validation and invalidation on attraction as a function of verifiability. *Journal of Experimental Social Psychology*, 1966, **2**, 98–107.

Byrne, D., & Rhamey, R. Magnitude of positive and negative reinforcements as a determinant of attraction. *Journal of Personality and Social Psychology*, 1965, **2**, 884–889.

Byrne, D., & Wong, T. J. Racial prejudice, interpersonal attraction, and assumed dissimilarity of attitudes. *Journal of Abnormal and Social Psychology*, 1962, **65**, 246–253.

Byrne, D., Young, R. K., & Griffitt, W. The reinforcement properties of attitude statements. *Journal of Experimental Research in Personality*, 1966, **1**, 266–276.

Calhoun, J. B. Population density and social pathology. *Scientific American*, 1962, **206**, 139–148.

Capaldi, E. J. A sequential hypothesis of instrumental learning. In K. W. Spence and J. T. Spence (Eds.), *The psychology of learning and motivation: advances in research and theory*. Vol. 1. New York: Academic Press, 1967. Pp. 67–156.

Carriero, N. J. The conditioning of negative attitudes to unfamiliar items of information. *Journal of Verbal Learning and Verbal Behavior*, 1967, **6**, 128–135.

Cartwright, D. The effect of interruption, completion, and failure upon the attractiveness of activities. *Journal of Experimental Psychology*, 1942, **31**, 1–16.

Cattell, R. B., & Nesselroade, J. R. Likeness and completeness theories examined by Sixteen Personality Factor measures on stably and unstably married couples. *Journal of Personality and Social Psychology*, 1967, **7**, 351–361.

Christian, J. J. The pathology of overpopulation. *Military Medicine*, 1963, **128**, 571–603.

Clore, G. L. Discrimination learning as a function of awareness and magnitude of attitudinal reinforcement. Unpublished doctoral dissertation, University of Texas, 1966.

Clore, G. L., & Baldridge, B. Interpersonal attraction: the role of agreement and topic interest. *Journal of Personality and Social Psychology*, 1968, **9**, 340–346.

Clore, G. L., & Baldridge, B. The behavior of item weights in attitude-attraction research. *Journal of Experimental Social Psychology*, 1970, **6**, 177–186.

Clore, G. L., & Byrne, D. The process of personality interaction. In R. B. Cattell (Ed.), *Handbook of modern personality study*. Chicago, Ill.: Aldine, in press.

Clore, G. L., & Gormly, J. B. Attraction and physiological arousal in response to agreements and disagreements. Paper presented at the meeting of the Psychonomic Society, St. Louis, November, 1969.

Clore, G. L., & Jeffery, K. M. Emotional role playing, attitude change, and attraction toward a disabled other. Paper presented at the meeting of the Midwestern Psychological Association, Detroit, May, 1971.

Clore, G. L., & Johnson. C. Black–white interactions in a summer camp for children. Unpublished manuscript, University of Illinois, 1971.

Cohen, A. R. Experimental effects of ego-defense preference on interpersonal relations. *Journal of Abnormal and Social Psychology*, 1956, **52**, 19–27.

Cohen, A., Stotland, E., & Wolfe, D. M. An experimental investigation of need for cognition. *Journal of Abnormal and Social Psychology*, 1955, **51**, 291–297.

Cole, D. "Rational argument" and "prestige-suggestion" as factors influencing judgment. *Sociometry*, 1954, **17**, 350–354.

Collins, B. E., Davis, H. L., Myers, J. G., & Silk, A. J. An experimental study of reinforcement and participant satisfaction. *Journal of Abnormal and Social Psychology*, 1964, **68**, 463–467.

Conant, J. B. *Modern science and modern man*. Garden City, N.Y.: Doubleday, 1952.

Corrozi, J. F., & Rosnow, R. L. Consonant and dissonant communications as positive and negative reinforcements in opinion change. *Journal of Personality and Social Psychology*, 1968, **8**, 27–30.

Corsini, R. J. Understanding and similarity in marriage. *Journal of Abnormal and Social Psychology*, 1956, **52**, 327–332.

Crespi, L. P. Amount of reinforcement and level of performance. *Psychological Review*, 1946, **51**, 341–357.

Cronbach, L. J. The two disciplines of scientific psychology. *American Psychologist*, 1957, **12**, 671–684.

Crowne, D. T., & Marlowe, D. *The approval motive*. New York: Wiley, 1964.

Curran, J. P., Jr. Analysis of factors affecting interpersonal attraction in the dating situation. Unpublished doctoral dissertation, University of Illinois, 1970.

Dahlke, H. O. Determinants of sociometric relations among children in the elementary school. *Sociometry*, 1953, **16**, 327–338.

Davie, M. R., & Reeves, R. J. Propinquity of residence before marriage. *American Journal of Sociology*, 1939, **44**, 510–517.

Deutsch, M. Socially relevant science: reflections on some studies of interpersonal conflict. *American Psychologist*, 1969, **24**, 1076–1092.

Deutsch, M., & Solomon, L. Reactions to evaluations by others as influenced by self-evaluation. *Sociometry*, 1959, **22**, 93–112.

Dickoff, H. Reactions to evaluations by another person as a function of self-evaluation and the interaction context. Unpublished doctoral dissertation, Duke University, 1961.

Dodd, S. C., & Garabedian, P. G. The logistic law of interaction when people pair off "at will." *Journal of Social Psychology*, 1961, **53**, 143–158.

Dollard, J. *Caste and class in a southern town*. Garden City, N.Y.: Doubleday, 1949.

Dollard, J., & Miller, N. E. *Personality and psychotherapy*. New York: McGraw-Hill, 1950.

Doob, L. W. The behavior of attitudes. *Psychological Review*, 1947, **54**, 135–156.

Duncan, S., Jr. Nonverbal communication. *Psychological Bulletin*, 1969, **72**, 118–137.

Dutton, D. G. Role performance and social perception. Unpublished doctoral dissertation, University of Toronto, 1969.

Dymond, R. F. Adjustment changes over therapy from self-sorts. In C. R. Rogers and R. F. Dymond (Eds.), *Psychotherapy and personality change*. Chicago, Ill.: Univ. of Chicago Press, 1954. Pp. 76–84.

Eddington, A. S. *The nature of the physical world*. New York: Wiley, 1928.

Edwards, A. L. Political frames of reference as a factor influencing recognition. *Journal of Abnormal and Social Psychology*, 1941, **36**, 34–50.

Edwards, A. L. Social desirability and probability of endorsement of items in the Interpersonal Check List. *Journal of Abnormal and Social Psychology*, 1957, **55**, 394–396.

Edwards, A. L. *Edwards Personal Preference Schedule manual*. New York: Psychological Corporation, 1959.

Edwards, J. R. Attitudinal reinforcement in a verbal conditioning paradigm. Unpublished master's thesis, McGill University, 1970.

Efran, J. Looking for approval: effects on visual behavior of approbation from persons differing in importance. *Journal of Personality and Social Psychology*, 1968, **10**, 21–25.

Efran, J., & Broughton, A. Effect of expectancies for social approval on visual behavior. *Journal of Personality and Social Psychology*, 1966, **4**, 103–107.

Efran, M. G. Visual interaction and interpersonal attraction. Unpublished doctoral dissertation, University of Texas, 1969.

Eisman, B. S. Attitude formation: the development of a color-preference response through mediated generalization. *Journal of Abnormal and Social Psychology*, 1955, **50**, 321–326.

Emerson, R. M. Deviation and rejection: an experimental replication. *American Sociological Review*, 1954, **19**, 688–693.

Ervin, C. R. Sex of evaluator as a determinant of reinforcement magnitude on interpersonal attraction. Unpublished master's thesis, University of Texas, 1967.

Ettinger, R. F. Personality correlates of interpersonal attraction. Unpublished master's thesis, Purdue University, 1967.

Ettinger, R. F., Nowicki, A., Jr., & Nelson, D. Interpersonal attraction and the approval motive. *Journal of Experimental Research in Personality*, 1970, **4**, 95–99.

Exline, R. V. Explorations in the process of person perception: visual interaction in relation to competition, sex, and need for affiliation. *Journal of Personality*, 1963, **31**, 1–20.

Exline, R. V., & Winters, L. C. Affective relations and mutual glances in dyads. In S. Tomkins and C. Izard (Eds.), *Affect, cognition, and personality*. New York: Springer Publ., 1965.

Eysenck, H. J. *Maudsley Personality Inventory*. San Diego, Calif.: Educational and Industrial Testing Service, 1962.

Farber, I. E. A framework for the study of personality as a behavioral science. In P. Worchel and D. Byrne (Eds.), *Personality change*. New York: Wiley, 1964. Pp. 3–37.

Farina, A., Sherman, M., & Allen, J. G. Role of physical abnormalities in interpersonal perception and behavior. *Journal of Abnormal Psychology*, 1968, **73**, 590–593.

Faunce, D., & Beegle, J. A. Cleavages in a relatively homogeneous group of rural youth: an experiment in the use of sociometry in attaining and measuring integration. *Sociometry*, 1948, **11**, 207–216.

Festinger, L. Informal social communication. *Psychological Review*, 1950, **57**, 271–282.

Festinger, L. A theory of social comparison processes. *Human Relations*, 1954, **7**, 117–140.

Festinger, L. *A theory of cognitive dissonance*. Stanford, Calif.: Stanford Univ. Press, 1957.

Festinger, L., Gerard, H., Hymovitch, B., Kelley, H., & Raven, B. The influence process in the presence of extreme deviates. *Human Relations*, 1952, **5**, 327–346.

Festinger, L., Schachter, S., & Back, K. *Social pressures in informal groups: a study of human factors in housing*. New York: Harper, 1950.

Festinger, L., & Thibaut, J. Interpersonal communication in small groups. *Journal of Abnormal and Social Psychology*, 1951, **46**, 92–99.

Filer, R. J. Frustration, satisfaction, and other factors affecting the attractiveness of goal objects. *Journal of Abnormal and Social Psychology*, 1952, **47**, 203–212.

Finley, J. R., & Staats, A. W. Evaluative meaning words as reinforcing stimuli. *Journal of Verbal Learning and Verbal Behavior*, 1967, **6**, 193–197

Fisher, R., & Smith, W. P. Conflict of interest and attraction in the development of co-operation. *Psychonomic Science*, 1969, **14**, 154–155.

French, E. G., & Chadwick, I. Some characteristics of affiliation motivation. *Journal of Abnormal and Social Psychology*, 1956, **52**, 296–300.

Galloway, J. Interpersonal attraction as a function of attitude similarity, ethnicity and topic relevance. Unpublished master's thesis, McGill University, 1970.

Galton, F. *Hereditary genius: an inquiry into its laws and consequences*. 1870. (Republished: New York, Horizon, 1952.)

Gebhard, M. E. The effect of success and failure upon the attractiveness of activities as a function of experience, expectation, and need. *Journal of Experimental Psychology*, 1948, **38**, 371–388.

Gebhard, M. E. Changes in the attractiveness of activities: the effect of expectation preceding performance. *Journal of Experimental Psychology*, 1949, **39**, 404–413.

Gewirtz, H. B. Generalization of children's preferences as a function of reinforcement and task similarity. *Journal of Abnormal and Social Psychology*, 1959, **58**, 111–118.

Gewirtz, J. L., & Baer, D. M. Deprivation and satiation of social reinforcers as drive conditions. *Journal of Abnormal and Social Psychology*, 1958, **57**, 165–172.   (a)

Gewirtz, J. L., & Baer, D. M. The effect of brief social deprivation on behaviors for a social reinforcer. *Journal of Abnormal and Social Psychology*, 1958, **56**, 49–56.   (b)

Goldstein. A. P. *Psychotherapeutic attraction*. Oxford, England: Pergamon, in press.

Golightly, C. The reinforcement properties of attitude similarity–dissimilarity. Unpublished doctoral dissertation, University of Texas, 1965.

Golightly, C., & Byrne, D. Attitude statements as positive and negative reinforcements. *Science*, 1964, **146**, 798–799.

Golightly, C., Huffman, D. M, & Byrne, D. *Liking and loaning.* To be published.

Gordon, J. E. Interpersonal predictions of repressors and sensitizers. *Journal of Personality*, 1957, **25**, 686–698.

Gormly, A. V., & Clore, G. L. Attraction, dogmatism, and attitude similarity–dissimilarity. *Journal of Experimental Research in Personality*, 1969, **4**, 9–13.

Gouaux, C. Interpersonal attraction as a function of induced affect and social dependence. Unpublished master's thesis, University of Texas, 1969.

Gouaux, C. Induced affective states and interpersonal attraction. Paper presented at the meeting of the Southwestern Psychological Association, St. Louis, April, 1970.   (a)

Gouaux, C. The influence of induced affective states on the effectiveness of social and nonsocial reinforcers in an instrumental learning task. Unpublished doctoral dissertation, Purdue University, 1970.   (b)

Gouaux, C., & Lamberth, J. The effect on interpersonal attraction of successive and simultaneous presentation of strangers. *Psychonomic Science*, 1970, **21**, 337–338.

Gouaux, C., Lamberth, J., & Friedrich, G. Affect and interpersonal attraction: a comparison of trait and state measures. To be published.

Grant, D. A. Testing the null hypothesis and the strategy and tactics of investigating theoretical models. *Psychological Review*, 1962, **69**, 54–61.

Greenberg, D. S. Biomedical policy: LBJ's query leads to an illuminating conference. *Science*, 1966, **154**, 618–620.

Greenberg, G. The effects of ambient temperature and population density on aggression in two strains of mice. Unpublished doctoral dissertation, Kansas State University, 1969.

Griffitt, W. Interpersonal attraction as a function of self-concept and personality similarity–dissimilarity. *Journal of Personality and Social Psychology*, 1966, **4**, 581–584.

Griffitt, W. Personality similarity, self-concept, and positiveness of personality description as determinants of interpersonal attraction. Unpublished doctoral dissertation, University of Texas, 1967.

Griffitt, W. Anticipated reinforcement and attraction. *Psychonomic Science*, 1968, **11**, 355–356.   (a)

Griffitt, W. Attraction toward a stranger as a function of direct and associated reinforcement. *Psychonomic Science*, 1968, **11**, 147–148.   (b)

Griffitt, W. Attitude evoked anticipatory responses and attraction. *Psychonomic Science*, 1969, **14**, 153–155.   (a)

Griffitt, W. Personality similarity and self-concept as determinants of interpersonal attraction. *Journal of Social Psychology*, 1969, **78**, 137–146.   (b)

Griffitt, W. Environmental effects on interpersonal affective behavior: ambient effective temperature and attraction. *Journal of Personality and Social Psychology*, 1970, **15**, 240–244.

Griffitt, W. Context effects in response to affective stimuli. *Personality: An International Journal*, 1971, **2**, 23–33.

Griffitt, W., & Byrne, D. Procedures in the paradigmatic study of attitude similarity and attraction. *Representative Research in Social Psychology*, 1970, **1**, 33–48.

Griffitt, W., Byrne, D., & Bond, M. H. Proportion of positive adjectives and personal relevance of adjectival descriptions. *Journal of Experimental Social Psychology*, 1971, **7**, 111–121.

Griffitt, W., & Guay, P. "Object" evaluation and conditioned affect. *Journal of Experimental Research in Personality*, 1969, **4**, 1–8.

Griffitt, W., & Jackson, T. The influence of ability and non-ability information on personnel selection decisions. *Psychological Reports*, 1970, **27**, 959–962.

Griffitt, W., & Jackson, T. Simulated jury decisions: the influence of jury-defendant attitude similarity–dissimilarity. To be published.

Griffitt, W., & Nelson, P. Short-term temporal stability of interpersonal attraction. *Psychonomic Science*, 1970, **18**, 119–120.

Griffitt, W., & Veitch, R. Hot and crowded: influences of population density and temperature on interpersonal affective behavior. *Journal of Personality and Social Psychology*, 1971, **17**, 92–98.

Grossman, B., & Wrighter, J. The relationship between selection–rejection and intelligence, social status, and personality amongst sixth-grade children. *Sociometry*, 1948, **11**, 346–355.

Guion, R. M. Personnel selection. In P. R. Farnsworth, O. McNemar, and Q. McNemar (Eds.), *Annual review of psychology*. Vol. 18. Palo Alto: Annual Reviews, 1967. Pp. 191–216.

Guthwin, J. Interpersonal attraction, interpersonal expectation, and self-esteem. Paper presented at Eastern Psychological Association, Atlantic City, April, 1970.

Hamilton, M. L. Affiliative behavior as a function of approach and avoidance affiliation motives, opinion evaluation, and birth order. Unpublished doctoral dissertation, University of Texas, 1964.

Haywood, C. H. Heterosexual perception and attraction as a function of personality cues. Unpublished manuscript, University of Texas, 1965.

Hebb, D. O., & Thompson, W. R. The social significance of animal studies. In G. Lindzey and E. Aronson (Eds.), *Handbook of social psychology*. (2nd ed.) Vol. 2. Reading, Mass.: Addison-Wesley, 1968. Pp. 729–774.

Heider, F. *The psychology of interpersonal relations*. New York: Wiley, 1958.

Hendrick, C., Bixenstine, V. E., & Hawkins, G. Race versus belief similarity as determinants of attraction: A search for a fair test. *Journal of Personality and Social Psychology*, 1971, **17**, 250–258.

Hendrick, C., & Brown, S. R. Introversion, extraversion, and interpersonal attraction. *Journal of Personality and Social Psychology*, in press.

Hendrick, C., & Page, H. A. Self-esteem, attitude similarity, and attraction. *Journal of Personality*, 1970, **38**, 588–601.

Hendrick, C., & Taylor, S. P. Effects of belief similarity and aggression on attraction and counter-aggression. *Journal of Personality and Social Psychology*, 1971, **17**, 342–349.

Hewitt, J., & Chung, B. J. Observed benevolence and hostility as determinants of interpersonal attraction. *Psychonomic Science*, 1969, **17**, 82.

Hodges, L. A. Verbal dogmatism as a potentiator of intolerance. Unpublished master's thesis, Purdue University, 1970.

Hodges, L. A., & Byrne, D. Verbal dogmatism as a potentiator of intolerance. *Journal of Personality and Social Psychology*, in press.

Hodges, L. A., & Byrne, D. Neutralization of attraction and evaluation responses by expression of feelings. Paper presented at the meeting of the Midwestern Psychological Association, Detroit, May, 1971.

Hoffman, L. R. Similarity of personality: a basis for interpersonal attraction? *Sociometry*, 1958, **21**, 300–308.

Hoffman, L. R., & Maier, N. R. F. An experimental re-examination of the similarity–attraction hypothesis. *Journal of Personality and Social Psychology*, 1966, **3**. 145–152.

Hogan, R., & Mankin, D. Determinants of interpersonal attraction: a clarification. *Psychological Reports*, 1970, **26**, 235–238.

Holmes, D. S. Amount of experience in experiments as a determinant of performance in later experiments. *Journal of Personality and Social Psychology*, 1967, **7**, 403–407.

Holton, G. The thematic imagination in science. In H. Woolf (Ed.), *Science as a cultural force*. Baltimore, Md.: Johns Hopkins Press, 1964.

Holtzman, W. H., & Young, R. K. Scales for measuring attitudes toward the Negro and toward organized religion. *Psychological Reports*, 1966, **18**, 31–34.

Hoult, T. F. Experimental measurement of clothing as a factor in some social ratings of selected American men. *American Sociological Review*, 1954, **19**, 324–328.

Huffman, D. M. Interpersonal attraction as a function of behavioral similarity. Unpublished doctoral dissertation, University of Texas, 1969.

Hughes, R. L. "Object" evaluation: a reinterpretation of affect conditioning in the reinforcement model of attraction. Unpublished master's thesis, University of Texas, 1969.

Hull, C. L. Differential habituation to internal stimuli in the albino rat. *Journal of Comparative Psychology*, 1933, **16**, 255–273.

Hull, C. L. *Principles of behavior*. New York: Appleton-Century-Crofts, 1943.

Hull, C. L. *A behavior system*. New Haven, Conn.: Yale Univ. Press, 1952.

Hunt, A. McC. A study of the relative value of certain ideals. *Journal of Abnormal and Social Psychology*, 1935, **30**, 222–228.

Hunt, D. E. Changes in goal-object preference as a function of expectancy for social reinforcement. *Journal of Abnormal and Social Psychology*, 1955, **50**, 372–377.

Izard, C. E. Personality similarity and friendship. *Journal of Abnormal and Social Psychology*, 1960, **61**, 47–51.   (a)

Izard, C. E. Personality similarity, positive affect, and interpersonal attraction. *Journal of Abnormal and Social Psychology*, 1960, **61**, 484–485.   (b)

Izard, C. E. Personality and similarity and friendship: a follow-up study. *Journal of Abnormal and Social Psychology*, 1963, **66**, 598–600.

Jackson, D. N. *Manual for the Personality Research Form*. Goshen, New York: Research Psychologists Press, 1967.

Janis, I. L., Kaye, D., & Kirschner, P. Facilitating effects of "eating-while-reading" on responsiveness to persuasive communications. *Journal of Personality and Social Psychology*, 1965, **1**, 181–186.

Jones, E. E. *Ingratiation*. New York: Appleton-Century-Crofts, 1964.

Jones, E. E. Conformity as a tactic of ingratiation. *Science*, 1965, **149**, 144–150.

Jones, E. E., & Daugherty, B. N. Political orientation and the perceptual effects of an anticipated interaction. *Journal of Abnormal and Social Psychology*, 1959, **59**, 340–349.

Jones, E. E., & Kohler, R. The effects of plausibility on the learning of controversial statements. *Journal of Abnormal and Social Psychology*, 1958, **57**, 315–320.

Joy, V. L. Repression-sensitization, personality, and interpersonal behavior. Unpublished doctoral dissertation, University of Texas, 1963.

Kantor, J. R. The current situation in social psychology. *Psychological Bulletin*, 1939, **36**, 307–360.

Kaplan, M. F., & Olczak, P. V. Attitude similarity and direct reinforcement as determinants of attraction. *Journal of Experimental Research in Personality*, 1970, **4**, 186–189.

Katz, D. Editorial. *Journal of Personality and Social Psychology*, 1965, **1**, 1–2.

Katz, I., Cohen, M., & Castiglione, L, Effect of one type of need complementarity on marriage partner's conformity to one another's judgments. *Journal of Abnormal and Social Psychology*, 1963, **67**, 8–14.

Katz, I., Glucksberg, S., & Krauss, R. Need satisfaction and Edwards PPS scores in married couples. *Journal of Consulting Psychology*, 1960, **24**, 205–208.

Keehn, J. D. Plain ol' superstition. *American Psychologist*, 1966, **21**, 916–917.

Kelly, G. A. *The psychology of personal constructs*. New York: Norton, 1955.

Kelly, J. G., Ferson, J. E., & Holtzman, W. H. The measurement of attitudes toward the Negro in the South. *Journal of Social Psychology*, 1958, **48**, 305–317.

Kendler, H. H. The influence of simultaneous hunger and thirst drives upon the learning of two opposed spatial responses in the white rat. *Journal of Experimental Psychology*, 1946, **36**, 212–230.

Kerckhoff, A. C., & Davis, K. E. Value consensus and need complementarity in mate selection. *American Sociological Review*, 1962, **27**, 295–303.

Kessel, F. S. The philosophy of science as proclaimed and science as practiced: "identity" or "dualism"? *American Psychologist*, 1969, **24**, 999–1005.

Kipnis, D. McB. Interaction between members of bomber crews as a determinant of sociometric choice. *Human Relations*, 1957, **10**, 263–270.

Kirkpatrick, C., & Stone, S. Attitude measurement and the comparison of generations. *Journal of Applied Psychology*, 1935, **19**, 564–582.

Krauss, R. M. Structural and attitudinal factors in interpersonal bargaining. *Journal of Experimental Social Psychology*, 1966, **2**, 42–55.

Kuhn, T. S. *The structure of scientific revolutions.* Chicago Ill.: Univ. of Chicago Press, 1962.

Lamberth, J. The effect of sequential variables on performance using attitudinal reinforcers. Unpublished doctoral dissertation, Purdue University, 1970.

Lamberth, J., & Byrne, D. Similarity–attraction or demand characteristics? *Personality: An International Journal*, 1971, **2**, 77–91.

Lamberth, J., & Craig, L. Differential magnitude of reward and magnitude shifts using attitudinal stimuli. *Journal of Experimental Research in Personality*, 1970, **4**, 281–285.

Lamberth, J., & Gay, R. A. Differential reward magnitude using a performance task and attitudinal stimuli. Paper presented at the meeting of the Western Psychological Association, Vancouver, June, 1969.

Lansing, J. B., & Heyns, R. W. Need affiliation and frequency of four types of communication. *Journal of Abnormal and Social Psychology*, 1959, **58**, 365–372.

Leary, T. *Interpersonal diagnosis of personality.* New York: Ronald Press, 1957.

Lefkowitz, M., Blake, R. R., & Mouton, J. S. Status factors in pedestrian violation of traffic signals. *Journal of Abnormal and Social Psychology*, 1955, **51**, 704–706.

Lerner, M. J. The effect of responsibility and choice on a partner's attractiveness following failure. *Journal of Personality*, 1965, **33**, 178–187.

Lerner, M. J., & Agar, E. The consequences of perceived similarity: attraction and rejection, approach and avoidance. To be published.

Leventhal, G. S. Reward magnitude, task attractiveness, and liking for instrumental activity. *Journal of Abnormal and Social Psychology*, 1964, **68**, 460–463.

Levine, J. M., & Murphy, G. The learning and forgetting of controversial material. *Journal of Abnormal and Social Psychology*, 1943, **38**, 507–517.

Levinger, G. Note on need complementarity in marriage. *Psychological Bulletin*, 1964, **61**, 153–157.

Levinger, G., & Breedlove, J. Interpersonal attraction and agreement: a study of marriage partners. *Journal of Personality and Social Psychology*, 1966, **3**, 367–372.

Levinger, G., & Gunner, J. The interpersonal grid: I. Felt and tape techniques for the measurement of social relationships. *Psychonomic Science*, 1967, **8**, 173–174.

Lewis, H. B. Studies in the principles of judgments and attitudes: IV. The operation of "prestige-suggestion." *Journal of Social Psychology*, 1941, **14**, 229–256.

Lindzey, G., & Byrne, D. Measurement of social choice and interpersonal attractiveness. In G. Lindzey and E. Aronson (Eds.), *Handbook of social psychology.* (2nd ed.) Vol. 2. Reading, Mass.: Addison-Wesley, 1968. Pp. 452–525.

Little, K. B. Personal space. *Journal of Experimental Social Psychology*, 1965, **1**, 237–247.

Liverant, S. The use of Rotter's social learning theory in developing a personality inventory. *Psychological Monographs*, 1958, **72**, No. 2.

Locke, E. A. The relationship of task success to task liking and satisfaction. *Journal of Applied Psychology*, 1965, **49**, 379–385.

Locke, E. A. The relationship of task success to task liking: a replication. *Psychological Reports*, 1966, **18**, 552–554.

Locke, E. A. Relationship of success and expectation to affect on goal-seeking tasks. *Journal of Personality and Social Psychology*, 1967, **7**, 125–134.

London, O. H. Interpersonal attraction and abilities: social desirability or similarity to self? Unpublished master's thesis, University of Texas, 1967.

Longmore, T. W. A matrix approach to the analysis of rank and status in a community in Peru. *Sociometry*, 1948, **11**, 192–206.

Loomis, C. P., & Proctor, C. The relationship between choice status and economic status in social systems. *Sociometry*, 1950, **13**, 307–313.

Lott, A. J. Learning and liking. Paper presented at the meeting of the Southwestern Psychological Association, Arlington, Texas, 1966.

Lott, A. J. The potential power of liking as a factor in social change. Paper presented at the meeting of the Southwestern Psychological Association, Austin, Texas, May, 1969.

Lott, A. J., Aponte, J. F., Lott, B. E., & McGinley, W. H. The effect of delayed reward on the development of positive attitudes toward persons. *Journal of Experimental Social Psychology*, 1969, **5**, 101–113.

Lott, A. J., Bright, M. A., Weinstein, P., & Lott, B. E. Liking for persons as a function of incentive and drive during acquisition. *Journal of Personality and Social Psychology*, 1970, **14**, 66–76.

Lott, A. J., & Lott, B. E. Group cohesiveness as interpersonal attraction: a review of relationships with antecedent and consequent variables. *Psychological Bulletin*, 1965, **64**, 259–309.

Lott, A. J., & Lott, B. E. Group cohesiveness and individual learning. *Journal of Educational Psychology*, 1966, **57**, 61–73.

Lott, A. J., & Lott, B. E. Liked and disliked persons as reinforcing stimuli. *Journal of Personality and Social Psychology*, 1969, **11**, 129–137.

Lott, A. J., Lott, B. E., & Walsh, M. L. Learning of paired associates relevant to differentially liked persons. *Journal of Personality and Social Psychology*, 1970, **16**, 274–283.

Lott, B. E., & Lott, A. J. The formation of positive attitudes toward group members. *Journal of Abnormal and Social Psychology*, 1960, **61**, 297–300.

Lundberg, G. A. Social attraction patterns in a rural village: a preliminary report. *Sociometry*, 1937, **1**, 77–80.

Lundberg, G. A., & Beazley, V. "Consciousness of kind" in a college population. *Sociometry*, 1948, **11**, 59–74.

Lundberg, G. A., & Steele, M. Social attraction-patterns in a village. *Sociometry*, 1938, **1**, 375–419.

Lundy, R. M. Self-perceptions and descriptions of opposite sex sociometric choices. *Sociometry*, 1956, **19**, 272–277.

Lundy, R. M. Self-perceptions regarding masculinity–femininity and descriptions of same and opposite sex sociometric choices. *Sociometry*, 1958, **21**, 238–246.

Lynes, R. After hours. Ouch! *Harper's*. 1968, **237** (1420), 23–26.

Mahaffey, P. L. Attraction affect as a cue for dispensing positive and negative behaviors to a stranger. Unpublished master's thesis, University of Texas, 1969.

Maisonneuve, J. A contribution to the sociometry of mutual choices. *Sociometry*, 1954, **17**, 33–46.

Mandler, G., & Sarason, S. B. A study of anxiety and learning. *Journal of Abnormal and Social Psychology*, 1952, **47**, 166–173.

Marlowe, D., & Gergen, K. J. Personality and social interaction. In G. Lindzey and E. Aronson (Eds.), *Handbook of social psychology*. (2nd ed.) Vol. 3. Reading, Mass.: Addison-Wesley, 1968. Pp. 590–665.

Mascaro, G. F. Interpersonal attraction and uncertainty reduction as functions of judgmental similarity. *Perceptual and Motor Skills*, 1970, **30**, 71–75.

Mascaro, G. F., & Lopez, J. A. The effects of delayed judgmental-similarity on evaluative attraction. *Psychonomic Science*, 1970, **19**, 229–230.

Masling, J., Greer, F. L., & Gilmore, R. Status, authoritarianism, and sociometric choice. *Journal of Social Psychology*, 1955, **41**, 297–310.

Mathes, R. C. "D" people and "S" people. *Science*, 1969, **164**, 630.

Matthews, V., & Weslie, C. A preferred method for obtaining rankings: reactions to physical handicaps. *American Sociological Review*, 1966, **31**, 851–854.

McDonald, R. D. The effect of reward–punishment and affiliation need on interpersonal attraction. Unpublished doctoral dissertation, University of Texas, 1962.

McGuire, W. J. Some impending reorientations in social psychology: some thoughts provoked by Kenneth Ring. *Journal of Experimental Social Psychology*, 1967, **3**, 124–139.

McWhirter, R. M. Inferred attraction as a positive linear function of attitude similarity. Unpublished master's thesis, University of Texas, 1966.

McWhirter, R. M. Interpersonal attraction in a dyad as a function of the physical attractiveness of its members. Unpublished doctoral dissertation, Texas Tech. University, 1969.

McWhirter, R. M., & Jecker, J. D. Attitude similarity and inferred attraction. *Psychonomic Science*, 1967, **7**, 225–226.

Meadow, B. L. The effects of attitude similarity–dissimilarity and enjoyment on the perception of time. Unpublished master's thesis, Purdue University, 1971.

Megargee, E. I. A study of the subjective aspects of group membership at Amherst. Unpublished manuscript, 1956.

Mehlman, B. Similarity in friendships. *Journal of Social Psychology*, 1962, **57**, 195–202.

Mehrabian, A. Relationship of attitude to seated posture, orientation, and distance. *Journal of Personality and Social Psychology*, 1968, **10**, 26–30.

Mendelsohn, G. A., & Rankin, N. O. Client–counselor compatibility and the outcome of counseling. *Journal of Abnormal Psychology*, 1969, **74**, 157–163.

Merritt, D. L. The relationships between qualifications and attitudes in a teacher selection situation. Unpublished doctoral dissertation, Syracuse University, 1970.

Miller, A. G. Role of physical attractiveness in impression formation. *Psychonomic Science*, 1970, **19**, 241–243.

Miller, N., Campbell, D. T., Twedt, H., & O'Connell, E. J. Similarity, contrast, and complementarity in friendship choice. *Journal of Personality and Social Psychology*, 1966, **3**, 3–12.

Mischel, W. *Personality and assessment*. New York: Wiley, 1968.

Mitchell, H. E. The effects of attitude similarity–dissimilarity and authoritarianism on simulated jury decisions. Unpublished master's thesis, Purdue University, 1970.

Mitchell, H. E., & Byrne, D. The defendant's dilemma: effects of jurors' attitudes and authoritarianism. Paper presented at the meeting of the Midwestern Psychological Association, Detroit, May, 1971.

Moos, R. H., & Speisman J. C. Group compatibility and productivity. *Journal of Abnormal and Social Psychology*, 1962, **65**, 190–196.

Morgan, C. L., & Remmers, H. H. Liberalism and conservatism of college students as affected by the depression. *School and Society*, 1935, **41**, 780–784.

Moss, M. K. Social desirability, physical attractiveness, and social choice. Unpublished doctoral dissertation, Kansas State University, 1969.

Moss, M. K. Interpersonal attraction and assumed similarity of attitudes. Unpublished manuscript, Wright State University, 1970.

Mowrer, O. H. *Learning theory and behavior*. New York: Wiley, 1960.

Mueller, L. M. Interpersonal attraction as a function of inferred similarity–dissimilarity: a reversal effect. Unpublished doctoral dissertation, University of Texas, 1969.

Munsinger, H., & Kessen, W. Uncertainty, structure, and preference. *Psychological Monographs*, 1964, 78 (9, Whole No. 586).

Murray, H. A. Studies of stressful interpersonal disputations. *American Psychologist*, 1963, **18**, 28–36.

Murstein, B. I. The complementary need hypothesis in newlyweds and middle-aged married couples. *Journal of Abnormal and Social Psychology*, 1961, **63**, 194–197.

Nelson, D. The effect of differential magnitude of reinforcement on interpersonal attraction. Unpublished doctoral dissertation, University of Texas, 1965.

Nelson, D. Attitude similarity and interpersonal attraction: the approval-cue hypothesis. Paper presented at the meeting of the Southwestern Psychological Association, Arlington, May, 1966.

Newcomb, T. M. An approach to the study of communicative acts. *Psychological Review*, 1953, **60**, 393–404.

Newcomb, T. M. The prediction of interpersonal attraction. *American Psychologist*, 1956, **11**, 575–586.

Newcomb, T. M. Individual systems of orientation. In S. Koch (Ed.), *Psychology: a study of a science*. Vol. 3. *Formulations of the person and the social context*. New York: McGraw-Hill, 1959. Pp. 384–422.

Newcomb, T. M. *The acquaintance process*. New York: Holt, Rinehart, and Winston, 1961.

Newcomb, T. M. Stabilities underlying changes in interpersonal attraction. *Journal of Abnormal and Social Psychology*, 1963, **66**, 376–386.

Newcomb, T., & Svehla, G. Intra-family relationships in attitudes. *Sociometry*, 1937, **1**, 180–205.

Novak, D. W., & Lerner, M. J. Rejection as a consequence of perceived similarity. *Journal of Personality and Social Psychology*, 1968, **9**, 147–152.

Nowicki, S., Jr. Interpersonal attraction, similarity and need for approval: an extension and attempt at the identification of new sources of variance. Unpublished doctoral dissertation, Purdue University, 1969.

Nowlis, H. H. The influence of success and failure on the resumption of an interrupted task. *Journal of Experimental Psychology*, 1941, **28**, 304–325.

Nunnally, J. C. *Popular conceptions of mental health*. New York: Holt, 1961.

Nunnally, J. C., Duchnowski, A. C., & Parker, R. K. Association of neutral objects with rewards: effect on verbal evaluation, reward expectancy, and selective retention. *Journal of Personality and Social Psychology*, 1965, **1**, 270–274.

Nunnally, J. C., Stevens, D. A., & Hall, G. F. Association of neutral objects with rewards: effect on verbal evaluation and eye movements. *Journal of Experimental Child Psychology*, 1965, **2**, 44–57.

Olczak, P. V. Balance versus reinforcement as determinants of attraction. Unpublished master's thesis, Northern Illinois University, 1969.

Oppenheimer, R. Analogy in science. *American Psychologist*, 1956, **11**, 127–136.

Orne, M. T. On the social psychology of the psychological experiment with particular reference to demand characteristics and their implications. *American Psychologist*, 1962, **17**, 775–783.

Osgood, C. E., Suci, G. J., & Tannenbaum, P. H. *The measurement of meaning*. Urbana, Ill.: Univ. of Illinois Press, 1957.

Palmer, J. Vindication, evaluation, and the effect of the stranger's competence on the attitude similarity-attraction function. Unpublished doctoral dissertation, University of Texas, 1969.

Palmer, J., & Byrne, D. Attraction toward dominant and submissive strangers: similarity versus complementarity. *Journal of Experimental Research in Personality*, 1970, **4**, 108–115.

Pearson, K., & Lee, A. On the laws of inheritance in man. I. Inheritance of physical characters. *Biometrika*, 1903, **2**, 357–462.

Perkins, C. C., Jr. An analysis of the concept of reinforcement. *Psychological Review*, 1968, **75**, 155–172.

Perrin, F. A. C. Physical attractiveness and repulsiveness. *Journal of Experimental Psychology*, 1921, **4**, 203–217.

Pervin, L. A. The need to predict and control under conditions of threat. *Journal of Personality*, 1963, **31**, 570–587.

Peterson, R. L. A videotape analogue for interpersonal attraction research. Unpublished master's thesis, Purdue University, 1969.

Pfaffmann, C. Behavioral sciences. *American Psychologist*, 1965, **20**, 667–686.

Picher, O. L. Attraction toward Negroes as a function of prejudice, emotional arousal, and the sex of the Negro. Unpublished doctoral dissertation, University of Texas, 1966.

Pickford, J. H., Signori, E. I., & Rempel, H. The intensity of personality traits in relation to marital happiness. *Journal of Marriage and the Family*, 1966, **28**, 458–459.   (a)

Pickford, J. H., Signori, E. I., & Rempel, H. Similar or related personality traits as a factor in marital happiness. *Journal of Marriage and the Family*, 1966, **28**, 190–192.   (b)

Pickford, J. H., Signori, E. I., & Rempel, H. Husband–wife differences in personality traits as a factor of marital happiness. *Psychological Reports*, 1967, **20**, 1087–1090.

Pintner, R., Forlano, G., & Freedman, H. Personality and attitudinal similarity among classroom friends. *Journal of Applied Psychology*, 1937, **21**, 48–65.

Polanyi, M. *Science, faith and society*. Chicago, Ill.: Univ. of Chicago Press, 1964.

Radin, N. S. Why not a draft for applied research? *Science*, 1966, **154**, 1276.

Razran, G. H. S. Conditioned response changes in rating and appraising sociopolitical slogans. *Psychological Bulletin*, 1940, **37**, 481. (Abstract)

Reagor, P. A., & Clore, G. L. Attraction, test anxiety, and similarity–dissimilarity of test performance. *Psychonomic Science*, 1970, **18**, 219–220.

Reilly, M. S. A., Commins, W. D., & Stefic, E. C. The complementarity of personality needs in friendship choice. *Journal of Abnormal and Social Psychology*, 1960, **61**, 292–294.

Reitz, W. E., Douey, J., & Mason, G. Role of homogeneity and centrality of attitude domain on reinforcing properties of attitude statements. *Journal of Experimental Research in Personality*, 1968, **3**, 120–125.

Reitz, W. E., & McDougall, L. Interest items as positive and negative reinforcements: effects of social desirability and extremity of endorsement. *Psychonomic Science*, 1969, **17**, 97–98.

Reitz, W. E., & Robinson, N. Effect of social desirability on interpersonal attraction. Paper presented at the meeting of the American Psychological Association, Washington, September, 1969.

Reitz, W. E., Robinson, N., & Dudley, L. Reinforcement properties of self-attitudes. Research Bulletin No. 110, January, 1969, University of Western Ontario.

Richardson, H. M. Studies of mental resemblance between husbands and wives and between friends. *Psychological Bulletin*, 1939, **36**, 104–120.

Richardson, H. M. Community of values as a factor in friendships of college and adult women. *Journal of Social Psychology*, 1940, **11**, 303–312.

Rohles, F. H. Environmental psychology: a bucket of worms. *Psychology Today*, 1967, **1**, 55–63.

Rokeach, M. (Ed.), *The open and closed mind*. New York: Basic Books, 1960.

Rokeach, M. Belief versus race as determinants of social distance: comment on Triandis' paper. *Journal of Abnormal and Social Psychology*, 1961, **62**, 187–188.

Rokeach, M., & Mezei, L. Race and shared belief as factors in social choice. *Science*, 1966, **151**, 167–172.

Rokeach, M., Smith, P. W., & Evans, R. I. Two kinds of prejudice or one? In M. Rokeach (Ed.), *The open and closed mind*. New York: Basic Books, 1960. Pp. 132–168.

Rosenblood, L. Information saliency: An explanation of the set size effect in impression formation and similarity-attraction research. Unpublished doctoral dissertation, Ohio State University, 1970.

Rosenfeld, H. M., & Jackson, J. Temporal mediation of the similarity-attraction hypothesis. *Journal of Personality*, 1965, **33**, 649–656.

Rosenthal, R. *Experimenter effects in behavioral research*. New York: Appleton-Century-Crofts, 1966.

Rosenzweig, S. Preferences in the repetition of successful and unsuccessful activities as a function of age and personality. *Journal of Genetic Psychology*, 1933, **42**, 423–441.

Rubin, Z. Measurement of romantic love. *Journal of Personality and Social Psychology*, 1970, **16**, 265–273.

Rychlak, J. F. The similarity, compatibility, or incompatibility of needs in interpersonal selection. *Journal of Personality and Social Psychology*, 1965, **2**, 334–340.

Rychlak, J. F. *A philosophy of science for personality theory*. Boston, Mass.: Houghton, 1968.

Sachs, D. H. The effects of manifest anxiety (drive) and attitude similarity–dissimilarity on attraction. Unpublished master's thesis, University of Texas, 1969.

Sachs, D. H., & Byrne, D. Differential conditioning of evaluative responses to neutral stimuli through association with attitude statements. *Journal of Experimental Research in Personality*, 1970, **4**, 181–185.

Sanford, N. Will psychologists study human problems? *American Psychologist*, 1965, **20**, 192–202.

Sapolsky, A. Effect of interpersonal relationships upon verbal conditioning. *Journal of Abnormal and Social Psychology*, 1960, **60**, 241–246.

Sapolsky, A. Relationship between patient–doctor compatibility, mutual perception, and outcome of treatment. *Journal of Abnormal Psychology*, 1965, **70**, 70–76.

Schachter, S. Deviation, rejection, and communication. *Journal of Abnormal and Social Psychology*, 1951, **46**, 190–207.

Schachter, S. *The psychology of affiliation*. Stanford, Calif.: Stanford Univ. Press, 1959.

Schiller, B. A quantitative analysis of marriage selection in a small group. *Journal of Social Psychology*, 1932, **3**, 297–319.

Schooley, M. Personality resemblances among married couples. *Journal of Abnormal and Social Psychology*, 1936, **31**, 340–347.

Schuster, E., & Elderton, E. M. The inheritance of psychical characters. *Biometrika*, 1906, **5**, 460–469.

Schwartz, M. S. Effectance motivation and interpersonal attraction: individual differences and personality correlates. Unpublished doctoral dissertation, University of Texas, 1966.

Scott, W. C. Response prediction and interpersonal attraction. Paper presented at the meeting of the Southwestern Psychological Association, Austin, April, 1969.

Sears, R. R. Transcultural variables and conceptual equivalence. In B. Kaplan (Ed.), *Studying personality cross-culturally*. New York: Harper, 1961. Pp. 445–455.

Secord, P. F., & Backman, C. W. Interpersonal congruency, perceived similarity, and friendship. *Sociometry*, 1964, **27**, 115–127.

Senn, D. J. Attraction as a function of similarity–dissimilarity in task performance. *Journal of Personality and Social Psychology*, 1971, **18**, 120–123.

Shaughnessy, J. M., & Levinger, G. Interpersonal search; a computer-assisted simulation. Technical Report, National Science Foundation, July, 1969.

Shaw, M. E., & Shaw, L. M. Some effects of sociometric grouping upon learning in a second grade classroom. *Journal of Social Psychology*, 1962, **57**, 453–458.

Sheffield, J., & Byrne, D. Attitude similarity–dissimilarity, authoritarianism, and interpersonal attraction. *Journal of Social Psychology*, 1967. **71**, 117–123.

Sherif, M., & Sherif, C. *Groups in harmony and tension*. New York: Harper, 1953.

Sherman, R. C. The effects of effectance arousal, patterning of information, and attitude similarity upon the intensity of interpersonal attraction responses. Unpublished doctoral dissertation, Iowa State University, 1969.

Signori, E. I., Rempel, H., & Pickford, J. H. Multivariate relationships between spouses' trait scores on the Guilford-Zimmerman Temperament Survey. *Psychological Reports*, 1968, **22**, 103–106.

Simon, B., & Lawton, M. P. Proximity and other determinants of friendship formation in the elderly. Paper presented at the meeting of the Eastern Psychological Association, Boston, April, 1967.

Simons, H. W., Berkowitz, N. N., & Moyer, R. J. Similarity, credibility, and attitude change: a review and a theory. *Psychological Bulletin*, 1970, **73**, 1–16.

Smith, A. J. Similarity of values and its relation to acceptance and the projection of similarity. *Journal of Psychology*, 1957, **43**, 251–260.

Smith, A. J. Perceived similarity and the projection of similarity: the influence of valence. *Journal of Abnormal and Social Psychology*, 1958, **57**, 376–379.

Smith, A. J. The attribution of similarity: the influence of success and failure. *Journal of Abnormal and Social Psychology*, 1960, **61**, 419–423.

Smith, R. E. Social anxiety as a moderator variable in the attitude similarity–attraction relationship. Paper presented at the meeting of the Western Psychological Association, Los Angeles, April, 1970.

Smith, R. E., & Jeffery, R. W. Social-evaluative anxiety and the reinforcement properties of agreeing and disagreeing attitude statements. *Journal of Experimental Research in Personality*, 1970, **4**, 276–280.

Smith, R. E., Meadow, B. L., & Sisk, T. K. Attitude similarity, interpersonal attraction, and evaluative social perception. *Psychonomic Science*, 1970, **18**, 226–227.

Smith, R. E., Smythe, L., & Lien, D. Inhibition of helping behavior by similar and dissimilar nonreactive fellow bystanders. Unpublished manuscript, University of Washington, 1971.

Sommer, R. Studies in personal space. *Sociometry*, 1959, **22**, 247–260.

Spear, N. E., & Spitzner, J. H. Simultaneous and successive contrast effects of reward magnitude in selective learning. *Psychological Monographs*, 1966, **80**, (10, Whole No. 618).

Spence, K. W. The nature of theory construction in contemporary psychology. *Psychological Review*, 1944, **51**, 47–68.

Spence, K. W. Theoretical interpretations of learning. In S. S. Stevens (Ed.), *Handbook of experimental psychology*. New York: Wiley, 1951. Pp. 690–729.

Spence, K. W. A theory of emotionally based drive (D) and its relation to performance in simple learning situations. *American Psychologist*, 1958, **13**, 131–141.

Spinoza, B. *The ethics*. New York: Dover, 1951.

Staats, A. W. Conditioned stimuli, conditioned reinforcers, and word meaning. In A. W. Staats (Ed.), *Human learning*. New York: Holt, 1964.

Staats, A. W. Social behaviorism and human motivation: principles of the attitude-reinforcer–discriminative system. In A. G. Greenwald, T. C. Brock, and T. M. Ostrom (Eds.), *Psychological foundations of attitudes*. New York: Academic Press, 1968. Pp. 33–66.

Staats, A. W. An outline of an integrated learning theory of attitude formation and function. In M. Fishbein (Ed.), *Readings in attitude theory and measurement*. New York: Wiley, 1969. Pp. 373–381.

Staats, A. W., & Staats, C. K. Attitudes established by classical conditioning. *Journal of Abnormal and Social Psychology*, 1958, **57**, 37–40.

Staats, C. K., & Staats, A. W. Meaning established by classical conditioning. *Journal of Experimental Psychology*, 1957, **54**, 74–80.

Staats, C. K., Staats, A. W., & Heard, W. G. Attitude development and ratio of reinforcement. *Sociometry*, 1960, **23**, 338–350.

Stalling, R. B. Personality similarity and evaluative meaning as conditioners of attraction. *Journal of Personality and Social Psychology*, 1970, **14**, 77–82.

Stapert, J. C., & Clore, G. L. Attraction and disagreement-produced arousal. *Journal of Personality and Social Psychology*, 1969, **13**, 64–69.

Stefaniak, D. Attitudinal effects on learning. Unpublished master's thesis, University of Texas, 1967.

Stein, D. D. The influence of belief systems on interpersonal preference: a validation study of Rokeach's theory of prejudice. *Psychological Monographs*, 1966, **80** (8, Whole No. 616).

Stein, D. D., Hardyck, J. A., & Smith, M. B. Race *and* belief: an open and shut case. *Journal of Personality and Social Psychology*, 1965, **1**, 281–289.

Stewart, R. H. Effect of continuous responding on the order effect in personality impression formation. *Journal of Personality and Social Psychology*, 1965, **1**, 161–165.

Taylor, H. F. *Balance in small groups*. Princeton, N. J.: Van Nostrand-Reinhold, 1970.

Taylor, J. A. A personality scale of manifest anxiety. *Journal of Abnormal and Social Psychology*, 1953, **48**, 285–290.

Taylor, M. J. Some objective criteria of social class membership. Unpublished manuscript, 1956.

Terman, L. M., & Buttenwieser, P. Personality factors in marital compatibility: I. *Journal of Social Psychology*, 1935, **6**, 143–171. (a)

Terman, L. M., & Buttenwieser, P. Personality factors in marital compatibility: II. *Journal of Social Psychology*, 1935, **6**, 267–289. (b)

Tesser, A. Attitude similarity and correlation as determinants of interpersonal attraction. Submitted for publication, 1971. (a)

Tesser, A. Evaluative and structural similarity of attitudes as determinants of interpersonal attraction. *Journal of Personality and Social Psychology*, 1971, **18**, 92–96. (b)

Tesser, A., & Brodie, M. A note on the evaluation of a "computer date." *Psychonomic Science*, 1971, **23**, 300.

Thiessen, D. D. Role of physical injury in the physiological effects of population density in mice. *Journal of Comparative and Physiological Psychology*, 1966, **62**, 322–324.

Thorpe, J. G. A study of some factors in friendship formation. *Sociometry*, 1955, **18**, 207–214.

Tornatzky, L., & Geiwitz, P. J. The effects of threat and attraction on interpersonal bargaining. *Psychonomic Science*, 1968, **13**, 125–126.

Townes, C. H. Quantum electronics, and surprise in development of technology: the problem of research planning. *Science*, 1968, **159**, 699–703.

Triandis, H. C. A note on Rokeach's theory of prejudice. *Journal of Abnormal and Social Psychology*, 1961, **62**, 184–186.

Triandis, H. C., & Davis, E. E. Race and belief as determinants of behavioral intentions. *Journal of Personality and Social Psychology*, 1965, **2**, 715–725.

Triandis, H. C., Loh, W. D., & Levin, L. A. Race, status, quality of spoken English, and opinions about civil rights as determinants of interpersonal attitudes. *Journal of Personality and Social Psychology*, 1966, **3**, 468–472.

U. S. Riot Commission. *Report of the National Advisory Commission on Civil Disorders*. New York: Bantam Books, 1968.

Van Dyne, V. E. Personality traits and friendship formation in adolescent girls. *Journal of Social Psychology*, 1940, **12**, 291–303.

Velten, E. The induction of elation and depression through the reading of structured sets of mood-statements. Unpublished doctoral dissertation, University of Southern California, 1967.

Velten, E. A laboratory task for induction of mood states. *Behavioral Research and Therapy*, 1968, **6**, 473–482.

Vreeland, F. M., & Corey, S. M. A study of college friendships. *Journal of Abnormal and Social Psychology*, 1935, **30**, 229–236.

Wallin, P., & Clark A. Cultural norms and husbands' and wives' reports of their marital partners' frequency of coitus relative to their own. *Sociometry*, 1958, **21**, 247–254.

Walsh, J. NIH: demand increases for applications of research. *Science*, 1966, **153**, 149–152.

Walster, E. Passionate love. In B. I. Murstein (Ed.), *Theories of love and attraction*. New York: Springer, in press.

Walster, E., Aronson, V., Abrahams, D., & Rottman, L. Importance of physical attractiveness in dating behavior. *Journal of Personality and Social Psychology*, 1966, **4**, 508–516.

Watson, D., & Friend, R. Measurement of social-evaluative anxiety. *Journal of Consulting and Clinical Psychology*, 1969, **33**, 448–457.

Watson, J. D. *The double helix*. New York: Atheneum, 1968.

Wehmer, G., & Izard, C. E. The effect of self-esteem and induced affect on interpersonal perception and intellectual functioning. ONR Technical Report No. 10, Vanderbilt University, 1962.

Wessman, A. E., & Ricks, D. F. *Mood and personality*. New York: Holt, 1966.

White, R. W. Motivation reconsidered: the concept of competence. *Psychological Review*, 1959, **66**, 297–333.

Whiting, J. W. M. Methods and problems in cross-cultural research. In G. Lindzey and E. Aronson (Eds.), *The handbook of social psychology* (2nd ed.), Vol. 2. Reading, Mass.: Addison-Wesley. 1968, Pp. 693–728.

Wiener, D. J. Effectance arousal and interpersonal attraction relating to a perceptual task: effects of certainty, consensual validation, and availability of verification. Unpublished doctoral dissertation, University of Texas, 1969.

Wiener, D. J. Failure of personality variables to mediate interpersonal attraction. *Psychological Reports*, 1970, **26**, 784–786.

Winch, R. F., Ktsanes, T., & Ktsanes, V. Empirical elaboration of the theory of complementary needs in mate-selection. *Journal of Abnormal and Social Psychology*, 1955, **51**, 508–513.

Winslow, C. N. A study of the extent of agreement between friends' opinions and their ability to estimate the opinions of each other. *Journal of Social Psychology*, 1937, **8**, 433–442.

Wong, T. J. The effect of attitude similarity and prejudice on interpersonal evaluation and attraction. Unpublished master's thesis, University of Texas, 1961.

Woodworth, R. S. *Dynamics of behavior*. New York: Holt, 1958.

Worchel, P. Adaptability screening of flying personnel: development of a self-concept inventory for predicting maladjustment. USAF School of Aviation Medicine Report, 1957, No. 56–62.

Worchel, P., & McCormick, B. L. Self-concept and dissonance reduction. *Journal of Personality*, 1963, **31**, 588–599.

Worchel, P., & Schuster, S. D. Attraction as a function of the drive state. *Journal of Experimental Research in Personality*, 1966, **1**, 277–281.

Wright, P. H. A model and a technique for studies of friendship. *Journal of Experimental Social Psychology*, 1969, **5**, 295–309.

Wright, P. H. Byrne's paradigmatic approach to the study of attraction: misgivings and alternatives. *Representative Research in Social Psychology*, 1971, **2**, 66–70.

Young, P. T., & Shuford, E. H., Jr. Quantitative control of motivation through sucrose solutions of different concentrations. *Journal of Comparative and Physiological Psychology*, 1955, **48**, 114–118.

Zander, A., & Havelin, A. Social comparison and interpersonal attraction. *Human Relations*, 1960, **13**, 21–32.

Zimbardo, P., & Formica, R. Emotional comparison and self-esteem as determinants of affiliation. *Journal of Personality*, 1963, **31**, 141–162.

Zuckerman, M., Lubin, B., & Robins, S. Validation of the Multiple Affect Adjective Check List in clinical situations. *Journal of Consulting Psychology*, 1965, **29**, 594.

Author Index

Numbers in italics refer to the pages on which the complete references are listed.

Subject Index